THE DARK DEFILE

The Dark Defile

Britain's Catastrophic Invasion of Afghanistan, 1838–1842

DIANA PRESTON

Walker & Company
New York

Published by Walker Publishing Company, Inc., New York
A Division of Bloomsbury Publishing

All papers used by Walker & Company are natural, recyclable products
made from wood grown in well-managed forests. The manufacturing processes
conform to the environmental regulations of the country of origin.

LIBRARY OF CONGRESS CATALOGING-IN-PUBLICATION DATA

Preston, Diana, 1952–
The dark defile : Britain's catastrophic invasion of Afghanistan,
1838–1842 / Diana Preston.—1st U.S. ed.
p. cm.
Includes bibliographical references and index.
ISBN 978-0-8027-7982-3 (alk. paper)
1. Afghanistan—History—British Intervention, 1839–1842.   2. Afghanistan—History,
Military—19th century.   3. British—Afghanistan—History—19th century.   I. Title.
DS363.P74 2012
958.1'03—dc23
2011024091

Visit Walker & Company's Web site at www.walkerbooks.com

First U.S. edition 2012

1 3 5 7 9 10 8 6 4 2

Typeset by Westchester Book Group
Printed in the U.S.A. by Quad/Graphics, Fairfield, Pennsylvania

To my husband, Michael

CONTENTS

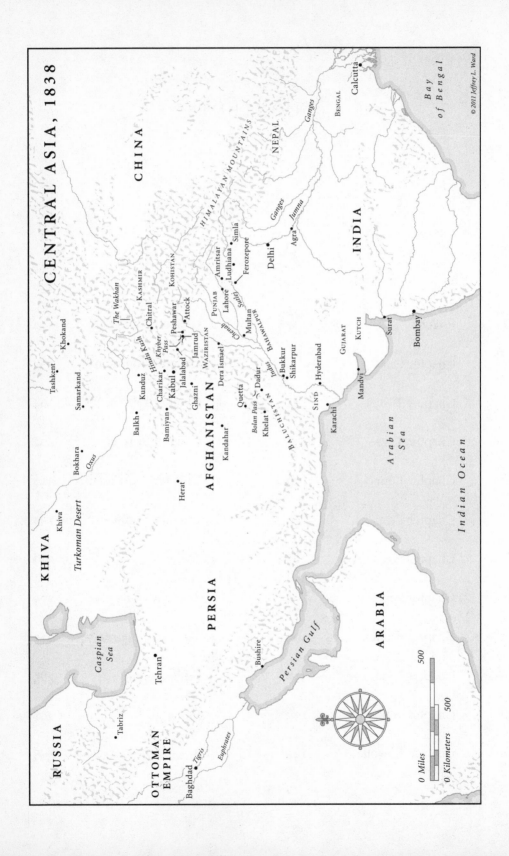

CENTRAL ASIA, 1838

© 2011 Jeffrey L. Ward

RUSSIA

OTTOMAN EMPIRE

Baghdad

Tigris

Euphrates

Tabriz

Tehran

Caspian Sea

KHIVA

Khiva

Turkoman Desert

Bokhara

Oxus

Samarkand

Tashkent

Khokand

Balkh

Kunduz

Hindu Kush

Charikar

The Wakhan

Chitral

KASHMIR

KOHISTAN

Peshawar

Attock

Khyber Pass

Jalalabad

Jamrud

WAZIRISTAN

Dera Ismael

PUNJAB

Amritsar

Ludhiana

Simla

Ferozepore

Lahore

Chenab

Sutlej

Multan

BAHAWALPUR

Delhi

Agra

Jumna

Ganges

NEPAL

HIMALAYAN MOUNTAINS

Ganges

BENGAL

Calcutta

Bay of Bengal

INDIA

PERSIA

Herat

AFGHANISTAN

Bamiyan

Kabul

Ghazni

Kandahar

Quetta

Bolan Pass

Khelat

Dadur

BALUCHISTAN

Indus

Bukkur

Shikarpur

SIND

Hyderabad

Karachi

GUJARAT

KUTCH

Mandvi

Surat

Bombay

Arabian Sea

Indian Ocean

ARABIA

Bushire

Persian Gulf

500

500

0 Miles

0 Kilometers

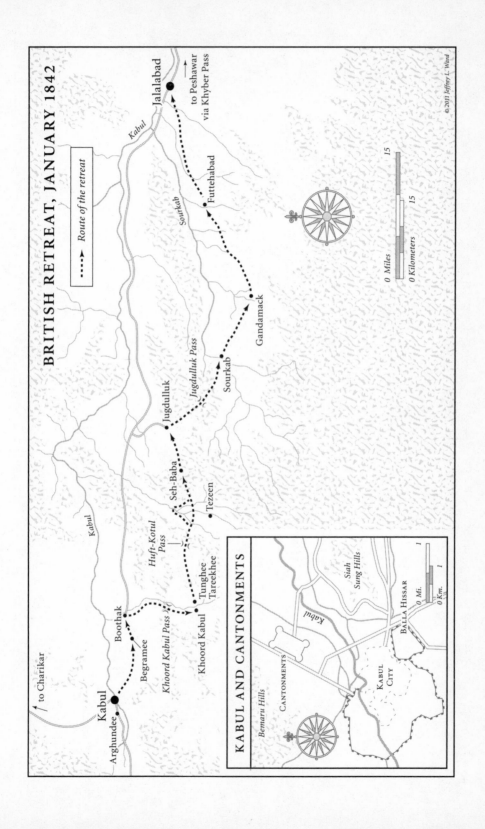

BRITISH RETREAT, JANUARY 1842

Route of the retreat

to Charikar

Kabul

Arghundee

Boothak

Begramee

Khoord Kabul Pass

Khoord Kabul

Tunghee
Tareekhee

*Huft-Kotul
Pass*

Tezeen

Seh-Baba

Jugdulluk

Jugdulluk Pass

Sourkab

Gandamack

Sourkab

Futtehabad

Jalalabad

to Peshawar
via Khyber Pass

Kabul

Kabul

0 Miles   15

0 Kilometers   15

© 2011 Jeffrey L. Ward

KABUL AND CANTONMENTS

Bemaru Hills

CANTONMENTS

Kabul

Siah
Sung Hills

BALLA HISSAR

KABUL
CITY

0 Mi.   1

0 Km.   1

PRELUDE

The consequence of crossing the Indus once to settle a government in Afghanistan will be a perennial march into that country.
—THE DUKE OF WELLINGTON, CONQUEROR OF NAPOLEON
AND FORMER BRITISH PRIME MINISTER, 1838

IN THE SUMMER heat of 1839 British forces marched, flags flying, into Kabul to replace Afghanistan's capable ruler, Dost Mohammed, with another, Shah Shuja, less able and less popular with his subjects but politically more acceptable in British eyes. Two years later, against their expectations, the British army was still mired in Afghanistan. At that time a no-nonsense major experienced an apparition while a senior officer was inspecting his regiment—the Forty-fourth Foot—and recorded it in his diary: "The colours of the regiment are very ragged and when they passed in review I was suddenly startled by what I took to be a large funeral procession. What put such a thing into my head I know not, as I was thinking of very different subjects."

Britain had sent an army into Afghanistan to protect its position in India, its most important overseas possession. Britain's involvement in the subcontinent was of long-standing. On the last day of 1600 Queen Elizabeth I granted a charter to "the Governor and Company of Merchants of London Trading in the East Indies." This became the Honourable East India Company, whose stated purpose was to win a share of the trade with the East—not only India but also China and what is now known as Indonesia—hitherto dominated by the Portuguese, Spanish and Dutch.

1

In 1608 Captain William Hawkins of the East India Company arrived on the west coast of India. The Portuguese merchants, established there for nearly a century, were determined to exclude rivals and attempted to waylay and murder Hawkins. However, in April 1609, he reached Agra, capital of the Mogul emperor Jahangir, who then ruled most of India and whose fabulous wealth—exemplified by rubies and emeralds the size of duck eggs—excited cupidity and admiration in equal measure throughout Europe.

Learning of Hawkins's arrival, Jahangir summoned him. Discovering that he spoke Turkish—"which he himself well understood"—the emperor, who was very curious about the wider world, enjoyed learning about the West from Hawkins. The Englishman was soon in high favor, and Jahangir even found him a wife. Such marks of distinction further worried "the Jesuits and Portugals," who, Hawkins claimed, "slept not, but by all means sought my overthrow." Nevertheless, Jahangir granted his request for trading rights for the company, which he permitted to establish a trading station at the port of Surat on the west coast. Other settlements followed—at Madras (Chennai)° and Calcutta (Kolkata) on the east coast and Bombay (Mumbai) on the west coast. Out in the Indian Ocean, the English navy safeguarded the company's merchant ships, impressing the Moguls by its ability both to defeat the fleets of European trading rivals and to fight off the increasingly powerful bands of pirates who preyed on ships carrying pilgrims across the Arabian Sea on the hajj to Mecca.

The company gradually prospered through a tripartite trade, bringing Indian products, including opium, to China and importing Chinese goods—in particular tea, not then grown in India, and silk, along with raw Indian cotton—to Britain. In time the British faced a new European rival in India—the French, who in 1664 had formed the French East India Company and who, from their base at Pondicherry, south of Madras, had ambitions to challenge Britain's growing commercial dominance. By the early eighteenth century the disintegration of the once all-powerful and centralized Mogul empire saw the British and French trading companies competing for allies among the Indian rulers striving to fill the

---

°One of the earliest governors of Madras was Elihu Yale, who acquired in India the fortune out of which he founded the university that bears his name.

vacuum left by the Mogul collapse. Although their purpose was avowedly commercial, the companies gradually began to control territory either directly or through vassal rulers. Writing in 1842 of this earlier period, Josiah Harlan, an American adventurer in India and Afghanistan, accurately observed that the British, ever ready to avail themselves of India's internal divisions, "stimulated the naïve chiefs, as the princes of India strove for independence against each other; and carrying out the maxim 'divide et impera' [divide and rule] they became the umpires of conflicting governments."

Political developments at home also affected the trading companies. In the middle of the eighteenth century, France and Britain fought each other in the War of the Austrian Succession and then in the Seven Years' War, with extensions of those conflicts in India as well as North America, making them perhaps the first world wars. In the early days, the East India Company had shipped modest numbers of soldiers from Britain to protect its property. Recognizing this was no longer sufficient, the company began recruiting soldiers in India, known as *sepoys* (from the Persian word for soldier, *sipahi*), and founded its own army. By the nineteenth century, with a quarter of a million men, the company's armies would be second in size among European-led forces only to those of Russia. Under the inspired generalship of Robert Clive and culminating in the Battle of Plassey in 1757, company forces crushed French ambitions, enabling the company to bring huge tracts of India, including Bengal, under its sway. The 1763 Treaty of Paris, which concluded the Seven Years' War, confirmed British supremacy in India as well as in North America. The Great Mogul had once dictated who was allowed to trade in India and on what terms; now the British would do so. Of the other European powers, only the French and the Portuguese retained toeholds in India.

The view in British ruling political circles, however, was that the company had become too important, too good a potential source of revenue to be allowed to remain independent. Company imports had risen more than threefold between the early 1700s and the 1770s. In 1773 the Regulating Act restrained the activities of senior company officials—the buccaneering, flamboyant *nabobs* who had unscrupulously amassed almost unimaginable personal fortunes through what an official report condemned as "the abandoned lust for universal wealth" in which "every spark and sentiment of public spirit was lost and extinguished." Then, in 1784, the India Act effectively subordinated the company to the British government, placing it under the newly created Board of Control; of the six men on the board, at least two had to be ministers of the British Crown.

The board's task was to monitor and, as the name implied, if necessary control the activities of the company's Court of Directors, which in turn transmitted orders to its officials in India through its Secret Committee. However, the time required for communication—dispatches took at least ten weeks to pass between England and India—was an obstacle to effective decision making from London. Senior officials in India were thus left with a great deal of autonomy, and the company's fortunes depended heavily on their individual abilities and characters.° The most senior British official in India was the governor-general, appointed under the terms of the 1784 act by the London government. He was based in Calcutta and was also head of the Bengal presidency. The other two presidencies—in Bombay and Madras—were subordinate to him. Each presidency maintained its own army with "native regiments," as they were known, of Indian sepoys commanded by British officers and some wholly European regiments. They were supplemented by a much smaller number of regiments of the British army posted to India for tours of duty— "Queen's regiments."

If Clive's victories had set the company upon an imperial path, the military triumphs of the future Duke of Wellington—on behalf of his brother Lord Wellesley, governor-general in India from 1798 to 1805— over the great Tipu Sultan,† ruler of the southern kingdom of Mysore, and over the once powerful Marathas of central India, completed that journey. Although the British never had any intention to settle in India, as they, the Spaniards and Portuguese had in the Americas, and although there were never more than fifty thousand Britons in the subcontinent of over 90 million people, by the early nineteenth century the company's

---

°By the start of the First Afghan War improvements to communications were close but not yet in place. In 1837 Samuel Morse exhibited his first electric telegraph in New York, and in 1838 the British ship *Sirius* was the first to steam continuously across the Atlantic.
†Among Tipu's prized possessions, seized by the British, was a near life-size mechanical model of a tiger consuming an English soldier. It is now in the Victoria and Albert Museum in London.

writ covered, directly or indirectly, almost two thirds of the subcontinent with a civil and military bureaucracy to match.

In barely more than two centuries India had become pivotal to Britain's aggressive pursuit of commerce, which, rather than a desire for territory, was the genesis of its growing empire. Additionally, the loss of the American colonies had enhanced India's status as both a totem and a projection of Britain's power and prestige, leading the radical politician Edmund Burke to describe the company's rule in India as "a delegation of the whole power and sovereignty of this kingdom sent into the East." Emblematic of the importance of commerce and of India to the British is that, having captured many colonies from their European rivals during the Napoleonic wars by dint of their command of the sea, at the end of the conflict they returned most of them. Those they retained protected their maritime mastery and routes to India, including the Cape Colony—the basis of South Africa—seized from the Dutch, and Mauritius and the Seychelles, taken from France.

Well safeguarded as India was by sea, the British became increasingly concerned that it was vulnerable to land invasion. By the early nineteenth century the East India Company had a two-thousand-mile-long northern frontier to defend, stretching from Bengal in the east to the line of the Sutlej River, a tributary of the Indus, in the northwest. To the company's Court of Directors and Britain's politicians, some parts of that border appeared more vulnerable than others. To the north and northeast, an inward-looking and isolationist China was no threat, while Nepal, although independent, had in 1815 signed a treaty of friendship with Britain and Nepal's Gurkha soldiers had become an important element of the East India Company's army.

However, to the northwest the situation looked potentially more threatening. Immediately beyond the northwestern borders of British India were the two largest Indian territories not yet bound to Britain—the Punjab and Sind—and beyond them, Persia (Iran) and Afghanistan, and beyond them Russia. Of all these, the British perceived the Russians as the greatest threat to India, either directly or through incitement of other of the states to act against the British presence.

❖　❖　❖

OF THE AUTOCRATS who at this time ruled much of continental Europe, Czar Nicholas I of Russia was the greatest and the most inflexible. Under his absolute and rigid rule, Russia remained a feudal society, half of its peasantry owned as serfs by their landlords. The Decembrist Rising at the time of his accession in 1825 had frightened Nicholas, already a man of a military cast of mind who throughout his life slept on a regulation military bed, into a reactionary conservatism. His fellow ruler Queen Victoria summed Nicholas up in the mid-1840s: "He is stern and severe—with fixed principles of duty which nothing on earth will make him change; very clever I do not think him, and his mind is an uncivilised one; his education has been neglected, politics and military concerns are the only things he takes great interest in; the arts and all softer occupations he is insensible to, but he is sincere, I am certain, sincere even in his most despotic acts, from a sense that it is the only way to govern."

Nicholas sought to impose Russian customs and language throughout his empire, in the process ruthlessly crushing nationalist risings such as those in Poland in 1830. He pushed outward the empire's boundaries in the south and east at the expense of the rulers of Ottoman Turkey and Persia. In the 150 years since the accession of Czar Peter the Great in 1689, the Russian empire's population had grown from 15 to 58 million, and its borders had advanced five hundred miles toward Constantinople and one thousand miles toward Tehran and Afghanistan.

It was this expansionary vision that Britain feared. Just as Britain had the world's most powerful navy, Russia in the nineteenth century had by far the largest army—well over half a million men. Most were conscripts. Although only 1 or 2 percent of eligible Russian males were conscripted annually, to be among them was a personal tragedy since service was for a period of twenty-five years. Britain, together with France, had for some time been struggling to prevent Russia from exploiting what seemed to be the inevitable breakup of the Ottoman Turkish Empire, which Czar Nicholas proclaimed "the sick man of Europe." A particular British concern was to keep Russia from securing access for its navy from the Black Sea through the Bosphorus and Dardanelles to the Mediterranean. From the difficulties in restraining Russia in its southern expansion, fears had grown in Britain—albeit based on sparse evidence—that to the southeast Russia might have ambitions beyond Central Asia, extending even to India.

Britain, at the time of the Afghan intervention, was a constitutional monarchy and well on the way to becoming the world's predominant commercial as well as naval power. Its share of the world's manufacturing output was on the rise from 9.5 percent in 1830 to its peak of some 20 percent in 1860.

Queen Victoria had come to the British throne in 1837 at the age of eighteen. "Poor little Queen," Thomas Carlyle wrote, "she is at an age at which a girl can hardly be trusted to choose a bonnet for herself; yet a task is laid upon her from which an archangel might shrink." Great Britain's population was some 18 million, excluding 8 million people in British-ruled Ireland. Britain's other overseas possessions covered some 2 million square miles with a population of well over 100 million. They spread from Canada, where in 1837 a crisis had been precipitated by Canadian troops sinking a U.S. warship transporting supplies across the Niagara River to Canadian insurgents, to Jamaica, Africa's Gold Coast and its southern tip, the Cape Colony, India, Ceylon (Sri Lanka), Malaya, the recently founded Singapore and Australia. In Britain, which had abolished slavery in 1834, only one in seven men had the vote, and no women were considered wise or strong enough to do so. Nevertheless, political life was lively, focusing not only on the wisdom of the Afghan intervention but also on further extensions of the franchise and the improvement of the lot of working people, both of which would give rise to considerable agitation, sometimes violent, by the Chartists and others over the next few years.

With a population of 2 million, London was the world's largest city and its financial center. Britain derived much of its commercial advantage from its mastery of the new coal-driven steam technology, which it used to power its burgeoning manufacturing industry and was developing to propel the railways and steamships that would export its manufactured products. These included the cotton goods that made up half the country's total exports. In 1814 Britain had exported 1 million yards of cotton cloth to India. By 1830 the figure had reached 51 million yards and would rise to 995 million yards in 1860, exemplifying the importance of India as a market as well as one of the main sources of raw cotton, the other being the southern United States.

Conditions both in the mines and in the factories producing Britain's new wealth were poor. In the mines, near-naked women and children pulled heavy wagons loaded with coal through the mineshafts. In the mills, children as young as eight or nine worked twelve-hour days, dodging beneath the whirring looms and other machinery, to clear blockages at great risk to their lives. In Manchester, the great "Cottonopolis," the average age of death of laborers and their families was seventeen, compared to thirty-eight for those in the countryside. As the First Afghan War ended, Friedrich Engels, the son of a German cotton mill owner, visited Manchester and the branch of the family firm there. Here, and in the other mills of the city, he experienced the appalling conditions and raged against the "brutally selfish" policy of mill owners holding wages down to enhance their own profits, writing that the only way the embittered masses could achieve justice was by violence. In 1848 he and Karl Marx would publish the *Communist Manifesto*.

The British had not yet become unequivocally committed to free trade because they were not yet convinced—although they soon would be—that they were unequivocally best placed to exploit it. Indeed, a leading politician maintained that he had no intention of making war in Afghanistan to promote the study among its inhabitants of Adam Smith, the first proponent of laissez-faire economics. However, during the Afghan War the British would also be involved in the First Opium War, aimed at forcing the Chinese to open their ports more fully to the import of opium, one of the most profitable products of their Indian possessions. The war at its end resulted in the secession by the Chinese of Hong Kong to the British.

British troops thus first entered Afghanistan at a time of worldwide commercial and territorial expansion and of intense international rivalry. This first war of Queen Victoria's reign proved more perilous than either the politicians who ordered the invasion or the generals who conducted it ever conceived as they set out. The outcome still affects us today.

CHAPTER ONE

When everyone is dead the Great Game is finished, not before.
—RUDYARD KIPLING, *KIM*

BRITAIN HAD BEEN worried about the intentions of other powers toward India long before British troops marched into Afghanistan. Until Napoleon's defeat in 1815, France seemed as great a threat as Russia. When in 1807 Napoleon and Czar Nicholas agreed to the Peace of Tilsit, there appeared a real risk of a joint Russo-Franco invasion of India. Both countries were also intriguing with Persia. Britain responded with a diplomatic offensive aimed at creating a series of buffer states through alliances with the rulers of lands lying in the path of a possible invasion of India. In 1807 the government instructed Lord Minto, governor-general of India, to seek the cooperation of the rulers of the territories across the Indus River: Afghanistan; the Punjab, ruled by the martial Sikhs; and Sind, which, controlling the delta of the Indus River, dominated access to the Arabian Sea. The British also dispatched an envoy to Persia, with which they had had a sometimes difficult trading and diplomatic relationship, to attempt to contain or neutralize Persian ambitions. With these missions began the so-called Great Game, the contest for control of Central Asia, which would extend from Persia to Tibet and last a century until an agreement between Britain and Russia, temporarily at least, defined their respective spheres of interest.*

---

*A young British officer, Captain Arthur Conolly, probably coined the term *the Great Game* in the 1830s before losing his life playing it, but Rudyard Kipling popularized it.

In Persia, the British first tried to bribe the shah to declare war on the Russians. When he wisely declined to do so, they attempted to cajole and bully him not to accept overtures from the French. In 1809 the choleric and undiplomatic Sir Harford "Baghdad" Jones—so-called because of his years of service there—arrived at the Persian court, reopened negotiations and when the Persian vizier annoyed him, called him an idiot; then, Jones reported, "[I] pushed him with a slight degree of violence against the wall . . . kicked over the candles on the floor, left the room in darkness, and rode home without any one of the Persians daring to impede my passage." Despite such unorthodox diplomacy and just possibly because of an enormous diamond Sir Harford had presented as a gift from King George III, in March 1809 the shah reluctantly agreed to a treaty with Britain. The Persians would not allow any European army to advance through their territory toward India and undertook to help the British defend India against the Afghans or any other power that invaded. In return, if any European power invaded Persia, the British promised to provide either soldiers or financial subsidies of the type they were deploying so successfully with more impecunious European countries in their war with Napoleon.

THE SUSPICIOUS AND independent-minded emirs who controlled Sind at first rebuffed British overtures with "imperious superiority." However, they were eventually induced to accept a treaty under which they promised not "to allow the tribe of the French" to settle in their lands. Negotiations with the ruler of the Punjab,[†] the one-eyed warrior Ranjit Singh, proved more complex. The "Lion of Lahore" had become the leader of his people in 1799 while still in his teens after successfully

---

cont. His world of secret agents and assassins, disguises and subterfuge, concealed messages and forged letters evoked in novels such as *Kim* was reasonably accurate, if pervaded with some of the romanticism that often clouded British perceptions of the region and its people.

[†]*Punjab* means "Land of the Five Rivers" and comes from the Persian *panj*, meaning "five," and *ab*, meaning "waters," because five tributaries of the Indus flow through it. The drink punch also derives from the word *panj* because it has five ingredients: rum, sugar, lemon, water and spice.

rallying the fractious Sikh brotherhoods, the *misls*, against an invading Afghan army that seemed about to overrun the Punjab. In 1801 he was proclaimed maharaja of the Punjab in his capital at Lahore, where his subjects showered him with silver and gold. By the time of the British mission his armies were second in size only to the company's on the Indian subcontinent.

The pockmarked and physically puny Ranjit Singh was as decisive in his private as in his public life. A great womanizer who maintained in his harem a regiment of women dressed in highly titillating costumes of his own devising, he nevertheless stabbed his mother with his sword for adulterous behavior, claiming "it was better that she should have died early than live a long life of guilt and shame." He was also a drinker of awesome proportions, consuming a regular mixture of opium, alcohol, meat juice and powdered pearls. He had ambitions to extend his kingdom southward across the Sutlej River, perhaps even to Delhi, where a weak Mogul emperor still nominally ruled, though at the pleasure of the British. Charles Metcalfe, a twenty-three-year-old company officer, was the Briton dispatched in 1808 to convince the Sikh leader of the threat of an invasion of India from the north and to warn him that if he tried to push his borders too far south the company's armies would confront him.

The Sikh maharaja suspected the British of using the threat of a foreign invasion to mask their own plans for expansion at his expense. Ranjit Singh was, however, a realist. Looking at a map of the Indian subcontinent on which British territories were marked in red, he prophesied that soon it would all be red. Recognizing that his armies were unlikely to defeat the company's, he renounced his ambitions for southern expansion and in 1809 signed the Treaty of Lahore with Britain, under which both sides swore "perpetual friendship." Ranjit Singh would keep his side of the bargain; nearly thirty years later, the British commitment to protect the Sikh alliance would be a major factor in the outbreak of the First Afghan War.

The British administration in Calcutta selected another young officer—the twenty-nine-year-old Scot, Mountstuart Elphinstone—as its envoy to Afghanistan. He was the first Briton to penetrate that remote region since a company official had traveled through it in disguise twenty-five years earlier on his way to Russia. The British therefore knew little of

Afghanistan's topography beyond that it was large, mountainous and land-locked. The country, of a similar size to the modern U.S. state of Texas, in fact consisted of several distinct zones. In the southwest an arid desert plateau around the Helmand River stretched toward Persia. In the north-west, plains ran across the Oxus River toward the khanates of Khiva and Bokhara. There were mountains in the center and the northeast including the six-hundred-mile-long Hindu Kush as well as mountains along the southeastern frontier with Baluchistan and with Ranjit Singh's territories. The few narrow passes leading through these mountains had often pro-vided a route for the invasion of India. Abul Fazl, friend and chronicler of Akbar, the greatest of the Moguls, called Kabul, the region's major city with the great Khyber Pass to its east, "the gate of Hindustan."

One of the first known invaders, Darius of Persia, led his army of Immortals down through the thirty-mile-long Khyber, whose bleak gray sides rising to five hundred feet overshadow a road in places just a few feet wide. Nearly two centuries later, in early 327 B.C., this inhospitable stone corridor resonated to the hoof beats of Alexander the Great's in-creasingly exhausted and fractious forces on the latest stage of their long march of conquest from Macedonia. The soon-to-be-defeated armies and war elephants of the Indian king Porus waited on the banks of the Jhelum River, a tributary of the Indus, in armor of silver and gold. Elphinstone, a classics scholar like most of the officers who would venture into Afghani-stan, for lack of more recent guides used the classical accounts of Alexan-der's expeditions for geographic reference.

Over the centuries other invasions followed Alexander's. Among the most significant was the conquest of most of northern India in 1001 by Mahmud, the Muslim ruler of Ghazni in the southeast of Afghanistan. He established the first of the series of Islamic sultanates that would grow to dominate much of the area. Fortified by his religion and its iconoclastic beliefs, he plundered Hindu holy places, melting down the golden idols at the shrine of Mathura and despoiling the great Hindu temple of Somnath on the Indian Ocean coast in what is now Gujarat. Here he destroyed the phallic stone lingam—symbol of the god Shiva—dispatching fragments to be incorporated in the steps of mosques in Mecca and Medina as well as in Ghazni. He also bore off to Ghazni the temple's massive ornate gates as a symbol of his triumph.

In 1398 Timur, or Tamburlaine as the West knows him from a corruption of "Timur the Lame," invaded India, where he defeated the sultan of Delhi and sacked the city so thoroughly, before leaving with a mass
of booty, that for two months "nothing stirred, not even a bird." In the
early sixteenth century, his descendant Babur floated down the Khyber
River from Kabul, holding drinking and cannabis parties as he went, to
found the Mogul empire using the cannons and muskets that he introduced to northwest India for the first time.

In 1739 the Persian Nadir Shah marched his armies through Kabul
and down the Khyber Pass to sack Delhi and carry off treasures such as
the Mogul emperor Shah Jahan's jeweled peacock throne. A few years
later, the Afghan king Ahmad Shah also sacked Delhi and removed most
of the treasures that Nadir Shah had left behind. His successors, albeit
less able and with a weaker grip on their dominions, had also shown an
enduring interest in invading from the northwest. Having witnessed these
incursions, by the early nineteenth century Britain determined to turn
the Afghans from potential aggressors to partners in providing a line of
defense for India against invaders, whether inspired by European geo-
politics or more local ambitions.

In March 1809, with thick snow still blanketing the peaks of the
surrounding mountains, Elphinstone and his party, which included 200
cavalrymen, 200 infantrymen and a string of 600 baggage camels, reached
the Afghan king's winter capital of Peshawar at the eastern end of the
Khyber Pass, then an Afghan possession. The Mogul emperor Akbar had
given Peshawar its name, meaning "Advanced Post," in the sixteenth century and saw it, as the British would, as key to the defense of his realm
against invaders from the northwest. The arrival of this British delegation
roused huge curiosity, and so many people pressed around that the king's
horsemen sent to escort the entourage through the city "charged the mob
vigorously, and used their whips without compunction," as Elphinstone
recalled. He was particularly struck by a tall thin man—"with swelling
muscles, a high nose, and an animated countenance," wearing a white
plumed conical red hat and mounted on a fine gray horse—who, brandishing a spear and shouting in a loud, deep voice, not only dispersed the
mob but rode furiously "at grave people sitting on terraces." His name,
Elphinstone was told, was Russool the Mad.

The new arrivals were comfortably accommodated in a large airy house and offered refreshments of sugared almonds and sherbet. The king, Shah Shuja, sent dishes from the royal kitchens for their meals. However, a week passed, and Elphinstone had still not seen him because of elaborate court protocol that even the mild-mannered Elphinstone found "a little unreasonable." He was told that "the ambassador to be introduced is brought into a court by two officers who hold him firmly by the arms. On coming in sight of the King, who appears at a high window, the ambassador is made to run forward for a certain distance, when he stops for a moment, and prays for the King. He is then made to run forward again, and prays once more; and after another run, the King calls out 'Khellut' (a dress) [meaning 'give him a dress of honor'] which is followed by a Turkish word 'Getsheen' (begone) from an officer of state, and the unfortunate ambassador is made to run out of the court and sees no more of the King, unless he is summoned to a private audience to his Majesty's closet."

This ritual was, however, "adjusted"—Elphinstone did not say how—and at last amid a great din, which he described as sounding like a charge of cavalry, he was brought before the ruler. Shah Shuja was sitting "on a very large throne of gold or gilding" covered with pearl encrusted cloth. "His appearance was magnificent and royal: his crown and all his dress were one blaze of jewels," and he was surrounded by eunuchs. He was "a handsome man, about thirty years of age, of an olive complexion, with a thick black beard. The expression of his countenance was dignified and pleasing, his voice clear and his address princely."

At first sight a dazzled Elphinstone thought that the king "had on armour of jewels." On closer inspection, he realized he was wearing "a green tunic, with large flowers in gold and precious stones, over which were a large breastplate of diamonds, shaped like two flattened fleur de lis, an ornament of the same kind on each thigh, large emerald bracelets on the arms . . . In one of the bracelets was the Koh-i-Nur, known to be one of the largest diamonds in the world." Shah Shuja's crown was nine inches high and "seemed to be radiated like ancient crowns, and behind the rays appeared peaks of purple velvet."

Before long Elphinstone had become a frequent visitor to the king, afforded the honor of meeting him in private in his harem. Elphinstone's mission was to persuade Shah Shuja to agree to an alliance to defend Afghanistan against invasion by France and Russia should they advance from the west through Persia. If pressed, he had permission to offer Shah Shuja arms and ordnance to defend his kingdom, though no troops. The two men got on well. On one occasion the king expressed his hope that Elphinstone would have a chance to see Kabul and all his territories, "which were now to be considered as our own." His manners impressed the envoy, who wrote, "It will scarcely be believed of an eastern Monarch, how much he had the manners of a gentleman, or how well he preserved his dignity, while he seemed only anxious to please." Courteous though he appeared, Shah Shuja had, however, little interest in either British fears or ambitions—his own position was far too precarious.

THE PRECEDING THIRTY years of Afghan history read like a particularly bloody revenge tragedy. Although travelers through Afghanistan would frequently pay tribute to the kindness, generosity, honor and bravery of those they met, blood feuds were common and disputes almost invariably settled by violence. A British soldier later killed during the First Afghan War observed, "They know no law but force and the sword; and every man among them is armed from head to foot—a state which they never quit by day or night, so insecure is life and property among them and so little dare they trust each other!"

Afghan society was feudal. In return for their lands, tribesmen paid their chief tribute in goods and money and when so ordered fought for their chief, who in turn was obliged to provide troops to the king when he needed to raise an army. However, the nature of "kingship" differed from Western tradition. Instead of being a united kingdom under a strong ruler, Afghanistan was—even when at its most unified—a loose grouping of semiautonomous tribes, some speaking different languages and looking physically different from their neighbors. Chiefs and elders ruled these tribes, and their support for the king in Kabul ebbed and flowed, depending on circumstances—something the British and, indeed, others would never quite fully understand. In each tribe the gathering of elders—the *jirgha*—played almost as important a role as the titular ruler. While Elphinstone admired the Afghans' independent spirit and belief that "all Afghans are equal," he deplored some of the consequences. "I once strongly urged on a very intelligent old man . . . the superiority of a quiet and secure life under a powerful monarch, to the discord, the alarms and the blood which they owed to their present system," to which the old man warmly replied, "We are content with discord, we are content with bloodshed, but we will never be content with a master."

For a brief period in the mid-eighteenth century, Shah Shuja's grandfather, Ahmad Shah, had melded an empire that included Kashmir, the Punjab, Sind and Baluchistan, and controlled the trade routes between Persia, Central Asia and India. Today Afghans regard him as one of the founding fathers of their state. The title Durr-i-Dauran (Pearl of the Age) was conferred on him, and the tribe to which his family clan—the Sadozai—belonged took the name Douranee (Pearl of Pearls). However, even before Ahmad Shah's death, the Douranee empire was fragmenting, and during the reign of his lackluster son the process accelerated. A particular obstacle to stability was "the dire results of polygamy." Afghan chiefs had many wives and so many children they often lost count of the number. Thus in each generation there were large numbers of brothers and half brothers who might sometimes combine in pursuit of a common goal, but who were just as likely to battle savagely among themselves on the slightest of pretexts.

Shah Shuja himself had many half brothers and one full brother, Zaman Shah, who between 1793 and 1801 ruled Afghanistan. However, in an unfortunate series of events that had all the usual complicated elements of blood feud and internecine rivalry, a half brother had ousted Zaman Shah. The cycle had begun in 1799 when Zaman Shah executed the leader of the powerful Barakzai family clan of the Douranee tribe for plotting against him. The dead chief left twenty-two sons, of whom the eldest, Futteh Khan, swore revenge. He persuaded Zaman Shah's half brother Mahmud, governor of the western city of Herat, to revolt. Together they toppled Zaman Shah and had him blinded, ordering his eyeballs to be pierced with the tip of a dagger—a traditional method of neutralizing rivals. Mahmud then ascended the throne with the powerful Futteh Khan by his side as his vizier.

When Shah Shuja learned what had happened to his full brother, he determined on revenge and proclaimed himself king, briefly seizing Kabul until forced to flee. In 1803 he tried again, this time successfully defeating and capturing his rival, Mahmud. He ordered him to be blinded but then rescinded the command—a rare humane gesture that proved to be a mistake. Futteh Khan escaped and by the time of Elphinstone's visit to Peshawar had raised a rebellion against Shah Shuja with the aim of restoring Mahmud to the throne.

Despite his initial welcoming of Elphinstone, Shah Shuja soon advised him to leave unless the British would agree to assist him against his enemies, just as they wished for his help against the French, Russians and Persians. Elphinstone had no authority to agree to such a thing, and in any case Shah Shuja and his advisers suspected the motives of the British and doubted whether they were half as powerful as they claimed. In a letter Elphinstone described a conversation with a court mullah: "Our reputation was very high for good faith and for magnanimous conduct to cornered princes," the mullah said, "but he frankly owned that we had the character of being very designing, and that most people thought it necessary to be very vigilant in all transactions with us."

However, while Elphinstone was still in Peshawar, news came that Shah Shuja's enemies had captured the southern city of Kandahar and that the armies he had sent to Kashmir to impose his authority there had been destroyed. In need of friends—even "very designing" ones—Shah Shuja agreed to conclude a treaty with the British that rejoiced that "the veil of separation" between the two countries had been lifted. Under the treaty he promised to prevent Britain's enemies entering his lands, while the British promised to reimburse any costs he incurred in so doing. What Elphinstone could not have known was that by this time, as a result of Baghdad Jones's efforts, the Persian shah had also signed a friendship treaty with the British.

Despite the fact that Shah Shuja would lose his throne to Mahmud within weeks of Elphinstone's departure, his mission had been highly useful. Though he had only visited the fringes of Afghanistan, never even penetrating the Khyber Pass, he had garnered a large amount of intelligence about the region. Using such information, the surveyor who had accompanied him drew the first map of what we now know as Afghanistan. Both his map and Elphinstone's reports, based as they were mainly on hearsay, would be carefully scrutinized by senior company officials and British politicians as the pace of the Great Game accelerated.

The following year, the displaced Shah Shuja retook Kandahar but was soon evicted by its nobles, who resented his hauteur and autocratic behavior—traits that would later bedevil British attempts to impose him on the Afghans. Not long after, he was imprisoned in Kashmir until "rescued" by the troops of Ranjit Singh, who coveted the fabulous Koh-i-Nur diamond that was still in Shah Shuja's possession. Despite yielding up this prize, Shah Shuja remained a prisoner in Lahore. Realizing that Ranjit Singh had no intention of helping him, he enterprisingly disguised himself as a beggar and escaped through the city's sewers. In 1816 he reached the British hill station of Ludhiana to join his blind brother Zaman Shah, who had also been given asylum there.*

Having ousted Shah Shuja, the pleasure-loving Mahmud spent most of his time in the harem, leaving the able Futteh Khan, his vizier, as the de facto ruler. It was a familiar pattern—a king from the Sadozai family clan of the Douranee tribe with a powerful adviser from the Barakzai family clan of the same tribe by his side. Futteh Khan restored order and then mounted a series of ambitious campaigns in which he was assisted by one of his younger brothers, Dost Mohammed. Eager to impress, he made himself useful to his older brother as an "enforcer." When only fourteen, Dost Mohammed killed a man whom he merely suspected of treachery. He also drank heavily. The American Josiah Harlan, who knew Dost Mohammed, described his drunken orgies when "friend and colleague, master, man and slave, all indiscriminate and promiscuous actors in the wild, voluptuous, licentious scene of shameful bacchanals, they caroused and drank with prostitutes and singers and fiddlers, day and night."

In 1816, on Futteh Khan's orders, Dost Mohammed seized the western city of Herat through subterfuge. However, he then violated the harem, stripping the women, noblewomen of the Sadozai royal house, of their jewels and even their clothes. Such an outrage by a member of one clan against another could not go unpunished. Dost Mahommed fled to Kashmir, and his elder brother, as head of the Barakzais, paid for his moment of madness. First, Mahmud's son Kamran blinded Futteh Khan

---

*Colin Mackenzie, a British officer who later met Zaman Shah, reported, "He still goes through the ceremony of having a glass held up before him during his toilette," even though he had been blind for many years. "So great a man cannot be vulgarly blind! This trifling trait shows the animus of his race, which is that of insane pride."

with the point of a dagger. Then, when he refused to write to Dost Mohammed ordering him to surrender, Mahmud had him slowly butchered before him. First his ears were sliced off, then his nose, then his hands, then—the unkindest cut of all—his beard, at which Futteh Khan at last broke down. A British officer to whom an eyewitness sent an account of the murder explained that "the beard of a Mahommedan is a member so sacred that honour itself becomes confounded with it; and he who had borne with the constancy of a hero the taunts and tortures heaped upon him, seemed to lose his manhood with his beard, and burst into a passion of tears." The torture finally ended when, after his feet had been cut off, Futteh Khan's throat was slit.

The cycle continued. Dost Mohammed and his brothers in turn swore to avenge Futteh Khan's death, raised an army, seized Kabul and forced Mahmud and Kamran to flee to Herat. Soon, however, fighting broke out between Dost Mohammed and his numerous brothers, from which by 1826 he finally emerged as the acknowledged head of the Barakzais, dominating what Josiah Harlan called "a community of scorpions." He renounced drinking and all his other former vices and devoted himself to the serious business of ruling, though at the time he only controlled Kabul and the territory of Ghazni to the south. One of his brothers ruled in Peshawar nominally on his behalf, but in effect independently, while several other brothers set themselves up as autonomous rulers in Kandahar and elsewhere.

Ranjit Singh had followed the civil wars in Afghanistan with close attention. In 1819 he had profited from the chaos to take Kashmir from the Afghans, and he also had designs on Peshawar, where a decade earlier Elphinstone had courted Shah Shuja. The Sikh ruler would find the British his firm friends as he pursued his goals because events in the wider world were moving to his advantage.

The Russian menace was growing. Russia had already wrung a number of concessions from Persia when in 1828 Czar Nicholas and his generals forced the Treaty of Turkmanchai on the Persians. This treaty not only annexed further territories to Russia, including Yerevan, the modern-day capital of Armenia and the surrounding area, but gave Russia territorial rights within Persia itself, among them the freedom to station "consuls" wherever it wished, as well as exclusive commercial privileges. A British

officer captured the contemporary British perception of Russia: "Peradventure that black and ominous eagle, which has so long been perched
upon the rocks overhanging the Caspian Sea, looking around with keen
eye, and in imagination devouring the rich provinces of Asia, may at last
take a daring flight towards the Indus, and at once settle all our worldly
affairs." British foreign secretary Lord Aberdeen put it more bluntly, writing of Russia's increasingly commanding position in Western and Central
Asia, "Russia holds the keys." He was determined they should not use
them to unlock the gates of India.

CHAPTER TWO

Commerce is the grand panacea . . . Not a bale of merchandise leaves our shores but it bears the seeds of intelligence and fruitful thought to the members of some less enlightened community.

—RICHARD COBDEN, ECONOMIST AND ADVOCATE
OF FREE TRADE

WITH RUSSIA SO close and Persia no longer an ally to be relied on, Ranjit Singh with his presence on the central Indus was becoming ever more important to British strategy. In January 1831, a young Scottish officer named Alexander Burnes was ordered to set sail up the Indus with a gift of English dray horses for Britain's Sikh ally.* However, the mission had another, deeper purpose. Burnes was to do a little espionage by assessing the navigability of the Indus and thus its suitability as a conduit for British trade and influence. As one British government minister wrote, "No British flag has ever floated upon the waters of this river. Please God it shall, and in triumph."

Alexander Burnes was born in Montrose, on Scotland's east coast, and his great-grandfather was the uncle of Scotland's national poet Robert Burns, who spelled his surname differently. He had arrived in India in 1821 as a sixteen-year-old East India Company cadet and followed the then standard advice to aspiring young officers: "Mind you study the

---

*Scots made a disproportionately large contribution to the making and the running of the British Empire at all levels.

native languages, sir!" He quickly learned Hindi and then Persian and Arabic. As a slight young man of only middling height who loathed exercise and throve on argument, he must have seemed quite unusual to the other cadets. Promotions came swiftly, and, deeply curious about the people and customs of India, he traveled whenever his duties allowed. In 1829 he was transferred to the company's elite Political Department, which provided far greater opportunities and excitement for able young officers than did garrison duty with their regiments, awaiting their turn for promotion. "Politicals," as they were known, habitually dressed in black frock coats. They served not only in the company's headquarters in Calcutta but also as advisers to rulers of states allied to the company, as well as undertaking special or secret missions. Burnes was delighted, seeing himself "on the high road . . . to office, emolument and honour." He was first appointed assistant to the company's resident in Kutch and then two years later to lead the survey of the Indus.

At this time British knowledge of the river was vague. The only available accounts of much of its course were, as Burnes noted, those of Arrian, Curtius and the other ancient historians of Alexander's expedition, which had returned eastward down it after defeating Porus. Yet a senior company official observed, "The navigation of the Indus is important in every point of view." The reason was commercial as well as political. If British cottons and woolens could be sent north up the river, Britain could challenge the Russians, who were able to convey their goods economically to Central Asia by way of the River Volga and the Caspian Sea. Thus Britain "might succeed in underselling the Russians and in obtaining for ourselves a large portion at least of the internal trade of Central Asia . . . our first object being to introduce English goods and not Englishmen into Kabul and Central Asia," wrote Lord Ellenborough, president of the Board of Control in London.

However, the emirs of Sind, through whose lands the lower portion of the Indus flowed, remained deeply suspicious of the British, and a British expedition could not pass through Sind without some plausible pretext. This was provided by the dapple gray stallion and four mares dispatched from England to Ranjit Singh in return for some Kashmiri shawls that he had sent to King William IV. There was no doubt that the safest way of transporting the horses to the maharaja's capital of Lahore was up the

Indus, and to allay the emirs' suspicions further, an official suggested that a large gilded carriage should also be sent "since the size and bulk of it would render it obvious that the mission could then only proceed by water."

Not everyone agreed with the subterfuge. Sir Charles Metcalfe, the man sent twenty years earlier to negotiate with Ranjit Singh and now a member of the governor-general's council, denounced "the scheme of surveying the Indus, under the pretence of sending a present to Rajah Ranjit Singh" as "a trick unworthy of our government, which cannot fail, when detected, as most probably it will be, to excite the jealousy and indignation of the powers on whom we play it . . . It is not impossible that it may lead to war."

Such objections were overruled. Alexander Burnes received secret instructions to conduct a clandestine but comprehensive survey of the Indus, including its depth, breadth and direction of flow, "its facilities for steam navigation, the supply of fuel on its banks, and the condition of the princes and people who possess the country bordering on it." Furthermore: "Your own knowledge and reflection will suggest to you various other particulars in which full information is highly desirable; and the slow progress of the boats up the Indus will, it is hoped, give you every opportunity to pursue your researches." As he prepared for the long journey to Lahore, Burnes decided that taking troops with him would only invite hostility and selected just three companions—Ensign J. D. Leckie of the Bombay Infantry, company surveyor Mohammed Ali and an Indian doctor—along with servants to look after them.

After shipping the horses and carriage up the coast from Bombay to Mandvi in Kutch, on the morning of 21 January 1831 Burnes and his party set sail from there in a flotilla of five vessels, hugging the coast before turning into the delta of the Indus. As they made their slow progress, Burnes went to work taking twenty bearings daily, but the emirs of Sind greeted his approach with the hostility and skepticism the British had anticipated. They shared the views of a holy man who, watching the vessels sail by, cried out, "Alas! Sind is now gone, since the English have seen the river, which is the road to its conquest." Fourteen years later the British indeed annexed Sind, but for the moment the emirs refused to allow Burnes into their lands and their soldiers harassed the expedition. While he waited impatiently for permission to proceed, storms battered his little fleet, and Sindi and Baluchi tribesmen fired off their matchlocks and promised to slit the throats of every man on board. The emirs only relented when the British authorities in India threatened them with invasion.

Mooring near Hyderabad, the principal city in Sind, Burnes was received by its superbly jeweled emir, to whom he presented a gun, a brace of pistols, a gold watch, two telescopes, a clock, some English shawls and cloths and two pairs of elegant cut-glass candlesticks. The emir was friendlier than Burnes had anticipated, perhaps because a few years earlier Burnes's doctor brother James, also traveling through the area, had cured him of a dangerous illness. He even allowed the expedition to voyage onward aboard his state barge, which was, Burnes wrote, "about sixty feet long, and had three masts, on which we hoisted as many sails, made of alternate stripes of red and white cloth." They sailed along, helped by a fair wind and a sixteen-man crew happily smoking *bhang*—marijuana.

At Khairpur, the ruler—a cousin of the emir of Hyderabad—sent gifts of sheep, spices, sugar, tobacco and opium, and a courtier told Burnes gravely that astronomers had foretold that "the English would in time possess all India . . . for the stars and heaven proclaimed the fortune of the English!" Toward the end of May 1831, Burnes and his party left the Indus and entered the Chenab River and on 8 June finally reached Ranjit Singh's borders. Here one of his courtiers, mounted on a magnificent elephant, welcomed them, assuring them that Ranjit Singh "was deeply sensible of the honour conferred upon him by the King of England, and that his army had been for some time in readiness on the frontier to chastise the barbarians of Sind," who had long arrested the progress of Burnes and his men. The Sikh soldiers impressed Burnes: "[They are] tall and bony men, with a very martial carriage: the most peculiar part of their dress is a small flat turban, which becomes them well; they wear long hair, and from the knee downwards do not cover the leg."

After branching off again, this time down the Ravi River, in mid-July Burnes and his party after a seven-hundred-mile river journey at last approached Lahore. The sun was going down, and on the distant horizon, he reported, "[I saw] the massy mountains which encircle Kashmir clothed in a mantle of white snow. I felt a nervous sensation of joy as I first gazed on the Himalayas." Three days later, Burnes and his companions rode into the city on elephants preceded by the great coach and the dray horses. Dismounting in the courtyard of Ranjit Singh's palace, they were conducted inside. "While stooping to remove my shoes at the threshold," Burnes recounted, "I suddenly found myself in the arms and tight embrace of a diminutive old-looking man—the great Maharajah Ranjit Singh."

The maharaja was, in fact, only forty-three. He was short—barely five feet three inches—but Burnes reflected that "there must be a mighty contrast between his mind and body." Taking Burnes by the hand, Ranjit Singh led him into a marble hall where a pavilion of silken cloth studded with gems had been erected and courtiers all dressed in yellow waited. Also present to participate in the festivities was the thirty-seven-year-old Captain Claude Wade, the company's political officer responsible for the Punjab. Wade had made the short journey from his headquarters at Ludhiana, the company's forward station for its northwestern territories, where his special responsibilities were keeping watch over both Shah Shuja and British relations with the Sikhs. Wade, son of a colonel in the Bengal army, had been serving in India since 1809 and was able but intellectually stubborn.

Burnes presented the cloth of gold bag containing the official letter he had brought from Lord Ellenborough. So gratified was the Sikh ruler with its protestations of friendship and admiration that he ordered a peal of artillery from sixty guns, each firing twenty-one times. With the cacophony still resounding, he and Burnes went to see the gift of "horses of the gigantic breed which is peculiar to England," described in Ellenborough's letter. The sight of them, "excited his utmost surprise and wonder, their size and colour pleased him: he said they were little elephants."

The gift had certainly been well chosen. Ranjit Singh, who was said to be fond of reciting the couplet:

Four things greater than all things are,
Women, and Horses, and Power, and War

was passionate about horses. Burnes soon had the opportunity to observe the maharajah's passion for women when, one evening, Ranjit Singh invited him to view his fabled female "soldiers." Something of a womanizer

himself, Burnes enjoyed the spectacle of thirty or forty bejeweled dancing girls, dressed like boys but in flowing silks, with bows and quivers in
their hands and gold dust around their eyes. "This is one of my regiments,
but they tell me it is one I cannot discipline," Ranjit Singh joked.

The maharaja was also keen to discuss more serious matters, quizzing Burnes about the navigability of the Indus and asking Burnes's opinion of his army and of the European officers he employed to train it. He
acknowledged frankly that he would like to make the rich provinces of
Sind his own and said he was curious to understand the relative strength
of the European powers.

The maharaja made much of Burnes, inviting him to breakfast on rice,
sugar, milk and preserved mangoes served on banana leaves, and sending
him the wine mixed with pearls and precious gems of which he himself
was "immoderately fond." In his turn, Burnes admired the maharaja,
whom he thought "an extraordinary character" whose two great weapons
of diplomacy were "cunning and conciliation." However, Burnes doubted
whether he had long to live since "his chest is contracted, his back is bent,
his limbs withered, and it is not likely that he can long bear up against a
nightly dose of spirits more ardent than the strongest brandy."

While in Lahore, Burnes explored the city, finding the tall houses
handsome but the streets narrow and "offensively filthy" from the open
sewers running down their center. He inspected the city's mosques,
where, as elsewhere in the Sikh Punjab, Muslims were required to pray in
silence. He also talked to some of Ranjit Singh's French officers who had
previously been in the service of the Persians and had traveled extensively. They talked of cities Burnes had never seen: Herat, Kandahar,
Ghazni and Kabul in Afghanistan and farther-flung near-mythic places
beyond the Oxus River like Bokhara. The Frenchmen's accounts caught
Burnes's imagination—especially when they described places vanquished
by his revered namesake Alexander—but good British agent that he was,
he also recorded regretfully that "the French have much better information of these countries than ourselves."

In mid-August, Burnes and his party took their leave of Ranjit Singh,
who showed him the Koh-i-Nur diamond that he had extorted from the
Afghan king Shah Shuja. It did not disappoint. "Nothing can be imagined
more superb than this stone; and it is of the finest water, and about half

the size of an egg." Ranjit Singh's final gift to Burnes was a silk pearl-hung bag containing the fulsome letter—a scroll nearly five feet long—which Burnes was to deliver to his masters in India. It rhapsodized about the English horses "of singular beauty, of mountainous form, and elephantine stature,"* hailed Burnes as "that nightingale of the garden of eloquence"— heady stuff for a young man not yet twenty-five—and hoped that the friendship between the Sikhs and the British would always continue to be firm.

From Lahore, Burnes traveled eastward to Ludhiana, where he met the deposed Afghan brothers Zaman Shah and Shah Shuja, living there in exile. Zaman Shah complained to Burnes of the inflammation in his eyes that he had suffered ever since being blinded and begged him piteously to intercede with the governor-general to put his brother back on his throne. Shah Shuja himself, dressed in pink gauze and wearing a green velvet cap, also received Burnes, who thought him corpulent and melancholy but affable. The Afghan spoke of his hopes of soon retrieving his fortunes, adding, "Had I but my kingdom, how glad should I be to see an En- glishman at Kabul and to open the road between Europe and India!" Burnes was unimpressed, writing farsightedly: "From what I learn, I do not believe the Shah possesses sufficient energy to seat himself on the throne of Kabul, and that if he did regain it, he has not the tact to dis- charge the duties of so difficult a situation."

Burnes traveled on a further hundred miles to the Himalayan hill station of Simla, where the governor-general, Lord William Bentinck, and his staff were escaping the hot weather of Calcutta and the plains. Bentinck congratulated him on his success in investigating the geography of the Indus and promised that his maps and reports would be brought to the attention of the authorities in England without delay. Burnes thought it a good moment to seek approval for a plan that had been forming in his mind of a journey to Kabul—one of Central Asia's greatest trading entrepôts—and on through the Hindu Kush to the kingdom of Bokhara and the Caspian Sea.

Burnes's timing was good, though not for the reasons he might have expected. While he had been sailing up the Indus, Arthur Conolly, the

*The horses are said to have soon died from a mixture of overfeeding and inactivity.

quiet, religious young officer generally credited with giving the Great
Game its name, had been returning overland to India after a period of sick
leave in England. From St. Petersburg he had gone to Tehran, then continued eastward through Persia and some of the small Central Asian states
into Afghanistan. In 1831 he had arrived in India convinced by what he
had seen that the Russians might—if they succeeded in taking the strategically placed walled city of Khiva, ruled over by a mentally unstable king
kept rich by slaving—be able to advance through Persia and Afghanistan
down into India unless the rulers of Afghanistan could be persuaded to
resist them. A powerful and united Afghanistan was, he argued, India's
best defense. The governor-general wanted to send someone quietly and
unobtrusively to find out more about Afghanistan and the lands beyond.
Once again, Burnes seemed an ideal candidate. He wrote jubilantly to
his sister, "The Home Government have got frightened at the designs of
Russia, and desired that some intelligent officer should be sent to acquire
information in the countries bordering on the Oxus . . . and I, knowing
nothing of all this, come forward and volunteer precisely for what they
want."

In December 1831 Burnes set out from Delhi on the new mission
that would shape the remainder of his life. This time his travel companions were the Indian surveyor who had accompanied him to Lahore, the
army surgeon James Gerard, who had traveled extensively in the Himalayas, and an Indian servant to cook for them. He also took with him as his
munshi, or secretary, a gifted young man whose life would become closely
interlinked with his own: Mohan Lal, a young Hindu Brahmin from
Kashmir whose father had been Elphinstone's *munshi* on his mission to
Shah Shuja and who was one of the first Indians to receive an English-
language education. At Burnes's request, Mohan Lal kept a diary of their
journey.

To avoid attention Burnes traveled simply, with the minimum of baggage. Pausing in Lahore, he was again lavishly entertained by Ranjit
Singh, who invited him tiger hunting and to wild drinking parties at which
tipsy dancing girls "tore and fought with each other." The Sikh ruler was
openly curious about the purpose of Burnes's new journey, but, knowing
his loathing for the Afghans, Burnes merely said that he was making a
leisurely journey home to Britain and was vague about his intended route.

A month later, Burnes and his companions were on the road again, having shaved their heads and donned turbans, long, flowing robes and sandals, and each taking only one saddlebag. At Attock they crossed the Indus and three miles farther on entered Afghan territory.

Their next destination was Peshawar, held by Sultan Mohammed Khan, rival and half brother of Dost Mohammed, who acknowledged Ranjit Singh as his overlord. Knowing they risked being robbed by bandits, Burnes secreted his few valuables, tying a bag of coins around his waist, fastening his passport to his right arm and disguising a letter of credit to look like an amulet which he wore on his left arm. However, they reached Peshawar unmolested. Sultan Mohammed Khan proved a good host, ordering his Kashmiri cook to make them sumptuous *pulaos*. Burnes thought him "an educated, well-bred gentleman, whose open and affable manner made the most lasting impression . . . his seraglio has about thirty inmates, and he has already had a family of sixty children. He could not tell me the exact number of survivors when I asked him!" Hearing where he was bound, Sultan Mohammed Khan urged Burnes to abandon his journey, warning that if he traveled to Bokhara "nothing could save [him] from the *ferocious* and man-selling Uzbeks: the country, the people, everything was bad." Burnes was not dissuaded but took Sultan Mohammed Khan's advice to dress yet more simply. In the bazaar the party bought the cheapest clothes they could find. Burnes dyed his beard black and henceforth called himself "Sekundur," Persian for Alexander, and claimed to be an Armenian. The Hindu Mohan Lal took the Muslim name Hassan Jan.

In mid-April the party set out for Kabul. Warned to avoid the Khyber Pass because of the wild Khyberee tribesmen infesting it, Burnes and his companions followed another route along the swift-flowing Khyber River, crossing it twice, once on "a frail and unsafe" raft which bore them a mile downstream before they were able to gain the opposite bank while their horses and pack animals swam across. After a week's hard journeying they found themselves plodding across the bone-dry, stony plain toward the town of Jalalabad. Burnes was told that in the summer months a hot wind known as the simoom scoured the land, driving men and animals insane and putrefying their living bodies. The only remedy was water poured violently down the victim's throat or a mixture of sugar and dried Bokhara plums. Burnes was skeptical but thought the plain a fear-some place best avoided in the summer heat.

From Jalalabad, which Burnes thought one of the dirtiest places he had ever seen, they moved on to Gandamack, where, according to the Afghans, the cooler climes began. Passing shepherds driving their flocks up to the summer pasturelands, they reached Kabul on 1 May 1832, to be welcomed by another of Dost Mohammed's half brothers, Nawab Jubbar Khan—a man of great influence over the Barakzai clan and known as a good friend to Europeans. He installed Burnes and his party in a wing of his mansion—not a moment too soon for Dr. Gerard, who was suffering badly from dysentery.

Almost immediately, Burnes learned of a European being detained in a nearby village and sent help. The man who arrived next day at Nawab Jubbar Khan's house was the disputatious Joseph Wolff. Though now a British citizen and Anglican clergyman married to an English noblewoman, he had begun life as the son of a German rabbi but, as intellectually curious as he was physically restless, he had converted first to Lutherism, then to Catholicism. When his endless questions in Rome proved too much for the Papal Curia, he was bundled into a coach and deported. Arriving in England, he found that Anglicanism suited him and decided to become a missionary. His tales of travels through Central Asia, during which he had been kidnapped, robbed, shipwrecked, threatened with being burned alive and stripped of all he possessed, and especially his account of the kingdom of Bokhara, fascinated Burnes.

Leaving Gerard to recover, Burnes and his new friend accepted an invitation to call on Dost Mohammed in the great gray fortress, the ancient Balla Hissar, overlooking the city. The Afghan leader, now in his midforties, was often described as resembling an Old Testament prophet. He had an aquiline nose, hazel-gray eyes and every Thursday had his thick beard dyed black ready for the Friday Muslim Sabbath. Seating his guests close by him, he showed a lively curiosity, questioning them about every-thing from how Europe's kings coexisted without destroying one another, the extent of Britain's wealth (which, he asserted, "must come from In-dia"), whether the British had designs on Kabul, the uses of steam en-gines and what the Chinese were like. He then asked the purpose of Burnes's journey and why he was dressed as he was. Burnes replied that he had a great desire to travel and was returning to Europe by way of Bokhara. He had changed his clothing for safety and comfort but had no intention of trying to conceal from Dost Mohammed that he "was an Englishman."

Burnes was soon enamored of populous, bustling Kabul, writing to his mother that "truly, this is a paradise." Together with Mohan Lal he wandered the narrow winding streets of baked-mud brick houses and admired the bazaars piled with the city's fabled fruit: grapes, pears, apples, apricots, quinces, melons and rhubarb. However, he was most interested in the people, sauntering about in sheepskin cloaks that made them look huge. Mohan Lal thought the Kabul women promiscuous despite their head-to-toe coverings and in his journal inscribed the proverb: "The flour of Peshawar is not without the mixture of barley; and the women of Kabul are not without lovers."

The two men visited the Armenian quarter, whose inhabitants complained that because of the prohibition on alcohol by Dost Mohammed— "a reformed drunkard"—they had lost their main means of support, though Burnes noted that wine could still be found and that it tasted like Madeira. They also explored the area in the shadow of the Balla Hissar inhabited by the Kizzilbashis, descendants of the soldiers left behind by the Persian Nadir Shah, of whom Dost Mohammed's mother was one. However, Burnes could not linger. He had hoped to join one of the great caravans traveling north from Kabul but learned that the northern passes were still snowbound and he would have to wait. Instead, he decided to form his own small caravan and hired "a hale old man who had grown grey in crossing the Hindu Kush" as their personal *cafila-bashee*, or "conductor." Nawab Jubbar Khan, who was convinced Burnes and his companions would all be slain or taken as slaves, pressed him to take with him his steward's brother and provided Burnes with letters of introduction to the emir of Bokhara.

At Burnes's final meeting with Dost Mohammed, the Afghan ruler laid bare his political difficulties, including his difficult relations with his half brothers in Peshawar and Kandahar. He was especially virulent about Ranjit Singh and asked Burnes whether the British would accept his help to destroy the maharaja—a question that would bedevil Dost Mohammed's relations with Britain and to which Burnes could only reply that the maharaja was a "friend" of the British. Changing tack, Dost Mohammed startled Burnes by offering him the command of his army, an honor he courteously declined. Before Burnes left, Dost Mohammed ordered a slave boy brought before them because he thought Burnes would want to see a member of the Kaffir tribe from the mountains north of Kabul, reputedly descended from the soldiers of Alexander the Great. Though the boy was pale and had bluish eyes, Burnes was unconvinced he had Macedonian ancestry.

Departing Kabul in mid-May, Burnes carried away with him an impression of Dost Mohammed as "the most rising man in Kabul"—an able man and a strong leader, far superior to Shah Shuja. He was convinced that "unless it be propped up by foreign aid," the old Sadozai regime with its exiled figurehead Shah Shuja languishing at British expense in Ludhiana had passed away "in favour of the more vigorous Barakzais whose supremacy seemed acceptable to the people." Events would prove him absolutely correct. However, his view of the Afghans in general was misjudged. He thought them "a nation of children; in their quarrels they fight, and become friends without any ceremony. They cannot conceal their feelings from one another and a person with any discrimination may at all times pierce their designs . . . their ruling vice is envy . . . No people are more incapable of managing intrigue."

As Burnes and his companions trudged north through hilly country, where the snows still lay five feet deep, toward the Hindu Kush, Burnes suffered agonies of snowblindness—the burning of the cornea—from the glaring reflection of the sun on the white landscape. However, reaching the valley of Bamiyan with its two Buddhist statues, a male figure 120 feet high and a female one 70 feet tall carved into the mountainside, he was sufficiently recovered to sketch them.* Soon they had passed from Afghan territory into lands controlled by slave-taking Uzbek tribes, fanatical in their observance of Sunni Islam. Burnes and his party had to be very careful not to cause offense. After being warned that they should never sleep with their feet toward Mecca, "which would be evincing [their] contempt for that holy place," Burnes took the precaution of consulting

---

*These are the statues recently destroyed by the Taliban, though Burnes noted that they had already suffered damage.

his compass indoors as well as out. He also trimmed the central part of his mustache to avoid being taken for a Shia Muslim.

By early June they were out of the towering defiles of the mountains and entering the plains sloping northward to the Oxus River. Ahead lay the lands of Murad Beg, ferocious Uzbek ruler of Kunduz, of which it was said, "If you wish to die, go to Kunduz." Burnes hoped to move swiftly onward without attracting attention. He and his party never changed their clothes, ignoring the lice, used their sleeves as towels and their nails as combs, ate hard bread and slept on dung-covered floors, but Burnes thought these just petty inconveniences "when compared with the pleasure of seeing new men and countries, strange manners and customs, and being able to temper the prejudices of one's country, by observing those of other nations." One of those customs, though, was the sale of sad, dejected slaves in the bazaars. Mohan Lal watched a prospective purchaser take a girl behind a wall to examine her body: "when her veil was lifted up by the seller and gradually her cap and sheet, the woman, turning her face towards the sky, began to rend the air by her screams."

However, through the officiousness of the Afghan that Nawab Jubbar Khan had sent with the party, Murad Beg learned of their presence and summoned Burnes to Kunduz, seventy miles away. Leaving Dr. Gerard and Mohan Lal behind, Burnes set out, uncomfortably aware that some years earlier another expedition led by an East India Company veterinary surgeon called William Moorcroft, the first Englishman to reach Bokhara, had been imprisoned by Murad Beg. Reaching Kunduz, Burnes put on a pair of high felt boots to conceal his "provokingly white ankles" and with some trepidation waited on the Uzbek chief, an ugly man "with harsh Tartar features." However, Murad Beg believed Burnes's story that he was just a poor Armenian traveler, and he returned with relief to his companions.

They traveled onward to Balkh—the ancient Bactria, homeland of Alexander's wife, Roxane—where an Uzbek customs official tried unsuccessfully to seduce Mohan Lal, sending him lovelorn Persian verses. By then they had exchanged their horses for camels, on which they were carried in woven panniers four feet long and three feet wide, banging against the camels' bony ribs. As they traveled over the arid desert toward the Oxus River, sand whipped their faces and their parched lips burned.

After being towed in a boat by swimming horses over the Oxus, they found themselves among nomadic Turkoman tribesmen, whose chief livelihood was plundering caravans and who purchased their wives; the price of a girl was five camels, while a woman could cost up to a hundred since experience counted for more than beauty.

Fearing that after their arduous journey they might be denied entry into Bokhara, Burnes dispatched a letter to the principal minister requesting the protection of the emir, whom he hailed as the "Commander of the Faithful." It was granted, and on 27 June, they passed through the city gates. Exchanging their turbans for Bokharan sheepskin caps to avoid attracting attention, they stayed in the city nearly a month. The slave markets, where on Saturday mornings human flesh was trafficked, shocked them. They also witnessed how justice was dispensed when they came across Muslims being flogged for sleeping after sunrise and missing their morning prayers or for smoking. Anyone caught flying pigeons on a Friday was paraded on a camel with one of their birds dead around their neck.

Yet they also found much to enjoy in this city intersected by canals, shaded by mulberry trees, bringing water from the Zerafshan River.* They lodged in a small house, one attraction of which was that "it presented an opportunity of seeing a Turkoman beauty, a handsome young lady, who promenaded one of the surrounding balconies." Burnes went to the hamman to be "laid out at full length, rubbed with a hair brush, scrubbed, buffeted and kicked," which was "very refreshing." In Bokhara's thriving bazaars they examined silks, spices, silver and tea, and Burnes discovered English chintz for sale, on which, so the merchants told him, they could make a 50 percent profit. They ate grape jelly with crushed ice and strolled in the Registan—the great square in front of the emir's palace—where a stranger only had to seat himself on a bench to "converse with the natives of Persia, Turkey, Russia, Tartary, China, India and Kabul."

Burnes was disappointed to be refused an audience with Bokhara's ruler, Emir Nasrullah, but observed him leaving the mosque, noting his pale gaunt face and small eyes. He was in fact a man of vicious habits already on the path to insanity, who had those who displeased him thrown into the *zidane*—a pit which he kept well stocked with flesh-biting insects, reptiles and rotting filth.

---

*The name Zerafshan means "gold-bearing." The river also flows past Samarkand.

Burnes left Bokhara in July 1832 convinced that, provided secure trade routes could be established along the Indus and through Afghanistan, English manufactured goods could compete on price as well as quality with those the Russians sent through their network of internal waterways. As Burnes and his party headed westward for the long trek across the feared Turkoman desert to Meshed in Persia, they passed lines of slaves trudging toward Bokhara. Mohal Lal saw a group "walking barefoot in the fiery desert. Their hands and necks were fastened together with an iron chain. They were completely exhausted with hunger, thirst and fatigue. They were crying and begging for something to eat and Burnes gave them a melon." Before long, though, their own plight was nearly as bad. Both people and animals were dying of thirst, and Burnes watched desperate men opening the veins of their camels to drink their blood. By September 1832, however, they finally reached Meshed, and the group now divided. Mohan Lal, to whom Burnes gave a testimonial praising his great tact and diplomacy, and Dr. Gerard set out back overland to India, while Burnes headed for the Caspian Sea and thence to Tehran.

He was received by the elderly Persian shah, who greeted him with the strange question demanded by court etiquette, "*Dumagh i shooma chak ust?*" (Are your brains clear?) before interrogating him closely. He was interested to know whether Burnes had taken notes to which he truthfully replied, "Yes, I have measured the roads . . . and sounded the rivers." The shah also inquired into such minutiae as whether the journey had been expensive and whether Burnes had sampled horseflesh while among Uzbeks. Having satisfied the shah's curiosity, Burnes finally headed south to the Persian Gulf, where he took a ship for Bombay.

Burnes's reports on all he had seen—in particular on the potential for British trade as a source both of profit and of influence to counter Russian ambitions and on the potential for military advances by the Russians toward Kabul—so impressed the governor-general that he sent him to London to tell his story to the government in person. When he arrived there in October 1833, a gratified Burnes found himself lionized by every society hostess anxious to secure "Bokhara Burnes," as he had become known, for her parties. He met the prime minister, was presented to the king and began preparing his journals for publication. However, if he expected promotion to some exalted position, he was mistaken; some, like Lord Ellenborough at the Board of Control, thought him cocksure and "immensely vain." Though promoted to the rank of captain, the young man who had "beheld the scenes of Alexander's wars, of the rude and savage inroads of Genghis and Timur" and "marched on the very line of route by which Alexander had pursued Darius," after turning down a subordinate post in the British mission at Tehran, accepted a posting back to the relatively junior position he had occupied before his travels up the Indus as assistant to the company's resident in Kutch. However, events would shortly thrust him forward again.

CHAPTER THREE

Everything tends to show the gigantic scale upon which Russia's projects of aggrandisement are formed, and how necessary it is for other nations to keep vigilant watch, and have their horses always saddled.

—LORD PALMERSTON, SEPTEMBER 1834

ALEXANDER BURNES SOON learned that he had underestimated Shah Shuja. While the Scotsman had still been traveling, the exiled Afghan king, whom he had thought too uncharismatic and lethargic to inspire his countrymen's support, had begun a bid to retake his throne. Encouraged by rumors that the Persians were planning to attack the western Afghan city of Herat and knowing this would distract Dost Mohammed, Shah Shuja had approached Ranjit Singh. Though by no means natural allies, each could offer something the other wanted. They negotiated a treaty under which Shah Shuja agreed to let the Sikh ruler have Peshawar and some surrounding territory—if he could take it from Dost Mohammed's half brother Sultan Mohammed Khan—while Ranjit Singh would help Shah Shuja oust Dost Mohammed himself from Kabul. During the negotiations Shah Shuja refused a request that he return to India the gates of the Hindu temple at Somnath removed to Ghazni eight hundred years previously by the emperor Mahmud. Conscious that he was under British protection, Shah Shuja also tested the British reaction to his plans. Governor-General Bentinck responded blandly that the British government "religiously abstains from intermeddling with the affairs of

37

its neighbours," but he did not attempt to dissuade him from his expedition and later granted Shah Shuja four months' advance on his pension to help him recruit an army.

In February 1833 Shah Shuja left Ludhiana with three thousand soldiers, crossed the Indus and advanced into Sind, where he defeated its rulers in battle, forcing them to acknowledge his supremacy and pay him a huge sum in tribute. Fortified financially and politically, Shah Shuja and his army, which had grown to twenty-four thousand, advanced through the Bolan Pass toward the southern Afghan city of Kandahar.

As increasingly urgent demands for help from Kandahar's rulers, his unreliable half brothers, reached Dost Mohammed, he debated what to do. Recalling Burnes's protestations of British goodwill, he wrote to the governor-general seeking an alliance but was gently rebuffed and decided to lead his armies to the relief of Kandahar. Arriving in the summer of 1834, he fell on his rival's besieging forces. According to some accounts, at the height of the battle, Shah Shuja, who had been viewing the fighting from a distance, lost heart and fled on elephant back, sparking panic among his men, who began streaming from the field. Whatever the case, Dost Mohammed was victorious. He was probably not surprised when among the captured baggage his men found letters written by the British political officer Claude Wade urging the Afghan tribal leaders, including Dost Mohammed's own chiefs, to support Shah Shuja.

However, Dost Mohammed had more pressing matters to deal with than British double-talk. Returning to Kabul, he learned that Peshawar had fallen to Ranjit Singh. Deploying his favored weapons of "cunning and conciliation," as Burnes had called them, the Lion of Lahore had gulled Peshawar's Sultan Mohammed Khan into believing he might assist him in dethroning his half brother Dost Mohammed. In May 1834 one of Ranjit Singh's most senior commanders, Hari Singh, had arrived outside Peshawar with nine thousand Sikh troops. The purpose of his visit was supposedly diplomatic, but there was nothing diplomatic about the way he occupied the city and ejected Sultan Mohammed Khan, who fled with his forces to Jalalabad. For a while he contemplated trying to capture Kabul from his half brother but learning of Dost Mohammed's victory at Kandahar instead sought his protection.

Although he had never ruled the city of Peshawar and its surrounding

territory, to Dost Mohammed its loss to the infidel Sikhs was a shameful blow to Afghan and Islamic prestige. He declared himself Amir-al-Mominin (Commander of the Faithful), and began striking coins bearing the words *Amir Dost Mohammed, by the grace of God*, ghazi (holy warrior). He also displayed to the populace, as a sign of his commitment to the cause, a cloak believed to have belonged to the prophet Mohammed.* Before long he had amassed a large army to engage in jihad, holy war, against the Sikhs. The American adventurer Josiah Harlan described how Dost Mohammed appeared "with fifty thousand belligerent candidates for martyrdom and immortality. Savages from the remotest recesses of the mountainous districts, who were dignified with the profession of the Mohammedan faith, many of them giants in form and strength, promiscuously armed with sword and shield, bows and arrows, matchlocks, rifles, spears and blunderbusses . . . prepared to slay, plunder and destroy for the sake of God and the prophet, the unenlightened infidels of the Punjab."

The thirty-three-year-old Harlan, born in Pennsylvania, had originally come to India as a supercargo on a merchant ship before finding employment—despite a lack of relevant academic qualifications—with the East India Company as a surgeon and then transferring to the company's artillery and serving in Burma. At this time he was in Ranjit Singh's service with the Sikh rank of general. He cultivated a dashing, buccaneering appearance. Dr. Richard Kennedy, a British army surgeon who encountered him later in Kabul, described "a tall manly figure, with a large head and gaunt face . . . dressed in a light, shining, pea-green satin jacket, maroon-coloured silk small-clothes, buff boots, a silver-lace girdle fastened with a large, square buckle bigger than a soldier's breast-plate, and on his head a white cat-skin foraging cap with a glittering gold band and tassels." But Kennedy also deduced that "though he dressed like a mountebank," Harlan was no fool. He had a vast amount of local knowledge and great shrewdness.

While Josiah Harlan observed events from the Sikh side, a British agent calling himself Charles Masson was accompanying Dost Mohammed. Masson was another of the eccentrics and mavericks who, like Harlan, flitted in and out of the Great Game. He had first come to the attention

---

*The next person to display it and to call himself Amir-al-Mominin would be Mullah Omar, the Taliban leader, in 1996.

of the British authorities at Bushire on the Persian Gulf in 1830 when he had claimed to be an American archaeologist born in Kentucky with important political information to impart about Russian ambitions in Central Asia. His assertion that he was American was, like his supposed name, false. He was, in fact, an English deserter named James Lewis who in 1827 had assumed an American identity to avoid detection. An educated man with a passion for archaeology and coin collecting, he had embarked on an extraordinary odyssey through the Khyber Pass to Afghanistan, where he had met and been impressed by Dost Mohammed.* Journeying onward to Kandahar, he had been repeatedly robbed and at one stage stripped completely naked, surviving only through the kindness of a stranger who gave him a sheepskin coat.

Deciding enough was enough, he had traveled through Sind and west to Bushire. Luckily for him, the East India Company's resident official at this Persian port readily believed his story and dispatched him to the British mission to the shah's court. Not only was his identity again accepted without question, but the British envoy offered to fund his archaeological studies in Afghanistan in return for intelligence on what was happening there. Masson had returned to Kabul in June 1832, only a few days after Burnes and his party had passed through on their way to Bokhara.

Claude Wade, in his headquarters in Ludhiana, had learned of Masson's existence and ordered his agent in Kabul, Seyyid Keramat Ali, to watch him. The behavior of the gray-eyed, red-haired, shabbily dressed Masson as he poked about old ruins was, as the agent reported to Wade, decidedly odd. Around this time Dr. Gerard and Mohan Lal, returning to India after parting from Burnes, also encountered Masson. From them Wade discovered how well connected Masson had become in Kabul. Dost Mohammed's favorite son, Akbar Khan, had become his patron, and many leading Afghans, including Dost Mohammed himself, were his friends.

However much Masson deceived his fellow countrymen, Josiah Harlan, a real American, knew he was a fraud. Harlan had earlier encountered Masson in the Punjab and warned Dr. Gerard that he was an imposter. Gerard duly told Wade, who soon identified Masson as the army deserter

---

*The British Museum in London has many specimens collected by Masson, including 6,200 coins.

James Lewis. Unmasking and punishing him if he returned to British jurisdiction was one option, but instead Wade decided to use Masson to
replace Seyyid Keramat Ali, whose activities were beginning to excite
suspicion in Kabul. In April 1834 Wade had therefore written to the
governor-general arguing that though desertion was a heinous crime, Masson should be pardoned if he agreed to spy for the British. Within weeks
Wade received permission to recruit Masson. The latter's feelings at being
essentially blackmailed were equivocal, but he recognized that he had no
choice.

Thus "Charles Masson," as he continued to call himself, was with
Dost Mohammed as he prepared to confront the army that Ranjit Singh
had assembled to defend Peshawar. Even more fearsome than Dost Mohammed's and certainly better disciplined, it consisted of sixty thousand
troops under the maharaja's own command, twenty thousand men commanded by French mercenary officers and a battery of twenty-four cannon
under the American Alexander Gardner. Dost Mohammed doubted his
ability to win and, at Masson's suggestion, asked the British to intervene.
His enduring hope that the British would help him against Ranjit Singh
despite so much evidence—both overt and covert—to the contrary would
be one of the most striking contributors to Dost Mohammed's behavior. In
March 1835 he received his reply: The British would not interfere over
Peshawar. Dost Mohammed was left feeling like a "fly facing an elephant."

However, the Afghan leader still hoped to find a diplomatic solution,
and Ranjit Singh exploited those hopes to trick him. The agent of his deceit was Josiah Harlan, who arrived in Dost Mohammed's camp in the
Khyber Pass ostensibly to initiate diplomatic discussions but with the secret purpose of trying to bribe the Afghan chiefs to desert Dost Mohammed's army. He later boasted of how he "divided his [Dost Mohammed's]
brothers against him exciting their jealousy . . . and stirred up the feudal
lords of his durbar, with the prospect of pecuniary advantages." In particular, he induced Dost Mohammed's half brother Sultan Mohammed
Khan, the former ruler of Peshawar, to defect and ride with his followers
under cover of darkness for the Sikh camp.

The result was everything Harlan had hoped. The desertion of such
a large body of soldiers threw Dost Mohammed's camp "into inextricable
confusion, which terminated in the clandestine rout of his forces, without

beat of drum, or sound of bugle or the trumpet's blast, in the quiet still-
ness of midnight. At daybreak no vestige of the Afghan camp was seen
where, six hours before, 50,000 men and 10,000 horses with all the busy
host of attendants were rife with the tumult of wild commotion," he
wrote. Even if Harlan exaggerated, which he almost certainly did, Dost
Mohammed could only retreat to Kabul, where for the moment he turned
his back on the world to contemplate the deceit of his close family members and to study the Koran.

Claude Wade, meanwhile, following events from Ludhiana, was
growing increasingly convinced that it was in the British interest for Shah
Shuja, not Dost Mohammed, to occupy the throne in Kabul. After years
of living under British protection and at British expense, Shah Shuja would
be more malleable in British hands. Also, to Wade, Shah Shuja's weak-
nesses were an asset. The younger, more able, more vigorous and charismatic Dost Mohammed was far more capable of stamping his authority
on Afghanistan's disparate tribal elements and creating a strong, united
country. Once he had done so, he might be tempted to play politics with
Britain's enemies. Far better, felt Wade, that Shah Shuja should preside as
a bland figurehead king of a weak Afghanistan whose feudal chiefs, preoccupied with their own affairs and rivalries, would be easier for Britain
to manipulate.

Although he shared much of Wade's assessment of Dost Mohammed's and Shah Shuja's characters, Burnes's views on the best course of
action ran directly counter to Wade's. Burnes thought Dost Mohammed's
competence and intelligence would make him a reliable ally. He firmly
believed in a strong Afghanistan under Dost Mohammed and thought
Ranjit Singh was growing far too powerful for the region's stability and for
Britain's prospects of developing the Indus as a trade route for British
goods. His ideal was political equilibrium between the Sikhs, the Afghans
and the Sindis.

However, changes in the political landscape at home in Britain made
Wade's views the more likely to prevail. In March 1835, just as Ranjit
Singh and Dost Mohammed were confronting each other, the Tory gov-
ernment of Sir Robert Peel was replaced by a Whig government under
Lord Melbourne. He selected his close friend Lord Palmerston as his for-
eign secretary, a position Palmerston had occupied and enjoyed previously.

A believer that "the law of self-preservation is a fundamental principle of the law of nations" and for whose policies the term *gunboat diplomacy* would later be coined, Palmerston had begun his political career with the Tories but to the surprise—discomfort even—of some within the Whig party had switched his allegiance to them. While previously at the Foreign Office, Palmerston had often dismayed his officials by his forceful, impulsive independence. Melbourne also selected two others who would influence—through acts of either commission or omission—the coming Afghan drama. The fifty-one-year-old George Eden, Lord Auckland, was appointed governor-general in place of Lord William Bentinck, whose five-year tour of duty had ended. Auckland, a former First Lord of the Admiralty and a man with no experience of India and its affairs, was a pleasant, cautious and kindly man who meant it when he spoke of his desire of "doing good to his fellow creatures—of promoting education and knowledge . . . of extending the blessings of good government and happiness to millions in India." Lord Ellenborough's successor as president of the Board of Control responsible for Britain's policy in India was Sir John Hobhouse.

In the autumn of 1835, the bachelor Lord Auckland sailed for India with his two spinster sisters Emily and Fanny, who were to act as his hostesses, to be greeted on his arrival five months later by disquieting reports that the Persians, actively encouraged by the Russians, and in particular their ambassador in Tehran, Count Simonich, were preparing to seize the Afghan cities of Kandahar and Herat. John McNeill, secretary to the British envoy in Tehran, argued in a pamphlet on his return to London that an independent Persia was absolutely essential to India's security. Otherwise, he predicted that (in what would become known as *a domino effect*) all other rulers between Persia and India would come under Russian influence, threatening India's security. He also asserted that "the right of interference in the affairs of independent states is founded on this single principle, that as self preservation is the first duty, so it supersedes all other obligations," before concluding, "it is the ambition of Russia that forces upon us the necessity of endeavouring to preserve that which is obviously necessary to our own protection. If she will not give us security for the future she can have no right to complain if we should take all practicable measures to impede and obstruct the course she has so perseveringly pursued. If she attempts to justify her own aggressions, on what principle can she complain of measures of defence, however extensive?" His rhetoric, at the same time utterly Machiavellian and Palmerstonian and utterly modern, struck a chord in official circles, especially when reports soon followed from the British mission in Tehran emphasizing the extent of Russian influence in Persia and also reporting that Dost Mohammed was offering to help the Persians take Herat if they would partition its territory with him and help him against the Sikhs.

These reports, seeming to confirm some of their worst fears, thoroughly alarmed the British. In June 1836 the Secret Committee of the East India Company dispatched a letter asking the newly arrived Governor-General Auckland to send an envoy to Afghanistan to assess whether the moment had come "to interfere decidedly in the affairs of Afghanistan" to halt Russian encroachment. The words *to interfere* meant only one thing: military intervention. When he received the letter some months later, Auckland was reluctant to take military action, even though he "would not under-rate the value of Afghanistan as an outwork to [Britain's] Indian possessions." He believed the most effective way to counter Russian influence was through expanding British trade on the Indus and beyond, and cultivating the friendship of the neighboring rulers. However, his three closest advisers all strongly favored an interventionist policy in Afghanistan and would over the critical months ahead manipulate a cautious and sometimes indecisive Auckland.

The most senior member of this trio was the forty-three-year-old Chief Secretary William Hay Macnaghten, an ambitious, scholarly archbureaucrat and old India hand who had served Bentinck. Auckland's sister Emily wryly nicknamed him "*our* Lord Palmerston," describing him as "a dry, sensible man, who wears an enormous pair of blue spectacles and speaks Persian, Arabic and Hindustani rather more fluently than English but for familiar conversation rather prefers Sanskrit." Macnaghten had been born in Calcutta and, after receiving his education in England, spent five years in undemanding posts as a junior officer in the East India Company's army before joining the administration, where he had made his mark in codifying laws before moving into more general policy work. An officer who had worked with Macnaghten described him as "dry as dry, like an old nut and so reserved as to be rude." The other two advisers were Henry Torrens, Auckland's assistant secretary, and John Colvin, his private secretary.

DOST MOHAMMED WAS hoping that the new governor-general would prove more sympathetic to him than had Bentinck, whom he blamed for the loss of Peshawar. In the spring of 1836 he had written to Auckland congratulating him on his appointment, saying, "The field of my hopes, (which had before been chilled by the cold blast of the times) has, by the happy tidings of your Lordship's arrival, become the envy of the garden of Paradise." He also asked Auckland's advice on dealing with the "reckless and misguided Sikhs" and concluded, "[I hope] your Lordship will consider me and our country as your own"—an offer he did not intend to be construed as one day it would be.

Auckland took several months to reply. When he did, his friendly but unhelpful letter assured Dost Mohammed that the British desired a thriving and united Afghanistan and hoped the Sikhs and Afghans could bury their differences; and then stated that the British would like Dost Mohammed's help to exploit the navigation of the Indus for the commercial benefit of both countries, to which end Auckland would "depute some gentleman" to go to Kabul. The letter concluded with a statement that must have struck Dost Mohammed as deliberately obtuse if not downright hypocritical: "My friend, you are aware that it is not the practice of the British Government to interfere with the affairs of other independent states; and indeed it does not immediately occur to me how the interference of my government could be exercised for your benefit [with the Sikhs]."

The envoy whom Auckland decided to send to Kabul to fulfill his promise to Dost Mohammed—which chimed with the desire of the Secret Committee, when it eventually became known to him, that someone should be sent—was Alexander Burnes, whom he had met in London but who had since returned to Kutch. Auckland told Dost Mohammed that Burnes's orders were to explore "the best means of promoting the interests of commerce, and facilitating the intercourse of traders between India and Afghanistan." His real mission, however, was to persuade Dost Mohammed both to be reconciled with Ranjit Singh and to keep the Russians and Persians out of his territories.

In November 1836 Burnes left Bombay. This time his companions were Lieutenant Robert Leech of the Bombay Engineers, a stout, good-natured man who would use the journey to produce one of the first detailed maps of the Khyber Pass, and Lieutenant John Wood of the Indian navy. Burnes would later be joined by his former traveling companion Mohan Lal and by Dr. Percival Lord. As before, Burnes found much to interest him on the journey. Sailing up the Indus, he decided that having tasted frog, horse, shark and camel, he might as well sample crocodile, but he found the flesh tasteless and dry. By June 1837 he had reached Dera Ismael on the Indus, where, resisting such diversions as almond-eyed dancing girls adorned with necklaces of cloves, he settled down to pen a letter to Dost Mohammed "enlarging on the advantages of peace."

Despite dangers including the "smart shock of an earthquake," Burnes and his companions were, by comparison with his previous journeys, clearly traveling in some comfort. After pitching camp by a "crystal rivulet" flowing through some once celebrated Mogul gardens, they charged their glasses with burgundy and toasted the beauty of their surroundings. All the time, however, Burnes was making detailed observations of the flow of the Indus, the depth of the fords, the strength of any fortifications they passed and evidence of mineral deposits like coal.

In late August, with the temperature touching one hundred degrees Fahrenheit and a haze low on the surrounding mountains, the party reached Lahore, where General Paolo Avitabile, an Italian mercenary employed by Ranjit Singh as governor, received them. Avitabile exercised his formidable authority through extortion. A shocked British officer described how "all fines being the perquisites of the governor, he is not chary of their infliction. Almost all crimes, even murder, may be atoned for by money, to extort which, torture is always applied." The hands and noses of those too poor or obstinate to pay were lopped off. In one case, where he had given up hope of extracting money from the miscreants, Avitabile allowed a mother whose son had been killed to slit the murderers' throats and drink their blood. However, Avitabile was exceedingly affable to his British guests, driving them in his own carriage on the next stage of their journey to Jamrud, three miles south of the mouth of the Khyber Pass, through which Burnes, having requested safe conduct from the local chiefs, proposed to travel.

Some weeks earlier, while still on the Indus, Burnes had learned of a battle between the Afghans and the Sikhs that had recently taken place at Jamrud, which, he noted, was in ruins. Dost Mohammed in a letter to Burnes claimed the Afghans had been provoked by the Sikhs' fortress building. Victorious in their initial assault, the Afghans had not felt able to press their advantage because of fear of the arrival of Sikh reinforcements. They had therefore fallen back on Kabul, leaving the Sikhs still in possession of Jamrud, where Burnes observed them busily constructing one of their new forts. Even though several thousand men had died on each side, the confrontation was more significant in political than in military terms because it further reinforced the British government's view that there was little chance of achieving a rapprochement between Ranjit Singh and Dost Mohammed and that any alliance with the latter would seriously endanger British-Sikh friendship.

Practical problems preoccupied Burnes at Jamrud. There was no sign of the Afghan escort he had optimistically asked "the chiefs of the pass" to provide. While they waited, his party had to endure "the effluvia from the dead bodies, both of men and horses" from the recent battle, which Burnes found "quite revolting." They were also given ample evidence of how dangerous these lands were when tribesmen attacked some of their camel drivers, drove off the camels and beheaded two of the men, whose mangled torsos were later brought into camp.

Running out of patience, Burnes decided, against Avitabile's earnest advice, to wait no longer, and on 2 September his party somewhat gingerly entered the Khyber Pass, an obstacle of legendary difficulty—in an officer's words, "a narrow defile of twenty-eight miles long, between lofty perpendicular hills, the road during its entire length passing over rocks and boulders, which render a speedy advance or retreat of any body of men impossible. The heights on either side entirely command the defile, and are scarped so that they cannot without great difficulty be scaled. They are also perforated with numbers of natural caves, the secure haunts of the savage robbers who have for ages held possession of the pass."

On this occasion the tribes, in return for payment, treated them well. Over the next few days they were passed from one tribe to the next. Burnes later wrote, "Our march was not without a degree of anxious excitement. We were moving among a savage tribe, who set the Sikhs at defiance, and who paid but an unwilling allegiance to Kabul . . . By the road they showed us many small mounds, built to mark the spots where they had planted the heads of the Sikhs whom they had decapitated after the late victory: on some of these mounds locks of hair were yet to be seen."

To Burnes's relief, they cleared the Khyber Pass safely, and as they drew nearer to Kabul enjoyed the cool pine-scented air and groves of ripe pomegranates. One of those who came to greet them along the road was the elderly *cafila-bashee* who had helped Burnes through the Hindu Kush on his way to Bokhara and who now brought with him several mule-loads of fruit from another old friend, Nawab Jubbar Khan. Burnes gave the man a comfortable tent and a good *pulao*. He was soon also joined by Charles Masson, with whom he had been corresponding regularly and of whose low opinion of himself he was unaware. An embittered Masson later wrote that from the first he derived little confidence that Burnes would succeed, "either from his manner, or from his opinion 'that the Afghans were to be treated as children.' A remark that drew from me the reply that he must not then expect them to behave as men."

Traveling on through steep-sided passes dotted with pines and holly trees, Burnes and his party at last saw "the distant hills over Kabul" emerge on the horizon. On 20 September 1837, a full ten months after departing from Bombay, they entered Kabul to be greeted "with great pomp and splendour by a fine body of Afghan cavalry," led by the emir's favorite son, Akbar Khan, who honored the envoy by placing Burnes beside him in the howdah of his own elephant. This was perhaps no more than Burnes ex-pected. Dost Mohammed had written to him, "My house is your house and if it pleases God, we shall soon know the secret wishes of each other."

The delegation was accommodated within the Balla Hissar fortress, and the next day Burnes presented a letter from Lord Auckland eulogiz-ing the benefits of commerce to Dost Mohammed, who greeted him warmly. When Burnes referred to "some of the rarities of Europe" that he had brought as gifts, he replied that Burnes and his companions "were the rarities the sight of which best pleased him." Josiah Harlan was by then in Kabul and in Dost Mohammed's service. He had been dismissed by Ranjit Singh for allegedly counterfeiting coins, pretending to have suc-ceeded in the old alchemist's trick of turning base metal into gold as well as demanding an extortionate fee from the maharaja to treat him after one of his many strokes. According to Harlan, Dost Mohammed actually thought Burnes's gifts, which included a brass telescope, a pair of pistols and trinkets and knickknacks for his harem such as a toy accordion, were tawdry. "Behold! I have feasted and honoured this Feringee to the extent of six thousand rupees, and have now a lot of pins and needles and sundry petty toys to show for my folly!" he complained in private.

The Afghan leader must have also been both confused and suspicious about British intentions toward him. He had hard evidence that the British had actively connived at Shah Shuja's attempt in 1833 to take his throne from him, and knew that they continued to be active supporters of his great enemy Ranjit Singh. However, he remained desperate for British help. To the southeast were the expansionist Sikhs, to the west Herat was ruled by a detested rival dynasty, while, to add a further complication, the oft-threatened Russian-backed Persian advance from the west on Herat seemed imminent. Dost Mohammed knew that if the Persians took the city, they were unlikely to halt there. Furthermore, his perennially disloyal half brothers at Kandahar were already making overtures to the Persians.

Over succeeding weeks, Dost Mohammed and Burnes met frequently. Just as before, the Afghan leader's quiet authority and thoughtful demeanor impressed Burnes. "Power frequently spoils men, but with Dost Mohammed neither the increase of it, nor his new title of Emir seems to have done him any harm. He seemed even more alert and full of intelligence than when I last saw him," he wrote of these encounters. The two men discussed a wide range of subjects, from the expansion of trade to the question of whether the Afghans were descended from the Jewish tribes as Dost Mohammed appeared to believe. The discussions of course turned frequently to Ranjit Singh and Peshawar. Dost Mohammed argued that Sikh aggression and expansionism were a barrier to the free flow of trade sought by the British.

What Dost Mohammed could not know was that, despite the impression he gave to contrary, the confident and articulate Burnes had no authority to make commitments such as those Dost Mohammed was seeking. While he had still been on the way to Kabul, Macnaghten, realizing somewhat late in the day that Burnes would be put on the spot, had dispatched further instructions: "In any case in which specific political propositions shall be made to you, you will state that you have no authority to make replies, but that you will forward them, through Captain Wade, to the Government. If applied to, as you probably may be, for advice by Dost Mohammed Khan, in the difficulties by which he is surrounded, you will dissuade him from insisting in such a crisis [on] pretensions which he cannot maintain, and you will lead him as far as may be in your power, to seek and to form arrangements of reconciliation for himself with the Sikh sovereign."

In late October Burnes received yet further instructions, by which he was to make clear that "under any circumstances our first feeling must be that of regard for the honour and just wishes of our old and firm ally Ranjit Singh." However, if Dost Mohammed would seek peace with the Sikhs and abandon all contact with Persia, the British would use their good offices with the Sikhs perhaps to restore Peshawar to one of Dost Mohammed's half brothers on payment of tribute to Ranjit Singh. As Burnes quickly discovered, the thought of Peshawar in the hands of one of his traitorous half brothers was as unacceptable to Dost Mohammed as "placing a snake in my bosom."

Burnes was in a difficult situation. The means of transport then available and the long distances involved inevitably meant that letters overlapped and fresh instructions arrived while previous questions remained unanswered. Under the circumstances Burnes allowed himself greater latitude than his superiors ever envisaged. Soon after his arrival he wrote to Lord Auckland suggesting that Dost Mohammed be promised Peshawar on the death of Ranjit Singh. Rightly convinced that Peshawar was the key, he wrote further in late December: "In a settlement of the Peshawar affair we have, as it seems to me, an immediate remedy against further intrigue, and a means of showing to the Afghans that the British Government does sympathise with them, and at one and the same time satisfying the chiefs, and gaining both our political and commercial ends." He therefore held out promises of British help to Dost Mohammed in the event of a foreign attack on his country, even suggesting that the British might mediate between the Afghans and the Sikhs.

Two months after Burnes's arrival, his position became yet more difficult when the Persians finally made their long anticipated advance on Herat. In his published account of his mission, Burnes wrote simply that "these circumstances had a prejudicial effect at Kabul," but he knew that if the Persians succeeded in taking Herat they would be only four hundred miles from Kabul. As a result, he took it upon himself to offer bribes to the rulers of Kandahar not to ally themselves with the advancing Persians and was jubilant over the cleverness of his strategy, boasting to a friend: "The chiefs of Kandahar had gone over to Persia. I have detached them and offered them British protection and *cash* if they would recede, and if Persia attacked them. I have no authority to do so but am I to stand by and see us ruined at Kandahar?" He sent Lieutenant Robert Leech to Kandahar to confirm its rulers' agreement and in late December 1837 wrote to Macnaghten, justifying his intervention: "In the critical position in which I was situated I saw no course left but that which I have followed . . . Herat may withstand the attack of the Persians, but if not, and the shah marches to Kandahar, our own position in the East becomes endangered and the tranquillity of all the countries that border on the Indus."

The arrival in Kabul of a Russian envoy, Captain Ivan Vickovich, convinced Burnes even more strongly that he had been right to act. "We are in a mess here," he wrote to a colleague. "Herat is besieged and may fall; and the Emperor of Russia has sent an envoy to Kabul, to offer Dost Mohammed Khan money to fight Ranjit Singh!!!!! I could not believe my eyes or ears; but Captain Vickovich—for that is the agent's name—arrived here with a blazing letter, three feet long, and sent immediately to pay his respects to myself. I, of course, received him, and asked him to dinner."

They dined together on Christmas Day. Burnes found the slight, thirty-year-old officer in his striking Cossack uniform both agreeable and intelligent. Of Lithuanian extraction, Vickovich had been exiled as a student for participating in Polish nationalist demonstrations but had later gained a commission in a Cossack regiment and, as able a linguist as Burnes, had undertaken successful missions in Central Asia. After receiving instructions from Count Simonich, the Russian envoy in Tehran, on his way to Kabul he stopped at Kandahar to encourage its rulers to cooperate with the Persians. Their Christmas dinner was to be the only meeting between the British and the Russian envoys. "I regret to say that I found it to be impossible to follow the dictates of my personal feeling of friendship towards him, as the public service required the strictest watch, lest the relative positions of our nations should be misunderstood in this part of Asia," wrote Burnes. To Lord Auckland he wrote that he "knew not what might happen, and it was now a neck-and-neck race between Russia and us."

Dost Mohammed, anxious to do nothing to offend the British, asked Burnes how he should treat the Russian emissary. He dutifully agreed to keep Vickovich at arm's length, gave Burnes—for onward transmission to Calcutta and London—copies of the introductory letters Vickovich had brought and even offered to send him packing. Burnes meanwhile was sending dispatch after dispatch to Calcutta, arguing that Dost Mohammed was "the one strong man" in Afghanistan and that "now is the time to bind him to our side." However, all Burnes's official letters passed through Ludhiana and the hands of Claude Wade, whose suspicion of Dost Mohammed remained unshakable. He would not accept that the only reason Dost Mohammed had made overtures to the Russians and the Persians was because the British refused to help him against Ranjit Singh. He also could not appreciate that Dost Mohammed would hardly regard Russia and Persia—with their aggressive ambitions toward the western Afghan city of Herat—as desirable allies. Therefore, in letters he forwarded with those from Burnes, he criticized Burnes's views to his superiors. Burnes found himself rebuked for his promises to the chiefs of Kandahar. A furious Macnaghten, writing on behalf of Lord Auckland, told him in future to "conform punctually in all points to the orders issued for your guidance" and to inform the Kandahar rulers that he had exceeded his instructions. Immediately Burnes did so, the Kandahar chiefs began negotiating with the Persians.

Dost Mohammed also received short shrift. He had written personally to Lord Auckland seeking British assistance over Peshawar—even offering to rule jointly over Peshawar with his untrustworthy half brother Sultan Mohammed Khan—but the governor-general told him bluntly that Peshawar was to remain in Sikh hands. If he wished British support, he had to promise to make no agreement with any other foreign powers without consulting the British. One of his chiefs commented that the British "asked much from Dost Mohammed, but granted nothing in return," while another observed that the emir "had often written to the British Government about his affairs, and that in reply they answered him about their own."

Even Burnes's good friend Nawab Jubbar Khan complained to him that the British appeared to value their offers "at a very high rate, since we expected, in return, that the Afghans would desist from all intercourse with Persia, Russia, Turkestan." "Were the Afghans . . . to make all these powers hostile, and receive no protection against the enmity raised for their adhering to the British?" he asked. Burnes's mission was falling apart, which, given his masters' "do-nothing" policy, as he called it, was always likely to be the case. The months he had spent in Kabul had done little except to convince Dost Mohammed that the British were not willing to be his friends and were very probably his enemies.

Yet despite all the frustrations, Burnes's fascination with the region and its people was deepening. He still found time to explore Kabul, examining Afghan claims to be able to turn base metal into gold, admiring sword blades so sharp that they could sever a silken handkerchief thrown into the air and observing the women, of whom he wrote: "Their ghost-like figures when they walk abroad make one melancholy; but if all be true of them that is reported, they make ample amends when within doors for all such sombre exhibitions in public." Masson would later accuse him of blatant philandering in Kabul, relating how a courtier of Dost Mohammed suggested that "I should follow the example of my illustrious superiors and fill my house with black-eyed damsels." "Illustrious superiors" clearly meant Burnes, though Mohan Lal later refuted the accusations against him.

Not long after their arrival, Burnes and his companions had made an expedition into foothills of the Kohistan mountains north of Kabul, where Burnes contrasted the beauty of the landscape with the "turbulent and vindictive" people, the Tajiks, who inhabited it, their lives governed by endless blood feuds so that it was "rare to see a man go to bathe, hunt or even ride out without a part of his clan attending him as a guard." On his return to Kabul, Burnes had been surprised to find an emissary from Murad Beg of Kunduz waiting for him. The psychopathic ruler, having learned of the presence of the British delegation in Kabul, had a favor to ask. His younger brother's eyesight was fading, and he wished to send him to Kabul to be treated by the British. Recognizing an opportunity to make an ally of the powerful Kunduz chieftain, Burnes replied that he would not dream of requiring a sick man to travel through the Hindu Kush to Kabul, but would send his colleagues, Dr. Lord and Mr. Wood, to offer what assistance they could.

In early November 1837 the two men set out on what would be an epic journey through snowstorms so bad that some of their attendants "went raving mad." Though Lord and Wood were unable to help Murad Beg's brother, they managed to establish friendly relations with the chief and learned much about Uzbek customs, such as their "truly enormous" eating habits: Two Uzbeks could easily down an entire sheep as well as rice and bread, "afterwards cramming in water-melons, musk-melons or other fruit." They also observed their passion for horse racing, claiming that the first prize for one race was a girl, the second prize fifty sheep, the third prize a boy and the booby prize a watermelon.

However, by the spring of 1838 there was clearly no reason for Burnes to remain in Kabul any longer. All his appeals on behalf of Dost Mohammed had failed, and the Afghan leader wrote bitterly to Burnes, "I expected very much from your government, and hoped for the protection and enlargement of Afghanistan. Now I am disappointed." On 21 April Dost Mohammed sent publicly for the first time for Vickovich, who made him lavish promises. On 26 April, as Burnes took his leave from Dost Mohammed—who embraced him, wished him long life and presented him with three horses—it seemed that the Russians had won.

The cynical Masson, who had decided to leave Kabul with Burnes, later wrote, "Thus closed a mission, one of the more extraordinary ever sent forth by a government, whether as to the singular manner in which it was conducted or as to its results." He added with an unfair swipe at Burnes, "The government had furnished no instructions, apparently confiding in the discretion of a man who had none."

The real problem was that the British authorities in India had already decided their next course of action while Burnes was in Kabul, and nothing he could say or do could change it. When in the city he had written to a friend, "I came to look after commerce, to superintend surveys and examine passes of mountains, and likewise certainly to see into affairs and judge of what was to be done hereafter; but the hereafter has already arrived." He had been overtaken by events.

CHAPTER FOUR

It is evident that Afghanistan must be ours or Russia's.
—LORD PALMERSTON, OCTOBER 1838

AS A DISAPPOINTED Alexander Burnes made his way back to India, events in the western Afghan city of Herat were gathering momentum. Forty-five thousand people lived within its moated mud-walls. One British visitor wrote, "If dirt killed people where would the Afghans be! . . . The residents cast out the refuse of their houses into the streets, and dead cats and dogs are commonly seen lying upon heaps of the vilest filth." The city was mercilessly governed by Shah Shuja's short, stocky and pockmarked nephew Kamran, who had blinded Dost Mohammed's elder brother Futteh Khan twenty years earlier. As a younger man, Kamran had been able to cut a sheep in half with a single slash of his saber, but he was now an aging alcoholic and the real power in Herat was his avaricious vizier Yar Mohammed, who patrolled the city accompanied by executioners bearing large knives and tiger-headed maces.

Herat occupied a strategic position at the confluence of the major routes into Central Asia from the west. The surrounding countryside, rich and fertile, was ideal for supplying a large army. However, Herat also derived its wealth from slave trading. Many of those sold in its market were Persians seized in border raids, and this had provided Persia, strongly encouraged by its Russian advisers, with a pretext for attacking a city that had once been part of the Persian Empire. Four years earlier, the elderly Persian shah, whom Burnes had met on his return from Bokhara, had died, to be succeeded by his ambitious grandson Mohammed Shah. In early 1836 the new shah had demanded hostages and tribute from Herat. Yar Mohammed had replied on behalf of Kamran: "We gave no hostages during the reign of the late shah, and we will give none now. You demand a present; we are ready to give as large a present as we can afford. If the shah is not satisfied with this, and is determined to attack us, let him come."

Yar Mohammed and Kamran next suggested to the Persians an alliance against both Dost Mohammed at Kabul and his half brothers at Kandahar. The shah's lofty response was that he would take Kabul and Kandahar for himself without their help—and Herat too. He also increased his demands: Kamran was to renounce his titles, sermons were to be read in Herat's mosques in the shah's name, the usual way of signifying a change of ruler, and his likeness, not Kamran's, was to be stamped on the city's coinage. As the shah must have anticipated, Kamran could not accept these demands, and in the summer of 1837 Herat readied itself for the Persian onslaught.

Yet on 18 August someone else arrived in Herat in advance of the Persians: Eldred Pottinger, a twenty-six-year-old Northern Ireland–born subaltern in the East India Company's Political Department and nephew of Henry Pottinger, British resident in Kutch, whose assistant Burnes had been. When his uncle had told him of Persia's ambitions toward Herat, Pottinger had volunteered to go to the region to gather intelligence and had set out for Afghanistan on his unofficial mission in the guise of a horse dealer. His appearance in Herat at this time was fortuitous. Taking a risk, Pottinger threw off his disguise and made himself known to the notoriously suspicious and vindictive Yar Mohammed, who might well have regarded him as a spy. Luckily for Pottinger, the vizier decided there were advantages in the presence of a British officer at this critical juncture and made him his military adviser.

By late November, with the air growing chill and a hard frost on the ground, thirty thousand Persian troops were encamped among the streams and orchards to the northwest of the city. Among them were Russian officers acting as military advisers and also a shadowy regiment of Russians claimed by one source to be deserters from the Russian army. On 23 November, two months after Burnes's arrival in Kabul, the Persian army began to bombard Herat. However, as Pottinger recorded in his journal,

Herat's defenses were strong, and to his critical eyes the attackers poorly led. At least as many cannonballs sailed over Herat as hit its mud walls, and though the Persian mortars were more accurate, the shells they hurled into the city were "carved out of slate-rock and their chamber contain[ed] little more than a bursting charge." When the Persians deployed their largest weapon, a massive 68-pounder gun, its carriage collapsed after it had fired only a few of its projectiles, rendering the weapon useless.

Pottinger also found much to criticize in Yar Mohammed's tactics. To encourage defenders to sally out under cover of darkness to attack outposts and destroy siege works, the vizier offered a reward for every Persian head brought into the city. "Barbarous, disgusting and inhuman," wrote the young officer. Sometimes bounty hunters tried to trick Yar Mohammed. Pottinger noted how one man presented a pair of bleeding ears, for which he duly received payment, then a little while later another man appeared with a head, for which he claimed a reward. Unfortunately for him, one of the vizier's attendants spotted that the mutilated head was earless and also, on closer inspection, that it was not Persian at all but belonged to a defender killed the previous night.

Both sides indulged in tit-for-tat brutality. When the Persian shah learned that Kamran and his vizier had sold all their Persian prisoners as slaves, he ordered the abdomens of all his Herati captives to be slit open and their heads forced into the gaping cavity until they suffocated. As for Herat's citizens, their plight worsened as famine and disease took hold. They also had to endure Yar Mohammed's sadistic attempts to extort money to pay his soldiers. The tortured corpses of those too stubborn to reveal where they kept their wealth, and of those who had none to offer but who had not been believed, were flung over the city walls. Sometimes the Russians in the Persian camp fired rockets "whose fiery flight as they passed over the city struck terror into the hearts of the people who clustered on the roofs of their houses praying and crying by turns."

During pauses in the sometimes desultory fighting, Yar Mohammed employed Pottinger as a go-between. Riding into the Persian camp, Pottinger was greeted by shouts of "Bravo! Bravo!" and loud protestations that the British had always been "friends of the King-of-Kings." In the camp he met another British officer, Captain Charles Stoddart, aide to John McNeill, now British envoy to the Persian court, who himself arrived at the camp from Tehran in early April 1838. McNeill hoped to convince the shah that he was violating Persia's treaty obligations to Britain and must lift the siege. At the very least he wished to mediate between the Persians and Heratis. However, in the midst of the diplomatic toing and froing, the Russian minister to the Persian court, Count Simonich, also appeared, offering the Persians rather more than the British did—funds and further military advice to pursue their conquests. By early June, after being repeatedly snubbed by the shah, McNeill decided he had no option but to break off relations with the Persian court and on 7 June departed, taking Stoddart with him. With Herat's fall to the Persians seeming increasingly likely, some of the Afghan chiefs began to talk of saving the city from the Persians by offering to become vassals of Russia, and it took much of Pottinger's energy to dissuade Yar Mohammed from such a course.

Meanwhile, with the strong possibility that Herat would fall and that the Persians, with Russian backing, would fulfill their threats to move on Kandahar and even on Kabul itself, British policy toward Afghanistan had been crystallizing. On 12 May Auckland had written from India to Sir John Hobhouse, president of the Board of Control in London, defining the options as he saw them. Britain could simply "leave Afghanistan to its fate" and concentrate on defending the Indus Valley, though that would encourage the Russians and Persians to "intrigue upon our frontiers." Alternatively, Britain could "attempt to save Afghanistan" by supporting the current rulers of both Kabul and Kandahar in an extension of a divide-and-rule policy of the type previously favored by Wade, except that might put Britain's treasured alliance with the Sikhs at risk because of the Afghan leaders' ingrained hostility toward them. Auckland's third option, running contrary to all the advice he had received and was to receive from Burnes, was to encourage Ranjit Singh—though regarded by most Afghans as their greatest foe—to invade Afghanistan and impose the elderly and unpopular Shah Shuja on the people as king instead of Dost Mohammed. This was a course mooted by Wade in one of his letters forwarding those of Burnes's favoring Dost Mohammed, and this was the solution Auckland considered the "most expedient" and decided to adopt, driven as he was by his desire above all to preserve the Sikh alliance.

Chief Secretary William Macnaghten and the more junior Henry Torrens and John Colvin had no doubt influenced Auckland's decision.

The governor-general and these three of his advisers were at this time at Simla escaping the summer heat in the northwestern foothills of the Himalayas near Ludhiana. Pleasant though Simla was, it was far from the rest of Auckland's staff in Calcutta. The nineteenth-century historian Sir John Kaye likened Simla to a cross between a sanatorium and a lunatic asylum "where our Governors-General, surrounded by irresponsible advisers, settle the destinies of empires without the aid of their legitimate fellow-counsellors . . . [Simla] has been the cradle of more political insanity than any place within the limits of Hindustan."

By the end of May 1838 Macnaghten, who had urged Auckland to lose no time, was on his way from Simla to see Ranjit Singh to set in motion Auckland's policy to depose Dost Mohammed and replace him with Shah Shuja. Auckland, whose natural inclinations were for peace, was left to worry whether he had done the right thing. Not only had he sent Macnaghten to the Sikh court on his own initiative without waiting for endorsement from London, but he started to fret that Ranjit Singh might suspect that the British proposals were a mask for actions to further their territorial ambitions on the Indus. Macnaghten, meanwhile, crossed the Sutlej River marking the boundary between British India and Sikh territory, traveling on elephant back in the extreme pre-monsoon summer heat, and in early June was received by Ranjit Singh in the welcome shade of a grove of mangoes at Adinanagar, northeast of Lahore. Auckland need not have worried; Ranjit Singh was receptive to the British proposals. Suitably encouraged, Macnaghten raised the question of whether the Sikhs would act alone to restore Shah Shuja or whether the British should also be a party to the operation. When Ranjit Singh unhesitatingly opted for a joint operation, wisely preferring to share the risks, Macnaghten suggested the device of adding Britain as a party to the treaty the Sikhs had signed four years previously with Shah Shuja at the time of his own attempt to retake his throne, thus turning it into a new tripartite treaty. Ranjit Singh graciously replied, "This would be adding sugar to milk."

Negotiations moved to Lahore, where Macnaghten was joined by Burnes, whose opinion he had sought on the policy to restore Shah Shuja. Burnes had replied that "to ensure complete success to the plan, the British Government must appear directly in it; that is, it must not be left to the Sikhs themselves." He pointed out that Shah Shuja was believed by his people to be an ill-starred man with "no fortune" but suggested "our name will invest him with it." Burnes also asserted that "the British Government have only to send him [Shah Shuja] to Peshawar with an agent, and two of its own regiments as an honorary escort, and an avowal to the Afghans that we have taken up his cause, to insure his being fixed for ever on the throne."

The latter was an odd opinion for such a vociferous supporter of Dost Mohammed. In fact, in his note he crossed out the words that he had *no very high opinion* of Shah Shuja. Burnes had perhaps decided that, given his superiors' apparent determination to cast off Dost Mohammed, the only way to advance his career as well as to achieve the united Afghanistan he favored was to fall in line and to back Shah Shuja. He later wrote to a friend that he decided to support Shah Shuja "not as what was best, but what was best under the circumstances which a series of blunders had produced." Yet even at this eleventh hour he again spoke up for Dost Mohammed, perhaps to salve his conscience, adding at the end of his note, "It remains to be reconsidered why we cannot act with Dost Mohammed. He is a man of undoubted ability, and has at heart a high opinion of the British nation; and if half you must do for others were done for him, and offers made which he could see conduced to his interests, he would abandon Russia and Persia tomorrow . . . Government have admitted that he had at best a choice of difficulties; and it should not be forgotten that we promised nothing, and Persia and Russia held out a great deal."

As he had no doubt anticipated, his plea was ignored. The talks continued against a background of opulent Sikh hospitality with military reviews, gunnery displays and much drinking of fiery spirits. All the time, reports were arriving of the deteriorating situation at Herat, including rumors that a large Russian force was on the way to help the Persians. Fear that two world powers—Britain and Russia—might be about to confront each other on his doorstep convinced Ranjit Singh yet further to throw in his lot with the British and agree to the detailed terms of the new tripartite treaty proposed by Macnaghten.

The enemies of one would be the enemy of all. Shah Shuja was to renounce all rights to Peshawar, Kashmir and other former Afghan territories appropriated by the Sikhs as well as, in return for an agreed payment by the emirs, all claims to suzerainty in Sind. He was to pay Ranjit

Singh a large sum of money—the word *tribute* was not used—in return for which, to enable Shah Shuja to save face, the Sikhs would keep five thousand troops at the ready to be sent to Shah Shuja's assistance in times of need. Shah Shuja was also to send annual gifts to Ranjit Singh, including "55 high-bred horses of approved colour and pleasant paces," turbans, shawls, rice and large amounts of Afghanistan's famous fruit, which, it was specified with a gourmet's attention to detail, should include "musk melons of a sweet and delicate flavour . . . grapes, pomegranates, apples, quinces."

Shah Shuja would "oppose any power having the desire to invade the British and Sikh teritories by force of arms to the utmost of his ability." He was also to promise not to negotiate with any foreign power unless sanctioned by the British and the Sikhs and not to encroach into Persia. As regards Herat, if Shah Shuja's nephew Kamran survived the Persian onslaught, he would be allowed to continue to rule there. In return for these concessions, British and Sikh troops would support Shah Shuja's invasion of his homeland, and he would be given funds to levy and equip an effective army, which would be trained and led by British officers from the company's army. On 26 June Ranjit Singh put his name to the new treaty, and Macnaghten set off to Ludhiana to coax Shah Shuja to sign as well.

In Herat, meanwhile, food and fuel were almost exhausted, and the population was starving and fever-ridden in the searing summer heat. On 24 June Pottinger thought that the city was about to fall when a determined Persian bombardment was followed by a simultaneous attack on the city's five gates. Though the attacking Persian columns, now said to be directed by Count Simonich himself, were repulsed from four of the gates, at the fifth they broke through. As Afghan troops fought desperately to hold off the Persians, Pottinger ran to the breached gate to see what was happening. On the way, he met Yar Mohammed. But far from attempting to rally his troops, some of whom were beginning to slink away, the vizier seemed to have given up. Lowering his bulky body, he sat down in despair, and according to Pottinger, it took all his energy to rouse him to action. Yar Mohammed got to his feet again, yelled at his men to hold their ground and for a while they obeyed, but as the Persians pushed forward, the vizier wavered once more. Pottinger seized his arm and, reviling him as a coward, dragged him toward the fighting around the gate. Suddenly Yar Mohammed became a man possessed, laying into his troops with a wooden staff and driving them forward like cattle to overwhelm the astonished attackers who fled back to their camp.

Unaware, of course, of the latest developments at Herat, Macnaghten was warmly welcomed by Shah Shuja in Ludhiana, which he reached on 15 July. Though the former king was startled by the extent of the concessions expected of him, excitement at the prospect of regaining his throne overruled his misgivings and he accepted the tripartite treaty without amendment, assuring Macnaghten that his supporters would rally to him. However, he insisted that his own troops must restore him to the throne, wisely pointing out that "the fact of his being upheld by foreign force alone could not fail to detract, in a great measure, from his dignity and consequence."

The invasion strategy discussed with both Shah Shuja and Ranjit Singh was that the former with his newly recruited British-officered army should pass down the Indus through Sind, whose emirs would have little choice but to cooperate while being, in Burnes's words, "squeezed like an orange" for funds to support the expedition. Subsequently the army would push up through the Bolan Pass to Quetta, Kandahar and then on to Kabul, while the Sikhs, accompanied by Shah Shuja's eldest son, Timur, would advance through the Khyber Pass. Auckland had originally envisaged only a minor role for British troops. However, his thinking and that of Macnaghten had changed. Reasonably enough, Auckland had begun to doubt whether Shah Shuja, who had thrice failed to retake his throne and whose military successes had been few, could succeed against Dost Mohammed, especially since he would be allied with the Afghans' traditional enemies, the Sikhs, which would have a unifying effect on the normally disputatious and divided Afghans. At the same time, Ranjit Singh had been subtly suggesting to Macnaghten that his men had little experience of fighting in the manner required to force the Khyber Pass and might require British assistance. He feared terrible carnage and confessed that he doubted his men "could be induced to march over the corpses of their countrymen."

Auckland sought the advice of Sir Henry Fane, his experienced military commander in chief, on the extent of direct British military involvement. Fane had pronounced views on intervention over the Indus: "Every advance you might make beyond the Sutlej to the westward, in my opinion adds to your military weakness." Instead, Britain should consolidate its position in India: "Make yourselves complete sovereigns of all within your bounds. *But let alone the far west,*" he had advised earlier that year. However, if the politicians had decided that an invasion was to go ahead, Fane considered the British had to be there in full and sufficient force to ensure success, especially if the army might in addition be required to dislodge the besieging Persians from Herat, which at the time seemed possible.

Thus by late August 1838 the reluctant Fane was already informing the regiments that were to make up the superbly titled Army of the Indus. They were to include both "native" and European regiments of the East India Company's armies as well as some Queen's regiments of the British army posted to India. A total of six regiments of cavalry and eighteen battalions of infantry, together with artillery, engineering and other support, were readied for the campaign. British officers began to recruit and train the levies who were to form Shah Shuja's army, while Auckland selected the political officers who were to accompany the expedition. Claude Wade was to go with the Sikh army. Burnes's hopes were high that he would be selected to accompany Shah Shuja. In late July, arriving at Simla to pay his respects to Lord Auckland, he wrote to his brother: "We are now planning a grand campaign to restore the Shah to the throne of Kabul . . . What exact part I am to play I know not, but if full confidence and hourly consultation be any pledge, I am to be chief. I can plainly tell them that it is *aut Caesar aut nullus* [I'll be Caesar or nothing], and if I get not what I have a right to, you will soon see me en route to England."

Burnes, however, was not to be Caesar. Instead, Auckland decided that Macnaghten, older and more experienced in the workings of the administration, should be "Envoy and Minister on the part of the Government," while Burnes would be chief political officer to Commander in Chief Sir Henry Fane and go in advance of the British expeditionary force to conciliate the rulers through whose territories it would pass. Auckland softened Burnes's disappointment by hinting that once Shah Shuja was firmly on his throne and Macnaghten returned to India, Burnes would replace him. Burnes was also mollified by receiving a double promotion to the rank of lieutenant colonel and a knighthood. The ambitious thirty-three-year-old—now Sir Alexander Burnes—thought no more of going home.

On 9 September 1838 the Persians broke off their siege of Herat and departed, meaning that one of the major reasons for the campaign into Afghanistan—the Russian-backed Persian menace—had disappeared.

This did nothing to disrupt British plans. Indeed, three weeks earlier John Colvin, Auckland's assistant, had written that "no result of the siege of Herat will delay the Shah's [Shuja's] expedition with our direct support," while a few days later Auckland himself stated that even if Herat held out, "I shall not be the less convinced that the Government is acting wisely." The truth was that, though the outcome of the siege would influence the number of British troops to be sent into Afghanistan, Herat had become an irrelevance. The British were set on invasion.

The Persian withdrawal from Herat was the result of robust action by the British against both the Russians and the Persians. Foreign Secretary Lord Palmerston had protested formally to the Russian foreign secretary, Count von Nesselrode, about the incitement by Count Simonich and his agents of the Persians and others in the region. Not wishing at this time openly to confront Britain in Persia or elsewhere, von Nesselrode effectively disowned many of the actions of both Simonich and his agents, making flimsy excuses for others. But most important, he asserted that Russia would now use all its influence to restrain the Persian shah and would do everything possible to preserve the peace in Central Asia. As a result, Count Simonich was recalled to Russia. Vickovich, returning to St. Petersburg from Kabul and expecting to be congratulated, found himself dismissed as "an adventurer . . . who, it was reported, had been lately engaged in some unauthorised intrigues at Kabul and Kandahar." According to the Russians, Vickovich retreated to his bedroom and shot himself in the head with his service pistol, although some British journalists of the time suggested that he had been murdered by the Russian government to prevent him from revealing the extent of Russian intriguing.

Following John McNeill's previous severing of his relations with the Persian shah over his attack on Herat in early June, Auckland had, at McNeill's prompting, dispatched a battalion of soldiers and marines in two ships from Bombay to the Persian Gulf as a show of force. The troops had occupied the strategically situated island of Karrack (Kharg)—close to the Persian mainland near Bushire—whose Persian governor had capitulated immediately. By July grossly exaggerated reports of the scale of the British landing on Karrack were filtering through to the Persians encamped with their shah outside Herat. Profiting from them, McNeill dispatched Charles Stoddart back to the shah's camp to inform him bluntly that the British would no longer tolerate any attempt by the Persians to take Herat or indeed to occupy any other part of Afghanistan and to warn him that his country risked full-scale invasion if he did not comply with British wishes. The shah took the point, observing to Stoddart, "The fact is, if I don't leave Herat, there will be war, is not that it?" Stoddart replied, "all depends upon your Majesty's answer." Two days later, the shah dissembled to Stoddart that had he realized his advance on Herat might upset the British, "we certainly would not have come at all." Thus by early September Stoddart had been able to report that "the Shah has mounted his horse 'Ameerj' and is gone."

On 1 October, several weeks before receiving official confirmation that the Herat siege was over, Auckland issued the so-called Simla Manifesto—his justification for invasion. The document placed the entire blame on Dost Mohammed in an interpretation of events so twisted it could have been penned by the Red Queen in the yet-to-be-written *Alice in Wonderland*. According to one of the young British heroes of the campaign to follow, it used the words *justice* and *necessity* "in a manner for which there is fortunately no precedent in the English language."

Dost Mohammed was accused of "sudden and unprovoked" aggression at Jamrud against Britain's "ancient ally" the Sikhs—despite the fact that Ranjit Singh had been the aggressor by seizing Peshawar. In striking contrast to the reality of Dost Mohammed's continuing solicitations of Britain as his ally in the region, he was charged with collusion with the Persians and with nurturing "schemes of aggrandizement and ambition, injurious to the security and peace of the frontiers of India." The manifesto further declared that "he openly threatened, in furtherance of those schemes, to call in every foreign aid which he could command. Ultimately he gave his undisguised support to the Persian designs in Afghanistan." Dost Mohammed and his Barakzai brothers—the rulers at Kandahar—had proved from their "disunion and unpopularity" that they were "ill-fitted under any circumstances to be useful allies to the British government," and so long as Kabul remained under Dost Mohammed's government, the British "could never hope that the interests of our Indian Empire would be preserved inviolate."

The manifesto maintained that Britain needed an ally on its western frontier who was "interested in resisting aggression and establishing tranquillity"—identifying Shah Shuja, who, while in power, "had cordially acceded to the measures of united resistance to external enmity which were at that time judged necessary by the British Government." The manifesto asserted in direct contradiction of all the sparse available information "his popularity throughout Afghanistan had been proved" and that "pressing necessity as well as every consideration of policy and justice warranted their espousing his cause." The document ended on a flourish. Shah Shuja, it promised, "will enter Afghanistan surrounded by his own troops, and will be supported against foreign interference and factious opposition by a British army . . . and when once he shall be secured in power, and the independence and integrity of Afghanistan established, the British Army will be withdrawn." The governor-general rejoiced that by these actions he would be assisting "in restoring the union and prosperity of the Afghan people."

The manifesto nowhere mentioned Russia, perceived both in London and India as the real enemy behind the actions of the shah of Persia and the alleged threat from Dost Mohammed. In a private letter to the British ambassador in Moscow Palmerston had said, "Auckland has been told to take Afghanistan in hand and make it a British dependency . . . we have long declined to meddle with the Afghans but if the Russians try to make them Russian we must take care that they become British." However, Russia was a major power, and Britain was enmeshed in a diplomatic struggle to contain its ambitions in the Caucasus, Eastern Europe and elsewhere at the expense of the Ottoman Turks. For Auckland to have cited Russia in a document attempting to justify war and invasion (although neither word is mentioned in the context of the British action) would have been embarrassing to the government in London, and the gentle and gentlemanly Auckland was not the man to embarrass them. He crafted his manifesto to cast the British action as a regional one designed to protect Britain's regional interest and not a strategic or imperial one with global repercussions.*

The contradictory and hypocritical manifesto was widely published in the British and Indian press and instantly condemned by many who

---

*In a similar way, in the twentieth-century the Western powers would be reluctant to name China and Russia as their enemy formally when engaging in proxy wars.

understood the true situation in India and Afghanistan. The clamor intensified when official confirmation came that the Persians had withdrawn from Herat. Macnaghten hastily drafted a fresh note for Auckland, issued on 8 November, stating that the governor-general would continue "to prosecute with vigour the measures which have been announced, with a view to the substitution of a friendly for a hostile power in the eastern provinces of Afghanistan, and to the establishment of a permanent barrier against schemes of aggression upon our north-west frontier."

Though the time consumed by communication and the pressure of events had prevented Auckland from obtaining prior sanction from London for each step of his strategy as it had evolved, Prime Minister Lord Melbourne and his cabinet in Britain and the governor-general and his advisers in India were in agreement about what had to be done. To Lord Palmerston it had become a question of who was to be master of Central Asia. When in December 1838 Melbourne and Palmerston received the Simla Manifesto that Auckland had sent home—with a humble cover letter suggesting others could judge it but he would only say, "I could have made it stronger if I had not had the fear of Downing Street before my eyes and thought it right to avoid direct allusion to Russia"—they approved it.

The East India Company's Court of Directors was more nervous at the prospect of war in its name. The directors had earlier warned Auckland to make no decision on Afghanistan until he knew the outcome of the siege at Herat, but he had disregarded their advice. Now they had no choice. The British law that regulated the relationship between government and company required them to agree to the proposals put to them by the Board of Control under its president, Sir John Hobhouse. Twenty years later, he would confess to the House of Commons, "The Afghan war was done by myself; the Court of Directors had nothing to do with it."

Many of the population, caught up in Russophobia, supported the invasion decision. The *Times* welcomed it as well, condemning "the Russian fiend" who "from the frontiers of Hungary to the heart of Burmah and Nepal . . . has been haunting and troubling the human race, and dilligently perpetrating his malignant frauds . . . to the vexation of this industrious and essentially pacific [British] empire."

As the future prime minister Lord Salisbury wrote, opinion was polarized: "You must either disbelieve altogether in the existence of the

Russians, or you must believe that they will be in Kandahar next year. Public opinion recognises no middle holding ground." Among the many knowledgeable and experienced dissenters from the invasion decision as unlikely to achieve its aim of increasing the security of India's north-west frontier, was Mountstuart Elphinstone, who, thirty years earlier had led the first British delegation to Afghanistan, and who wrote to Burnes, "You will guess what I think of affairs in Kabul . . . If you send 27,000 men up the *Durra-i-Bolan* [Bolan Pass] to Kandahar (as we hear is intended), and can feed them, I have no doubt you will take Kandahar and Kabul and set up [Shah] Shuja; but for maintaining him in a poor, cold, strong, and re- mote country, among a turbulent people like the Afghans, I own it seems to me to be hopeless." He continued, not being afraid, unlike the mani- festo, to mention Russia, "If you succeed, I fear you will weaken the posi- tion against Russia. The Afghans were neutral, and would have received your aid against invaders with gratitude—they will now be disaffected and glad to join any invader to drive you out."

To Lord William Bentinck, Auckland's predecessor as governor- general, the war was "an act of incredible folly." To Charles Metcalfe, who had headed the administration of India in the interregnum between the two, "We have needlessly and heedlessly plunged into difficulties and embarrassments not without much aggression and injustice on our part from which we can never extricate ourselves without a disgraceful retreat which may be more fatal in its consequences than an obstinate persever- ance in a wrong course. Our sole course is to resist the influence of Rus- sia, and our measures are almost sure to establish it." Lord Wellesley, also a former governor-general, dismissed what he regarded as a wild expedi- tion into a distant region of "rocks, sands, deserts, ice and snow" as an "act of infatuation." However, the most percipient, prophetic condemnation of all came from Wellesley's brother, the Duke of Wellington, who predicted to one of the company's directors that Britain's difficulties would com- mence where its military successes ended: "The consequences of crossing the Indus once, to settle a government in Afghanistan, will be a perennial march into that country."

CHAPTER FIVE

What is the cause of all this bustle and war I hardly know . . . How
it will turn out I know no more than the man in the moon.
                    —LIEUTENANT TOM HOLDSWORTH, 1838

IN LATE NOVEMBER 1838, Lord Auckland and Ranjit Singh pre-
sided over a grand ceremonial gathering, or durbar, at Ferozepore on the
Sutlej River—the boundary between the Sikh and British territories. The
occasion was both an affirmation of British-Sikh friendship and a demonstration of the splendors of the Army of the Indus about to depart for Afghanistan. The leaders paid reciprocal visits to each other's camps and
reviewed each other's troops. Auckland's sister Emily, who accompanied
him, found the sights dazzling, especially the maharaja's thousands of followers "all dressed in yellow or red satin, with quantities of their horses
trapped in gold and silver tissues, and all of them sparkling with jewels."

Sometimes the presence of so many thousands of soldiers, elephants
and horses brought chaos. The British camp, Emily complained, was
"dreadfully noisy . . . The cavalry have pitched themselves just behind our
tents; one horse gets loose, and goes and bites all the others, and then they
kick and get loose too, and all the *syces* [grooms] wake and begin screaming, and the tent pitchers are called to knock in the rope pins, and the
horses are neighing all the time . . . Then the infantry regiment has got a
mad drummer . . . He begins drumming at five in the morning and never
intermits till seven . . . It was so like dear Shakespeare specifying the
"'neighing steed and the spirit-stirring drum.'"

The forces participating in the durbar were 9,500 men of the company's Bengal army including some attached Queen's regiments such as the Sixteenth Lancers, known as the Scarlet Lancers, resplendent in their tight-fitting scarlet tunics and plumed helmets. They were to be accompanied in the forthcoming invasion by 6,000 Indian levies, including one regiment of Nepalese Gurkhas, recruited, trained and officered by the British for Shah Shuja. The plan was that the joint force would march southwest from Ferozepore through the princely state of Bahawalpur and into Sind, where it would cross the Indus. Meanwhile, 5,600 men of the company's Bombay army would embark in Bombay to sail five hundred miles northwest to Karachi—at that time a small fishing village at the mouth of the Indus—and thence march three hundred miles northeast up the river to rendezvous with their comrades at the town of Shikarpur, after which the whole army would move on through Baluchistan and the Bolan Pass to Quetta, Kandahar and finally Kabul.

This combined army would total just over 21,000, fewer than the number originally planned because following the Persian withdrawal from Herat its strength had been reduced by one division of 4,500 men. Auckland's commander in chief, Sir Henry Fane, had used the reduction to suggest that he should no longer head the army, writing to Auckland, "I do not think that for *this* my service is needed." Fane was anyway in poor health, doubtful of the wisdom of the mission and his tour of duty in India was soon due to end. In addition, unusually and to Fane's displeasure, Auckland had given the task of organizing food and sufficient horse and camel transport for the advancing army not to the officers of the military commissariat but to Macnaghten and his team of political officers who would be traveling with the army. Fane foresaw that this and other delegations of authority to Macnaghten would cause friction between the military and political leaders, adding in his letter to Auckland, "I think too that your instructions to Sir William Macnaghten and to me are such as an officer of my rank could hardly submit to serve under."

The sixty-year-old Sir Jasper Nicolls would, after much discussion in London, be selected to replace Fane and would arrive in India the following year. In the meantime, Fane planned to sail downriver for a while with his staff, keeping parallel with the Bengal force to oversee its progress. General Sir John Keane, commander in chief of the Bombay army, was to assume the supreme command after the rendezvous of the Bombay and Bengal forces.

In addition to the main Army of the Indus, the troops to be commanded by Shah Shuja's son Prince Timur, who was to be accompanied by Claude Wade as political agent, were being assembled at Peshawar. Six thousand of the eleven thousand men would be Sikhs, but this was as far as the Sikh military contribution would go. This force was to take the most direct route to Kabul, marching through Ranjit Singh's territories and the Khyber Pass.

Ranjit Singh, however, had announced that his dignity would be injured if the main Army of the Indus were to pass that way, hence the reason for its circuitous route through the Bolan Pass. The British were not overly concerned. As Captain Henry Havelock, aide-de-camp to Sir Willoughby Cotton, commander of the Bengal army, observed, "It was the policy of the hour to humour and caress the old ruler of the Punjab." The British government had anyway decided that a detour through Sind might provide an opportunity to bring its still restive and resistant emirs to heel. As it advanced north through Sind, the Bombay force was to attempt to impose on the emirs a treaty of Macnaghten's devising obliging them to allow the British unrestricted navigation of the Indus and—in return for Shah Shuja abandoning his claim to suzerainty over them or to the payment of any future tribute—to make him a large single payment to support his war effort.

There was thus only rejoicing at Ferozepore and a mutual exchange of gifts. Ranjit Singh gave Auckland a bed with gold legs and encrusted with rubies and emeralds, while Lord Auckland presented him with a portrait of Queen Victoria in a solid gold jeweled frame painted by his sister Emily. A British officer captured the magnificence and chaos as the maharaja made a courtesy visit to the British camp: "From beneath a massive canopy of dust emerged the motley array of Ranjit's elephants and cavalcade. Now hundreds of gaily-clad Sikh horsemen—some in bright chain armour, others in various coloured silks and cloths of gold, brandished their long spears, flung back their brass embossed shields, and galloped with headlong fury around the maharaja's elephants," which were covered with "gorgeously-embroidered gold cloth" and on whose backs swayed howdahs inlaid with ebony and ivory. The red-robed and

turbaned Ranjit Singh himself was wearing the fabled Koh-i-Nur diamond on his arm. To the watching officer, the red and blue uniforms of
the British looked somewhat dull by comparison. In Auckland's durbar
tent, Ranjit Singh reclined on a sofa. To Emily Eden's artist's eye he looked
"exactly like an old mouse, with grey whiskers and one eye." An English
officer thought him "slight in form, and his face expressive of the shrewd-
est cunning. The leer that occasionally escaped from his single optic
seemed to tell a clear tale of his debauchery."

In his own durbar tent of cashmere cloth supported by silver poles
and with furniture "of frosted silver, inlaid with gold," Ranjit Singh gave
lavish parties for the British grandees, treating them to fireworks and per-
formances by hoards of female singers and dancers. Emily wrote, "I could
not help thinking how eastern we had become, everybody declaring it was
one of the best-managed and pleasantest parties they had seen. All those
screaming girls and crowds of long bearded attendants, and the old tyrant
drinking in the middle—but still we said; 'What a charming party!' just as
we should have said formerly at Lady C.'s or Lady J's." Ranjit Singh, whose
own "unbridled devotion to ardent spirits" was obvious to all, pressed her
to taste the fiery brew of pounded emeralds, brandy and oranges—a "horrible spirit, which he pours down like water. He insisted on my just touching it . . . and one drop actually burnt the outside of my lips. I could not
possibly swallow it." Yet at the military reviews she noted how the Sikh
soldiers outshone the British in both dress and discipline: "Nobody knows
what to say about it, so they say nothing except that they are sure the Sikhs
would run away in a real fight. It is a sad blow to our vanities!"

On 10 December 1838 the Bengal army under Sir Willoughby Cotton set out on the twelve-hundred-mile circuitous trek to Kabul via
Quetta, with Shah Shuja and his levies for symbolic reasons keeping two
or three marches ahead. Cotton was a stout, good-natured, not overly
bright man, of whom Fane had written, "I don't think Cotton has a mind
which carries away much of verbal instructions." Macnaghten, who remained with Auckland, was to catch up with them later. The 9,500-strong
column with its thousands of bullock carts, horses and mass of camp
followers—an average of at least three for every soldier—stretched nearly
forty miles. There were also thirty thousand camels. "What a sea of camels! What a forest of camels' heads and humps and grain bags!" wrote one

officer of the procession. "What resounding of sticks as the vast mass is driven slowly along, browsing as they go and leaving not one green leaf behind them." Each camel took up fifteen feet of road and could advance at a speed of only two miles an hour, making them, as events would prove, easy targets for raiding tribesmen.

Fane's request to his officers and men to travel light was comprehensively ignored. Cotton, riding in a horse-drawn buggy, had 260 camels for his baggage, making Sir John Keane's personal baggage train of 100 camels as he later advanced up the Indus from Karachi appear quite modest. J. H. Stocqueler, editor of the *Bombay Times* who for a while traveled with the Bombay troops, thought the officers "regarded the expedition as little else than an extensive pleasure promenade—an enormous picnic" and that many "would as soon have thought of leaving behind their swords and double-barrelled pistols as march without their dressing-cases, perfumes, Windsor soap and eau-de-cologne." The Sixteenth Lancers, who were leading the Bombay force, even brought a pack of foxhounds so they could go hunting. When Stocqueler offered the officers' mess some boxes of fine cigars, he was politely rebuffed on the grounds that they already had two camel-loads of the best Manilas.

This was still a time when officers in the British, or "Queen's," army purchased their commissions and often their promotions. Officers paid for their own uniforms and equipment, making it almost impossible to be an officer without at least a modest private income. A young ensign had to spend almost all his first year's pay to rig himself out. The arrangements, however, differed for the officers of the East India Company's army. The company had its own military academy at Addiscombe in Surrey in England, where potential officers spent two years studying military matters, Hindi, mechanics and mathematics. They did not purchase either their commissions or their promotions. They were career soldiers mainly from middle-class backgrounds, in contrast to many of the Queen's army officers who were often from more wealthy and aristocratic families and served for shorter periods. Queen's army officers tended to look down on their East India Company colleagues, who were excluded from some of the highest-level posts in India such as that of commander in chief. Unsurprisingly, many company officers considered the Queen's officer "always a mere bird of passage" who "should never command in India."

The comforts of an officer's life contrasted sharply with the lot of the private soldier, whether in either the British or the company army. Despite the heat, each European or Indian infantryman was required to wear a rigid leather stock around his neck to keep his head up and his eyes ahead. On his head was a tall shako of black cloth stretched over a wicker or wire frame with a leather visor and secured by a chin strap. He wore stiff white trousers whitened with pipe clay, his "red coat"—a serge swallow-tailed garment buttoned to the throat—and a white cross belt from which hung his sword and sixteen-inch steel bayonet. His cartridge belt held sixty musket balls, each an ounce and a third in weight, for his "Brown Bess" flintlock musket. A muzzle-loaded weapon, it was unchanged since the Battle of Waterloo and had an effective range of only up to 150 yards.[*] On his back—unless he paid to have it carried by camel as some members of the Army of the Indus did in contravention of their orders—he carried a heavy rucksack holding the rest of his equipment.[†]

The private soldier was subject to harsh discipline—death by firing squad for striking an officer, refusing to obey orders or for cowardice, and public flogging with a knotted cat-o'-nine tails for lesser offenses. Although in 1812 the commander in chief of the army, Frederick, Duke of York, had ordered that no man should receive more than three hundred lashes, military courts retained powers to inflict up to three thousand. If a man fainted during punishment or was considered by doctors to be unfit to endure any more blows, he was given a few days to recover before the rest of the lashes were delivered. However, as recently as 1835, the then governor-general Lord William Bentinck had ordered that sepoys should not be flogged—a concession greatly resented by their British army brothers-in-arms, who were still so regularly flogged that the East India Company soldiers nicknamed them "bloody-backs."

In Afghanistan, the soldiers of the Army of the Indus would encoun-

---

[*]The origin of the name Brown Bess isn't certain, although some claim it derives from an order by the Duke of Wellington to his soldiers at Waterloo to paint their gun barrels brown so the enemy would not be alerted to troop movements by seeing them gleaming in the sun.
[†]The majority of British soldiers were illiterate, but for those who were not and were willing to carry the extra weight in their packs, newly available novels included works by Charles Dickens such as *The Pickwick Papers, Oliver Twist* and *Nicholas Nickleby*.

ter a very differently armed and equipped enemy. Dost Mohammed's forces consisted primarily of mail-clad, metal-helmeted irregular cavalry armed with sword and lance. The standard firearm of both horsemen and foot soldiers was the long-barreled matchlock jezail, which not only was more accurate than the Brown Bess but fired a heavier bullet and had more than four times its range. A British officer examining a captured jezail was surprised to find that "the ramrod, when put down the barrel, extended fully a foot from the muzzle. There must have been four or five times as much powder in the charge as is contained in one of our cartridges." The jezail took two or three minutes to fire and reload, compared with the British musket's more rapid rate of fire of two, even three, rounds a minute when in practiced hands. The jezail was thus an ideal weapon for a long-range sniper on a hillside but less suited to conflict on the open battlefield, where its bearer would be unable to withstand the more frequent disciplined volleys from the Brown Bess musket. Afghans usually carried two, even three, loaded weapons with them. Having fired them, rather than stand and reload, they either retreated or advanced to fight hand-to-hand with sword and small, round shield.

Morale was high as Cotton's forces passed into Bahawalpur, whose ruler Alexander Burnes, traveling in advance of the army, had persuaded to cooperate. However, as the terrain changed from tamarisk bushes to sand and date palms and the Indus drew nearer, some of the sepoys became unsettled. Sita Ram, a high-caste Brahmin of the Bengal Native Infantry seconded to Shah Shuja's levies, explained why in his memoirs of the campaign: "[To cross the Indus] is forbidden by our religion and the very act means loss of caste. Consequently many sepoys obtained their discharge and many deserted." He was also speaking for many of his countrymen when he wrote that the people of Sind, whose lands they would soon be entering, "were all Mohammedans whose language we did not understand and everything belonging to them was unclean." Lieutenant Tom Holdsworth expressed doubts of another kind that were probably also quite typical. Though he wrote to his father, "I should like very much to see Kabul, Kandahar and all that part of the world, which so few Europeans have visited," he added, "What is the cause of all this bustle and war I hardly know . . . How it will turn out I know no more than the man in the moon."

From Bahawalpur, the Bengal force crossed into northern Sind, where, in late December, Burnes and Mohan Lal pressured the elderly and reluctant ruler of the rocky fortified island of Bukkur in the middle of the Indus into allowing the British forces to occupy it. Meanwhile, on receiving the not entirely unexpected news that the emirs of Sind were rallying their forces at their capital of Hyderabad and intending to oppose Keane's advance through their lands from Karachi and the mouth of the Indus, Fane, still accompanying the force, ordered Cotton and the bulk of his Bengal troops to move down to support the Bombay army.

This show of force backed up by stern diplomatic threats was enough to convince the Sindi emirs to accept the imposition of Macnaghten's treaty obliging them to let the British troops pass through their territories, to permit free navigation of the Indus and to make the required large payment to release themselves for all time from any claim from Shah Shuja of suzerainty or for tribute. When the emirs had rightly remonstrated that these demands ran counter to an agreement made only a year earlier, they were informed that "neither the ready power to crush and annihilate them, nor the will to call it into action, were wanting, if it appeared requisite, however remotely, for the safety or integrity of the Anglo-Indian Empire or frontier." Cotton, like many of his officers and men, had hoped for prize money from the capture of wealthy Hyderabad, whose treasuries were reputed to contain 8 million pounds sterling in coin. Instead, he returned disappointed to Bukkur to oversee the construction of boat bridges to enable the army to cross the Indus.

The task was completed within eleven days and with considerable ingenuity. An officer of engineers described how they seized 120 boats, felled trees for beams and planks and in the absence of any rope made "500 cables out of a peculiar kind of grass which grows 100 miles from here," by twisting the long fibrous stems together. They then made anchorage points in the river from "small trees joined and loaded with half a ton of stone. [Their] nails were all made on the spot. [They] then anchored the boats in the middle of the stream, in a line across, leaving twelve feet between each; strong beams were laid across the boats, and planks nailed on these for a roadway. This is the largest military bridge which has ever been made." By 18 February 1839, the army, its equipment and supplies, as well as its thousands of camp followers, had passed over the Indus.

Reaching Shikarpur—a small, hot and dirty town of mud-brick houses where Shah Shuja and his levies had already arrived safely—Cotton halted. He did so to wait for Keane and the Bombay force to rendezvous with him and to allow supplies of grain, water and animal forage to be organized at regular intervals along his route across the 150-mile stretch of bleak, salt-rimed desert that lay between Shikarpur and the formidable Bolan Pass. Macnaghten, who had caught up, was fretting at the delay caused by what he considered the needless diversion of Cotton's forces to Hyderabad. He was also alarmed by reports that Baluchi tribesmen planned to block the pass, and pressed Cotton to go on while he remained with Shah Shuja and the king's levies until Keane arrived, when they would advance together. The reason Shah Shuja was to stay behind was insufficient baggage animals. Macnaghten had sought an additional one thousand camels from Cotton, who had refused him, claiming he could not spare them.

In fact, Macnaghten was soon barely on speaking terms with Cotton, who, he complained in a dispatch to Auckland a few weeks later, was a terrible defeatist: "Not content with telling me we must all inevitably be starved, he assures me that Shah Shuja is very unpopular in Afghanistan and that we shall be opposed at every step of our progress. I think I know a little better than this." Cotton in turn accused the envoy of wishing to take over command of the army. The friction between the political and military leadership foreseen by the now departed Fane was only too evident.

On 22 February Cotton led his forces onward again, taking with him provisions for only six weeks and leaving Macnaghten and Shah Shuja behind with one of his own brigades, under the recently widowed fifty-six-year-old Major General William Nott, to guard his rear. Burnes and Mohan Lal traveled ahead of the main force, their task to try to negotiate with the Baluchi tribes through whose lands the army had to pass.

As the army plodded westward toward the Bolan Pass across the unforgiving scorpion-infested desert, temperatures touched one hundred degrees Fahrenheit, relieved only by occasional thundery showers when "the cool drops fizzed as they fell on the burning sand." Two officers were found dead of heat stroke in their tents, their bodies blackened. Eleven men who lost their way and unwisely halted under a tree to drink brandy also collapsed and died. Such water as existed was muddy and brackish, and there was no food for the livestock. Lieutenant Henry Durand, an officer of engineers, later complained that they "marched into this tract of land as if possessed of miraculous powers of abstinence." Pack animals died in their hundreds, while straggling beasts were seized by Baluchi tribesmen who were tracking the progress of the strange and cumbersome procession. Sita Ram wrote of the general despair, "Our sufferings were frightful and the livers of all the Hindustanis were turned to water."

Macnaghten had requested Cotton to do nothing to inflame the local population as his army approached Afghanistan, but when robbers attacked a hospital wagon, killing and wounding its occupants, Cotton ordered any raiders to be shot on sight. Sixteen days after leaving Shikarpur the army reached Dadur at the mouth of the Bolan Pass. According to an agreement just negotiated by Burnes and Mohan Lal with Mehrab Khan of Khelat—the powerful Baluchi ruler who controlled the pass—food supplies adequate for the ten-day transit of the Bolan should have been waiting, but there was barely enough to feed the army for a day. Though the khan was blamed for this, the lack of supplies was not entirely his fault. The advancing army had already consumed much of his people's crops as well as using up precious water supplies at a time of drought, and though he could not supply much grain, the khan did provide thousands of sheep. He also told Burnes that the British venture was foolhardy, even hopeless, saying that Dost Mohammed was an able and resourceful ruler and that though the British might displace him and set up Shah Shuja, they "could never win over the Afghan nation." Such gloomy predictions did not endear the khan to Macnaghten, who wrote to Auckland urging that Khelat's most important provinces be annexed to Shah Shuja's kingdom—when he again had one.

Cotton, meanwhile, decided to push on into the Bolan Pass, knowing that there he would at least find water and hoping that when the army reached Quetta at the other end of the pass, supplies would be easier to come by. On 16 March the column began the arduous climb into the seventy-mile-long pass, which at its highest point reaches nearly six thousand feet. Heavy rains turned the stream running through the Bolan into a dangerous torrent, which the advancing force had to cross repeatedly. The ground behind them was soon littered with the carcasses of animals unable to stumble any farther, especially camels, which, Henry Havelock wrote, "never feel at home but on a plain and on soft ground" and which suffered horribly as they toiled uphill over bleak, stony terrain with "not a blade of grass, not a tree to be seen." Another officer claimed that a tot of whiskey had a miraculously reviving effect on any beast that collapsed. The column also faced attack by tribesmen lying concealed with their long-barreled jezails behind the jagged outcrops above the pass, and whose behavior the khan of Khelat, whatever he might claim, was unable to control. The Reverend George Gleig, principal chaplain to the Army of the Indus, caught the menace of the wild desolate pass, "overlooked in all its narrower veins by clefts among which marksmen may stand, and high precipices, from the summits of which loosened rocks may be hurled."

Yet at last the army emerged from the Bolan Pass into meadows of aromatic herbs and nodding tulips and irises, but so few cultivated fields of barley and wheat that one officer in desperation purchased ghee (clarified butter) from some passing Afghan merchants to keep his camels alive. On the chill morning of 27 March the hungry and somewhat demoralized army reached the mud-walled town of Quetta, having lost in the pass two thousand camels and the valuable supplies the animals had been carrying. Learning that Quetta held no more than two days' supply of corn and that little more was to be found in the hinterland, Cotton put his men on half rations while he waited for the Bombay force and Shah Shuja's levies to arrive. Camp followers struggled to exist on fried sheep skins, congealed animal blood and whatever roots they could grub up. Some of Cotton's officers, though, spent their time shooting woodcock, while the botanists among them examined the wild anemones, buttercups, poppies and dandelions growing around Quetta that were such a relief after what one officer called the "dismal sterility" of the Bolan Pass.

On 4 April Sir John Keane finally arrived with the Bombay contingent and Shah Shuja's levies and immediately assumed command of the entire Army of the Indus. Keane was a choleric man of nearly sixty who liked to be carried in a palanquin. He had fought in Wellington's army during the Peninsula War and been wounded while leading an attack on New Orleans in the Anglo-American War of 1812. He had risen with the help of influential friends and was disliked by many for his coarse behavior and foul language. Henry Havelock wrote of Keane's "open parade of private vices," hinting that they were "only a cloak for darker features of his character." The fact that Keane was not an East India Company officer was also held against him, given the rivalry between the officers of Queen's regiments and those of the company.

Keane had had to pick his way under sniper fire around piles of rotting animal carcasses and human corpses "in every degree of putrefaction" as he advanced through the defiles of the Bolan Pass in Cotton's wake. He had also experienced severe communications problems because the Baluchi tribesmen were attacking the *cossids*—native messengers employed by the British—and according to Lieutenant Holdsworth stealing official dispatches "to wrap their kebabs in." Keane was therefore not in the best frame of mind when he reached Quetta and took command. He and Cotton quarreled immediately because Keane saw at once that the situation in Quetta was critical. Neither his own nor Cotton's forces had any supplies. Keane decided his best option was to push on at once to Kandahar in the hope that their few remaining provisions would last until then.

Despite his reservations, he appointed Cotton to command the Bengal infantry, which till then had been led by the able but irascible Major General Nott, who, having rejoined the main force, was—so Keane informed him—to be left to garrison Quetta with a brigade. Keane appointed Major General Thomas Willshire, like Cotton and himself a British army officer, to command the two brigades of the Bombay infantry. Nott, who was senior to both Cotton and Willshire, was predictably convinced that Keane was sidelining him because he was a company, not a Queen's, officer. From a relatively humble tenant-farmer background, Nott was deeply critical of the posting of Queen's officers to India. Some years earlier, in 1834, he had warned in one of the Bengal newspapers of the consequences "if the long-tried and experienced Company's officer is to be superseded and commanded by the silly and weak scions of the aristocracy, or by the men of interest, whom the whim or caprice of the Horse Guards may send across the Ocean." A furious scene between Nott and Keane ended with the latter roaring that he would never forget Nott's conduct "as long as I live!"

In the early morning of 7 April 1839, the Army of the Indus moved out, Shah Shuja's levies in the lead once again for presentational reasons. The formidable Khojuk Pass lay between the army and the plains of Kandahar. Although shorter than the Bolan Pass, it was steeper, rising to almost 7,500 feet. In the thinning air a tangled mass of exhausted men and beasts struggled for breath as they ascended the narrow precipitous track. Moving the heavy artillery was a particular nightmare. Stripped to the waist and working in teams of one hundred alternating in thirty-minute shifts, sweating soldiers man-hauled the guns on long ropes. Once they had pulled one gun to the top of the pass, there was the even more difficult and dangerous task of getting it down the slope on the other side, which had a gradient of one in three, without it running away with itself. It took a week, but after a remarkable display of endurance and sheer grit, the guns were safely through the pass. Along the way, however, twenty-seven thousand musket balls and fourteen barrels of gunpowder had had to be abandoned—army engineers exploded them to keep them out of enemy hands—and three thousand long-suffering camels had either tumbled into precipices, collapsed through sheer exhaustion or been rustled by raiders.

Shah Shuja was once more in his ancestral territory. His attendants pitched his brilliantly colored royal tents close to the British encampment but not near enough to discourage a group of Afghan horsemen from galloping through the tents one evening. The raiders shot down twelve men and carried off two women and a pair of elephants—one of them Shah Shuja's own mount. It was hardly an auspicious start to his renewed reign. To mark his return as king, the British invited him to tour their camp. Henry Havelock watched as Shah Shuja was carried on men's shoulders "in a gilded litter fenced from the sun by a kind of circular dome, guarded by about sixty attendants in scarlet armed with javelins or drawn sabres, some carrying silver sticks, others touting their master's title and all running along at a fast pace." He thought "the most singular part of the costume of the monarch's retinue" was their caps "of red cloth ornamented with long horns of black felt, which give the wearers the air of representing in masquerade the great enemy of the human race [i.e the devil]." He was unimpressed by the king himself—a "rather stout man of the middle size, his chin covered with a long, thick, and neatly trimmed beard, dyed black to conceal the encroachments of time."

Havelock also found fault with the king's manner, which to his critical eye suggested "that mixture of timidity and duplicity so often observable in the character of the highest order of men in Southern Asia." Though the king's behavior toward the British was "gentle, calm and dignified," his demeanor toward his own people was such that they "invariably

complained of his reception of them as cold and repulsive even to rudeness." Havelock also noted what Burnes had in vain pointed out to his
superiors: that the Afghans regarded Shah Shuja as "a man of evil destiny,
a *kum nuseeb*, or *bud bukht*."

On 20 April a large body of horsemen approached the camp. Ignoring
sentries' warning shots, their splendidly armed and clad leader, gold-fringed
turban on his head, trotted forward and indicated that he had come in
peace to wait upon Shah Shuja. The man was Haji Khan Kakur, an influential Afghan chief, who prostrated himself before a gratified Shah Shuja and
received permission to pitch his tents nearby. Haji Khan claimed that the
rulers of Kandahar—Dost Mohammed's half brothers—had been planning
to attack the British column but that he had convinced them they would be
defeated and to flee. Haji Khan was a noted and notable liar who, according
to one British officer, had "commenced life in the humble capacity of a melon
vendor and raised himself to the highest rank by cunning and enterprise . . .
invariably changing sides when his interest prompted him to do so." It is
unclear whether on this occasion his claims were true. Yet before long,
more chiefs arrived to pledge allegiance to the returning king.

With daytime temperatures still well above one hundred Fahrenheit,
the Army of the Indus continued toward Kandahar, moving slowly across
an arid and still mountainous landscape where the wells held only brackish
and salty water. One officer noted in his diary, "no sweet water . . . great
suffering among the soldiers, European and native, and the cattle." Two
days later, when the green ribbon of water that was the Dori River near
Kandahar came in sight, parched men and animals rushed toward it. In
their eagerness, horses tumbled down its steep banks, and many too weak to
right themselves drowned. Keane ordered his army to make camp on the
banks of the Dori, intending the following day to enter the walled city of
Kandahar, whose rulers had indeed fled across the Helmand River toward Persia and which clearly would offer no resistance. However, next
morning, 25 April, to Keane's anger he awoke to discover that Macnaghten and Shah Shuja had, without any consultation with him, set off during
the night with some of their men to Kandahar, into which Shah Shuja had
made a ceremonial entrance at dawn.

Two weeks later, on 8 May, seated on a canopied platform and, as the
army surgeon Dr. Richard Kennedy described, with "the chief and general

staff of the British army on his left, and some half-a-dozen shabby-looking, dirty, ill-dressed Afghan fellows on his right," Shah Shuja was formally proclaimed king of Afghanistan to a 101-gun salute. The moment passed "without, however, any symptom of the interest or enthusiasm which we were led to expect," another officer noted. Though the crowds dutifully attended the ceremony, a subsequent military review before the Afghan king attracted few spectators. Sita Ram captured what many had known in their hearts for months: "The truth began to dawn on us that despite all the assurances Shah Shuja had given us in Hindustan that the Afghans were longing for his return, in reality they did not want him as their ruler." In particular they resented that "he had shown the English the way into their country and that they would shortly take possession of it. They would use it as they had done all Hindustan and introduce their detested rules and laws." The hatred of the foreign invader became soon and bloodily obvious. A young officer wrote home of his sense of vulnerability, describing "horrible" murders of those unwise enough to stray too far and how he always carried loaded pistols when he rode out.

MEANWHILE IN LONDON in the New Year of 1839, the British government faced an incessant clamor from Sir Robert Peel, the head of a critical Tory opposition, for the publication of all relevant documents justifying the Afghan invasion, citing the precedent of government publication of previous important documents relating to Indian policy.

Release would have been difficult enough since the government did not wish to expose the disagreements of Burnes, among others, with the proposed way forward, but there was also a further complication. Relations with Russia had thawed to such an extent that Britain was preparing to receive a state visit from the Czsarevitch, the future Alexander II and liberator of the serfs. Under the circumstances, publishing documents too openly critical of Russia seemed out of the question to the authorities. Hobhouse, the president of the East India Company's Board of Control, summed up some of the objections to total disclosure in familiar terms: foreign relations difficulties, national security, impeding the progress of ongoing military operations and the impossibility of entrusting the public with sensitive information. "First—it would necessarily raise most embarrassing questions regarding the state of our relations with Russia. Secondly—it would put the Enemies of Great Britain in possession of most important information regarding the means of conquering the Indian Empire and of counteracting the measures in progress for defending it, and Thirdly—it might embarrass and weaken those measures by raising a premature discussion, and create unnecessary alarm in the Public Mind."

In Parliament the prime minister claimed the opposition was playing party politics in asking for such disclosure and in so doing entirely disregarding the national interest. Eventually, however, the government had to give way. Bolstering itself with the comforting thought that previous disclosures on other matters had been selective, over the next few months it released a selection of papers both partial and edited. Palmerston, newly married to his long-term mistress Lady Cowper, himself masterminded the dilution of the anti-Russian content of the published material. Similarly, Hobhouse omitted key dispatches from Burnes promoting Dost Mohammed's merits and claims and edited others that were published without making clear where the editing had taken place. When Burnes came to hear of it, he was deeply upset, believing, as did the great historian of the period, Sir John Kaye, that officials had "dug the grave of truth . . . The character of Dost Mohammed has been lied away; the character of Burnes has been lied away. Both by the mutilation of the correspondence of the latter." The official records—"the sheet-anchors of historians"—had been falsified. Burnes himself wrote, "All my implorations to Government to act with promptitude and decision had reference to doing something when Dost Mohammed was King, and all this they have made to appear in support of Shah Shuja being set up!"

However, these concerns seemed to evaporate with the successful 1839 springtime visit of the Czarevitch to London and the opening of promising discussions between Russia and Britain about the vexed "Eastern question" of the two countries' relations with Ottoman Turkey, as well as initial positive reports of the military campaign in Afghanistan. Few questioned whether, with a seeming new diplomatic détente having been reached with Russia, the Afghan intervention remained necessary. Yet when catastrophe struck, what one critic called "the garbled," and others "the mutilated" and "eviscerated," nature of the disclosures would return to haunt the government.

CHAPTER SIX

We may fairly say that the game is over.

—SIR JASPER NICOLLS,
COMMANDER IN CHIEF IN INDIA, 1839

THE ARMY OF the Indus stayed for nearly two months in Kandahar, where crops ripening in the surrounding fields and meadows provided food for the near-starving men and animals. This puzzled Dost Moham-med, who wondered whether the British were intending to defer their advance on Kabul until the following year, perhaps while they went west-ward to Herat. However, in late June his doubts about British immediate intentions ended when he learned that the replenished Army of the Indus had set out northeast toward the fortified city of Ghazni, ninety miles south of Kabul. Ironically, the day the army marched out, 27 June, was the very day when—unbeknownst to them—Ranjit Singh died in his capi-tal of Lahore, where his diminutive body was cremated on a sandalwood pyre shared with four wives and seven slave girls who committed suttee for him.*

Army commander Keane left behind at Kandahar his only siege guns—four 18-pounders weighing sixty hundredweight—and their al-most one thousand shells that had been dragged through the passes with

---

*Suttee—the rite whereby living wives and concubines joined their dead husbands on their funeral pyres, sometimes voluntarily, sometimes not—was practiced by Sikhs and Hindus but had been outlawed in British India.

such agonizing effort, taking with him only his 6- and 9-pounder guns. Assured by Macnaghten that the defenders of Ghazni would surrender without a fight and by an officer of engineers that the fortress walls were weak anyway, he had bowed to the arguments of his artillery commander that the bullocks were still too exhausted to drag the heavy guns any farther. That decision—wrong as it would prove—was one of choice. However, Keane had no option but to leave behind three thousand camel-loads of grain. Despite all his threats and protestations, the camel drivers refused to move beyond Kandahar because they feared Dost Mohammed's retribution.

A further setback had occurred two weeks earlier when Shah Shuja had sent a copy of the Koran and ten thousand rupees to the Ghilzais, who controlled the country through which the Army of the Indus would shortly pass. The Ghilzais were feared by the British as "a numerous and warlike tribe" whose chiefs, according to the Reverend Gleig, inhabited "towers or castles that lie scattered in great numbers through the valleys, while the hills which overlook them abound with glens and deep recesses, whence sudden outbursts might easily be made on a line of march conducted otherwise than cautiously." The Ghilzai chiefs had returned the Koran but kept the money, a sign that they rejected Shah Shuja's request for safe passage. Mohan Lal thought one reason for their contemptuous refusal was that they knew the British had already broken faith with other tribal leaders by failing to reward them for their help. Soon after the army had left Kandahar, Ghilzai horsemen were observed stalking the column, and Keane posted additional cavalrymen as pickets around it in case of attack.

Daytime temperatures of 120 degrees Fahrenheit, a hot searing wind and clouds of choking dust became as great a trial as the Ghilzais. So too did the perennial problem of insufficient supplies. On 20 July, with three days' supply of food left, the force was a day's march from Ghazni. Keane dispatched a reconnaissance party ahead, which reached within half a mile of Ghazni but saw only a few horsemen moving about in the surrounding hills. On their return they fell in with an Afghan rider, who told them he had visited the British camp and not been impressed and added what was becoming a familiar warning: "You are an army of tents and camels; our army is one of men and horses. What could induce you to squander crores [tens of millions] of rupees in coming to a poor rocky country like ours, without wood or water and all in order to force upon us a *kumbukht* (unlucky person), as a king, who, the moment you turn your backs, will be upset by Dost Mohammed, our *own* king?"

The next morning Keane himself rode ahead with some of his officers to take a closer look at Ghazni and its great citadel, but as they drew near, marksmen in the surrounding orchards forced them back. Keane ordered infantry forward to dislodge them and some of his artillerymen to bring up their 9-pounder guns within range of the fortress to test its defenses with their shrapnel shells—hollow balls filled with shot surrounding a fused powder charge.* Ghazni's Afghan defenders responded by firing back solid shot, and Keane ordered his own gunners to retreat. In contradiction to what Macnaghten and others had told him, Ghazni would not fall without a fight. What's more, Ghazni's walls stood on a mound 120 feet high surrounded by a moat and themselves rose to a height of seventy feet and looked strong. In fact, they were twenty feet thick in places. Through his telescope, Keane also saw signs of recent attempts to reinforce the defenses. These were the work of one of Dost Mohammed's sons, Hyder Ali Khan. Sent by his father to organize the defense of Ghazni, he had ordered the moat to be dug around the fortress and screening walls thrown up to protect its gates. He had also brought in enough supplies to enable Ghazni to withstand a six-month siege if necessary. Dost Mohammed had also sent another son, Mohammed Afzal Khan, with a force of cavalry and orders to deploy in the vicinity of Ghazni. According to intelligence reports reaching Keane, he was less than a two days' ride away.

With his supplies almost exhausted, Keane had little time to decide what to do. The arrival in his camp of Dost Mohammed's nephew Abdul Rashid Khan, whom Mohan Lal had met many years earlier and to whom he had written coaxing him to come over to the British, decided him. Abdul Rashid Khan assured Keane that while three of Ghazni's four gates— all of which were constructed as strongpoints and through which the path turned at a right angle to impede onrushing forces—had been bricked up,

---

*Shrapnel shells—devices which explode in flight, scattering lead shot and other lethal materials—were invented by the British artillery officer Henry Shrapnel in the 1790s.

the Kabul Gate on the north side was only lightly barricaded in anticipation of the arrival of reinforcements from Kabul. After Keane's chief sapper, Major George Thomson, had taken a good look at the Kabul Gate through his telescope and agreed that it might well be possible to blow it open, Keane decided to risk all by storming it without delay and on the afternoon of 21 July moved his army up to Ghazni.

Just before dawn on 22 July, however, a force of some three thousand *ghazis*—fundamentalist Islamic holy warriors determined to drive out the infidels and if necessary ready to martyr themselves in the process and thereby win their place in paradise—came galloping in from the east and fell on Shah Shuja's camp. Their attack was supported by artillery fire from within Ghazni, including rounds from a giant brass 48-pounder that the Afghans called Zubur-Zun (Hard-Hitter) and that the British quickly nicknamed "Long-Tom." Eventually, after some heavy fighting the *ghazis* were driven off and about fifty captured and dragged before Shah Shuja. According to Burnes, one *ghazi* yelled at Shah Shuja that he was an infidel and had brought infidels into the country and pulling out a knife stabbed one of his attendants. Shah Shuja's response was to order all but two prisoners, whom for some reason he pardoned, to be beheaded. A horrified British officer stumbled upon the scene. The prisoners "were huddled together pinioned, some sitting, some lying on the ground, some standing, and four or five executioners, armed with heavy Afghan knives [*tulwars*]—a something betwixt a sword and a dagger, the shape of a carving knife, two feet long in the blade, broad and heavy—were very coolly, and in no sort of hurry, hacking and hewing at their necks, one after the other, till all were beheaded."

Keane meanwhile was making final plans for his assault on Ghazni. An explosives party consisting of three officers, three sergeants and eighteen Indian sappers was to cross the bridge over the moat to the Kabul Gate and place twelve leather bags containing three hundred pounds of gunpowder at its foot. The men were then to detonate the explosives with a seventy-two-foot-long fuse. As soon as the gate was blown in, a storming party of 240 handpicked men under Colonel William Dennie was to charge in, supported by further troops under Brigadier "Fighting Bob" Sale, a disciplinarian no-nonsense officer, loved by his men, who would emerge as one of the most unlikely heroes of the First Afghan War. Sale was to command the whole assault force, with Cotton commanding the reserve. Meanwhile, three infantry companies of the Thirty-fifth Bengal Native Infantry were to circle around to Ghazni's Kandahar Gate on the south side and feign an attack to divert the defenders' attention from what was happening at the Kabul Gate. Keane had also deployed a detachment of cavalry to watch for the return of the *ghazis* or for any sudden advance on Ghazni by Dost Mohammed's forces, and to cut off anyone trying to flee the town.

As the time for the attack approached, the atmosphere in the camp was nervous. Tom Holdsworth, writing to his father afterward, caught the mood: "There was a nervous irritability and excitement about us the whole day; constantly looking at the place through spy-glasses, etc.; and then fellows began to make their wills and tell each other what they wished to have done in case they fell; altogether it was not at all pleasant and everyone longed most heartily for the morrow, and to have it over." In the moonless, windy early hours of 23 July, the explosives party was waiting a few hundred yards from the Kabul Gate with its bags of gunpowder. Artillery had earlier been moved into position on rocky heights overlooking the Kabul Gate to provide covering fire to the assault forces, the gunners grateful for the sound of the high winds to mask the creaking of the gun carriages.

Just after three o'clock, "when the morning star was high in the heavens and the first red streak of approaching morning was on the horizon," the demolition party crept across the bridge over the moat. When the group was still fifty yards from the walls, a shout from the ramparts ahead was followed by a shot from a jezail. The men had been spotted. At almost the same moment the diversionary attack on the Kandahar Gate began, and Keane's artillery opened fire. The explosives party continued its approach, managing to deposit all the bags of gunpowder against the Kabul Gate and to position and light the long fuse. However, in the high wind, at first it failed to ignite properly. One of the officers, Lieutenant Henry Durand, blew on the guttering flame and scraped at the fuse with his nails to make it easier to spark fully. Finally, at the third attempt it caught.

The demolition party dashed back the way they had come before flinging themselves to the ground as a tremendous explosion reverberated around them. Certain that the gate had been breached, Durand looked around for his bugler to signal for the storming party to advance, only to find the man had been shot through the head. Luckily Colonel Dennie took the initiative. Without waiting for the signal, he charged at the head of his men over the bridge and into the fallen debris of the shattered gateway. In the still-choking smoke the fighting was fierce and hand-to-hand as Dennie's men pressed onward into the town. Hyder Ali Khan, who had been discussing with his counselors where best to place the women for their protection, had been taken completely unawares. By the time he heard the explosions and musket fire, it was too late to organize effective resistance.

As Dennie's men pushed on, the main storming party under Brigadier Sale advanced across the bridge. Holdsworth described how it felt to rush toward the still-smoking breach and, as he did so, to try to make himself as small a target as possible: "The fire on both sides was at its height. The noise was fearful, and the whole scene the grandest and, at the same time, the most awful I ever witnessed . . . As we got nearer the gate it grew worse and the enemy, from their loopholes began to pepper us." They "threw out blue lights in several places which looked beautiful, and the flames of their and our artillery, together with smaller flashes from the matchlock men added to the roar of their big guns . . . the whizzing of their cannon-balls and ours . . . the singing of the bullets." Then, as so often, the fog of war descended. As Brigadier Sale's men pushed in over the smoking beams and tumbled stones of the great gate, Captain Alexander Peat of the initial explosives party, "stunned and bewildered by concussion," called out, "Don't go on, it's a failure!" Sale at once ordered his bugler to sound the retreat. As his men began falling back, another officer told Sale that Peat was wrong and Dennie had got inside the citadel, at which the brigadier ordered the bugler to signal the advance once more, causing his column to turn and again rush across the bridge.

A group of Afghan defenders had in the meantime gathered in the ruins of the gateway and tried valiantly to hold off Sale's men with their *tulwars.* One young lieutenant recalled how in the vicious hand-to-hand fighting some of the attackers were "*literally* cut to pieces." Sale himself, although in his late fifties, was in the thick of the fighting. He was wounded twice and escaped death at the hands of his Afghan attacker, who had knocked him to the ground and pinioned him, only by wrenching his sword arm free and cleaving the Afghan's skull to his eyebrows. However, the sheer force and unexpectedness of the attack had broken the defenders' resistance. Some trying to flee through the ruins of the gateway tripped over the still-blazing timbers and were burned alive; others were bayoneted by the attackers or trampled beneath the hoofs of terrified Afghan cavalry horses, which the defenders had brought into the city and which were now running loose in the streets. The British took the citadel itself without a fight and captured Hyder Ali Khan. His women, who were in one officer's view neither "pretty or interesting," were taken into safe custody as the British troops began to loot, finding, as well as fine quilts and ladies' "inexpressibles," large quantities of gunpowder, weapons, grain and other food. The whole operation had taken less than two hours with 600 of the enemy killed and 1,600 captured, against British casualties of 182 killed or wounded.

The Army of the Indus had been fortunate. Anticipating that his enemies were most likely to take the shorter route through the Khyber Pass, Dost Mohammed had stationed his best troops under his son Akbar Khan to watch that pass. Even so, as Keane later discovered, Dost Mohammed's son Mohammed Afzal Khan, at the head of five thousand Ghilzai horsemen, had been only six miles from Ghazni when he had heard the sounds of the attack. Instead of advancing, he had ordered his men to ride as hard as they could for Kabul, leaving many baggage elephants and much of his equipment behind him. Keane lost no time in dashing off a report to Lord Auckland describing the capture of Ghazni: It was "one of the most brilliant acts it has ever been my lot to witness, during my service of 45 years in the four quarters of the globe."

British officers meanwhile went on sightseeing expeditions around Ghazni, admiring the exquisite brick workmanship of two ancient towers, one of which was at least 180 feet high, and visiting the eleventh-century polished white marble tomb of Sultan Mahmud, who had invaded India on ten separate occasions. The tomb lay within a walled garden planted with mulberries. As well as a giant tiger skin and strings of ostrich eggs interwoven with peacock's feathers, officers inspected the tomb's massive gates, which were eight feet wide and fourteen feet high. Reputedly plundered by Sultan Mahmud from the Hindu temple of Somnath in Gujarat, these were the gates Ranjit Singh had once demanded as the price for assisting Shah Shuja. The gates were said to be cedar or sandalwood, but one officer, sniffing them hopefully, found "the smell is entirely gone."

News of the fall of the supposedly impregnable Ghazni made a profound impression within Afghanistan. Burnes's old friend Nawab Jubbar Khan arrived from Kabul bearing Dost Mohammed's offer to surrender if he were given the post of vizier, held by his murdered brother Futteh Khan and which he regarded as the hereditary right of the Barakzais. Scenting complete victory, Macnaghten rejected Dost Mohammed's suggestion, offering him instead honorable exile in British India. He also dismissed any idea of releasing the emir's son, Hyder Ali Khan. For once Nawab Jubbar Khan's usual good nature deserted him. Dost Mohammed, he said, would rather throw himself on the point of a British bayonet than accept exile. As a parting shot, he demanded of Shah Shuja, with whom he was granted an audience, "If you are to be king, of what use is the British army here? If the English are to rule over the country, of what use are you here?"

On 30 July 1839, leaving twelve hundred men behind to garrison Ghazni, the Army of the Indus set out on the final ninety-mile march northeastward to Kabul, climbing in blustering winds and with hands and feet aching with cold up to a rugged defile known as Sheer Dundau (Lion's Teeth), nine thousand feet above sea level, before descending toward their goal of Kabul, itself at six thousand feet. As the column passed the fortlike villages of mud brick, people crowded the roadsides to watch. Crossing the foaming Kabul River, the army advanced through cultivated valleys with groves of willows, poplars and cypresses. Then came reports that Dost Mohammed had fled Kabul.

In fact, informed by Nawab Jubbar Khan that his proposed peace terms had been rejected, Dost Mohammed had advanced at the head of thirteen thousand troops, including tribal chieftains and mercenaries and accompanied by thirty guns, to the narrow valley of Arghundee. Here he had ridden through the ranks, brandishing a copy of the Koran and exhorting his men to rid the country of the infidel invaders and their puppet king, against whom his clerics had issued a fatwa. However, with the Army of the Indus so close, his chiefs had refused to fight, and the mercenaries he had recruited had slipped away from the camp. That same night, 2 August, accompanied by his son Akbar Khan, whom he had recalled from keeping watch on the Khyber Pass, other family members and a few hundred still-loyal supporters, he rode north for the Hindu Kush, leaving his camp to be looted while those who had once vowed loyalty to him hurried away to declare allegiance to Shah Shuja.

Keane dispatched a combined contingent of British cavalry and Shah Shuja's levies under Captain James Outram to pursue Dost Mohammed and another force to secure his abandoned guns. Meanwhile, on 6 August the Army of the Indus camped within three miles of Kabul. The soldiers gorged on "peaches, apples, plums, pears and grapes . . . all equal to any hot-house fruit in England," and Mohan Lal gazed upon "emerald-like gardens . . . intersected and washed as they are by brooks of crystal-like water," which had captivated him on his earlier visits to Kabul.

Hearing of the safe arrival of the Army of the Indus at Kabul, Sir Jasper Nicolls, the new commander in chief in India, wrote in his journal, "We may fairly say that the game is over."

CHAPTER SEVEN

Be silent, pocket your pay, do nothing but what you are ordered,
and you will give high satisfaction. They will sacrifice you and me,
or anyone, without caring a straw . . . I can go a good way, but my
conscience has not so much stretch as to approve of this dynasty.
But, mum—let that be between ourselves.

—ALEXANDER BURNES, 1839

ON THE AFTERNOON of 7 August 1839, mounted on a white charger with saddle and bridle embellished with gold and at the head of his
levies and the Army of the Indus, Shah Shuja approached the city he had
not seen for thirty years. He was wearing a jeweled coronet. According to
Henry Havelock, yet more jewels sparkled on his arms and chest, while
around his waist was "a broad and cumbrous girdle of gold in which glit-
tered rubies and emeralds not a few." Riding close to the king were
Keane, Macnaghten and Burnes, the latter pair in the full diplomatic
dress of "a cocked hat fringed with ostrich feathers, a blue frock coat with
raised buttons, richly embroidered on the collar and cuffs, epaulettes not
yielding in splendour to those of a field-marshal, and trousers edged with
very broad gold lace." Mohan Lal, also on horseback, was wearing "a new
upper garment of very gay colours" and "a turban of very admirable fold
and majestic dimensions."

As the procession entered Kabul's narrow streets, Havelock thought
that "never was any town seen more closely thronged by men; of women,
glimpses only could be caught as they peeped furtively from the tops of

houses. The extent of the population and the eagerness of all ranks to behold the spectacle, was as apparent in the few open spaces of the city as in the narrow lanes, the passages of the covered bazaars, and on the bridge of the clear and rapid Kabul River. An ocean of heads was spread in every direction. They were for the most part cleanly and becomingly turbaned. The features of the spectators were generally comely, and all lighted up with the emotion of curiosity."

However, like many of the British, he was struck by the subdued mood. There was none of the noisy shouting that would have come from a British crowd. He decided it was not only because the Afghans were, like other Muslims, "grave, sedate, and slow in their demeanour" but because "the prevailing feeling was not one of much affection for Shah Shuja, who will probably as a ruler be less popular than the ex-Emir." The army surgeon Kennedy also found the king's reception unenthusiastic: "I can honestly say that the Kabulis did not fling him either a crust or a nosegay, or shouted a single welcome that reached my hearing: a sullen surly submission to what could not be helped, and an eager determination to make the most that could be made of existing circumstances, and turn them to account, appeared to be the general feeling."

The procession ascended toward the Balla Hissar, built on a commanding promontory overlooking the eastern approaches to the city. Henry Havelock described it as both "the royal palace and fortress" of Kabul. The complex was about half a mile long and a quarter of a mile wide; its lower portion housed barracks and stables, while on the highest point sat the citadel itself, overlooking the royal palace amid its spacious gardens. As the cavalcade advanced into the Balla Hissar, Kennedy described how "a tremendous discharge of camel artillery—jinjals [small cannon] fixed on swivels and mounted on camels—saluted our entrance into the citadel, and as they were fired at random, in the very midst of the procession, the helter-skelter and confusion of the horses of the staff officers and the native horsemen was anything but agreeable: most happily no accident occurred."

Arriving outside his former palace, Shah Shuja could not contain his excitement. Havelock described him rushing up the great staircase and running "with childish eagerness from one small chamber to another," but weeping at what he took as signs of neglect and damage during the

Barakzais' tenure there, especially the removal of the little pieces of mirror-glass once set into the walls to reflect the flickering candlelight and the sparkle of gems. In fact, the palace was not in good condition, and in forthcoming days Shah Shuja would narrowly escape being crushed to death when the rafters of his audience chamber collapsed shortly after he had left to go to pray. Several weeks later, on 3 September, Shah Shuja was reunited with his son Timur, who arrived with Claude Wade and their army, having marched through the Khyber Pass from Peshawar. This meant that the shorter communication route to India through the Khyber Pass, rather than around through the Bolan Pass, was now open.

The Army of the Indus settled in an encampment connected to the city by a narrow road "hemmed in by huge masses of rock on the left hand and dense groves of mulberry-trees on the right bordering the Kabul River." This road soon thronged with "men from the city hawking about camp, grapes, apples, melons, silks, furs and calling out most vociferously as if determined to compel us to buy," an officer noted. Many soldiers were curious to venture into the city of which they had heard so much, but "owing to instances of irregularities committed by Europeans entering Kabul," officers were instructed to issue passes only to soldiers "on whose sobriety and steadiness dependence can be placed." One of the problems was the cheap wine and fiery brandy that were readily available despite the re-formed Dost Mohammed's prohibition of alcohol. The moralistic Baptist and teetotaller Havelock feared the citizens of Kabul would soon learn "the difference between Britons drunk and Britons sober."

The army surgeon James Atkinson paid his first visit to the city on 10 August, marveling at the magnificent fruit piled up in shops "little better than sheds." He watched cooks preparing kebabs, confectioners making sweetmeats, gun makers, swordsmiths and farriers making guns, *tulwars* and horseshoes, while the carpet and silk dealers peddled rugs, furs, lace and chintz. It seemed to him that "nothing could exceed the industry that appeared everywhere around us; everybody employed and intent on his calling." Crossing a bridge over the Kabul River that ran through the city, he saw that, though some thirty yards wide, at this time of year it was only a foot deep. Kabul's Grand Bazaar, built in the early seventeenth century of burned brick richly painted with images of fruit and trees, was "a gem amidst the edifices of mud" that surrounded it. In fact, the city's great markets formed the main thoroughfares linking the residential areas with one another.

Kabul reminded Atkinson of Paris because people "[live] a good deal out of doors, and eat their meals constantly at the benches, where the cooks, a numerous class, fry their kebabs, and are as expert and active as a French artist in the subterraneous kitchen of a café. Then there are the ice-shops and *falood* shops, where you see the rugged Afghan regaling on summer dainties, crunching a lump of ice, with the usual quantity of cherries, grapes, or other fruit, and a goodly portion of his brown cake of bread, everything of the kind being what is called dog-cheap."

However, Atkinson deplored the "most disgusting" public baths, dismissing the Afghans as "generally an exceedingly dirty people" with "a sort of hydrophobia, a horror of water in its capacity of cleansing the person." He was also unimpressed by the people's houses of timber and sun-dried brick: "The middle part of the city is a collection of dwellings, two and three stories high, with almost inaccessible zigzag streets and blind alleys, a black offensive gutter creeping down the centre of the greater part of them. Walls across, with gateways, are common in all the streets, so that, by closing the doors, the city is divided into numerous distinct quarters of defence. The roofs of the houses have commonly a parapet-wall round them, to allow the women of the family to take an airing unveiled, and they are generally also applied to the nastiest of purposes." These warrenlike residential areas were known as *mahallas*, where a maze of narrow, winding, dead-end alleys, or *kuchas*, led to the individual houses, built like fortified dwellings with bare external walls, only one point of entry or exit and, at the heart, a secluded inner courtyard.

While his troops explored Kabul, Auckland was already planning their withdrawal. He had meant it when, in the Simla Manifesto, he had promised that as soon as Shah Shuja was back on his throne and "the independence and integrity of Afghanistan" established, the Army of the Indus would return to India. Two weeks after Shah Shuja's delighted return to his palace within the Balla Hissar, Auckland—although still awaiting confirmation that the Army of the Indus had safely arrived in Kabul—was already writing to Macnaghten of his hopes for the speedy return of the regiments to India. In fact, Auckland intended to withdraw the entire Bombay contingent and some of the Bengal forces almost

immediately, leaving only a single brigade as a token of British support for
Shah Shuja.

Before Auckland's letter reached Kabul in September, Sir John
Keane had independently reached similar conclusions, that most of the
British forces could return swiftly. However, as the weeks passed, those
in Kabul came to see that this would be impossible. Among the reasons
was the failure to capture Dost Mohammed as he fled toward the Hindu
Kush. The force led by Captain James Outram that had set out in pursuit had been led on a wild goose chase by the Afghan chief Haji Khan
Kakur, who had accompanied him in command of two thousand of the
shah's cavalry and was a supposedly knowledgeable guide. Haji Khan
Kakur had, it seems, decided to keep his future options open by allowing
Dost Mohammed sufficient time to disappear into the lands of the independent Uzbek tribes beyond the mountains. Outram wrote to Macnaghten that Haji Khan Kakur was guilty of "either the grossest cowardice or
the deepest treachery" and clearly believed the latter. On 18 August Outram and his men returned crestfallen to Kabul, where Keane told the officers that "he had not supposed there were thirteen such asses in his
whole force!" Haji Khan Kakur was accused of deliberate deceit and ban-
ished to India.

Initially Macnaghten and Keane were not especially concerned that
Dost Mohammed was still at large. However, by September Dr. Percival
Lord—Burnes's erstwhile traveling companion, who had been dispatched
north toward the Hindu Kush as a political officer to gather intelligence—
was sending alarming reports that the emir was attempting to raise the
tribes beyond the Hindu Kush to fight on his behalf. As a precaution
Keane, to whom Auckland had given authority to vary troop dispositions,
decided after discussion with Macnaghten to retain the principal portion
of the Bengal division in Afghanistan under Sir Willoughby Cotton. The
decision disappointed many of the officers who were eager to leave a place
where, as shown by the exorbitant prices realized at an auction of the possessions of a deceased brigadier, seeming necessities such as wine and
cigars were scarce.

Before any troops departed, a bizarre ceremony was enacted. Macnaghten had persuaded Shah Shuja to inaugurate the Order of the
Douranee Empire, after the name by which the Afghan Empire had

been known in its heyday under Shah Shuja's forebears. An earlier idea had been to call it the Order of the Douree Douranee so that, as the army surgeon Kennedy wrote, "the knights were to have written themselves 'D. D.'; but some wicked wag announced it to mean 'the dog and duck!' so it was changed." Shah Shuja sat on an old camp chair wearing a yellow tunic, billowing crimson gown and a purple velvet crown and flanked by two stout eunuchs, each bearing a dish. The ceremony commenced with Sir John Keane kneeling before the king. Then, as Kennedy described, "one of the fat eunuchs waddled to the front and uncovered his dish, in which was the decoration and ribbon of the 'Order of the Douranee Empire.' The Emperor with great difficulty stuck it on; and Sir John's coat being rather too tight, it cost him some effort to wriggle into the ribbon: but the acorn in time becomes an oak, and Sir John was at last adorned . . . a Knight Grand Cross of the Douranee Empire!" Macnaghten and Cotton were invested next, but Burnes was told he would have to wait for his decoration because the goldsmiths had not been able to work fast enough. Neither were decorations ready for the fifty or so officers created Knights Commander and Companions, but a cavalry officer of the Bengal army read out their names, at which each man stepped forward and bowed to the king.

In Calcutta, Lord Auckland had issued his own, less flamboyant congratulations in the form of a General Order lauding Keane and the Army of the Indus and exulting that "the plans of aggression by which the British empire in India was dangerously threatened, have, under Providence, been arrested. The Chiefs of Kabul and Kandahar, who had joined in hostile designs against us, have been deprived of power, and the territories which they ruled have been restored to the government of a friendly monarch." Later in London, the British government would make its own awards to those deemed to have engineered the first victorious campaign of young Queen Victoria's reign. Auckland was to become an earl. Keane's reward was a barony, Macnaghten's a baronetcy and Wade's a knighthood.

On 18 September Major General Willshire left for India at the head of the Bombay Division. His orders were to divert en route to punish the khan of Khelat, who was judged, not entirely fairly, to have reneged on his promises to supply and assist the Army of the Indus as it had advanced through the Bolan Pass. In mid-November Willshire's forces arrived before the walls of Khelat—a citadel nearly as strong as Ghazni—and stormed it, losing one in seven of his men in the process. The khan was discovered with a musket ball through his heart, a fate that Mohan Lal thought exceeded his crime. A young British sublieutenant, William Loveday, moved by a request from one of the khan's retainers for a shroud to cover his dead master, donated a brocade bedcover that he had purchased in "days of folly and extravagance at Delhi." A rival claimant to Khelat was installed, who, as the price for his throne, agreed to the annexation of Khelat's richest provinces to the kingdom of Afghanistan, just as Macnaghten had recommended to Lord Auckland. To "assist" Khelat's new ruler, Loveday was appointed his adviser. However, the dead khan's young son Nussar Khan had escaped and would soon return in force to challenge these cosy new arrangements.

Claude Wade was the next to depart homeward, taking with him those of Prince Timur's levies who were no longer considered necessary and the six thousand Sikhs who were returning to an increasingly unstable homeland, now that Ranjit Singh was dead. The unrequired contingents of the Bengal Division left on 15 October with Keane. He was glad to be going, but something deeper than mere satisfaction at departing a wild and alien place seems to have been going through his mind. He famously remarked to Lieutenant Durand, hero of the storming of Ghazni, who was returning to India with him, "I wished you to remain in Afghanistan for the good of the public service, but since circumstances have rendered that impossible, I cannot but congratulate you on quitting the country; for mark my words, it will not be long before there is here some signal catastrophe!" Perhaps in making his gloomy prophesy he had in mind the recent murder of Lieutenant Colonel Herring and some of his men, ambushed by Ghilzai tribesmen while escorting a treasury convoy to Kabul from Kandahar.

On the very eve of departure another of Keane's officers, Lieutenant Colonel Macdonald, wrote to a friend, "Shah Shuja, I am sorry to say, is not popular and to maintain him on the throne it was absolutely necessary to have left some of our troops in support of him. It is to be hoped that it will be otherwise by and by and that we will be able to leave him to 'the holy keeping' of his own subjects."

❖   ❖   ❖

AS THE DUST clouds raised by the last of the departing troops finally settled, those left behind took stock of their situation and responsibilities. The total number of regiments left in Afghanistan was one Queen's regiment—the Thirteenth Light Infantry—seven regiments of the Bengal Native Infantry and one of Native Cavalry with between seventy to eighty artillery pieces. Their task, which they were to share with Shah Shuja's soldiers, was to garrison the principal cities of his kingdom—Kabul, Jalalabad, Kandahar, Quetta, Ghazni—and guard other strategic positions such as the approaches to the passes. The Reverend Gleig estimated the total strength "of armed men, natives, and foreigners" at some twenty thousand.

It was a modest force for the task it faced, especially when dispersed around the country. Twenty-eight-year-old Lieutenant Vincent Eyre—a capable and handsome officer who was among those remaining in Kabul—called the forces left behind "a miserable moiety" and complained that troops had been precipitately withdrawn "before any steps had been taken to guard against surprise by the erection of a stronghold on the approved principles of modern warfare" or to secure the lines of communication with India hundreds of miles away. Sir John Keane had, he wrote bitterly, "left behind him, in fact, an army whose isolated position and reduced strength offered the strongest possible temptation to a proud and restless race to rally their scattered tribes in one grand effort to regain their lost independence."

Eyre was right that the British in Kabul were isolated. Everything—supplies, reinforcements, orders from Calcutta—depended on keeping open the lines of communications through the narrow Afghan passes. Furthermore, messages took some five weeks to travel between Kabul and Calcutta. Should a crisis arise, those in command in Kabul would have to act on their own initiative—a situation conferring both considerable power and responsibility. The two senior men were Cotton, to whom the departing Keane had handed command of the remaining forces in Afghanistan, and Macnaghten. The relationship between them remained as uneasy as it had been during the advance on Kabul. As envoy to the court of Afghanistan, Macnaghten claimed the right to impose his will on the military where political necessity required, something the Reverend Gleig deplored: "One of the great principles of the English constitution, the subserviency of the military to the civil power, was applied to a case for which it was altogether unsuited . . . all authority over the troops, both in regard to the choice of their positions and the manner of using them, was vested in civilians . . . in Afghanistan it was wholly out of place." He also pointed out such an arrangement was bound to cause tension since many of the political officers were military officers of a subordinate rank. He thought Alexander Burnes the ablest of the diplomatic corps and noted that he had early protested the absurdity of the arrangement and "foretold the results to which it would lead."

The Reverend Gleig additionally disapproved of the appointment of what he called "a whole army of British political agents." The chaplain believed that in Afghan eyes, "not only was the King of Kabul supported on his throne by British bayonets" as if the British government doubted his military strength, but it also appeared as if the British "reposed no confidence whatever in his sagacity or political firmness." The problem was that the British did doubt Shah Shuja's sagacity. As Mohan Lal later wrote, "We neither took the reins of government into our own hands, nor did we give them in full powers into the hands of Shah Shuja. Inwardly or secretly we interfered in all transactions," though "outwardly we wore the mask of neutrality. In this manner we gave annoyance to the king upon the one hand, and disappointment to the people on the other."

Shah Shuja's subjects were not the only ones alienated by events. In October Major General Nott, who had been appointed to command in Kandahar, had been ordered to cooperate with Willshire, a Queen's officer, in the attack on Khelat. He had agreed to provide troops but had protested to the deputy adjutant general at Kabul, "I conceive myself to be senior to local Major-General Willshire, and therefore can obey no orders originating with that officer, nor can I serve under him."

Unknown to Nott, he was at that very time being considered as successor to Sir Willoughby Cotton. However, when his complaint was brought to Auckland's attention, the governor-general decided that Cotton had to stay on until another successor was found. He gave Nott the option to resign his command if he was so discontented, but he was not in a financial position to do so. However, from his headquarters in Kandahar, he would observe events with growing disapproval and alarm.

As the weather turned cooler, Shah Shuja and Macnaghten departed

for Jalalabad to winter there, as had been the tradition of the kings of
Kabul. However, before the snows began to fall, ten thousand soldiers,
still living in their lightweight campaign tents, needed to be properly accommodated. The most sensible place to billet troops, given its strong,
high walls and preeminent position above the city, was the Balla Hissar.
Henry Havelock certainly thought so, writing that the fortress was "the
key of Kabul" and that whoever held it could hold the city. This too was
the recommendation of the army engineers. Indeed, so obvious did this
seem that Brigadier Sale had already ordered the erection of mud barracks within the Balla Hissar to accommodate the Thirteenth Light Infantry. Yet when Shah Shuja learned of this, he objected. His enormous
harem of royal wives and concubines, children, elderly female relations
and the mass of attendants and eunuchs required to run this department
of the royal household was on its way to Kabul from the Punjab, and he
insisted that he needed the space in the Balla Hissar for them. He also
claimed that to have foreign troops in close proximity to the ladies of his
household would be an affront to his dignity.

Cotton's indignant response was that "in Persia, in Egypt, in Muscat,
the greatest sovereigns allow the officers to occupy palaces [but] Shah
Shuja declares he will resign his throne if he be so insulted by the con-
tamination of those men who bled for him, and placed him where he is!"
Macnaghten, though, supported Shah Shuja, and somehow—accounts
vary as to who made the final decision—cantonments were instead built
on low swampy ground a mile north of the city, between the Kabul River
and a broad canal on the one side and the road leading to the northern
province of Kohistan on the other. While these were being built, a few
troops were permitted to remain within the Balla Hissar, but the majority
passed the winter in ramshackle, chilly quarters that were hastily impro-
vised beneath its walls.

The cantonments soon under construction could not have been farther from the "stronghold on the approved principles of modern warfare" that Eyre wanted. Indeed, he later attributed "almost all the calamities
that befell our ill-starred force" to the arrangements which he called "a
disgrace to our military skill and judgement." The cantonments were to
be contained within a rectangular area measuring some thousand yards
by six hundred yards and surrounded by a low mud wall with bastions at

each corner and a narrow ditch that, as a senior officer later sneered, could be leaped by any Afghan "with the facility of a cat." At the north end of the cantonments was the "Mission Compound," roughly half the size of the main area and again bounded by a low wall. Here in the envoy's residence Macnaghten would hold court.

Surrounding gardens and orchards, which could not be cleared for fear of giving offense to the Afghans, obstructed the line of fire from the cantonments and provided cover for any would-be attackers, while barely four hundred yards from the southern corner was a mud-brick village bounded by a low wall that also provided excellent cover. Even worse, the cantonments were close to several Afghan forts, so that in times of trouble, as Eyre noted, soldiers "could not move a dozen paces from either gate without being exposed to the fire of some neighbouring hostile fort garrisoned by marksmen who seldom missed their aim." The cantonments were also overlooked by the Siah Sung Hills a mile to the east and by the even more commanding Bemaru Hills to the west. Strangely, though it was decided to post troops in the Siah Sung Hills, no plans were made to defend the cantonments from potential attack from the west.

Shah Shuja's unwillingness to house his allies also extended to their grain, which he ordered to be removed from the Balla Hissar. In an act of incredible stupidity, the British high command had the main commissariat stores placed in an indefensible old fort outside the main compound and opposite a walled garden, the Shah Bagh. When the chief commissariat officer complained and asked for storage within the cantonments, according to Lieutenant Eyre he was told that "no such place could be given him, as they were far too busy in erecting barracks for the men to think of commissariat stores."

Not everyone was to live in the ill-conceived cantonments. Alexander Burnes, no doubt anxious to be as free of Macnaghten as possible, had early found himself a spacious house in the Kizzilbashi area near the center of Kabul, with Mohan Lal only a few houses away. Opposite Burnes's mansion was a small, fortified building selected as a suitable place for Captain Hugh Johnson, the paymaster and head commissariat officer of Shah Shuja's army, to protect Shah Shuja's treasury with the help of a few guards. Also close by was the headquarters of Brigadier Abraham Roberts, the commander of the shah's army, while Captain Robert Trevor, commander of the king's Life Guards, occupied a small tower between Roberts's and Burnes's residences.

As these eccentric and insecure arrangements were made, with key command posts scattered willy-nilly about the city and the main force located in a ludicrously indefensible position, the British set out to enjoy themselves that autumn and winter. The departure of the sixteenth Lancers and their small pack of foxhounds with Keane was a cause for regret, but they held gymkhanas and races and went shooting and boating. They played cricket while the Afghans watched, but the latter, according to the Reverend Gleig, were not "tempted to lay aside their flowing robes and huge turbans and enter the fields as competitors." The officers staged plays to which Afghan nobles were invited, with Alexander Burnes and others translating the dialogue for their guests.

Sometimes the British organized wrestling contests with the Afghans, and one officer constructed a boat complete with oars, masts and rudder, in which to go sailing on the lake. When the lake froze, young officers went sliding with the Afghans over the ice—something which the Reverend Gleig thought the Afghans did "far more skilfully, as well as gracefully, than their European visitors." The Afghans had believed that "heat, and not cold, was the white man's element" until the British officers made skates for themselves. "The Afghans stared in mute amazement while the officers were fastening on their skates, but when they rose, dashed across the ice's surface, wheeled and turned, and cut out all manner of figures upon the ice, there was an end at once to disbelief in regard to the place of their nativity. 'Now,' cried they, 'we see that you are not like the infidel Hindus that follow you: you are men, born and bred like ourselves, where the seasons vary, and in their changes give vigour both to body and mind. We wish you had come among us as friends, and not as enemies, for you are fine fellows one by one, though as a body we hate you.'"

Some of the British also thought the Afghans "fine fellows." In those first months, Henry Lawrence was impressed by their individual courage, hospitality and generosity, their fine appearance and horsemanship, their love of sport, frank demeanor and affability. However, as the army of occupation settled down, early bonhomie faded as aspects of British behavior began to cause huge offense. Although sepoys were allowed to have their wives with them, European private soldiers were not, and large numbers of prostitutes were soon observed streaming into the cantonments. To the Afghans this was "rending the veil of religious honour." As for the officers, some formed liaisons with Afghan women, who, Surgeon Atkinson claimed, were "notoriously given to intrigue," taking advantage of their all-covering burkas to slip about the city without being recognized "even, it is said, by their own husbands!"

Atkinson certainly displayed a detailed knowledge of their habille beneath the burka: "They wear a loose yellow, blue, or red jacket, muslin or silk, which hangs down below the waist, and wide trousers of silk or other coloured material. They are particular in having their hair minutely arranged. It is plastered down stiff with gums in various forms on the head, and from the roots behind, plaited into numerous long tails which hang over the shoulders and back. The outer margin of the ears, all round, is pierced and decorated with rows of small silver rings. Larger rings hang from the lobes of the ear. The neck and chest are tattooed, and dotted over with shapes of flowers and stars. The lids of the eyes are loaded with *soorma* (black antimony), and they use rouge. The face is often adorned with little round moles of gold and silver tinsel and vermilion fixed on with gum. The jacket and trousers are all that is worn in the house." According to rumurs, the women's willingness to risk death by consorting with the British had something to do with an Afghan predilection for homosexuality. Proverbs and songs were quoted hinting at such proclivities, for example "A beautiful boy with a bottom like a peach stands across the river, and I can't swim" and "A woman for mating, a boy for love."

Occasionally, the intentions of British officers were honorable. Captain Robert Warburton of the Bengal artillery fell in love with and married a beautiful niece of Dost Mohammed, with Burnes and Macnaghten acting as witnesses. However, most relationships were casually promiscuous. The Reverend Gleig, who found so much to commend in the interactions between the British and the Afghans, deplored the distrust and alienation resulting from British womanizing, while Sita Ram wrote that more than one officer "was stabbed or fired at" by outraged husbands. Alexander Burnes was, once again in his career, believed by contemporaries to be seducing local women, and yet again Mohan Lal defended him, asserting in his memoirs that Burnes and the several other officers living with him—his brother Lieutenant Charles Burnes, who had recently arrived in Kabul, his military secretary William Broadfoot and his political officer Lieutenant Robert Leech—had brought Kashmiri girls with them from India and therefore had no need to run after Kabul women.

Whatever Burnes's personal activities at the time, his attitude to the philanderings of his British comrades made him enemies. When angry Afghan men sought justice from him as the British resident in Kabul, he always supported his fellow countrymen and, Lal frankly acknowledged, "gave no justice" and "wounded the feelings of the chiefs." Abdullah Khan, the powerful head of the Achakzai clan, was so enraged when Burnes refused to intervene over the seduction of one of his women that he declared a blood feud against him. Such insensitive and offhand behavior toward Afghans from a man once so well attuned to understanding local attitudes seems strange. Perhaps the good judgment that had served him previously had been diminished, distorted by his feeling that he was being marginalized, his advice was being ignored and that the overall situation was deteriorating. For all this he blamed Macnaghten. He was so disenchanted that he wrote to his friend Dr. Lord, "I have begun the year with a resolution of making no more suggestions, and of only speaking when spoken to." Later he told Lord, "Be silent, pocket your pay, do nothing but what you are ordered, and you will give high satisfaction. They will sacrifice you and me, or any one, without caring a straw . . . I can go a good way, but my conscience has not so much stretch as to approve of this dynasty. But, mum—let that be between ourselves."

The arrival of the wives of British officers, perhaps surprisingly, did not ease the growing resentment at British behavior. Though their presence might have been expected to have a restraining influence on philandering, to the watching Afghans it suggested a worrying permanence about the occupation. British forces were supposed to have left after Shah Shuja's restoration. Instead a sizable number had stayed on, and now their women had come. Among the first to arrive in late 1839 was Macnaghten's wife, Fanny, by common repute as pushy and ostentatious as he was reserved and studious, who moved in with her husband in his house adjoining the perimeter of the cantonment. Early in the new year came the tall imposing figure of fifty-two-year-old India-born Florentia Sale, wife of Brigadier "Fighting Bob" Sale, now the second-in-command in Kabul.

Her experiences in Afghanistan would make her a national heroine. With her, besides a household staff of forty servants, was one of her daughters, Alexandrina, shortly to marry Lieutenant John Sturt of the Royal Engineers. Florentia had grand ambitions to plant a flower and vegetable garden in her new home, and her gardeners were soon at work.

CHAPTER EIGHT

There is nothing more to be dreaded or guarded against I think in our endeavour to re-establish the Afghan monarchy than the overweening confidence with which Europeans are too often accustomed to regard the excellence of their own institutions and the anxiety that they display to introduce them in new and untried soils.

—CLAUDE WADE, JANUARY 1839

DURING THE WINTER months of 1839, Macnaghten's focus turned increasingly on events beyond Afghanistan's borders. He was alarmed by news that the Russians, despite their promises and protestations to Palmerston, were continuing to press forward in Central Asia, mounting an expedition from their frontier base at Orenburg, in the southern Ural Mountains, against the khanate of Khiva. The Russians' declared aim was to punish its tribes for their raids into Russian territory to abduct its citizens for sale in the slave markets of Khiva, but in considerable part the expedition was sparked by the British invasion of Afghanistan and consequent Russian fears about British intentions for further expansion. On hearing of the British capture of Kandahar, Czar Nicholas I told the Austrian ambassador, "Much good may it do them; they said I wanted to occupy those countries. It's their army that is there. They always describe me with my arms stretched out wishing to seize all . . . it is they who are everywhere." Equally, the Russians had long regarded the Central Asian khanate of Khiva as pivotal to the control of trade in the region and a desirable imperial acquisition. A Russian envoy who had visited Khiva twenty years before had written that if Russia could take Khiva, "It would become the point of reunion for all the commerce of Asia, and would shake to the centre of India the enormous commercial superiority of the dominators of the sea [the British]."

Macnaghten saw no reason why, if the Russians indeed took Khiva, they would halt there. His nightmare vision was of Cossack armies advancing to the northern slopes of the Hindu Kush and pushing down into Afghanistan toward India. The way to stop them, he believed, was for Britain to mount a major preemptive military expedition through the Hindu Kush to annex the petty states lying between the mountains and the Oxus River. He said as much to Auckland in secret dispatches written with a pen dipped in rice water that could only be read by the application of a solution of iodine. Without even waiting for Auckland's sanction, he sent part of a brigade northward toward Bamiyan to watch the passes leading down from the Hindu Kush.

Auckland, who had known of the Russian plans to advance on Khiva for some time, thought Macnaghten was exaggerating the danger. Neither, as Macnaghten wanted, was Auckland tempted to deploy troops westward to annex Herat, where, despite earlier promises to the British, the vizier Yar Mohammed was again putting out feelers to the Persians. While the Army of the Indus had been on its long journey to Kabul, Charles Stoddart and Eldred Pottinger had quarreled with Yar Mohammed, jeopardizing the British position in the territory instead of safeguarding it, which had been one of the key aims of their intervention. Liberal men of conscience, the two had tried to dissuade Yar Mohammed from continuing the slave trade that was so crucial to Herat's economy. The administration in India had disowned Stoddart and Pottinger's stance, claiming that they were acting in a purely personal capacity. Auckland's private secretary, John Colvin, had written, "Why is it that Englishmen everywhere are rough, overbearing, without tact . . . and more disliked by foreigners than any other people? Pottinger endeavoured to make an Utopia of justice and forbearance among these rude . . . Afghans, fresh as they are from a prolonged and desperate contest and the result is that he with his schemes is sent out of the country and the check that he might by wiser means have maintained is totally lost."

Claude Wade thought similarly: "There is nothing more to be dreaded or guarded against I think in our endeavour to re-establish the Afghan monarchy than the overweening confidence with which Europeans are too often accustomed to regard the excellence of their own institutions and the anxiety that they display to introduce them in new and untried soils . . . The people of these countries are far from ripe for the introduction of our highly refined system of government or of society and we are liable to meet with more opposition in the attempt to disturb what we find existing than from the exercise of our physical force."

Auckland was more charitable toward Stoddart and Pottinger, acknowledging that it was "extremely difficult to fix our relations with a government so loose and suspicious as that of Herat upon a satisfactory and secure footing." Writing to Macnaghten in December 1839, Auckland set out what he believed the real priorities to be: "I only want to know of Shah Shuja that he is becoming an Afghan king and drawing his subjects about him, that his Afghan levies are making progress towards efficiency, that his contingent is in a condition to give him support." In other words, the most important thing was for Shah Shuja to gain respect by consolidating his position within Afghanistan, and there could be no question of dispatching yet more troops from India for the further aggrandizement of the erstwhile pensioner king. Apart from anything else, Auckland was already concerned at the costs thus far of Britain's Afghan adventure.

In early 1840, however, following news of the expedition against Khiva, London began to share Macnaghten's reservations about Russian intentions. Palmerston, feeling he had been deceived by Russian protestations of goodwill the previous year, thought like Sir John Hobhouse that action against them in Central Asia might be necessary and approved a letter sent by Hobhouse and the Secret Committee to Auckland in late February 1840, promising that "should you be called upon to extend your direct influence, whether to Herat or to the north of the Hindu Kush, we shall support you with an entire confidence in the judgement which has hitherto characterised all your proceedings."

Nevertheless, the optimistic Auckland still believed that in only a few more months Shah Shuja would be firmly in control of the administration of his kingdom and that he would be able to withdraw the bulk of the remaining troops from Afghanistan by October, leaving Shah Shuja as a bulwark against the Russians. In March 1840 he again came under pressure from Macnaghten when reports arrived that the Russian force advancing on Khiva was much larger than the British had anticipated, but he held firm, stating that "we must mainly look to the exertion of our power in Europe for the purpose of checking, beyond the limits of Afghanistan, the unjustifiable advances of Russian aggression." His caution was vindicated when in the late spring of 1840 news arrived that the Russians' Khivan expedition had failed, turning back starved and frozen in subzero temperatures when only halfway toward its objective. By the time the expedition returned to Orenburg it had lost a fifth of the five thousand men who had set out. Indeed, Khiva would soon cease to be an issue between Britain and Russia. That summer, the British officer Richmond Shakespear negotiated with the Khivans the release of four hundred Russian slaves and provided Russia, with whom Palmerston was now taking a hard line, with a face-saving way of abandoning its Khivan ambitions at least for the present.*

Gradually, however, Auckland's hopes of an early withdrawal from Afghanistan faltered. In May Hobhouse, after studying a report by Macnaghten on the attitudes of the Afghan chiefs, wrote from London to tell him bleakly, "If what he says is strictly true I see no chance of your being ever able to withdraw your troops from Kabul and Shah Shuja appears to entertain no such wish or expectation. Yet a permanent or even a prolonged occupation of that country is not and was not contemplated by any of us."

The truth was that Shah Shuja was already showing himself a poor ruler compared with Dost Mohammed. The latter had consciously made himself approachable to his people. After becoming emir he had "protested to his friends that he would not become a king after the manner of the Sadozais, to be secluded in his harem and to take no cognizance of public affairs . . . and that all classes of people should have access to him." Even Hindus had been unafraid to approach him in the street, and according to

*Another young British officer, Captain James Abbot, had earlier tried but failed to secure the release of the Russian slaves at Khiva. Abbot later had a successful military career in British India. Abbottabad, where Osama Bin Laden was killed, was named for him.

Mohan Lal "any man seeking for justice" could "stop him on the road by holding his hand and garment and may abuse him for not relieving his grievances" and the emir would continue to listen to him "without disturbance or anger." His reputation for fair dealing had been so widespread that a common saying had been "Is Dost Mohammed dead, that there is no justice?" Though the emir had remained almost pathologically suspicious and wary of his courtiers, he had been careful to treat them as equals and had done away with the elaborate court ceremonial of the Sadozais. To many looking back on his reign, he seemed to have established a degree of political stability so that travelers to Kabul had been able to speak of it as *"abad wa fariman"* (flourishing and plentiful).

By contrast, Shah Shuja's stiff haughty manners and cold demeanor toward his own people, noticed and criticized by British army officers during the advance of the Army of the Indus, had become yet more pronounced since his return to Kabul. One officer observed, "Our friend Shah Shuja, I am sorry to say, does not take well with his Afghan subjects . . . and he will I fear be to the Indian Government a very expensive bird to keep on his perch." Shah Shuja expected his nobles to stand for hours on end, hands folded and at a respectful distance waiting to see whether he would deign to notice them. Often they had to retire without having been allowed to address one word to him. As a result, within the first weeks he had already alienated a number of important tribal leaders who had initially been in favor of his return. In particular he had offended some of the influential Kizzilbashi community within Kabul. Many of them had initially readily agreed to serve Shah Shuja in their traditional roles as tax gatherers, clerks and suppliers of stores but were soon complaining that the new king treated them with less respect than Dost Mohammed had done.

Corruption was rife among Shah Shuja's family and followers. Several of his sons, whom he had appointed to key positions, abused them. One of these, Sufter Khan, who was made governor of the province of Kandahar, increased his salary by terror and extortion and spent the proceeds on homosexual orgies. A letter by his medical attendant published in the *Bombay Times* of 21 October 1840 alleged that he enticed British soldiers to his palace, where he drugged and sexually abused them.

As well as members of his family, Shah Shuja selected other corrupt favorites as ministers. Burnes wrote that "bad ministers are in every government solid grounds for unpopularity" and lamented, "I doubt if ever a King had a worse set than Shah Shuja." One of the most detested was the elderly Mullah Shakur, who had accompanied Shah Shuja from Ludhiana and whom he had appointed his chief minister. Mullah Shakur, whose cropped ears were a sign that in earlier years he had displeased his master, allowed his officials to exact higher taxes from Kabul's merchants than agreed by the British. Those who complained were beaten or imprisoned, while in the countryside, Mullah Shakur dispatched royal tax gatherers to live off the local people until their extortionate demands were met.

Resentful of outside interference, Mullah Shakur spread rumors that Britain would never allow Shah Shuja full power to reign and was intent on attacking Islam. By late 1840 Macnaghten would demand his replacement by a pro-British minister, but by then much damage had been done, especially by Mullah Shakur's highlighting of Shah Shuja's reliance on the British, which ran directly counter to what Auckland wanted. People joked that coins struck in Shah Shuja's name depicted him as "the apple of the eye of the British." Surgeon Atkinson understood the problem exactly, writing that "the power which raised him to the throne is the principal drawback on his popularity. It is difficult for the people rightly to comprehend the policy which influenced that measure. They can see nothing in our advance to Kabul but a scheme of conquest, and no denial can convince them that we are not now the masters and the controllers of the country." When Burnes learned that the king's name had been omitted from the Friday prayers in one of the mosques, he sent Mohan Lal to find out why. The mullah told Lal that Shah Shuja was not the true king according to Muslim law because he ruled only by the grace of foreign troops.

A further and very real source of grievance against the king and the British occupiers was that the presence of large numbers of foreign troops had immediately sent up the prices of the daily necessities of life. In particular, the purchase by the army commissariat of large amounts of grain had soon pushed the price beyond what ordinary people could afford. Mohan Lal wrote that before long, "the cry of starvation was universal, and there were very many hardly able to procure a piece of bread even by begging in the streets." People recalled how in the days of Dost Mohammed, price levels had been controlled. Nawab Jubbar Khan had ordered a butcher convicted of charging more than he should to be nailed by his ear to his butcher's block so that "he was forced to stand there for a whole day, passing a stream of blood from his ear; and the meat was next morning so cheap as to be within the reach of all classes." Shah Shuja himself took no such measures, although on one occasion Burnes on his own initiative ordered the distribution of a thousand loaves to a hungry crowd milling outside his house and pleading for help.

And all the time, there was the specter of Dost Mohammed's return. By early 1840 he was in Bokhara, having decided to throw himself on the unreliable mercy of its emir, Nasrullah Khan—the sinister young man whom eight years earlier Burnes had observed leaving the mosque in Bokhara. It was a dangerous move, and Dost Mohammed had only turned for help to wealthy Bokhara in desperation. However, he was no more deceived by Nasrullah's true character than Burnes had been. When the emir urged him to bring his entire family with him to Bokhara, Dost Mohammed thanked him gracefully. However, he wrote secretly to Jubbar Khan, in whose charge he had left them, that he would rather see his family dead than sent to Bokhara and asked him instead to give them into the keeping of the British. Nasrullah, who had hoped to seize the family's jewels, was enraged when they failed to arrive, and flung Dost Mohammed into jail. Also detained in Bokhara at that time was Colonel Charles Stoddart, sent in late 1838 by John McNeill to negotiate a treaty of friendship with Nasrullah.

As 1840 wore on, the situation in Afghanistan worsened with a rash of uprisings and attacks. Baluchi tribesmen ambushed British troops on the road from Quetta to Kandahar, killing 148 men, while the western Ghilzais, who inhabited the country between Kandahar and Ghazni and had rebelled the previous autumn, again rose up, cutting the fragile communication lines. When Nott sent a force against them from Kandahar, the Ghilzais were only beaten off with difficulty. Later, after some negotiations, Macnaghten agreed to pay the chiefs an annual stipend in return for guarantees of their future good behavior. But most alarming of all was the news in the summer of 1840 that Dost Mohammed had left Bokhara and was raising a force ready to invade Afghanistan. This was what Macnaghten had feared, noting that "the Afghans are gunpowder, and the Dost is a lighted match."

CHAPTER NINE

It requires the most cautious steering to refrain, on the one side
from alarming popular prejudices, and on the other from leaving
the Government in the same imbecile state in which we found it.
                                    —SIR WILLIAM MACNAGHTEN, 1840

ACCOUNTS OF DOST Mohammed's escape vary. Some suggest
that the emir of Bokhara, bowing to pressure from other local rulers who
believed Dost Mohammed the only leader capable of organizing resistance to the infidel British, allowed him to escape. However, Nasrullah
was not a man given to rational decisions nor to being told what to do by
other people. More likely, Dost Mohammed engineered his escape after
first negotiating the release of Akbar Khan and another of his sons who
had gone with him to Bokhara.

Whatever really happened, as Surgeon Atkinson noted, news of Dost
Mohammed's escape "produced a deep sensation throughout Afghanistan,
revived the spirit of the rebellious, and gave a new stimulus to our military
operations against the anticipated movements of the restless Emir," who
now declared "his object to be a holy war, a crusade against the infidels,"
and began recruiting troops paid for by taxes and customs dues that he
began levying on caravans heading north from Kabul. Macnaghten and
Burnes learned what had occurred on 17 July. Though most of Dost Mohammed's extensive family was by now in their custody, they never expected this to inhibit the emir since the British were known for their
scrupulous treatment of such "guests." By contrast, it was common practice

among the Afghans to punish a rebellious chief by giving any of his wives who were taken prisoner to mule drivers of the lowest and most despised tribe, the Hazaras.*

On 6 August the first reports reached Kabul of serious disturbances to the north beyond Bamiyan, and the following day came news that Baluchi tribes commanded by Nussar Khan had besieged the fortress of Khelat in the southwest recently annexed to Shah Shuja's kingdom. The young political officer William Loveday, who had donated his silk bedspread as a shroud for the dead khan, had surrendered the fort and was taken prisoner, beaten and abused as his captors paraded him near naked and in chains through the villages. Several months later British troops, pursuing Baluchi marauders, would discover his still-warm, naked and emaciated body chained to a camel pannier, "his head cut off, and his servant sitting crying at his feet." By his side were two letters: one to his sister, bidding her adieu, and the other to a friend, which his captor had not given him time to complete before decapitating him.

At around this time, intelligence arrived that to the west in Herat Yar Mohammed was planning to profit from the situation by attacking Kandahar, while to the southeast in the Sikh domains Ranjit Singh's successors were obstructing the movement of British supplies intended for Afghanistan and plotting with Ghilzai chiefs, who had taken refuge with them, and with the Sindi rulers against the British. Macnaghten complained to a colleague, "Herat on the one side and the Sikhs on the other are terrible thorns—and I do not anticipate that we shall ever have fair play from either until we find ground and opportunity for coercing them into good behaviour." Under pressure from all directions, he urged Auckland to restore Peshawar and the lands up to the Indus to Afghan rule—the very thing for which Dost Mohammed had asked and been refused on the grounds that it would alienate the now dead Ranjit Singh, and which, had it been granted, would have saved many thousands of lives.

At this critical time Macnaghten also dispatched a long note to

---

*The Hazaras, who inhabit western Afghanistan, are believed by some to be the descendants of the Mongol cavalry of Genghis Khan. As an ethnic minority and as Shia Muslims in a country where the majority follow Sunni Islam, they were traditionally servants, even slaves, and were and are still looked down on by other tribes.

Auckland's aide Henry Torrens in Calcutta, setting out the manifold problems that had confronted the British since arriving in Kabul, perhaps with the intention of fending off criticisms of his management of affairs thus far. "The Afghans are a nation of bigots," he asserted. "Besides an intolerance of our creed [religion] there is an intolerance of our customs, and it behoves us therefore to be very wary in our attempts at innovation: nor ought it ever to be forgotten that a system, though excellent in itself, may not be good as applied to this country, nor though good, may it be such as to admit the due appreciation of its advantages. It requires the most cautious steering to refrain, on the one side from alarming popular prejudices, and on the other from leaving the Government in the same imbecile state in which we found it."

Macnaghten railed that "our enemies try to impress the people with a belief that we are the rulers of the country" and suggested it was difficult for Shah Shuja—though "there is not an abler or better man than himself in all his dominions"—to live up to his subjects' expectations since, impoverished by the campaign to restore him, he lacked "the means either of rewarding his friends or conciliating his enemies." Just as Western officials would do in regard to President Hamid Karzai more than 160 years later, he urged a publicly deferential approach toward Shah Shuja so that he should not appear to be just a puppet of the British, though adding that in private "I have never ceased to urge upon his Majesty the great importance of selecting a competent minister, of reforming his army, and of reducing his expenditure within the limits of his income."

However, before Torrens had time to receive and digest Macnaghten's note, the local situation had deteriorated yet further. In early September, according to Atkinson, "information reached Kabul that the whole country between the Hindu Kush and the Oxus River had risen in favour of Dost Mohammed who, with his eldest son Akbar Khan, was advancing with a force of horsemen supplied by Uzbek tribal leaders towards Bamiyan." The emir's approach frightened a detachment of Shah Shuja's levies into falling back from their remote northern outpost to Bamiyan, whence, on 7 September, Cotton hastily dispatched reinforcements under Colonel William Dennie, who had distinguished himself at the assault on Ghazni. Five days later, a depressed and anxious Macnaghten wrote to Auckland reporting Cotton's view that unless the British army was instantly strengthened, "we cannot hold the country"—a view with which he strongly agreed. The menace of Dost Mohammed seemed only too real. Atkinson wrote that "so completely had the enemy closed up every source of intelligence and so difficult was it to collect the least exact information of his whereabouts at the time that Dost Mohammed actually slept about three miles from our camp at Bamiyan on the night of 17 September, and the first knowledge our troops had of his proximity was furnished next morning, by some hundreds of Uzbeks on the heights and others descending into the valley."

However, on 18 September, a day when Macnaghten had never felt "so much harassed in body and mind," came a turn for the better. If the British had been uncertain of Dost Mohammed's intentions, he had been similarly anxious about theirs, writing to a chief, "For God's sake, tell me the news! Will the Feringhees run or fight?" Unclear also of the exact British whereabouts, he had begun advancing toward Bamiyan. When Dennie in turn learned that some of the emir's men had been sighted, he concluded they could only be an advance party and sent troops and artillery to confront them, before following himself with further troops. After rendezvousing with his own men, together they encountered their enemy in a narrow valley. Dennie realized by their numbers that this was no advance guard but Dost Mohammed's entire force. He ordered his artillery to fire on the densely packed mass of enemy cavalry. Dost Mohammed's six thousand Uzbek horsemen fled, leaving behind tents, baggage, kettledrums, standards and his only artillery piece. He himself only escaped destruction or capture because of the speed of his horse, but many of his followers were pursued and cut down.

Macnaghten could breathe again, and when the news reached Auckland he wrote to London praising "this brilliant achievement . . . which with reference to the small number of our troops engaged . . . cannot fail to be productive of the best moral effect." In the aftermath of the emir's flight, Dr. Percival Lord persuaded the wali of Kulum, one of the most important local tribal leaders, to withdraw his support from Dost Mohammed. The emir, though, remained defiant, claiming he was as indestructible as a wooden spoon: "You may throw me hither and thither, but I shall not be hurt." He must have been heartened when an entire recently and locally recruited regiment of Shah Shuja's infantry took advantage of the disturbances to desert to him. Their defection reinforced Burnes's view that "Sheets of foolscap are written in praise of the Shah's contingent, and, as God is my judge I tremble every time I hear of its being employed . . . Shah Shuja never can be left without a British army, for his own contingent will never be fit for anything."

Meanwhile in Kabul, despite news of the rout of Dost Mohammed's men at Bamiyan, the atmosphere remained tense. Atkinson believed that had Dost Mohammed been able to get close to Kabul, "our game with our handful of troops would have been a desperate one." So many soldiers had been sent north that the city itself had been left vulnerable. "Great excitement prevailed everywhere. Our camp was about two miles from the Balla Hissar, and we had constantly an alarm that a night attack would be made upon us; picquets were strengthened and a sharp look-out was kept . . . In the Balla Hissar, artillery was placed, and the gates and magazine were doubly guarded. During the whole of September and October, the city continued in a state of extreme agitation; armed men in the streets, sharpening their swords at the cutlers' shops, looked fierce and threatening; and day after day a revolt was whispered to be at hand. Under such circumstances, no one could feel at ease. The Kizzilbashis and Afghans who had joined the Shah were in dismay, and with good reason, for should the conspiracy meet with even temporary success, their heads would soon have been severed from their bodies, or their bowels ripped up."

He described how an "active system of espionage" was set up "to discover the plans of the conspirators . . . known to be meditating mischief." Learning of a plot to seize Shah Shuja during one of the visits he was fond of making to a garden two miles from the citadel, the British discouraged him from going there, while across the city key plotters were arrested. According to Atkinson, this "had a talismanic effect . . . their followers, as is generally the case in eastern conspiracies, became at once paralyzed and powerless."

Deciding that Kohistan had to be subdued before the situation there grew any worse, in late September Macnaghten dispatched a brigade under "Fighting Bob" Sale. His mission was to discourage the chiefs from supporting Dost Mohammed as well as to punish them for having defied orders to muster levies and pay taxes by destroying the many fortresses and strongholds studding the valleys of Kohistan. This demonstration of military might was to go hand in hand with a softer, subtler approach.

Alexander Burnes and Mohan Lal, accompanying Sale, were to send agents
into the forts and villages to try to bribe Dost Mohammed's adherents to
desert his cause. However, despite their efforts and though by late October Sale had reduced several forts to rubble, the main rebel chiefs were
at large and, as Macnaghten had always feared, joined forces with Dost
Mohammed.

The situation appeared grave when, on 2 November 1840, an advance party of Sale's cavalry unexpectedly encountered Dost Mohammed
and several hundred horsemen in the valley of Purwandurrah, north of
Kabul. The emir ordered his men to attack, and in response Captain Fra-
ser, leading the British forces, commanded, "Front! Draw swords!" Yet
though the British officers charged toward the enemy, not all their troops
followed. Two squadrons of the Second Bengal Native Cavalry dawdled
behind, then, seeing their officers—including Dr. Lord, who had been accompanying the party as an observer—cut down in fierce fighting, turned
and fled. Some of Dost Mohammed's men pursued the escaping cavalry
for more than a mile, while the emir with the rest of his force almost
reached the British infantry and artillery positions. However, Dost Mohammed decided not to expose his men to the guns and, ordering a retreat, galloped away victorious, blue standard fluttering. Alexander Burnes
was so alarmed that he at once dispatched a messenger to Macnaghten
urging him to recall all troops immediately to Kabul to resist what he
predicted would be a full-scale rising in Kohistan on behalf of Dost
Mohammed.

According to Atkinson, an eyewitness, two days later Macnaghten
was taking his customary evening ride and pondering Burnes's advice. As
he was approaching the gate of his residence "a horseman, passing his
escort . . . rode suddenly up to him, and said, 'Are you the Envoy?' 'Yes, I
am the Envoy.' 'Then,' rejoined the horseman, 'here is the Emir.' 'What
Emir? Where is he?' 'Dost Mohammed Khan!' was the reply." The amazed
Macnaghten then saw "the very ex-chief himself alighting from his horse,
and claiming his protection. The whole scene was truly electrical." Macnaghten invited Dost Mohammed to accompany him into the residence.
When the envoy asked him why he had defied the will of the British government for so long, he replied that it was his fate—he could not control
destiny.

Dost Mohammed's decision to surrender himself at this critical point is puzzling. Perhaps, having won the encounter at Purwandurrah, he had decided that honor was satisfied and that there was no point continuing to resist a more powerful enemy. Perhaps he had simply grown weary or fallen into the despondency to which Josiah Harlan claimed he was prone. The Reverend Gleig concluded that Dost Mohammed "felt that for the present his game was played out." Later Afghan historians would blame him for giving up at the very moment when the British were vulnerable and he might have gone on to rally mass support against them, but he had probably not fully appreciated how exposed the British were at the end of long supply and communication lines to India.

For the moment, the emir seemed genuinely relieved to be in British custody. He offered Macnaghten his sword, commenting that he had no further use for it, but the envoy just as graciously begged him to keep it. In fact, Dost Mohammed had taken the precaution, while on his way to Kabul to surrender, of exchanging his own fine sword for the more ordinary blade of his attendant. Atkinson, observing the fallen leader closely, thought that he looked haggard and careworn. Instead of the tall, spare, handsome man he had imagined from the accounts of others, Dost Mohammed "[is] on the contrary, robust, and large-limbed; his nose is sharp and aquiline; his eye-brows are highly-arched, and his forehead falls back at a striking angle. His moustache and beard are grey. They had not been dyed, he said afterwards, from the time he quitted Kabul." However, he was clearly not without vanity, saying to Macnaghten, "They told me you were an old man; but I do not think so; how old are you?" When Macnaghten replied that he was nearly fifty, Dost Mohammed responded, "Ah! That is just my age." He was, in fact, nearer sixty. Macnaghten ordered a tent to be pitched in the gardens for Dost Mohammed, who, after eating a hearty meal after the sun had gone down since it was Ramadan, slept soundly. Macnaghten's military secretary Captain George Lawrence, who kept guard during the night, found him deep asleep every time he checked on him.

The next day, as the astonishing news spread throughout the city that Dost Mohammed was in British custody, Atkinson noticed Kabul had become suddenly tranquil, "totally free from the least trace of agitation." Dost Mohammed was not to remain there for long. On 12 November Sir Willoughby Cotton left with some of his forces for Jalalabad, where he intended to winter with Shah Shuja. With him went Dost Mohammed, beginning his journey into exile in India. Shah Shuja had refused to see the emir before his departure, which probably spared both of them some embarrassment. Shah Shuja had, of course, wanted his enemy dead. He had told Lawrence that several of his men had offered to bring in Dost Mohammed and had asked slyly, "If in apprehending the Emir, it should so happen that he should be killed, what then would be the Envoy's opinion?"

WHILE DOST MOHAMMED had still been at large, Macnaghten had declared that "no mercy should be shown to the man who is the author of all the ills that are now distracting the country" and had mentioned the possibility of his execution. However, with Dost Mohammed safely in custody, Macnaghten made clear to Shah Shuja that there was no question of executing the man whom he was treating more as a guest than a prisoner. Indeed, Macnaghten had undergone an extraordinary change of heart, praising the emir as "a wonderful fellow" and asking Auckland to treat him generously. As if his earlier disputes with Burnes over the respective merits of the two rulers had never occurred, he wrote urging that Dost Mohammed should be treated "with liberality," saying Shah Shuja "had no claim upon us. We had no hand in depriving him of his Kingdom, whereas we ejected the Dost, who never offended us, in support of our policy of which he was the victim." Burnes had an affectionate meeting with Dost Mohammed before the latter departed Kabul, and gave his old friend an Arab horse.

Meanwhile, as the emir left his erstwhile capital behind him, Atkinson noticed that he talked incessantly and seemed "exceedingly cheerful." He even asked Atkinson, a skilled artist, to draw his likeness but returned to a pet subject: "You must make my beard black. It is now much shorter than it used to be for since my troubles began, no attention has been paid to it, and it has not been dyed." Although Atkinson captured the vivid yellow of his turban, the emir complained that "his beard did not look black enough."

At Peshawar, Dost Mohammed was joined by a huge number of family members—318 according to the meticulous records of the British officer in charge of them—including nine wives, thirteen sons, seven daughters, ten grandchildren and all their attendants and slaves. From there the party continued on the journey into protective custody in India, where, the following May in Calcutta, Dost Mohammed would be one of Auckland's most honored guests at the birthday ball for Queen Victoria. However, though Dost Mohammed had formally ordered his eldest and favorite son, Akbar Khan, to surrender to the British, he had refused to obey—perhaps as his father had intended he should. He was still free somewhere beyond the Hindu Kush.

CHAPTER TEN

For God's sake clear the passes quickly, that I may get away.
—MAJOR GENERAL WILLIAM ELPHINSTONE, OCTOBER 1841

WITH AFGHANISTAN APPARENTLY quiescent following Dost Mohammed's surrender, Macnaghten planned to devote more time to improving the country's internal government, especially the raising of revenue. "We have hitherto been struggling for existence without any leisure to turn to the improvement of the administration," he wrote to the governor-general's private secretary John Colvin in November 1840.

However, his hope of leisure was illusory. In late 1840 the Douranee tribes around Kandahar rebelled. Under the Sadozais they had once enjoyed special privileges, but Dost Mohammed had squeezed them relentlessly for taxes. With the restoration of the Sadozai Shah Shuja they had expected better, and indeed he had promised it. However, despite Shah Shuja's assurances, the Douranees found themselves still oppressed by the same tax gatherers as before.

The rebellion was also a sign of a wider dissatisfaction in Afghanistan with a "double" system of government, in which an Afghan king ruled but only nominally and at the pleasure of foreign and infidel invaders who held his reins. The tribal chiefs were particularly opposed to British meddling with the feudal arrangements for levying irregular cavalry. Under Afghan tradition the ruler gave the chiefs subsidies in return for which they promised to equip and train a certain number of cavalrymen to fight on his behalf. The chiefs made a good profit from the difference between what they received and their actual additional costs. However, Macnaghten, by nature a centralizer and a bureaucrat, was interfering in these arrangements.

He had several reasons for doing so, all seemingly sensible if the effects on the chiefs were ignored. He knew that before the British could safely withdraw from Afghanistan, Shah Shuja had to be provided with troops more immediately available and more reliable and effective than the feudal cavalry. In addition, Macnaghten wanted to save Shah Shuja money; paying for cavalry levies was expensive, and Shah Shuja could not afford it. Macnaghten complained that the king's revenue was "hardly enough for the maintenance of his personal state," and yet the Indian government was "perpetually writing . . . that this charge and that charge [was] to be defrayed out of his 'Majesty's resources!' God help the poor man and his resources." Reducing the feudal levies and the creation of new cavalry corps, paid for by and dependent on the British, were means of eroding the power of the chiefs, who derived status as well as money from the number of troops they provided, and of relieving the financial pressures on the king. All this, and the perceived British aim of eventually replacing the feudal cavalry, angered the chiefs.

Macnaghten, however, failed to appreciate the depths of the chiefs' concern. When the Douranees rebelled, he dismissed them as "perfect children," just as Burnes had done, and continued that they "should be treated as such. If we put one naughty boy in the corner, the rest will be terrified. We have taken their plaything, power, out of the hands of the Douranee chiefs, and they are pouting a good deal in consequence."

General Nott, the commander in Kandahar, was given the job of disciplining the naughty children. On 3 January 1841 his men defeated fifteen hundred Douranee horsemen, who fled across the Helmand River. However, though the Douranee insurgents had been scattered, their rebellion was not over. Evidence soon emerged that their leader, Aktur Khan, was plotting with Herat's vizier, Yar Mohammed, who had, indeed, helped incite their original rebellion. At the same time, Yar Mohammed was yet again courting the Persians, even though the British were still paying him hefty sums in return both for promises that Herat would not collude with other states and in the as-yet-unfulfilled hope of their being allowed to station a British garrison in the city. When Yar Mohammed demanded still more money, making it insultingly clear he would cooperate no further until it was paid, in February 1841 Major D'Arcy Todd, the political officer who had replaced Eldred Pottinger in Herat, decided unilaterally to withdraw the British mission. Hearing the news, Macnaghten, who continued to believe the British could never be truly secure in Afghanistan until they had annexed Herat, immediately sought permission to dispatch a force there, which would also hunt down Aktur Khan and his rebels. However, the normally acquiescent Lord Auckland castigated Todd for his actions and refused to sanction any campaign against Herat, again telling Macnaghten he "must be strong in Afghanistan" before any such venture could be contemplated.

Macnaghten regretfully abandoned the campaign against Herat but still had Aktur Khan to deal with. The Douranee leader was coaxed into making terms under which he agreed to disband his followers in return for a conditional pardon and some fiscal concessions, among them an end to the detested system of billeting tax collectors on communities until they paid what the collectors demanded. He also insisted on the replacement of Shah Shuja's chief minister and tax gatherer, the corrupt, earless and avaricious Mullah Shakur, whom the British had long distrusted anyway.

The terms notwithstanding, Macnaghten's political officer at Kandahar, Major Henry Rawlinson, rightly anticipated that all that had been gained was "temporary tranquillity." Indeed, Aktur Khan was soon gathering forces for a renewed struggle. When Rawlinson warned that however many times the British beat the Douranees, doing so would only aggravate the widespread national feeling against the British, Macnaghten reproved him for his "unwarrantably gloomy view," warning against "idle statements" that might "cause much mischief" and complaining that "we have enough of difficulties and enough of croakers without adding to the number needlessly." The Douranees were mere "ragamuffins," and there was no national feeling against the occupying forces. He advised Rawlinson to view matters with a little more *couleur de rose*—one of his favorite expressions.

A rebellion by the Ghilzais of western Afghanistan in the spring and summer of 1841, provoked by the British appropriation and rebuilding of a fortress at Khelat-i-Ghilzai in their heartlands, did not alter

Macnaghten's views. Neither did a further Douranee rebellion at the end
of which Aktur Khan was again put to flight. To Macnaghten, Douranee
and Ghilzai discontent were minor flare-ups and not signs of more concerted resistance to come. On 20 August 1841, with both tribes apparently peaceable, he famously boasted in a letter to friends, "The country
is perfectly quiet from Dan to Beersheba." Elsewhere he wrote, "All
things considered, the perfect tranquillity of the country is to my mind
perfectly miraculous. Already our presence has been infinitely beneficial
in allying animosities and pointing out abuses . . . we are gradually placing matters on a firm and satisfactory basis."

Burnes, however, saw things differently. Though he maintained in
correspondence that he got on well with Macnaghten, perhaps so as not to
damage his prospects of succeeding him, he knew that the envoy continued to marginalize him. As he himself described, he was in the "most
nondescript of situations"—"a highly paid idler, having no less than 3,500
rupees a month as Resident at Kabul, and being, as the lawyers call it,
only counsel, and that, too, a dumb one—by which I mean that I give paper
opinions, but do not work them out." At least he was living well. At his
weekly dinners he could offer his guests champagne, hock, Madeira, sherry,
port, claret, sauternes, curacao and maraschino. He regularly dined on
such delicacies as "smoked fish, salmon grills, devils, and jellies" and was
putting on weight; "if rotundity and heartiness be proofs of health, I have
them," he wrote to a friend.

Burnes's unwanted leisure had given him a more detached view than
Macnaghten, and he realized that the country was not quiescent as the
envoy claimed. He also thought the British were making mistakes in the
internal running of Afghanistan, especially with regard to taxation and
the administration of justice, both fundamental to achieving stability.
Writing critically to an officer who had attacked a Ghilzai fort simply because its occupants had dared him to, he expressed his opposition to military adventurism: "I am one of those altogether opposed to any further
fighting in this country, and I consider we shall never settle Afghanistan
at the point of the bayonet." When Burnes set such opinions down frankly,
he annoyed Macnaghten, who warned Auckland that Burnes was painting
a less favorable picture of the state of things in Afghanistan for only one
reason: because "when he succeeds me his failures would thus find excuse
and his successes additional credit."

Having already read the government's published selective and expurgated versions of the documents leading to war in Afghanistan and
denounced the publication as "pure trickery," Burnes was clearly worried
that, whatever the outcome in Afghanistan and whatever his own career
prospects, his personal views on what had happened might be "massaged"
or suppressed. Indeed it had already happened. In the summer of 1841 he
contemplated writing an account of the political events that had brought
the British to Kabul. Even if he could not publish it in his lifetime, he
could leave the manuscript to his executors "and thus furnish food for reflection on the wisdom of the world when I am food for worms." Burnes
did not write his account, but helped by his younger brother Charles, he
transcribed every public document he had written about the Afghan invasion and occupation and sent the copies to his elder brother James, in
Bombay.

In the autumn of 1841 Burnes learned that Macnaghten had finally
got his reward for his endeavors in Afghanistan: the governorship of
Bombay, one of the most prestigious appointments in British India.
Other changes in the top command in Afghanistan had also been made.
With Sir Willoughby Cotton anxious to retire and pleading ill health a few
months earlier, Lord Auckland had offered the post of commander in
chief to the fifty-nine-year-old lame, gout-ridden Major General William
Elphinstone, suggesting he might find the bracing air of Kabul better for
his health than the hot plains of India. Somewhat to Auckland's surprise,
he had accepted. The new commander in chief was a Queen's officer and
first cousin of Mountstuart Elphinstone, who had journeyed to Shah
Shuja's court at Peshawar more than thirty years earlier. John Colvin,
Auckland's private secretary, wrote confidently to Macnaghten that he
was "the best general we have to send you." Others who knew him better
had a different opinion. John Luard, one of the staff officers in Calcutta
who had served under Elphinstone when he commanded the sixteenth
Lancers in the 1820s, wrote that he was then "a very gentlemanly and
agreeable person but from want of decision and never trusting in his own
opinion unfit to command even a regiment." Now he was "feeble in health
as well as in mind, wanting in resolution and confidence in himself, no
experience of warfare . . . totally unfitted to the command of the force at
Kabul."

William Nott would have been a far better choice, but, as he himself knew, he had alienated too many people. He had never bothered to conceal his contempt for Shah Shuja, whom he thought "as great a scoundrel as ever lived," while directing vitriol at Macnaghten and his "silly" political officers, who resembled "small birds [Nott had] seen frightened in a storm, ready to perch upon anything, and to fly into the arms of the first man they meet for protection . . . what will they do when *real* danger comes?" Of the envoy himself he wrote, "It would take many years to *undo* what that man, Macnaghten, has done . . . bringing into contempt everything connected with the name of Englishmen."

At the time of his appointment Elphinstone was commanding a division of the Bengal army near Delhi. He had not seen action since the Battle of Waterloo, had been in India a mere two years and spoke not a word of Hindustani. One of the reasons for selecting Elphinstone was Auckland's belief that his "remarkably mild and conciliatory manners" would help him work effectively with Macnaghten and his successors in the divided, ambiguous senior politico-military hierarchy. The very traits that made Elphinstone appear preferable to the tempersome Nott—amiability, courtliness and preference for consensus rather than confrontation— were not, of course, the qualities required in a crisis. However, a crisis was not what Auckland, lulled by Macnaghten's *couleur de rose* assurances, anticipated. He wrote to Elphinstone, "The part which we shall have to play will I trust be rather that of influence than of war . . . the duty of the officer in command in Afghanistan will be rather that of maintaining a strong attitude, and of directing the distribution of the troops and the measures necessary for their health and comfort, than of conducting active operations." He went on that Elphinstone should be cautious in deploying British troops and focus on building up Afghanistan's own army so that the British army was not regarded "as its sole support and dependence." It all must have seemed so much easier in Calcutta than Kabul.

Elphinstone had arrived in Kabul to assume command in late April 1841, to be assured by the eager-to-depart Cotton, "You will have nothing to do here. All is peace"—a view not shared by Cotton's Persian interpreter, Captain Henry Palmer, who, when offered the chance to transfer to Elphinstone's staff and remain in Kabul, refused on the grounds that it would not be "more than a few months before every European soldier is murdered." He was not the only one to have a sense of impending catastrophe. Not long after, Major Hamlet Wade had recorded in his diary the disturbing image that had filled his mind while watching Sale review his regiment: "The colours of the regiment are very ragged, and when they passed in review I was suddenly startled by what I took to be a large funeral procession. What put such a thing into my head I know not, as I was thinking of very different subjects. I cannot help recording this, it has made such an impression."

Almost as soon as he arrived, Elphinstone was struck down by fever and chronic rheumatic gout and regretted ever coming to Kabul. The arrival in July of his second-in-command, Brigadier John Shelton, did nothing to cheer him. Like Cotton, Shelton was a veteran of Wellington's Peninsular Wars, where he had lost his right arm at the Battle of San Sebastian, apparently standing unflinching outside his tent while surgeons cut it from its shoulder socket. Shelton was also a bad-tempered martinet with contempt for almost everyone else's views except his own. He had reached Kabul after marching a relief brigade, including a Queen's regiment, the Forty-fourth Foot of which he was colonel, up through the Khyber Pass with such severity that his bullying had sparked a brief mutiny. However, he had succeeded along the way in destroying more than a hundred forts used by rebel tribesmen.

Another to depart was Brigadier Abraham Roberts, the commander of the shah's contingent who had disagreed with Macnaghten about how best to train and recruit an Afghan national army and been treated with scant respect by Macnaghten, who had considered the expression of his views little short of mutiny. As a consequence Roberts had resigned, to be replaced by the sixty-year-old Brigadier Thomas Antequil. Auckland, knowing that there had been, to say the least, faults on both sides, urged Macnaghten to treat the new appointee with more consideration.

It was soon obvious to all that Elphinstone and Shelton, who was to command the Kabul garrison, were grossly mismatched. Shelton was openly rude to the mild and courtly major general, whose response was to have as little to do with his second-in-command as possible. However, one matter on which both Elphinstone and Shelton could agree was the poor siting of the cantonments, where the main body of British troops was billeted. Elphinstone was so worried by their exposed position that he offered to purchase several surrounding orchards and gardens at his own expense so that they could be razed to deny potential enemies cover. When his offer was turned down—none of the extant records or memoirs explain why—he suggested purchasing the land to the south of the cantonments so that a fortress could be built there to hold weapons and stores. Macnaghten, himself a little anxious about the vulnerability of the cantonments, supported Elphinstone's plan, and work began. However, when Lord Auckland learned it would cost £2,400, he at once ordered the project to be abandoned.

The growing desire for economies would be a crucial factor in the disaster about to unfold. The cost of the Afghan occupation was approaching £1.25 million per annum.* In London the company's Court of Directors and the Board of Control had early begun to doubt whether keeping an unpopular king on his throne was worth the cost. In December 1840 they had recorded their view that the restored monarchy would for years to come need British forces "to maintain peace in its own territory, and prevent aggression from without" and that "to attempt to accomplish this by a small force, or by the mere influence of British Residents, will, in our opinion, be most unwise and frivolous and . . . we should prefer the entire abandonment of the country, and a frank confession of complete failure, to any such policy." To them, the only options were a speedy retreat or a considerable increase in military forces. Even after learning of Dost Mohammed's surrender—news of which had reached London on 6 January, hastened on the last stage of its journey by the newly introduced French telegraph from Marseilles—they wrote again to Auckland stating that they had not changed their views.

When these letters reached Calcutta in March 1841, Auckland had convened his Supreme Council to debate whether the British should remain in Afghanistan. Auckland had neither the kind of strength of character nor the depth of experience to go against the advice of those on the ground in Kabul and to authorize a withdrawal. Therefore, bolstered by his council's conclusion, albeit one reached with no great enthusiasm, that the British should remain, Auckland assured the Court of Directors and

---

*Updating monetary values is notoriously difficult, but if one uses the Bank of England calculator, £1.25 million equates to £108 million in today's values, or $178 million if converted at current exchange rates.

Board of Control that he would keep a strong force in Afghanistan while fostering the development of an effective Afghan army and discouraging any attempt by Shah Shuja to expand his territories. However, Auckland had not consulted Sir Jasper Nicolls, the military commander in chief in India, who was not in entire agreement. In his private journal Nicolls wrote that the Afghan occupation was untenable in the long term: "We cannot afford the heavy, yet increasing drain upon us. Nine thousand troops between Quetta and Karachi; at least 16,000 of our army and the Shah's to the north of Quetta. The king's expenses to bear in part—twenty-eight political officers to pay, besides Macnaghten . . . To me it is alarming."

Macnaghten, though, was relieved; withdrawal from Afghanistan would have associated him forever with failure rather than success. Others too had their own interests to consider. Speaking in the west country of England in June 1841, Foreign Secretary Lord Palmerston boasted that "a distinguished military officer" recently returned from Afghanistan had assured him that "accompanied by half a dozen attendants, but without any military escort, [he] had ridden on horseback many hundreds of miles through a country inhabited by wild and semi-barbarous tribes who but two years ago were arrayed in fierce hostility against the approach of the British arms . . . with as much safety as he could have ridden from Tiverton to John O'Groats."

Meanwhile, Auckland had floated a bond in Calcutta to raise funds to pay for the costs of the occupation. Despite a favorable rate of interest, take-up was slow but eventually reached more than £2 million. Macnaghten was so divorced from financial realities that when he learned of the bond he assumed it was intended to raise funds for the British expeditionary force currently off the coast of China intent on forcing the Chinese to open their ports to Indian opium. However, Auckland left the envoy in no doubt that he too had to make economies. Lady Sale wrote in her journal of letters arriving from Calcutta by every post urging retrenchment. Macnaghten accepted that the cost of the occupation was "an awful outlay." Perhaps that was why in August 1841, believing the tribes had by then been brought to heel, he canceled his earlier request to Auckland to send five extra regiments to Afghanistan and even suggested that "part of those now in the country might be withdrawn." As a result, Brigadier Sale was ordered to take his brigade back to India, effectively cutting the Army of the Indus stationed around Kabul by almost a half. However, Macnaghten's change of heart was very much against the views of Nott, watching events from Kandahar, who believed that "unless several regiments be quickly sent, not a man will be left to note the fall of his comrades."

In Britain a series of poor harvests and a downturn in home demand for manufactures, together with rising government costs including those of the military, had led to an economic crisis. Sir Robert Peel, leader of the opposition in Parliament, derided the chancellor of the exchequer's (treasury secretary's) position: "Can there be a more lamentable picture than that of a Chancellor of the Exchequer seated on an empty chest—by the pool of a bottomless deficiency—fishing for a Budget?" In the early summer of 1841 Lord Melbourne, the Whig prime minister, called a general election, which Peel and the Tories (Conservatives) won. Peel succeeded Melbourne as prime minister.

Also at around the time of the election, Britain agreed to a treaty, whose other signatories included the Ottoman Turkish Empire and Russia, which stipulated that no naval vessels other than Turkish ones could transit the Bosphorus and Dardanelles, thus ending British concern that the Russian navy had free passage from the Black Sea to the Mediterranean. This treaty, together with a further one signed earlier in 1841 guaranteeing Ottoman Turkey's sovereignty, marked a further relaxation of tensions between Britain and Russia over the "Eastern question," making the possibility of any Russian move toward India remote for the present.

However, many on both sides saw the détente between Britain and Russia as a pause, not a cessation, in their confrontation. The wife of the Russian foreign minister wrote to her husband, "We coax the English too much, they are always false brothers and desert you as soon as it is not in their interest to be with you." The *London Morning Herald* declared of Russia, "A power driven by the spirit of insatiable conquest and whose dominance is based on darkness and error, does not seem to us to be the right ally for England in the settling of the affairs of other nations." The *Times* thundered, "There is poison in the hilts of [Russian] swords and the blades are stained with the blood of the Poles."

The news of the election's outcome reached Lord Auckland, a Melbourne appointee, in India on 16 August. Four days later he dispatched a letter of resignation to Hobhouse in London, expressing his hope that

he could sail home the following March. In this letter he noted that matters remained to be settled in India, and in regard to Afghanistan warned
Hobhouse that Elphinstone's health was failing and that Macnaghten, who
claimed his health was also poor, should not remain much longer in Kabul.
The following day, probably as a consequence of the change of government, he wrote to Macnaghten emphasizing that the situation of the British in Afghanistan was now much more at risk "from financial than from
military difficulties."

Macnaghten took the point and a little later made the fateful decision to cut the subsidies the British had earlier agreed to pay to the tribes
controlling the passes leading in and out of Afghanistan. As Henry Havelock wrote, the payment of these subsidies—the equivalent of "protection
money"—was integral to Afghan life. The tribes "cared not which of their
rulers, whether Barakzai or Sadozai, lorded it in the Balla Hissar, provided they were left in their undisturbed enjoyment of their ancient
privileges of levying tribute from caravans, or of mercilessly plundering
all who resisted . . . or received from the existing Government a handsome
annual stipend." Macnaghten knew eliminating the subsidies might back-
fire, but decided that "the necessities of his Majesty, and the frequent
prohibitions I have received against further reliance on the resources of
the British government, appeared to admit of no alternative."*

The most ill-judged economy of all was to dock the payments to the
Ghilzais who controlled the shortest route to India through the eastward
passes, including the Khyber, even though, as Macnaghten admitted, they
had been scrupulous in keeping their side of the bargain. For months,
convoys and caravans "of all descriptions had passed through these ter-
rific defiles, the strongest barriers of mountains in the world," in safety, as
Havelock wrote. In early October 1841 Macnaghten summoned the Ghilzai chiefs to Kabul. They received with apparent indifference the news
that henceforth they would receive only half the annual agreed subsidy of
eighty thousand rupees (eight thousand pounds) and left Kabul quietly.
However, they at once occupied the eastern passes, declared jihad (holy
war) and plundered the next caravan to attempt to reach Kabul.

---

*Auckland is often blamed for specifically instructing Macnaghten to take this step but in
fact only argued for economy, learning of the particular measure after the event.

The Ghilzai rising delayed the planned departure from Kabul of Sale's brigade, together with a number of sick and wounded, back to India. The Macnaghtens were also intending to accompany it on their way to their new life in Bombay, as were Lady Sale and Elphinstone. The elderly major general was so crippled by rheumatism and gout that he could no longer mount his horse unaided, and openly admitted to his officers that he was no longer fit to command. He had been pressing Auckland to relieve him on the grounds that, as he had written to his cousin Mountstuart, his presence in Kabul was "useless to the public service and distressing" to himself. His replacement, at least temporarily, was—to Brigadier Shelton's chagrin—to be Major General Nott, who was ordered up to Kabul from Kandahar.

Macnaghten stubbornly dismissed repeated warnings from Mohan Lal and his network of spies that the Ghilzai rising was not an isolated event but the forerunner of a more widespread and concerted insurrection. Increasingly, Shah Shuja's writ scarcely extended beyond Kabul and its immediate hinterland.* He also ignored the advice of Eldred Pottinger, the new political officer in Kohistan, who was convinced that the Douranee, Ghilzai and Kohistani chiefs had formed an alliance, and predicted a "coming tempest." Just as he had dismissed the Douranees as "children," Macnaghten assured Auckland that the eastern Ghilzais were rascals who would be easily trounced. Brigadier Sale was the man ordered to do the trouncing and to secure the vital route through the Khyber Pass before escorting his charges safely to Peshawar as previously planned.

On 9 October a vanguard of eight hundred men under Colonel Thomas Monteith set out from Kabul to secure the Khoord Kabul Pass, a narrow defile hemmed in by high rock walls some ten miles east of the city. Among this advance guard was Captain George Broadfoot, who commanded a regiment of Indian, Gurkha and Afghan sappers among Shah Shuja's levies. His orders were to accompany Monteith with a hundred of his men, but worried by the vagueness of his instructions, he wanted to know whether the column was likely to be opposed and whether there would be forts to be assaulted so he could decide what equipment his sappers should bring.

---

*In early 2009, U.S. vice president Joseph Biden is said to have suggested to President Karzai in a similar vein that he was little more than "mayor of Kabul."

Broadfoot went first to Monteith, who told him that he had received no specific orders himself and was in no position to give advice. Broadfoot then went back and forth between Macnaghten and Elphinstone, discovering nothing except that he would get no help from either. The envoy and the major general each referred him repeatedly back to the other and declined to take any responsibility. Their attitudes betrayed their mutual lack of trust and understanding. A peevish Macnaghten complained that Elphinstone seemed to expect him "to turn prophet"—it was impossible for him to predict whether there would be any hostilities or not—while the increasingly agitated major general appeared exhausted and unable to concentrate, claiming he was being "reduced to a mere cipher" and that Macnaghten had tormented him from the very start. At their fifth and final meeting Elphinstone, who by then had taken to his bed, abrogated his responsibilities entirely and told Broadfoot to use his own judgment while imploring him, "For God's sake clear the passes quickly, that I may get away. For, if anything were to turn up . . . I am unfit for it, done up body and mind, and I have told Lord Auckland so."

According to Reverend Gleig, Sale was also worried about his men's equipment and asked Elphinstone for new muskets since their "old flint and steel muskets had become, through much use, so imperfect in their hands, that numbers were in the habit of missing fire continually, and the best and most serviceable in the whole brigade was just as likely to carry its ball wide of the mark as in a straight line towards it." Although four thousand new muskets were in storage in Kabul, Elphinstone turned Sale down.

In fact, Ghilzais attacked Monteith and the advance guard in their camp at Boothak near the entrance to the Khoord Kabul Pass on the very first night of their march. The sounds of gunfire were heard in the city, and the following day Sale marched to their relief. He then advanced into the five-mile-long pass under constant fire from Ghilzai tribesmen, concealed behind rocks high above, who, out of range of the obsolete British muskets, astutely appeared to be picking off the officers. Reverend Gleig described their skill at squatting behind rocks, "showing nothing above the crag except the long barrels of their fusils and the tops of their turbans." Sometimes they were so well concealed that "except by the flashes which their matchlocks emitted, it was impossible to tell where the marksmen lay." Though their "every step was disputed," Sale doggedly pushed on, clearing the Ghilzais from the heights and reaching the end of the pass after five hours' fighting, with nearly seventy wounded or killed. Broadfoot thought the fighting had been far more serious than anyone anticipated. Sale himself was among the first to be wounded, shot in the left ankle as he rode through the pass. Hamlet Wade, who was beside him, recalled how Sale turned to him and said coolly, "Wade, I have got it." Luckily the wound, though painful, was not serious.

After sending his sick and wounded back to Kabul, Sale—traveling in a litter because of his ankle—pursued the Ghilzais through bleak, barren terrain overhung by soaring rocks to a fort at Tezeen, east of the town of Khoord Kabul, where they had taken refuge. He was about to give the order to attack when the Ghilzais' leader, Khoda Bakhsh, offered to parley. On the advice of his political officer George Macgregor, Sale called off the assault. Macgregor then negotiated a peace under which Khoda Bakhsh was not only allowed to retain his fort but promised payment of the full subsidy once more if the Ghilzais would guarantee free passage through the passes. However, Khoda Bakhsh's offer of peace had only been intended to prevent the imminent destruction of his fort by a vastly superior force, and he had no intention of giving up the fight and observing their agreement. To him and the other watching tribal chiefs, the generous terms offered by Macgregor on his own initiative and without reference to Kabul were a sign not of British moderation but of weakness. Thus, as Sale resumed his march eastward toward Gandamack in late October, the Ghilzais repeatedly attacked his force. Only his decision to avoid the narrow, dangerously tortuous Pass of the Fairy, where, as he suspected, the Ghilzais had planned to launch a mass attack, saved him and his men from annihilation.

Sale pressed on while ordering the Thirty-seventh Infantry, a Queen's regiment, back to Kabul to fetch Elphinstone, the Macnaghtens, Lady Sale, the sick and wounded and bring them to his column so that he could escort them, as originally planned, through the Khyber Pass to Peshawar. Once again, though, the futility of the treaty with Khoda Bakhsh was proved when Ghilzais ambushed the troops in the Khoord Kabul Pass. Only with great difficulty did they manage to reach Boothak at the mouth of the pass before continuing back to Kabul.

In the Kabul cantonments those who mistakenly thought they were about to depart had been making their final preparations despite evidence of unusual activity in and around the city. One officer told Macnaghten that "a number of Ghilzai chiefs had left Kabul for hostile purposes." A constant stream of horsemen was seen riding off in the direction of the Khoord Kabul Pass, while others were observed moving about in the Bemaru Hills overlooking Kabul. In the city itself British officers were being insulted on the streets, and some narrowly escaped attempts to assassinate them—one officer evaded death only because of the speed of his horse. A sentry on guard duty was killed. When his belt and other belongings were discovered in the possession of three Afghans and Elphinstone demanded the culprits' execution, Macnaghten argued that this would only incite trouble and they were released.*

Macnaghten himself was warned not to ride for leisure "so early in the morning or so late in the evening as was his wont" and that three men had sworn on the Koran to take his life. Shopkeepers were refusing to sell their goods to the foreigners, claiming that if they did so they would be murdered by the rebels as collaborators. However, a sign of the general confidence still felt in the cantonments was that auctions of the personal possessions that Elphinstone and Macnaghten intended leaving behind fetched high prices.

Anticipating being able to leave Kabul in early November, Macnaghten predicted on 21 October, "The storm will speedily subside," although "there will be a heaving of the billows for some time, and I should like to see everything right and tight before I quit the helm." Lady Sale thought he was out of his depth in the face of what she perceived as a growing and very real crisis. On 26 October she wrote in her journal that "the general impression is that the Envoy is trying to deceive himself into an assurance that the country is in a quiescent state. He has a difficult part to play, without sufficient moral courage to stem the current singly." He was refusing to believe reports from one of his political officers that Dost Mohammed's son Akbar Khan had been sighted near Bamiyan, where he had joined forces with the Douranee rebel chief, Aktur Khan, and apparently

---

*An Irish private would later claim to have spotted one of the men in Jalalabad. Perhaps more confident in his powers of identification than he should have been, he would administer his own justice by holding him facedown in a deep pool until he drowned.

saw no significance in the fact that Akbar Khan's father-in-law was among
the foremost leaders of the eastern Ghilzai rebels.

A few days later, on 1 November, Burnes called on Macnaghten and,
according to Lady Sale, congratulated him "on leaving Kabul in a perfect
state of tranquillity" and wished him Godspeed back to India. Soon after
Burnes returned to his own house in the Kizzilbashi area of the city, an
agitated Mohan Lal arrived to warn him that a group of influential chiefs
led by Abdullah Khan, leader of the Achakzais, was plotting to kill him.
Abdullah Khan was the chief whom Burnes had offended by refusing to
intervene over the seduction of his favorite concubine by a British officer.
More recently, learning that Abdullah Khan had encouraged the rebellion of the eastern Ghilzais, Burnes had called him to his face a traitorous
dog and threatened to ask Shah Shuja to slice off his ears.

Burnes shrugged the warning off. Perhaps he was distracted by his
hopes of succeeding Macnaghten—hopes that in recent weeks had muted
his criticisms of the envoy's rose-tinted depiction of a tranquil Afghanistan.
A week earlier Lawrence had found Burnes "in high spirits at the prospect
of . . . exercising at last the supreme authority in Afghanistan." An entry in
Burnes's diary on 31 October reads: "Ay! What will this day bring forth . . .
It will make or mar me, I suppose. Before the sun sets I shall know whether
I . . . succeed Macnaghten." In fact, the sun had set that night, and he still
had not heard. Lady Sale later wrote that the hopes of the man who had
once insisted *"aut Caesar aut nullus"* were futile since another man was
said to have been nominated for the post.

Like Caesar before the Ides of March, Burnes continued to ignore
repeated warnings. His servants told him "there was a stir in the city and
that if he remained in it, his life would be in danger; they told him he had
better go to the cantonments; this he declined doing, giving as his reason,
that the Afghans never received any injury from him, but on the contrary,
he had done much for them, and that he was quite sure they would never
injure him." An Afghan friend called to tell him that if he did not take
shelter in the cantonments he would not live to see the sun rise, while
another friend, Nawab Mohammed Sharif, sent word that Burnes's house
was about to be attacked and offered the services of his son and a hundred of his retainers to defend it. Shortly before dawn, and with crowds of
people already milling in the streets outside, Shah Shuja's chief minister,

who had replaced the corrupt Mullah Shakur, arrived to beseech Burnes, his brother Charles and his secretary William Broadfoot, George Broadfoot's brother, who were also in the house, to seek safety in the Balla Hissar.

Burnes still refused to leave, though he wrote belatedly to Macnaghten requesting troops. He also sent a messenger to Abdullah Khan offering to reconsider his complaints. Unknown to Burnes, the Achakzai chief had the messenger killed instantly. During his first visit to Kabul as a younger man Burnes had called the Afghans children, asserting that they were incapable of concealing their feelings or managing an intrigue. But during those final hours he at last seems to have realized his error, and his confidence wavered. Mohan Lal was again trying to convince him an attack was imminent, describing how one of the conspirators had predicted Burnes's house would soon go up in flames, when yet another warning letter, this time anonymous and written in Persian, arrived. According to Lal, Burnes rose from his chair, sighed and said that "the time is not far when we must leave this country."

CHAPTER ELEVEN

We must see what the morning brings, and then think what can be
done.

—MAJOR GENERAL WILLIAM ELPHINSTONE,

2 NOVEMBER 1841

ON THE NIGHT of 1 November 1841, just as Mohan Lal had warned
Burnes, a small group of rebel chiefs met secretly in Kabul. The ringleaders included Abdullah Khan, leader of the Achakzais, and Amenoolah
Khan, the son of a camel driver who had become one of the country's
leading landowners, with ten thousand fighters loyal to him. He was sufficiently ruthless to have, as a younger man, rid himself of a brother he
feared as a rival by having him buried up to his chin in sand, one end of a
rope tied around his neck and the other to a wild horse, which he had then
ordered to be driven round and round until his brother's head had been
twisted off. Following the reinstatement of Shah Shuja, Amenoolah had
maintained the pretense of supporting him, but privately he despised the
king he saw as a puppet and hated the foreigners who tweaked his strings.
To encourage others to join the conspiracy, Abdullah Khan had written to
warn them that the British were about to seize them and send them as
prisoners to London. To add to the confusion, the rebel leaders circulated
a letter they had forged bearing Shah Shuja's seal, from which it appeared
that the king was calling on his people to rise up and destroy the infidels.

The rebels sensed Kabul was ripe for insurrection. They knew that
for the present they lacked the strength to attack the British in their can-

tonments, but other more vulnerable targets were nearer at hand. Abdullah Khan, smarting from Burnes's insults, suggested that their first move should be to attack his residence in the city. Such an attack would have the added benefit that in the same street was the equally lightly guarded house of Captain Johnson, paymaster of Shah Shuja's troops, where there would be much coin to loot.

Thus, as the pale light of a chilly dawn rose on 2 November—the third Tuesday of the Muslim holy fasting month of Ramadan—crowds began to gather around Burnes's house. Mohan Lal, whose own dwelling was also close by and who was woken early by his servant shouting, "You are asleep and the city is upset," at first counted no more than about thirty men milling about. However, as rumors of plunder spread throughout the city, the numbers grew. Captain Johnson, who had wisely spent the night in the cantonments, believed, "The plunder of my treasury, my private property and that of Sir Alexander . . . was too great a temptation to the inhabitants of Kabul."

Before long, peering from an upstairs window of his mansion, Burnes saw nearly three hundred men. They were growing louder, angrier and more excited by the moment while he had only twenty-nine guards to defend him. Trusting in his ability to calm the crowds, he ordered his men not to fire and went out on a balcony overlooking the street to address the mob with his brother Charles and friend William Broadfoot beside him. However, the rioters would not listen, and the first shots rang out from within the crowd. Burnes's guards returned fire, as did Broadfoot, who killed six Afghans before falling back, shot through the heart. By then the mob had set fire to the stables and servants' quarters, and smoke was billowing from them. Rioters were surging over walls and fences into the gardens below, screaming at the foreigners to come down. A desperate Burnes shouted offers of money if they would spare the lives of himself and his brother, but the only and repeated response was that he should come outside.

According to an Indian servant who later escaped, someone told Burnes that soldiers were on their way to help him. Hurrying up the stairs to the flat roof to see for himself, Burnes met a man descending who assured him "that there was not the least sign of a regiment." Disappointed, he turned back. At this point, a Kashmiri man who had somehow managed to get into the house stepped forward to proffer his help. He swore on the Koran that if Burnes and his brother would disguise themselves, he would smuggle them outside and through the garden to safety. Hastily, Burnes and his brother donned native dress and during a lull in the firing followed their protector out of the house. They had taken only a few steps when the man suddenly called out, "This is Sikunder Burnes," and the mob fell on them. According to one eyewitness, a mullah lunged at Alexander Burnes before killing his brother Charles. The mob then turned on Alexander again to finish him off. Mohan Lal, watching in horror from the roof of his house, gave a more colorful account of Burnes's last moments, claiming that "he opened up his black neckcloth and tied it on his eyes, that he should not see from whom the death blows struck him." What is certain is that within barely a minute the mob had hacked both brothers to pieces with their knives. An old Kizzilbashi friend of Burnes later retrieved the bloody remnants of their bodies at some personal risk and buried them.

The mob thoroughly looted Burnes's mansion before turning its attention to Paymaster Johnson's residence, carrying off seventeen thousand pounds in coin intended for Shah Shuja's troops and burning Johnson's meticulous accounts for the previous three years. The mob also attacked Mohan Lal's house. He escaped only by hacking a hole through an interior wall and scrambling into the adjoining house. He ran from there out into the street full of rioters. Several of them grabbed him and were about to kill him when one of his friends, Nawab Zaman Khan, recognized him and came to his aid. Pulling him beneath his voluminous garments, he somehow smuggled Mohan Lal into his own house. Here the women of his harem served their traumatized guest a sumptuous *pulao* which, having just witnessed the hacking to death of his old friend Burnes, he found impossible to eat.

The first reports of disturbances in the city reached the cantonments shortly after seven A.M. Macnaghten's political assistant, Lieutenant John Conolly, was with the envoy helping him prepare for what he still hoped would be his imminent departure to Bombay when an Afghan brought news that rioting had broken out. Dashing outside, Conolly heard the sound of firing from the direction of the city, and a few minutes later Burnes's note requesting military assistance arrived. He had written that there was uproar in the city, particularly in the vicinity of his residence, but had added that it would be easily quelled.

Although the sanguine tone of Burnes's note convinced Macnaghten that nothing serious was amiss, he nevertheless went to consult Elphinstone. Macnaghten's military secretary, Captain George Lawrence, soon joined them to report that his servant had just returned from the city breathless "and in the greatest excitement" with news that the shops were all closed and that crowds of armed men were filling the streets and surrounding Burnes's and Johnson's houses. Lawrence urged the envoy to send troops to Burnes's aid at once and also to arrest Abdullah Khan and Amenoolah Khan—a suggestion that Macnaghten immediately denounced as "pure insanity and under the circumstances utterly unfeasible." However, Macnaghten and Elphinstone did agree to order Brigadier Shelton, who was camped in the nearby Siah Sung Hills, to lead a force at once to the Balla Hissar to act "as circumstances required" and to send the rest of his troops back to the cantonments. Lady Sale's son-in-law, Lieutenant John Sturt, set out with the orders for Shelton, while Lawrence was told to ride at once to Shah Shuja to inform him what had been agreed. As Lawrence spurred his horse toward the city an Afghan brandishing a huge *tulwar* leaped at him out of a ditch, but he rode him down and galloped on toward the Balla Hissar on its high promontory with musket balls hissing past his head fired by other insurgents who had run from the city's Lahore Gate to try and head him off.

With the commotion within the city growing ever louder and smoke from burning shops and houses billowing into the sky, Shah Shuja tried to make out from his vantage point in the Balla Hissar what was happening in the narrow winding streets below. What he saw so alarmed him that he ordered one of his sons to take a regiment and some artillery into the city—the only prompt and timely military action taken that day to suppress the rising. When a breathless Lawrence reached the Balla Hissar, he found the king angrily pacing about and exclaiming, "Is it not just what I always told the Envoy would happen if he would not follow my advice?" by which he meant his frequent urgings to lock up or preferably execute the chiefs suspected of disloyalty. When Lawrence told him the action the British proposed to take, Shah Shuja replied that he had already sent troops led by his son into the city and had no doubt they would suppress

the revolt. He also told Lawrence that he had been informed that Burnes
had escaped.

Reassured, Lawrence sent a message to Shelton telling him to delay
his march to the Balla Hissar. Annoyed by the confusing and contradictory orders reaching him, Shelton dispatched Lieutenant Sturt to the
Balla Hissar to find out exactly what was going on. Just as Sturt was dismounting in the fortress within Shah Shuja's palace's precincts, a well-
dressed young Afghan leaped at him, stabbing him several times in the
shoulder, side and face before escaping with the aid of some confeder-
ates among the palace staff. Pouring blood and "crying out that he was
being murdered," the lieutenant stumbled into the palace, where Lawrence set to work staunching his wounds and then arranged for him to
be returned to the cantonments with a strong escort in one of the king's
palanquins. Those in the Balla Hissar learned that, despite earlier optimistic reports, the king's troops were faltering in their advance into the
city. They had found it almost impossible to drag their guns through the
crooked, winding streets and were pinned down under heavy fire. Shah
Shuja's advisers pleaded with him not to risk further the life of his son and
his soldiers and to recall them. Despite Lawrence's arguments to the contrary, he did so. However, Shah Shuja at last agreed to allow Lawrence to
ride personally to Shelton's camp with orders for him to march at once to
the Balla Hissar.

At Lawrence's urging, Shelton set off, but his mood was not improved when he reached the Balla Hissar, where to his surprise Shah
Shuja demanded to know "who sent me, and what I came there for" but
did ask him to cover the retreat of his own troops from the city. Shelton
did so, preventing further casualties and saving their guns. He then set up
two cannon on the walls of the Balla Hissar and began firing somewhat
indiscriminately down on the city. When Lawrence, who had been back to
the cantonments to report on events, arrived, the two men had a furious
argument. Lawrence later wrote of a nonplussed Shelton who "seemed almost beside himself, not knowing how to act and with incapacity stamped
on every feature of his face." He asked Lawrence what he should do, but
when the latter replied, "Enter the city at once," snapped back with "my
force is inadequate, and you don't appear to know what street fighting
is." Shelton refused to take any further action to quell the disturbances

beyond repositioning his guns to fire more accurately at the area where the disturbances had broken out and seemed "in fact quite paralysed." In disgust, Lawrence returned to the cantonments once more, skirting the city, which was now fully in the hands of the rebels.

By this time Shah Shuja was repeatedly demanding why the British were not taking action and shouting that if they did not crush the insurrection, he would burn the city down. Yet angry though he was, Shah Shuja knew his best hopes of survival still rested with the British, especially as some of his own guards had taken advantage of the commotion to desert him.

As darkness fell on the cantonments Elphinstone and Macnaghten had accepted that the fate of Burnes, his brother and his friend was beyond doubt, but had still done nothing. Lady Sale and her daughter were busy nursing Sturt, taking turns to wipe away the congealing blood from his wounds. He could not open his mouth because of damage to the nerves in his face. His tongue was so swollen he could not swallow, and if he tried to lie flat, blood threatened to choke him. Writing that day, Lady Sale thought it "a very strange circumstance that troops were not immediately sent into the city to quell the affair in the commencement; but we seem to sit quietly with our hands folded and look on . . . The state of supineness and fancied security of those in power in cantonments is the result of deference to the opinions of Lord Auckland whose sovereign will and pleasure it is that tranquillity do reign in Afghanistan . . . Most dutifully do we appear to shut our eyes on our probable fate."

However, if Lady Sale and others in the cantonments were surprised by British inertia, the leaders of the insurrection were amazed. One of the chiefs present at the meeting of 1 November later told a British officer that they had been so fearful of the revenge the British would exact that they had taken no personal part in the murdering and pillaging but throughout 2 November had remained quietly in their houses, horses saddled and waiting should they need to flee.

From his hiding place in the town that day, Mohan Lal sensed people's fear and apprehension as every minute they waited for British troops to arrive and "blow up the town to revenge the murder of Sir Alexander Burnes." Captain Johnson later wrote in his journal that though he had spoken to many Afghans, their unanimous view was that "the slightest exhibition of energy on our part" during the revolt's early stages would have snuffed it out. However, as a result of the paralysis that seized the British, though "300 men would have been sufficient in the morning to have quelled the disturbance, 3,000 would not have been adequate in the afternoon." Lady Sale blamed the influence of some of Macnaghten's Afghan informants, who, as she complained in her journal "flatter him into the belief that the tumult is *bash* (nothing) and will shortly subside."

The conspirators' confidence grew as that of the British diminished, and they lost little time spreading the news of their success. Their letter to the tribes of the Khyber Pass boasted that "stirring like lions, we carried by storm the house of Sekundur Burnes. By the grace of the most holy and omnipotent God the brave warriors, having rushed right and left from their ambush, slew Sekundur Burnes with various other Feringees of consideration . . . putting them utterly to the sword, and consigning them to perdition." The British were permitting what had started as perhaps little more than a violent demonstration to turn into something far more serious. Remarkably in this time of crisis and although the Macnaghtens had moved from their vulnerable residence into the cantonments, General Elphinstone and Macnaghten were still communicating principally by means of notes. "Since you left I have been considering what can be done tomorrow," Elphinstone wrote to the envoy that first night of the rising. "Our dilemma is a difficult one. Shelton, if reinforced tomorrow, might, [advancing from the Balla Hissar] no doubt, force in two columns on his way towards the Lahore gate [of the city], and we might from hence force that gate and meet them. But if this were accomplished what shall we gain? It can be done, not without very great loss, as our people will be exposed to the fire from the houses the whole way . . . but to march into the town, it seems, we should only have to come back again; and as to setting the city on fire, I fear, from its construction, that it is almost impossible. We must see what the morning brings, and then think what can be done."

The following morning brought panic when in the dawn light clouds of dust on the skyline and the crack of muskets suggested an attack on the cantonments was imminent. Drums were beaten to call the men to arms as a large body of horsemen approached. But as it drew nearer, those watching anxiously from behind the cantonments' flimsy defenses recognized the colors of the Thirty-seventh Regiment, which Sale had ordered back to the cantonments the previous day. Though three thousand Ghilzais had pursued and harassed them all the way to Kabul, their commanding officer had managed to bring his column and all its baggage safely in.

The arrival was a fillip to British morale, and Elphinstone agreed with Macnaghten that troops should be readied for an assault on the insurgents, but it was too late. As the news of Burnes's murder and of the looting of the treasury had spread to the surrounding villages, in Mohan Lal's words it had brought "thousands of men under the standard of the rebels." The area between the British camp and the city teemed with insurgents, and enemy horsemen were observed massing in the hills, among them Nawab Jubbar Khan, once Burnes's friend and the most steadfast supporter of the British in Kabul who, according to Mohan Lal, had also been seen in the city "beating a drum and haranguing the faithful to stand up to us." Three companies dispatched by Elphinstone to Kabul in midafternoon on 3 November met heavy opposition and were forced to fall back on the cantonments without even entering the city.

In the cantonments themselves, belated attempts were being made to improve the defenses. Lieutenant Eyre positioned the only available guns—six 9-pounders, four howitzers and three 5 ¼-inch mortars—as best he could, but clearly the British had insufficient artillery to protect themselves. Neither did they have enough artillerymen. According to Eyre there were only eighty, all Shah Shuja's men and, to make matters worse, "very insufficiently instructed, and of doubtful fidelity." Alive at last to the danger, Macnaghten sent letters imploring Brigadier Sale, by then well on the way to Jalalabad, to return forthwith to Kabul. He also wrote to General Nott at Kandahar asking him to send troops under his command, who were on the point of returning to India, to his aid as fast as possible.

Not only men and artillery were in short supply. The folly of placing all the commissariat stores in a fort four hundred yards beyond the southwest corner of the cantonments was finally apparent to all. Elphinstone increased the number of commissariat guards to eighty, but this was still not enough to defend it against a determined and numerous enemy to whom its cornucopia of everything from grain and hospital stores to spirits, wine, rum and beer was irresistible, and who had already occupied the orchards and gardens that lay between it and the camp. By 4 November four hundred Afghans had also taken over another nearby tower—the Mohammed Sheriff Fort—lying between the cantonments and the commissariat fort. Its forty-foot-high sunbaked mud walls pierced with loopholes provided excellent cover for Afghan marksmen. Elphinstone had suggested occupying the fort while it was still empty, but Macnaghten had argued against garrisoning it with British troops on the grounds that such a move might cause offense and hence "be impolitic."

On 4 November the Afghans besieged the commissariat fort in earnest and began mining beneath its walls. The officer in command there was Lieutenant Warren, a calm, taciturn young man who liked to go about with a pair of bulldogs at his heels. Realizing he was on the brink of being overwhelmed, Warren warned Elphinstone that unless he was reinforced at once he would have to abandon the fort. Elphinstone sent out two companies, whose somewhat ambiguous orders were to reinforce the fort's defenders or—if that proved impossible—to help them to evacuate it safely. The relief party at once came under heavy fire from marksmen concealed in the Mohammed Sheriff Fort and the surrounding gardens; they shot the two company commanders dead and forced the remaining troops to retreat back to the cantonments without reaching the commissariat fort. Later that day Elphinstone tried again, this time sending out a detachment composed principally of cavalry and with orders to help Warren evacuate the fort. However, as one eyewitness recorded: "From the loopholes of Mohammed Sheriff's fort—from every tree in the Shah's garden—from whatever cover of wood or masonry was to be found—the Afghan marksmen poured, with unerring aim, their deadly fire upon our advancing troops." They too were forced back.

Captain Boyd, the chief commissariat officer, pleaded with Elphinstone not to contemplate evacuating the fort but instead to renew his efforts to reinforce it. Lady Sale agreed with Boyd, writing in her journal that if the fort—"an old crazy one undermined with rats"—were abandoned, they would lose all their provisions. With only three days' food supplies left in the cantonments, this move could prove fatal. Elphinstone at first agreed with Boyd but then changed his mind. Boyd tried a second time, and Elphinstone again agreed with him, only to be swayed by the arguments of others that reinforcing the commissariat fort was impossible until the British took the Mohammed Sheriff Fort.

Dost Mohammed, ruler of Afghanistan, temporarily deposed by the British.

Shah Shuja, restored to the Afghan throne by the British as their puppet king.

George Eden, Lord Auckland, British governor-general of India.

Sir William Hay Macnaghten, British envoy in Kabul. (© National Portrait Gallery, London.)

Lord Melbourne, a member of the Whig
Party and British prime minister at the
beginning of the First Afghan War.

Sir Robert Peel, a member of the Tory
Party and British prime minister at the end
of the First Afghan War.

Lord Palmerston, foreign secretary
under Lord Melbourne.

The narrow defile of the Bolan Pass. (© The British Library Board [X 614 pl.5].
"Entrance from the Bolan Pass from Dadur," by James Atkinson.)

The Khyber Pass. (© The British Library Board [X 562 pl.28]. "Khyber Pass. Lundikana," by James Atkinson.)

Bala Hissar Gate, Kabul, photographed in 1879. (© The British Library Board [Photo 197/31]. "Bala Hissar Gate, Leading to City [of Kabul]," by Bengal Sappers and Miners.)

Kabul Bazaar, fruit season.

City of Kandahar, in southern Afghanistan. (© The British Library Board [Folio 11, 1840]. "City of Kandahar, Its Principal Bazaar and Citadel, Taken from the Nakkara Khuana," by Robert C. Carrick.)

One of the two giant statues at Bamiyan, destroyed by the Taliban in March 2001.

Alexander "Bokhara" Burnes, renowned traveler, political officer and British resident in Kabul.

Maharaja Ranjit Singh of the Punjab, Britain's ally and ruler of the Sikhs.

Captain Colin Mackenzie, hostage and survivor.

General George Pollock.

Campbell Smyth Gift 1936   SIR ROBERT AND LADY SALE.

Lady (Florentia) Sale, spirited diarist of the conflict, and her husband, Brigadier "Fighting Bob" Sale.

While Elphinstone asked the advice of anyone he could find—even junior officers—a further message came from Warren. He reported that the enemy were so close to breaking into the fort that some of his men were deserting their positions and fleeing over the walls, and that unless reinforced at once he would have no option but to abandon the commissariat. Elphinstone promised that soon after midnight he would send troops both to take the Mohammed Sheriff Fort and to reinforce Warren. But having issued the orders, on the advice of others he postponed the action until the following morning. According to Lieutenant Eyre, who had been among those pressing Elphinstone to act, the general had "an insuperable repugnance to nocturnal expeditions, and could tell of numberless instances where they had failed in Europe. It was an inconceivable trial to one's patience to be doomed to listen to such stories . . . when every moment was of infinite value."

The next morning, as Eyre had feared, was indeed too late. It was daylight before the troops were ready, by which time Warren and what was left of his beleaguered garrison had escaped from the commissariat fort by digging a hole through its wall and had struggled back to the cantonments, leaving the stores to looters. Very soon, according to Captain Johnson, the fort resembled "a large ant's nest. Ere noon, thousands and thousands had assembled from far and wide, to participate in the booty of the English dogs, each man taking away with him as much as he could carry—and to this we were all eye-witnesses." According to an officer in the Balla Hissar, Shah Shuja was watching from the rooftop of his palace "from where with the naked eye, the melancholy and heart-rending sight was distinctly visible. Grain, wine, hermetically sealed provisions and stores of every kind were being thrown over the walls in one common mass, and seized and carried away by the Afghans below. The King was dreadfully agitated, and turning to his Vizier said, 'The English are mad.'" Shah Shuja was so despondent that he was asking the advice of even the most junior officers, permitting them to sit by him and sending them warm quilts to keep out the extreme cold because, pride and dignity for the moment pushed aside, he "had forgot for the time that he was a king," just as Elphinstone in the cantonments seemed to have forgotten he was a general.

Also on 4 November supplies for Shah Shuja's troops, including a large quantity of grain, were lost. In the early days of the occupation the

British had sensibly planned to store the grain in specially erected warehouses in the Balla Hissar, but Shah Shuja had objected. Instead, the grain sacks had been stacked in a ramshackle fort, partly consisting of converted camel sheds, about a mile and a half from the cantonments on the outskirts of Kabul. Two days before, on the morning of 2 November, Captain Colin Mackenzie, who was living at the fort, had been about to ride to the cantonments when he was told that riots had broken out in the town. He had immediately ordered his troops to stand to arms but, as he later wrote, "suddenly a naked man stood before me, covered with blood, from two deep sabre-cuts in the head and five musket-shots in the arm and body." He proved to be a messenger sent by Macnaghten to another officer, Captain Robert Trevor, living with his extensive young family in a fort nearby.

Taking this as "rather a strong hint as to how matters were going," Mackenzie had immediately ordered the gates of his fort to be secured and prepared to resist an attack. He had also managed to get a message to the cantonments asking urgently for reinforcements or at least for some more ammunition. Lawrence, who was with Elphinstone when Mackenzie's message arrived, volunteered to lead a relief force, but his proposal was, he later complained, universally condemned by the other officers present as imprudent because "they feared exposing their men to street fighting." Mackenzie and his men had strained their eyes in vain "looking for the glittering bayonets through the trees." However, what they could see—and it brought them no comfort—was smoke rising from the direction of Burnes's house. They realized that the rumors of his murder that had begun reaching them must be true.

Mackenzie succeeded gamely in hanging on for the next thirty-six hours. The defenders numbered 160, including 90 Afghan mercenary musketrymen—*jezailchis*—handpicked by Mackenzie, to whom they were devoted. He in turn admired how they fought unflinchingly against their own countrymen, only occasionally breaking off "to refresh themselves with a pipe" or sometimes drowning out the sounds of battle and of women wailing over the dead and dying by twanging "a sort of rude guitar, as an accompaniment to some martial song which, mingling with the above notes of war, sounded very strangely."

When some of Mackenzie's other soldiers began dismantling parts of the fort's defenses so that they could make off, he seized a double-barreled gun and threatened to shoot the first man who disobeyed the order to return to his post. However, when on 3 November the leader of his *jezailchis* came to him and said, "I think we have done our duty; if you consider it necessary that we should die here, we will die, but *I* think we have done enough," even Mackenzie was forced to admit that if they stayed, they would all be massacred. Waiting until dark, with the *jezailchis* in the lead, a crowd of women and children in the center, and Mackenzie in the rearguard, they moved stealthily out into the darkness to try to find their way through to the cantonments. When a woman abandoned her child by the roadside in preference to leaving her pots and pans, Mackenzie drew his sword and thumped her with the flat of it until she again picked up her child.

This action may have saved his life because it meant he had his sword in his hand when moments later he was attacked by a party of Afghans crying out, *"Feringhee hust"* (Here is a European). Spurring his horse, Mackenzie wheeled around, cutting from right to left with his sword and severing the hand of the boldest assailant. After a bitter struggle during which Mackenzie received two saber slashes, he extricated himself from the mélee and galloping on found himself in the midst of another group of Afghans. It took him a moment to realize they were his own *jezailchis*, and it seemed to him his life had been preserved by a miracle. Soon afterward he reached the cantonments. Miracle or not, it had been a remarkable achievement. George Broadfoot noted admiringly that Mackenzie had fought for two days "and then cut his way to the large force, who did not seem able to cut their way to him."

Captain Trevor, commander of Shah Shuja's Life Guards, had also been besieged in his fort five hundred yards to the east of Mackenzie, together with his wife and seven children. At midday on 3 November Mackenzie had seen "the enemy enter Captain Trevor's tower and a report was brought by two of his servants that he and his family had all been killed." In fact the Trevors, together with a small sepoy escort, had managed to flee and eventually reached the cantonments, fording a river to get there. When an Afghan attempted to cut Mrs. Trevor with his sword, a mounted sepoy riding next to her put out his arm to protect her and lost his hand. Though weak from loss of blood, he remained by her side all the way to the cantonments.

Such instances of bravery, selflessness and resourcefulness contrasted sadly with the timid behavior of the British leadership. Their continued inaction convinced many chiefs who had been watching the
insurrection and trying to divine the outcome to join it. They would have
been amazed, if heartened, to learn that within just seventy-two hours of
the start of the rebellion, General Elphinstone was already contemplating
negotiating terms with the enemy. When on 5 November Lieutenant Eyre
urged him to send a force to capture the Mohammed Sheriff Fort by
blowing in the gate as a prelude to trying to regain the commissariat fort,
the general wrote to Macnaghten that he had agreed, but added: "It behoves us to look to the consequences of failure: in this case I know not
how we are to subsist, or, from want of provisions to retreat. You should,
therefore, consider what chance there is of making terms."

An initial attack on the Mohammed Sheriff Fort failed. The following day the British at last had some reason for optimism when a party
succeeded in storming it and driving out the occupiers, who fled into the
hills pursued by British cavalry. However, though the cantonments were
now a little more secure, the commissariat fort in which some supplies
still remained could not be retaken. The bare facts were that the troops
had lost most of their supplies and faced starvation. Yet, greatly to their
surprise, the commissariat officers were able to purchase grain from the
inhabitants of the nearby village of Bemaru at reasonable prices—a sign
that these people at least did not consider that the British were finished.
With these extra supplies and with the troops put on half rations, the immediate danger of being starved out of the cantonments had been averted,
though men, especially the Indian sepoys, were starting to fall ill because
of the intense cold. Sita Ram described how as the temperature dropped
some of his fellow sepoys "became helpless. Men lost the use of their
fingers and toes which fell off after great suffering." Lady Sale pitied the
troops, who were being constantly harassed by the enemy but "had no
cover night or day, all being on the ramparts." The defenders of the Balla
Hissar, led by Brigadier Shelton, were also suffering: Sixty sepoys had contracted pneumonia, and "there was hardly a grain of medicine, or a single
case of amputating instruments in the whole fort! And this with gun-shot
wounds occurring almost hourly," an officer lamented.

Elphinstone was yet again in despair. On 6 November he wrote to
Macnaghten that even though the immediate problem of finding enough

provisions had been overcome, a further "very serious and indeed awful" problem loomed: lack of ammunition. He urged Macnaghten not to tarry in seeking terms. "Do not suppose from this I wish to recommend or am advocating humiliating terms, or such as would reflect disgrace on us," he tried to justify himself, but his postscript revealed his acute anxiety: "Our case is not yet desperate . . . but it must be born in mind that it goes very fast."

Elphinstone's concern about ammunition was misplaced—there was, in fact, enough within the cantonments to last for twelve months, as even Lady Sale knew—and Macnaghten was not inclined to open negotiations with the rebel chiefs anyway. Instead the envoy was hoping that he might be able to bribe them and used Mohan Lal as his agent. Lal had, by then, taken refuge with a friend of Burnes's, the Kizzilbashi leader Shirin Khan, and had been sending intelligence reports to the envoy in the cantonments. Macnaghten's first targets included the Ghilzai leader Mohammed Hamza, to whom he instructed Lal to offer large sums if he could persuade the Ghilzais to withdraw from the insurrection. Macnaghten also told Lal to promise money to the Kizzilbashis and to a rival of the rebel leader Amenoolah Khan in return for exerting their influence in favor of the British.

However, a more permanent and reliable solution than bribery soon occurred to Macnaghten: political assassination. Perhaps what drove him to this was his acceptance at last of reports that Dost Mohammed's son Akbar Khan had appeared at Bamiyan in the north and was raising troops. Macnaghten instructed Lal to offer rewards for the killing of the principal leaders of the rebellion. In a letter of 5 November to Mohan Lal, Macnaghten's political assistant, Lieutenant John Conolly, promised "10,000 rupees for the head of each of the principal rebel chiefs." A few days later Conolly wrote to Lal that "there is a man called Haji Ali who might be induced by a bribe to try and bring in the heads of one or two of the *mufsids* [rebels]. Endeavour to let him know that 10,000 will be given for each head—or even 15,000 rupees."

As these plans developed, the British forces unlucky enough to have been sent to remote outposts were fighting for their lives. Two lieutenants commanding at Dardurrah, twenty miles north of Kabul, were murdered by Kohistani tribesmen while their soldiers fled. Also in Kohistan, insurgents occupied the plains between Kabul and the British post at Charikar, which was garrisoned by a regiment of Gurkhas. Eldred Pottinger, the political officer for Kohistan whose residence, an old castle, was only two miles from Charikar, had been warning Macnaghten for some time that trouble was imminent. He had requested reinforcements but received none. In desperation, Pottinger had tried to buy the support of the local chiefs but soon understood that, far from being potential allies, the chiefs were hostile. Pottinger's assistant, Lieutenant Charles Rattray, unwise enough to agree to join a group of petty Afghan chiefs who had gathered in a field adjoining the castle to discuss what they would be required to do in return for the proffered subsidies, was shot and wounded. As his attackers fled, a horrified Pottinger, looking out from the ramparts to see what had happened, watched helpless as other horsemen galloped up and dispatched the wounded Rattray. They then attacked his residence. A force from Charikar under Captain Codrington arrived in time to beat the attackers off, but only with heavy losses.

With no signs of any help arriving from Kabul, Pottinger had no option but to abandon the castle under cover of darkness and fall back on Charikar. However, here the position of the defenders quickly became untenable. Thousands of insurgents besieged the flimsy barracks, which were still in the process of being fortified and which had very limited supplies of water. Codrington commanded the troops while Pottinger took over the artillery until he was hit in the leg by a musket ball, but it was futile. A Gurkha soldier later wrote of the "*beegahs* [acres] of gleaming swords" moving toward them. Codrington was mortally wounded and spent his final hours composing a letter to his wife, which he entrusted, together with a portrait of her, to Pottinger, lying in the next bed, for safekeeping.

On 8 November the attackers, who had brushed off several gallant and determined sorties by the Gurkhas, offered terms provided the defenders agreed to become Muslims. Pottinger refused, saying, "We came to this country to aid a Mohammedan sovereign in the recovery of his rights. We are therefore within the pale of Islam, and exempt from coercion on the score of religion." The siege resumed with lack of water now as great a danger as the attackers. On 10 November each fighting man received only half a glass, and the following day many had to go without. Some men sucked pieces of raw mutton to deaden their thirst, while others stole out after dark in a bid to reach a nearby spring but returned empty-handed.

With over half the officers dead, only two hundred fighting men left and barely thirty rounds of ammunition apiece for their muskets, the wounded Pottinger knew they had to leave. On the night of 13 November, weak and dazed with thirst, the garrison left Charikar. As one survivor recalled, "Most of the wounded who were unable to move out . . . with us were slaughtered next day." Those who did get away owed their lives to a brave Gurkha bugler. Because of him, "the enemy either did not discover our retreat or were afraid to venture near, till long after daylight. We had all throughout the siege sounded our bugles with the regularity of peaceful times, by way of a hint to the enemy that we were all right. On this last fatal morning the Bugle Major . . . who was too severely wounded to leave with us, crawled up to a bastion and sounded the customary bugle at dawn."

As it turned out, Pottinger would be one of only four members of the garrison to make it safely back to Kabul, but when he arrived there two days later with his tales of hardship and massacre, he found little comfort.

CHAPTER TWELVE

It is not feasible any longer to maintain our position in this country.
—MAJOR GENERAL WILLIAM ELPHINSTONE, NOVEMBER 1841

AS THE INSURRECTION entered its second week, the mood in
the Kabul cantonments grew bleaker. Elphinstone's precarious physical
condition had been worsened by a bad fall from his horse, and he was no
longer able to ride around the cantonments to inspect the defenses. On 9
November he reluctantly recalled his second-in-command, Brigadier Shelton, from the Balla Hissar to take charge of the cantonments. The Afghans made no attempt to oppose Shelton, who brought his men in safely,
though there was some momentary alarm when Shelton, who had ridden
ahead, spied in the distance what he thought was a group of jezail-toting
Afghans. It turned out to be only a pack of pariah dogs.

Many welcomed Shelton's arrival, expecting "wonders from his
prowess and military judgement," as Lady Sale wrote. However, as she
also observed, the new arrangement was not a happy one. Shelton was
openly contemptuous of Elphinstone and "often refused to give any opinion when asked for it by the general." He brought his bedroll to councils
of war so that when he became bored he could simply curl up and go to
sleep. Elphinstone, who found Shelton "contumacious" and "actuated by
ill feelings" toward him, often interfered with or countermanded his orders, leaving more junior officers confused as to their instructions.

The brigadier was not a man who bothered to hide his feelings. Having
decided that the British could never survive the winter in Kabul, he told

everyone so, further lowering the morale that his arrival in the canton-ments had been expected to enhance. Shelton was also openly rude to Macnaghten. When Mackenzie took him to task about it, Shelton replied, "Damn it, Mackenzie, I *will* sneer at him, I *like* to sneer at him!" Lady Sale quickly grew to dislike Shelton and was irritated by his determina-tion to get out of Afghanistan and back to India at the earliest opportu-nity, writing: "It may be remarked that, from the first of his arrival in the country, he appears to have greatly disliked it, and his disgust has now considerably increased. His mind is set on getting back to Hindustan." She likened his presence to "a dark cloud shadowing us." Eyre wrote that, "from the very first, [Shelton] seemed to despair of the force being able to hold out the winter in Kabul and strenuously advocated an immediate retreat to Jalalabad. This sort of despondency proved unhappily very in-fectious. It soon spread its baneful influence among the officers and was by them communicated to the soldiery. The number of *croakers* in garri-son became perfectly frightful, lugubrious looks and dismal prophesies being encountered everywhere."

Shah Shuja, abandoned by Shelton and besieged in the Balla Hissar, knew that if the British indeed departed Afghanistan, either death or ex-ile would be his likely fate. Mohan Lal, in one of his stream of intelligence reports from his hiding place in the city, reported that Shah Shuja had told the 860 women of his *haram* that he would poison every one of them if the insurgents captured the cantonments. The king's gloom only deep-ened when he learned that the insurgent chiefs—a confederacy including Barakzais, Ghilzais and Sadozais—had elected Nawab Zaman Khan— the cousin of Dost Mohammed who had spirited Mohan Lal to safety beneath his bulky apparel—as their new king. It was obvious the nawab was a caretaker, warming the throne for the eventual return of Dost Mo-hammed himself. Abdullah Khan was appointed the nawab's commander in chief and Amenoolah Khan his vizier.

Within the cantonments the British debated how they could best preserve not only their lives but their honor. Unlike Shelton, Elphinstone and Macnaghten were for the moment convinced the British should re-main where they were. They still hoped for the arrival of reinforcements from General Nott or indeed for the return to Kabul of Brigadier Sale's brigade. The envoy had sent yet further messages to Sale, sometimes writing in French or Latin in case the message fell into enemy hands. He had also persuaded Elphinstone to write as well, though a critical Lady Sale thought the general's instructions highly ambiguous: "From the very cautious wording of the order, it appears doubtful whether [Sale] can take such responsibility upon himself as it implies. He is, if he can leave his sick, wounded and baggage in perfect safety, to return to Kabul, if he can do so without endangering the forces under his command. Now, in obeying an order of this kind, if Sale succeeds, and all is right, he will doubtless be a very fine fellow; but if he meets with a reverse, he will be told, 'you were not to come up unless you could do so safely!' "

On 10 November the British had a much needed success when Shelton led two thousand soldiers to assault the Rikabashi Fort, a small tower lying a mere three hundred yards from the northeast corner of the cantonments. Afghan marksmen had occupied it and were picking off unwary troops within the cantonments. Many of these sharpshooters were not soldiers but ordinary tradesmen from the city. Lady Sale noted that two of the most accurate were a barber and a blacksmith: "They completely commanded the loopholes with their long rifles; and although the distance is probably 300 yards, yet they seldom fail to put a ball through the body or into the clothes of anyone passing them . . . and it became an amusement to place a cap on the end of a pole above the walls, which was sure to be quickly perforated by many balls."

The attack on the Rikabashi Fort nearly failed when a captain, who had volunteered to blast open the main gate, in error blew in a small wicket gate wide enough to allow only one man at a time to crawl inside. A few did so, but they were left isolated when a sudden cry went up among those troops still outside that Afghan cavalry were coming, causing them to flee in panic. Shelton on this occasion, in Lady Sale's words, "proved a trump," coolly rallying his men and leading them back to capture the fort with its ample store of grain and to rescue their colleagues trapped within.

For some of these men it was too late. Also according to Lady Sale, Shelton's troops found an elderly officer who had struggled back outside severely hacked about the body by Afghans with their sharp *tulwars*. The officer's attackers had even pulled off his boots and severed two toes. "This is not battle," he groaned, "it is murder." He died after surgeons amputated both his arms in a futile bid to save him. Among the enemy corpses the British found sprawled on the ground was the headless body of a man who by his rich dress they identified as a chief. The unsqueamish Lady Sale was intrigued to observe that when it was too dangerous or difficult for the Afghans to carry away their dead from the battlefield, they contented themselves with cutting off the heads so that they could bury at least that part of the body with the due religious rites.

Emboldened by their success, the British captured, ransacked and destroyed four further nearby forts and brought a large amount of grain back to the cantonments. Though two hundred men had been killed or wounded, their confidence began to return, and many felt a turning point had been reached. For three days the Afghans hung back and allowed long lines of commissariat camels to tramp unmolested through the countryside close to the cantonments as the officers of the commissariat gathered up more food. There was jubilation when two dogs known to belong to officers who had marched with Sale trotted into the cantonments. Rumors flew that Sale and his column were coming. Yet, as day followed day, those looking toward the eastern passes saw no sign of the returning column, and on closer inspection, it was clear that the dogs had been running wild for quite a time—one had rabies.

Unknown to his compatriots waiting anxiously in Kabul, on 11 November Sale had moved out from Gandamack, but his destination was Jalalabad, not Kabul. Faced by Macnaghten's and Elphinstone's passionate and repeated entreaties and with his wife and daughter trapped in Kabul, it had been a hard decision. Sale had consulted his senior officers. Though some, including George Broadfoot, favored returning, the near-unanimous view was that if they tried to retrace their steps the seventy miles to Kabul, the waiting Ghilzais would fall on them. Even if they did turn and try to fight their way back through the passes to Kabul, it would mean leaving behind their three hundred sick and injured. Thus Sale chose to march resolutely on—a decision for which many would later criticize him. On 13 November he and his men reached Jalalabad, a little more than halfway between Kabul and Peshawar and on the south side of the Kabul River. They swiftly occupied its decrepit fortress and began repairing the town's defenses to ready it to withstand a siege and to act as a base for British troops coming up from India or back from Kabul. That same day, Sale sent a force out to reconnoitre. They came across a lone Afghan sitting among some rocks overlooking Jalalabad and playing what looked and sounded like bagpipes. From that point on, the British called his eyrie Piper's Hill.

Unaware of the true position, Elphinstone, Macnaghten and others continued to hope not only that Sale and his men were coming but also that General Nott, 290 miles away in Kandahar, would send help. Macnaghten's message to Nott asking him to send a relief column did not reach Kandahar until 14 November. Nott thought the envoy was asking for the near impossible—it was late in the season and some of the passes were already blocked by snow. The cold was so intense that his men felt as if their heads were freezing solid. But dutiful soldier that he was, he recalled a brigade that had departed six days earlier for India under its commander, Brigadier James Maclaren, and ordered them instead to march for Kabul. Nott's personal feelings are clear from a letter to his daughters: "I have received a *positive* order from the Envoy and Elphinstone to send troops to Kabul . . . This is *against my* judgment; 1st because I think at this time of year they *cannot* get there, as the snow will probably be four or five feet deep . . . besides which, it is likely they will have to fight every foot of the ground . . . I am obliged strictly to obey the orders of such stupid people, when I know these orders go to ruin the affairs of the British Government, and to cut the throats of my handful of soldiers . . . How strange that Macnaghten has never been right, even by chance!" He was equally open to Brigadier Maclaren, telling him, "The despatch of this brigade to Kabul is none of my doing. I am compelled to defer to superior authority but in my own private opinion I am sending you all to destruction."

In Kabul, although the British had taken the Rikabashi Fort and other strongholds, the insurgents, encouraged by Abdullah Khan and Amenoolah Khan, had merely been regrouping and had not gone away. Angry that the villagers of Bemaru, half a mile to the north of the cantonments on the road to Kohistan, were continuing to sell grain to the British, the insurgents drove them from their houses, seized their possessions, then positioned two guns—a 4-pounder and a 6-pounder—in the hills above the village, from where they began firing into the cantonments below. Macnaghten insisted the guns be captured. When Shelton objected that the risks were too great, Macnaghten replied, "If you will allow yourself to be thus bearded by the enemy, and will not advance and take these two guns by this evening, you must be prepared for any disgrace that may befall us."

The reluctant Shelton assembled four cavalry squadrons, seventeen infantry companies and two guns and on 13 November led them up into the hills around Bemaru. Charged by Afghan horsemen, the leading British troops held their fire, not discharging their Brown Bess muskets until the enemy was only ten yards away, but their volley failed to topple a single man or horse. Lady Sale, watching from her flat-topped roof where the chimney offered some protection from the bullets whizzing by, was terrified: "My very heart felt as if it leapt to my teeth when I saw the Afghans ride clean through them. The onset was fearful. They looked like a great cluster of bees." Unlike many of her male compatriots, she admired Afghan fighting tactics, astutely identifying some of the reasons for their success: "Every horseman [carries] a foot soldier behind him to the scene of action, where he is dropped without the fatigue of walking to his post. The horsemen have two or three matchlocks or jezails each, slung at their backs, and are very expert in firing at the gallop. These jezails carry much further than our muskets."

The broken British ranks fell back under the ferocious onslaught but managed to re-form. As the British guns under the command of Lieutenant Eyre began to fire, providing them with cover, their own cavalry galloped into action, scattering the Afghans and capturing their 4-pounder gun. Eyre would have liked to seize the other gun as well but had to content himself with spiking it before obeying the order to withdraw to the cantonments because night was falling. The action had been a success but only a temporary one. Though both guns had been dealt with, the enemy almost immediately reoccupied the Bemaru Hills, shutting off the supply of grain from the villagers who lived there. Eyre wrote: "This was the last success our arms were destined to experience. Henceforward it becomes my weary task to relate a catalogue of errors, disasters and difficulties, which, following close upon each other, disgusted our officers, disheartened our soldiers, and finally sunk us all into irretrievable ruin, as though heaven itself . . . had planned our downfall."

On 15 November the seriously wounded Eldred Pottinger and his three companions reached the cantonments to confirm the rumors that the garrison at Charikar had been overrun and to be welcomed, in Eyre's words, as "men risen from the dead." While they recovered from their wounds, the increasing cold and the fatigue of constantly manning the large perimeter of the cantonments took their toll on the garrison.

On 22 November the British tried to retake the Bemaru Hills from the enemy, whose morale had been boosted by the news that Akbar Khan, at the head of six thousand Uzbeks, was advancing on Kabul from Bamiyan in the north. However, the detachment of men sent out was too small, and their commander, Major Stephen Swayne, too indecisive. Eyre, who was again commanding the artillery, described with some bitterness how Swayne, "whose orders were to storm the village, would neither go forward nor retire; but concealing his men under the cover of some low wall, he all day long maintained an useless fire on the houses of Bemaru village, without the slightest satisfactory result."

The British cavalry were drawn up behind Eyre's guns, "where as there was nothing for them to do, they accordingly did nothing" except provide sitting targets for the Afghan sharpshooters, who picked off both men and horses. Eyre found his artillery also "exposed to the deliberate aim of the numerous marksmen who occupied the village and its immediate vicinity, whose bullets continually sang in our ears, often striking the gun, and grazing the ground on which we stood." Two of his six gunners were wounded, and later a bullet shattered Eyre's left hand and put him out of action. Shelton arrived with some reinforcements, but judging the forces available too few to dislodge the Afghans, he ordered them back to the cantonments.

That evening Macnaghten and Elphinstone convened a council of war, at which the envoy argued hard for a further attempt to drive the enemy from the Bemaru Hills. This time Shelton was to command the assault from the start and to deploy a much larger force. At two A.M. on 23 November, taking advantage of the darkness of a moonless night, the brigadier led his men silently out of the cantonments toward Bemaru once more. He was taking with him only a single field gun in contravention of standing orders stipulating that at least two were always to be deployed. He had wanted to take a smaller mountain gun as well, but this had been damaged and could not be repaired in time. Among Shelton's officers was the brave but corpulent and gloomy Colonel Thomas Oliver, whose customary response to inquiries about his well-being was to mutter, "Dust to dust!"

Initially, the assault force did well. Before the first light crept over the hills, Shelton had managed to get his men and their single gun up the steep rugged slopes to hills above the village. He ordered his gunners to fire grapeshot down on their surprised enemy, who dashed for cover inside the village's towers and houses before returning fire with their jezails. However, though several officers suggested that, with the benefit of darkness and the enemy in disarray and few in number, this was the moment to storm the village, Shelton delayed too long. Dawn was breaking by the time he sent a detachment under Major Swayne to take the village. This time the hapless Swayne unaccountably lost his way and instead of reaching the main gate—open and unguarded—led his men to a small barricaded wicket gate that he had no means of forcing. They were caught in a storm of jezail fire, and Swayne was shot in the neck. After half an hour, with full daylight approaching, Shelton recalled them.

By now all surprise had been lost. Those in the city could see and hear what was happening, and armed men—many again artisans—ran and rode from Kabul to aid the insurgents. Before long, the British were facing at least ten thousand men who occupied the village and surged up a neighboring hill separated by only a narrow gorge from the high ground occupied by Shelton. Meanwhile, on the plains below, "swarms of their cavalry" were deploying. As the Afghans opened a galling fire on his men, Shelton rejected the suggestion by some of his officers that the hundred engineers who had accompanied the force for this purpose should throw up a *sangar*—or stone breastwork—to provide protection and firing positions. Instead he ordered his infantry to stand and to form two squares, two hundred yards apart and with the cavalry between them but slightly to their rear. Eyre thought that forming squares—a tactic by which the British army had successfully repelled Napoleon's cavalry—was wholly inappropriate against "the distant fire of infantry" with their long-range muskets. The British troops simply presented "a solid mass against the aim of perhaps the best marksmen in the world."

By nine A.M. Shelton's single artillery piece had become too hot from repeated firing to be operated. Unless the gunners could cover the touch hole—or "serve the vent," as it was known—with their thumb as they rammed the charge home down the barrel, the backdraft they created was likely to ignite smoldering particles from previous firings and cause a premature discharge. With the metal red-hot, serving the vent was impossible. In any case, ammunition was short, and the gunners were exhausted.

The Afghans had by now advanced so close to the British troops that one of them defiantly planted a flag in the ground a mere thirty yards from the front square. Shelton offered one hundred rupees to any man who could seize it, but no one moved. Seeing the straits the British were in, the attackers, whose ranks included fearless and fanatical *ghazis* (holy warriors), rushed, yelling wildly, toward the British gun and seized it despite the fierce resistance of the artillerymen. Shelton ordered his cavalry to charge them, but the demoralized troopers would not follow their officers. Also, the infantrymen in the first square began falling back without orders on the second square, and it took all their officers' forcefulness to rally them.

But at this critical moment, the Afghan onrush suddenly faltered as news spread through their ranks that Macnaghten's bête noire, the Achakzai leader Abdullah Khan, had been wounded. Some began to fall back in great confusion, abandoning the British gun, though others had already made off with the horses and limber. This precipitate and unexpected retreat heartened the British, who recaptured their gun. By now it had cooled sufficiently for them to load it with fresh ammunition that had arrived from the cantonments and begin firing once more. Down in the cantonments, Macnaghten and Elphinstone had observed the sudden flight of the Afghans, and the envoy was eager to profit from it. Lady Sale overheard him ask Elphinstone to send troops to pursue the enemy, but the general dismissed the idea as "a wild scheme and not feasible."

In the hills the British seemed paralyzed. The cavalry still refused the orders of the officers to advance, while the infantry seemed too exhausted to move forward. Noting that the British were not following up their advantage, the Afghans paused in their flight and rallied. The consequence, as Eyre described, was that "not only did the whole force of the enemy come on with renewed vigour and spirits, maintaining at the same time the fatal jezail fire which had already so grievously thinned our ranks, but fresh numbers poured out of the city, and from the surrounding villages, until the hill occupied by them scarcely afforded room for them to stand." Before long, the front ranks of the first British square "had been literally mowed down," and a few minutes later another rush by *ghazi* fighters completely broke the square.

Shelton still would not signal the retreat. Standing there seemingly impervious to death or serious injury, he shouted to his men to hold firm, even though, as he later described, he was struck by no less than five balls, "none of which did much harm; one spent ball hit me on the head and nearly knocked me down; another made my arm a little stiff." Colonel Oliver, though, had had enough. Shouting that he was too fat to run, he began, rather than retreat, to walk doggedly toward the enemy, who duly shot him dead. When the British later recovered his body, his head had been cut off, together with the finger on which he had habitually worn a handsome diamond ring.

A panic-stricken retreat by the British infantry and cavalry followed, captured graphically by Eyre: "All order was at an end; the entreaties and commands of the officers, endeavouring to rally the men, were not even listened to, and an utter rout ensued down the hill in the direction of cantonments." The Afghan cavalry galloped after them, slashing and firing until ordered to desist by their commander, Osman Khan, another of Dost Mohammed's numerous nephews. Lady Sale, peering from her rooftop, was surprised to see him circling around clusters of British soldiers, waving his sword above his head but for some reason not attempting to kill them. As the exhausted troops ran back toward the cantonments, Elphinstone tottered outside the gates to attempt to rally them, but to no avail. Lady Sale overheard him complain later to Macnaghten, "Why Lord, Sir, when I said to them 'Eyes right,' they all looked the other way."

The battle for Bemaru had been an unqualified disaster, exposing British ineptitude and low morale to the Afghans and to the British themselves. Three hundred British troops had been killed or left lying in the field, to be killed and mutilated by the Afghans. Those still living felt themselves, in Captain Lawrence's words, to be "doomed men." To Eyre, 23 November was the day that finally "decided the fate of the Kabul force" when "even such of the officers as had hitherto indulged the hope of a favourable turn in our affairs began at last reluctantly to entertain gloomy forebodings as to our future fate."

That fate rested in the hands of three men who could not agree and none of whom was "the able pilot" Eyre thought essential to steer them from disaster. Elphinstone wished to negotiate as he had been advocating almost from the start of the rising. Macnaghten, however, was determined to wait a little longer before taking a humiliating step that would, in his eyes, be mere capitulation. Shelton, who had amply demonstrated what Eyre called his "dauntless" personal bravery at Bemaru, still wanted to march immediately from Kabul to Jalalabad, an idea from which, according to Captain Lawrence, Macnaghten recoiled as both disastrous and dishonorable and "to be contemplated solely in the very last extremity." It would mean abandoning vast amounts of British property and Britain's ally Shah Shuja, "to support whom was the main object of our original entrance into Afghanistan." Also, the troops would suffer immensely from the bitter cold, while the thousands of camp followers would "inevitably be destroyed."

Shah Shuja, watching from the Balla Hissar the rapidly declining fortunes of the allies on whom his life and fortunes depended, and alarmed by evidence that the insurgents were bribing some of his own men to desert their posts, added his opinion to the debate. Overcoming his earlier objections, he sensibly suggested that the British garrison should withdraw from the cantonments and join him in the Balla Hissar. As Henry Havelock had observed in happier times, the citadel was "the key to Kabul. The troops who hold it ought not to suffer themselves to be dislodged but by a siege; and they must awe its populace with their mortars and howitzers; for, in a land where every male has in his house, or about his person, a musket . . . , a sword and shield, a dagger . . . a contest in crooked lanes of flat-roofed houses with a population estimated at sixty thousand souls, would be unequal, excepting for very numerous forces indeed; in any case injudicious."

Elphinstone objected that the troops would never survive the two-and-a-half-mile contested march to the fortress, despite Shelton and his much smaller contingent having successfully made it in reverse two weeks before. Shelton himself argued that such a move would be pointless since they should quickly depart to India. Macnaghten, though, was torn. According to Lawrence, he thought "it might be the wisest ultimate course" but fretted that it "might also be to some extent disastrous." Again it would mean abandoning large amounts of British and East India Company property—an issue that evidently loomed large in Macnaghten's bureaucratic mind. He also feared the British would have to abandon their heavy artillery since it would be nearly impossible to drag it under fire to the citadel. Furthermore, in the Balla Hissar there would not be sufficient food or firewood to sustain so many. Macnaghten therefore decided to hang on in the cantonments in the hope that "something may turn up in our favour" and argued for remaining there a further eight to ten days.

Macnaghten still hoped Sale might answer his call. Even after learning that the brigadier had marched from Gandamack for Jalalabad, he had sent a message to Captain George Macgregor, Sale's political adviser, asking again for help. He complained that both he and Elphinstone had repeatedly written asking for the return of Sale's brigade, to no avail: "We learn to our dismay, that you have proceeded to Jalalabad. Our situation is a desperate one if you do not immediately return to our relief, and I beg you will do so without a moment's delay." Though he could not know it, this letter would cross with one from Macgregor finally dashing any hopes that Sale's men would return. The bearers of these messages were again the native messengers, the *cossids*, traveling on horseback or on foot. The risk of being intercepted was great, and their methods for concealing messages were ingenious. They bound the notes into their hair or hid them in lumps of wax they could swallow if captured. Captain Mackenzie wrote of "many a poor wretch" found lying by the roadside "with his throat cut from ear to ear and his body otherwise mutilated."

In the cantonments many listened to the debate about withdrawing to the Balla Hissar with anger and incredulity. Eyre thought it the most sensible course, and Lieutenant Sturt, recovering remarkably well from his stab wounds, urged "the absolute necessity of our now withdrawing our forces from the cantonments into the Balla Hissar" but, according to his mother-in-law, Lady Sale, was met by the cry of "How can we abandon the good buildings and property?" Mohan Lal also thought it bizarre that anyone should think it too dangerous to march to the Balla Hissar while believing that "to travel eight to ten days to Jalalabad through the frozen passes . . . occupied by the ferocious and plundering Ghilzais was . . . far from dangerous." He had also grown convinced that the British would have no option but to negotiate their departure from Kabul unless "a portion of the people or chiefs wished [them] to remain."

Mohan Lal himself had been busy trying to buy support for the British, as Macnaghten had ordered. His attempts to encourage the Kizzilbashi community, under its leader Shirin Khan, to declare for the British had faltered in the face of the obvious inability of the British to suppress the rising. However, he had evidently fared better with his plans to purchase the assassination of some of the insurrection's ringleaders. By the end of November both Abdullah Khan and another leading conspirator, Mir Misjidi, were dead. Abdullah Khan had died of those injuries sustained during the battle for the Bemaru Hills which had caused the insurgents temporarily to fall back. Mir Misjidi had simply vanished. One Afghan employed by Mohan Lal claimed to have shot Abdullah Khan with a poisoned musket ball from behind a wall during the fighting, while another asserted he had strangled Mir Misjidi while he slept and then disposed of his body. Both demanded the promised blood money. Mohan Lal refused to pay up—in Abdullah Khan's case because he doubted the truth of the supposed killer's story and in the case of Mir Misjidi because the assassin could not produce the head as proof.

Whatever his precise role in engineering what were clearly political killings, Mohan Lal rightly assessed that the fate of the British depended on the wishes of the Afghan people and their chiefs. On 24 November Osman Khan sent an envoy to the cantonments offering terms. As Lady Sale wrote that day, "They say they do not wish to harm us, if we will only go away; but that go we must and give them back the Dost; that Mohammed Akbar Khan (his son) will be here tomorrow with 6,000 men; and that if we do not come to terms, they will carry the cantonment; and that they are ready to sacrifice 6,000 men to do so."

Despite the bellicose undertones, the offer was a relief to Elphinstone at least. Macnaghten asked him for his formal opinion in writing, presumably to produce in any future inquiry, on whether the British could maintain a military presence in Afghanistan any longer. Elphinstone for once was utterly decisive: "I beg to state that, after having held our position here for upwards of three weeks in a state of siege, from the want of provisions and forage, the reduced state of our troops, the large number of wounded and sick, the difficulty of defending the extensive and ill-situated cantonment we occupy, the near approach of winter, our communications cut off, no prospect of relief, and the whole country in arms against us, I am of the opinion that it is not feasible any longer to maintain our position in this country, and that you ought to avail yourself of the offer to negotiate which has been made to you."

CHAPTER THIRTEEN

We shall part with the Afghans as friends, and I feel satisfied that any government which may be established hereafter will always be disposed to cultivate a good understanding with us.

—SIR WILLIAM MACNAGHTEN, DECEMBER 1841

THE SPEED WITH which Macnaghten followed up their offer of talks must have gratified Osman Khan and the Afghan chiefs and perhaps encouraged them to take a tough line when, on 25 November, they met in a gatehouse to the cantonments. During a tense and ill-tempered encounter, they asserted that the British were prisoners of war. As such they must surrender unconditionally and hand over all their arms, ammunition and treasure. The astonished envoy refused, and when the chiefs threatened him with meeting again on the field of battle, he retorted, "At all events we shall meet at the day of judgment." After the meeting broke up, Macnaghten wrote to the chiefs making clear the conditions he would consider acceptable, but their response was again to threaten hostilities, to which, according to Lady Sale, he replied grandly "that death was preferable to dishonour,—and that we put our trust in the God of battles."

At the same time, unaware that negotiations were stalling, Afghan fighters and their British opponents—both Europeans and sepoys—were socializing as if their differences were forgotten and the British would soon be on the road to India. Afghans even offered cabbages to the hungry British until a British officer stopped them in case they had some sinister motive like concealing bottles of alcohol among the leaves to intoxicate and thereby incapacitate the garrison. Even when the inhabitants of the cantonments discovered the talks had failed, they continued to believe that something would be settled. On 30 November Lady Sale wrote, "The politicals are again very mysterious, and deny that any negotiations are going on etc; but letters come in constantly; and we know they are treating with the Ghilzais."

Yet beyond the cantonments' insubstantial walls things were changing. Dost Mohammed's able, charismatic son Akbar Khan had just entered Kabul to scenes of rejoicing and a celebratory storm of jezail fire. With a kingdom to reclaim for his father he was not in a conciliatory mood and would from then on be a major force in directing the Afghans' policy toward the detested army of occupation.

With the air growing ever chillier, conditions in the cantonments were deteriorating. Soldiers on guard duty in exposed positions found their clothes became stiff with frost. Though there was plenty of wood within the cantonments, Elphinstone, who seems to have been confused about many things including how much ammunition and how many stores remained, would not, for fear of scarcity, even permit fires to be lit at night for warmth. The soldiers were to use wood only for cooking their food. With scarcely any forage left, starving horses began eating their own dung, the bark of trees, even gnawing tent pegs and cart wheels. According to Lady Sale, one artillery horse ate another's tail. However, the horses could at least provide food for humans. On 3 December she noted that a committee was being set up "to value all useless horses . . . which are to be destroyed; so there will be plenty of cheap meat, as tattoos [ponies] and camels have for some time past been eaten; even some of the gentlemen ate camel's flesh, particularly the heart, which was esteemed equal to that of the bullock." As always, the camp followers suffered worst and were soon existing on the carcasses of camels that had themselves died of starvation.

All the time the cantonments buzzed with rumors: that an all-out attack was imminent, that Akbar Khan had fallen gravely ill, that the alliance between the chiefs was fracturing beneath the strain of their age-old rivalries, that British reinforcements were advancing on Kabul. Meanwhile, the Afghans had occupied the hills and villages around the cantonments from which the British had on occasion still been able to obtain supplies. However hard they tried, the artillerymen could not dislodge them. With starvation a real and immediate threat and the intentions of the Afghan chiefs unclear, the so-called British councils of war were acrimonious sessions filled with mutual recriminations. Brigadier Shelton was often rolled up in his bedding on the floor, either genuinely asleep or simulating it to annoy Elphinstone, and few decisions were made. Lady Sale thought that "the General, unsettled in his purposes, delegates his power to the Brigadier, and the Brigadier tries to throw off all responsibility on the General's or any body's shoulders except his own."

Every day seemed to bring some further crisis. On 5 December the Afghans destroyed the one and only bridge over the Kabul River. It had been built out of wood by the British to speed communication between the cantonments and the Balla Hissar and was less than a quarter of a mile from the cantonments. Nevertheless, "our imbecile military leaders," as Lawrence called his superiors, did nothing to prevent the Afghans setting fire to it. On the following day a small party of Afghans placed makeshift ladders against the mud-brick walls of the nearby Mohammed Sheriff Fort, now occupied by the British, and clambered inside. Lady Sale thought "a child with a stick" could have repulsed them, but the terrified garrison bolted back to the cantonments, abandoning everything. There exaggerated reports of the attack on the fort caused such panic that sentries from Shelton's all-European regiment—the Forty-fourth—fled their posts. They were replaced by sepoys whose nerves, it seems, were stronger.

Macnaghten complained, "Our troops are behaving like a pack of despicable cowards, and there is no spirit or enterprise left amongst us." Confronted by the disastrous collapse in morale and the ever-dwindling supplies—by this time barely three days' provisions remained—he found it increasingly hard to withstand Elphinstone's pleas to seek a solution through negotiation. On 8 December, clearly still anxious to preserve a paper trail of responsibility for contentious decisions, he asked Elphinstone, "[Will you] be so good as to state, for my information, whether or no I am right in considering it as your opinion that any further attempt to hold out against the enemy would merely have the effect of sacrificing both His Majesty [Shah Shuja] and ourselves, and that the only alternative left is to negotiate for our safe retreat out of the country on the most favourable terms possible."

Elphinstone replied that the envoy understood his views perfectly: "The present situation of the troops here is such, from the want of provisions and the impracticability of procuring more, that no time ought to be lost in entering into negotiations for a safe retreat from the country." As far as Shah Shuja was concerned, Elphinstone insisted that his responsibility extended only to "the honour or welfare" of his troops—in other words, Shah Shuja was the envoy's problem. His note, which ended with a further plea to Macnaghten to "lose no time in entering into negotiations," was also signed by Elphinstone's three senior officers: Brigadiers Shelton and Thomas Antequil and Colonel Robert Chambers, commander of the cavalry.

Macnaghten, though, had not given up and later that day persuaded a reluctant Elphinstone to mount a final sortie to attempt to bring back grain from a village four miles away. Troops were readied, but a few hours later the general abandoned the plan as too risky. Still Macnaghten resisted, writing to his brother-in-law on 9 December, "The military authorities have strongly urged me to capitulate. *This I will not do till the last moment.*" However, his final justification for delaying talks—the hope that reinforcements might yet get through from Kandahar—was destroyed when, on 10 December, a messenger brought news that thick snows were delaying Brigadier Maclaren's advance.

The following day, 11 December, Macnaghten accepted the inevitable. Accompanied by his three staff officers—Captains Lawrence, Mackenzie and Trevor—he rode out to a meeting with Akbar Khan and the other leading chiefs on the plain southeast of the cantonments, taking with him a draft treaty that he had crafted carefully in Persian. After a brief exchange of courtesies, Macnaghten began reading the text of the treaty aloud to the assembled chiefs. It opened by acknowledging that the continued presence of the British army in Kabul in support of Shah Shuja was "displeasing to the great majority of the Afghan nation." It declared that the British government had only sent troops to Afghanistan to secure "the integrity, happiness and welfare of the Afghans" and that the British had no wish to stay if their presence was defeating that object.

Macnaghten then moved on to his detailed proposals. The British garrison in Kabul would withdraw "with all practical expedition" to Peshawar and thence to India. For their part, the chiefs would guarantee that the British should be "unmolested in their journey" and given "all possible assistance in carriage and provisions." At this point Akbar Khan demanded to know why the Afghans should give the British anything when they could depart the very next day. However, other chiefs rebuked him for so rudely interrupting, and Macnaghten continued. His treaty promised that the British garrisons at Jalalabad, Kandahar and Ghazni would also leave Afghanistan and that as soon as they had withdrawn in safety, the British would make immediate arrangements for the return of Dost Mohammed and his family to their homeland. As for Shah Shuja, he could choose whether to stay or to leave with the British. There was to be a general amnesty and eternal friendship between the Afghan and British nations "so much so that the Afghans will contract no alliance with any other foreign power without the consent of the English, for whose assistance they will look in the hour of need." As soon as the treaty was signed, the Afghans were to provide the British with all the provisions they needed for which the British would pay.

After two hours of haggling, the chiefs accepted Macnaghten's main proposals. The British would depart in three days, and meanwhile the Afghans would send into the cantonments everything the British needed. In addition, an exchange of hostages was agreed: The British would surrender Captain Trevor in return for an Afghan chief. As Macnaghten and his party rode the one mile back to the cantonments, a random bullet whizzed over their heads.

Macnaghten had done what Elphinstone wanted. Although he knew it was capitulation, that chilly day he must have believed that at least he had saved the lives of the 4,500 British troops, both European and Indian, and 12,000 camp followers in Kabul. In a long and never completed note justifying his actions he wrote: "The whole country . . . had risen in rebellion; our communications on all sides were cut off . . . We had been fighting forty days against very superior numbers, under most disadvantageous circumstances, with a deplorable loss of valuable lives, and in a day or two we must have perished from hunger, to say nothing of the advanced season of the year and the extreme cold . . . I had been repeatedly apprised by the military authorities that nothing could be done with our troops . . . The terms I secured were the best obtainable, and the destruction of fifteen thousand human beings [sic] would little have benefited our country, whilst the government would have been almost compelled to avenge our fate at whatever cost. We shall part with the Afghans as friends, and I feel satisfied that any government which may be established hereafter will always be disposed to cultivate a good understanding with us."

The next day the chiefs approached Shah Shuja with a proposition: He could remain as king provided he gave several of his daughters as wives to the leading chiefs and dispensed with some of the cumbersome ceremonials that they so much resented but that he so enjoyed. Shah Shuja, after some thought, accepted. However, Macnaghten's *couleur de rose* confidence that all would be well was challenged almost at once when, on the "exceedingly dark and freezingly cold" evening of 13 December, the six hundred British troops who still remained in the Balla Hissar departed for the cantonments to prepare for what they believed would be their imminent departure from Kabul. As the tail of the British column was passing through the gates of the citadel, some of Akbar Khan's men tried to rush through them. Shah Shuja's own soldiers only closed the gates against them with difficulty and in so doing stranded a number of British troops inside, as well as some much needed supplies of wheat and flour intended for the cantonments.

Outside the citadel, British soldiers were caught in the crossfire. Akbar Khan, who had promised to provide a safe escort for them, suddenly announced that with the surrounding area teeming with bandits, he could not guarantee their safety. They must halt for the night while he negotiated their safe passage with the local chiefs. Several officers walked up to the gates of the Balla Hissar to demand that the troops be allowed to reenter, but Shah Shuja's soldiers immediately fired on them. When they demanded to know on whose authority they were being thus attacked, the answer came that the king had ordered the gates to be held whatever the cost.

The troops had no option but to bed down beneath the walls of the citadel without food, fuel or tents on ground that was white with hoarfrost. When morning finally came, the numb and frozen men at last set out for the cantonments. Although Akbar Khan kept up some semblance of honoring his promise to protect the troops, threatening to cut down any man who molested them, Afghans still attacked the rear of the column.

Lieutenant Eyre recorded the fate of "a poor sick European artillery-man who, for want of a more suitable conveyance, had been lashed to the gun, [but] was unmercifully butchered." However, by ten A.M., the starving and exhausted force finally reached the cantonments. By then Shah Shuja, terrified by Akbar Khan's assault on the Balla Hissar, had changed his mind about the wisdom of accepting the chiefs' offer.

As yet, Akbar Khan and the other Afghan leaders had produced none of the promised supplies. When the British protested that this was delaying their preparations for departure, they claimed it was not their fault—that every time they collected food and animals to bring to the cantonments, the uncontrollable *ghazis* stole them. Lady Sale, sharper witted than many of her male colleagues, understood what was behind the shrugging off of responsibility: "Our allies, as they are now called, will be very magnanimous if they let us escape, now that they have fairly got us in their net."

The day stipulated in the treaty for the British departure passed without any sign of the agreed-upon provisions. Macnaghten sought another meeting with the chiefs at which he insisted they honor their commitments. Their response was that the British must first demonstrate their own good faith by handing over any forts they still occupied in the vicinity of the cantonments. Macnaghten knew that to do so would leave the cantonments even more exposed and vulnerable. He urged Elphinstone instead to take advantage of the extra troops recently arrived from the Balla Hissar to mount an attack on the city. The general insisted that such an action could only end in disaster. And so on 16 December the forts were surrendered as a goodwill gesture to the supposed "allies" of the British. Lawrence watched with tears in his eyes as "these strongholds, the last prop of our tottering power in Kabul, which it had cost us so much blood to seize and defend," were surrendered. By four o'clock the new occupants were sitting on the walls of one fort "from which every point of cantonment was visible" and passing "remarks and jokes on the conduct of those within." Four more officers were handed over as hostages, and a new date—22 December—was fixed for the British departure.

On 18 December thick snow began to fall in Kabul, adding to the misery of life within the cantonments. Eyre called it "a new enemy . . . which we were destined to find even more formidable than an army of rebels." The following day, Macnaghten received confirmation that Brigadier Maclaren had indeed given up his attempt to get through the snow-filled passes to Kabul and was returning to Kandahar. Meanwhile, in a further tightening of the screw, the Afghan chiefs declared that they would not permit the British to leave Kabul until Macnaghten and Elphinstone had ordered the other British garrisons in the country—at Kandahar, Jalalabad and Ghazni—to retreat to India as well. With few options left, the general and the envoy did as they were told.

At this low point—a time when Lady Sale was confiding to her journal, "We have very little hope of saving our lives"—Macnaghten decided on one final attempt to salvage the situation by manipulating the shifting loyalties and ingrained rivalries of the Afghans. For this delicate task he turned again to Mohan Lal, still living concealed in the Kizzilbashi quarter of the city, to try and lure the Kizzilbashis and the Ghilzais to the British cause. On 20 December he wrote to Lal, "You can tell the Ghilzais and Khan Shirin [chief of the Kizzilbashis] that after they have declared for his Majesty [Shah Shuja] and us and sent in 100 *kurwars* of grain to cantonments, I shall be glad to give them a bond for five lakhs of rupees." The following day, he wrote even more explicitly: "If any portion of the Afghans wish our troops to remain in the country, I shall think myself at liberty to break the engagement which I have made [i.e., with Akbar Khan] to go away, which engagement was made believing it to be in accordance with the wishes of the Afghan nation. If the Ghilzais and Kizzilbashis wish us to stay, let them declare so openly in the course of tomorrow."

Leaving Mohan Lal to try to detach the Ghilzai and Kizzilbashi leaders, Macnaghten continued his ever more humiliating exchanges with Akbar Khan. As the envoy well knew, time was not on his side. Akbar Khan and his supporters were making increasingly aggressive demands, even asking for Brigadier Shelton as a hostage. A few days earlier they had also asked for all the married men and their families to be handed over as surety for Dost Mohammed's safe return. Lady Sale was relieved to learn that Macnaghten had refused to give up any woman. Shelton was also extremely unwilling to be surrendered, so two lieutenants—Conolly and Airey—were given in his place. Macnaghten also agreed under pressure to hand over some of the British military stores and in a bid to mollify

Akbar Khan, even made him a gift of his own carriage and horses. In the increasingly menacing atmosphere and with no sign of the Ghilzais and Kizzilbashis responding to Mohan Lal's overtures, Macnaghten got cold feet about his intriguing, writing anxiously to Lal that he must refuse any presents of grain: "The sending [of] grain to us just now would do more harm than good to our cause; and it would lead the Barakzais to suppose that I am intriguing with a view of breaking my agreement"—as, indeed, he was.

Macnaghten was right to be cautious in a place where little remained secret for long—Lady Sale was convinced that the cantonments teemed with spies. Akbar Khan had indeed learned of the envoy's "intriguing" and duly set a trap for him. On 22 December—the new day set for the British to depart from Kabul—he offered Macnaghten a secret deal. His envoy was Captain "Gentleman Jim" Skinner—a British officer so nicknamed for his charm and courteous manners. Trapped in the city at the start of the insurrection, Skinner had at first been protected by friends but later had fallen into the hands of Akbar Khan, who had treated him well. Skinner was accompanied to the meeting by two Afghans—one a merchant and former acquaintance of Alexander Burnes who in better times had sold camels to the British army, and the other a first cousin of Akbar Khan's. Macnaghten and Skinner dined together while the Afghans waited in another room. During the meal, according to Captain Mackenzie, who was present, Skinner hinted that he and his companions were bearers of a "most portentous" message and that he himself "felt as if laden with combustibles." Mackenzie noticed how "the Envoy's eye glanced eagerly towards Skinner with an expression of hope . . . like a drowning man clutching at straws."

As soon as the envoy and Skinner rejoined the Afghans and the four were alone, Akbar Khan's cousin revealed the contents of the "portentous" message. Akbar Khan proposed that the next day he and the Ghilzais should unite with the British troops to mount a joint attack on the Mahmud Khan Fort, which commanded the road between the cantonments and the Balla Hissar, and to seize Amenoolah Khan, the Barakzai chief instrumental in the murder of Alexander Burnes. Akbar Khan even offered, in return for payment, to send Macnaghten Amenoolah's head. Though Shah Shuja could remain as king, he himself was to be appointed vizier and receive a lump sum of 3 million rupees as well as a handsome lifelong stipend. As for the British, they could remain until the following spring when, as the snows cleared from the passes, they could depart with honor as if of their own accord. Finally Akbar Khan asked that Macnaghten keep his offer secret, lest news of it reach Amenoolah Khan. Macnaghten eagerly took what one officer called "the gilded bait." Though balking at the John the Baptist–like delivery to him of Ameenolah's head, he accepted everything else, then naively penned and signed a document in Persian confirming it. He also promised to meet Akbar Khan the following day to ratify this in person.

At first, Macnaghten told no one—not even his three staff officers Mackenzie, Trevor, whom the Afghans had released, and Lawrence— what he had done. Mackenzie later wrote, "It seemed as if he feared that we might insist on the impracticability of the plan which he must have studiously concealed from himself." Early the following day, Mohan Lal learned from one of his informants that Akbar Khan had "laid a deep scheme to entrap the Envoy" and was even contemplating shooting him with the handsome brace of double-barreled pistols the envoy had just given him. Mohan Lal wrote at once to Macnaghten imploring him not to meet the Afghan chief outside the cantonments. On reading Lal's note, the envoy is said to have paled. However, it did not cause him to reconsider.

Lal's warning was, in fact, only the first of many. A little later that morning, when Macnaghten finally told Mackenzie of his secret pact with Akbar Khan, the captain's immediate response was that it must be a trick, to which Macnaghten snapped back, "A Plot! Let me alone for that, trust me for that!" Elphinstone, too, was also deeply skeptical when Macnaghten told him what he had agreed. He asked what part the other Barakzai leaders, who had been involved in the previous negotiations, had played in these, to which Macnaghten replied that they were "not in the plot." Macnaghten's choice of language revealed more clearly than anything else the dangerous path he had chosen. Elphinstone suggested that Akbar Khan could well be playing a double game himself, but Macnaghten dismissed his fears and requested that he have two regiments and two guns standing by ready to capture the Mahmud Khan Fort. When Elphinstone objected that the troops were not to be relied on and he still suspected treachery, Macnaghten turned impatiently away, saying, "Leave it all to me—I understand these things better than you."

The usually hesitant Elphinstone continued to be so worried that he sat down and wrote a letter to Macnaghten, again dwelling on the risks and asking what guarantees the envoy had received for the truth of what he had been told. He even made one last attempt to intervene in person. Just as Macnaghten was preparing to leave the cantonments, he came to find him and again expressed his misgivings. Lawrence heard Macnaghten reply, "If you will at once march out the troops and meet the enemy, I will accompany you, and I am sure we shall beat them; as regards these negotiations, I have no faith in them," to which Elphinstone responded, with a shake of his elderly head, "Macnaghten, I can't; the troops are not to be depended on."

And so at midday on 23 December, immaculate in gray trousers, black frock coat and top hat, the bespectacled Macnaghten rode out of the cantonments accompanied by Captains Lawrence, Trevor and Mackenzie in their scarlet uniforms and tall black shakos to his appointed meeting place with Akbar Khan about six hundred yards east of the cantonments near the banks of the Kabul River. He had an escort of only ten horsemen since the much larger one he had requested was not ready and he chose not to wait. Macnaghten was by this point mentally and physically exhausted. When Lawrence again asked whether there was a risk of betrayal, he wearily replied: "Of course there is; but what can I do? The General has declared his inability to fight, we have no prospect of aid from any quarter, the enemy are only playing with us . . . and I have no confidence whatever in them. The life I have led for the last six weeks, you, Lawrence, know well; and rather than be disgraced and live it over again, I would risk a hundred deaths; success will save our honour, and more than make up for all risks." Like a desperate gambler, he was prepared to stake all on one throw of the dice.

Suddenly Macnaghten remembered an Arab mare, belonging to a British captain, that Akbar Khan had admired and that he had subsequently purchased from the officer so he could present it to the chief as a goodwill gesture, and sent Mackenzie back to fetch it. By the time he returned, Macnaghten and the rest had already reached the riverbank. Akbar Khan and a large group of beturbaned Afghans in sheepskin

coats—Amenoolah's brother among them, which should have been a warning in itself—were waiting. After the usual salutations of "*Salaam Aleikum*"
(Peace be with you), Macnaghten presented the mare to Akbar Khan,
who also thanked him for his recent gift of pistols, which—he pointed
out—he was wearing. He suggested to Macnaghten that they dismount
and take their ease on some horse blankets that his men had spread on
the far side of a hillock sloping down to the river where the snow was less
thick. To Mackenzie, the atmosphere was sinister: "Men talk of presenti-
ment; I suppose it was something of the kind which came over me, for I
could scarcely prevail upon myself to quit my horse." However, whatever
his own fears and feelings, Macnaghten dismounted, scrambled up the
slope and reclined on a blanket, Trevor and Mackenzie beside him. Lawrence remained standing behind him until, at the chiefs' insistence to be
seated, he knelt on one knee close behind Macnaghten, ready to spring up
if necessary.

      With the other chiefs clustering close around so that they could hear,
Akbar Khan asked Macnaghten whether he was still prepared to abide by
what he had agreed the preceding night, to which Macnaghten replied,
"Why not!" Mackenzie, Lawrence and Trevor meanwhile found themselves being engaged in conversation by various Afghans chatting to them
of this and that. As Mackenzie later wrote, one of them was an old acquaintance who "betrayed much anxiety as to where my pistols were, and
why I did not carry them on my person." Alarmed by the "unusually large
numbers of armed men" starting to crowd around, Lawrence suggested to
Macnaghten that as the conference was supposed to be a secret one, they
should be told to pull back. Macnaghten complained to Akbar Khan, who
replied, "Oh, we are all in the same boat, and Lawrence Sahib need not
be the least alarmed."

      Suddenly Macnaghten and the three officers found themselves
grabbed from behind and their arms pinioned as Akbar Khan yelled, "*Bigir! Bigir!*" (Seize! Seize!). Glancing wildly about him, Mackenzie saw
Akbar Khan "grasp the Envoy's left hand, with an expression on his face
of the most diabolical ferocity," while another chief grabbed his right
hand. Then "they dragged him in a stooping posture down the hillock,
the only words I heard poor Sir William utter being, '*Az barai khuda!*'—
('For God's sake!'). I saw his face, however, and it was full of horror and

astonishment." Mackenzie himself was soon surrounded by "a circle of *ghazis* with drawn swords and cocked jezails," while the acquaintance with whom he had just been conversing was holding a pistol to his temple. Together with Trevor and Lawrence, he was dragged by his captors through a mass of hostile tribesmen shouting "Kill the Kafir[s]" and "Why spare the accursed!" and demanding that they be given up as *koorban*—a sacrifice.

The three officers were bundled onto horses behind riders who forced their way through crowds of Afghans who, according to Lawrence, were "armed to the teeth." They wheeled their mounts on the frozen snowy ground that was "slippery as glass" to try and dodge the saber thrusts and blows from the butts of jezails aimed at their prisoners. Trevor, who had brought his young and numerous family to safety in the cantonments at the start of the insurrection, was on this occasion not so fortunate. The horse carrying him away stumbled, and he fell, to be at once cut to pieces by a man exclaiming, "*Suggee*, Trevor" (Die, dog Trevor). (Trevor had been especially detested by some Afghans for his role in reforming the levying of cavalry.) Mackenzie and Lawrence, however, got away thanks to the skill of their abductors. Mackenzie described how at one point his captor unwound his turban—"the last appeal a Musalman [Muslim] can make"—to beg the attackers to spare his captive's life. Meanwhile, the small British escort, seeing what was happening, had bolted back to the cantonments. Only one man—Rajput Ram Singh—rushed forward sword in hand but was cut to pieces.

Lawrence and Mackenzie were taken to the Mahmud Khan Fort, where, according to Mackenzie, Akbar Khan had also arrived and was "receiving the gratitude of the multitude." Suddenly a *ghazi* rushed at Mackenzie and tried to strangle him. Akbar Khan drove the man off with his sword but then turned to Mackenzie to sneer "in a tone of triumphant derision, '*Shuma mulk-i-ma me-girid! (You'll* seize my country, will you!).'"

CHAPTER FOURTEEN

Man will not help us—God only can.
—LIEUTENANT JOHN STURT, ON THE EVE OF DEPARTURE,
5 JANUARY 1842

THOSE WATCHING FROM the ramparts of the cantonments could see that the supposed peace conference—just over a quarter of a mile away—had descended into tumult. Nevertheless, as Lawrence wrote, "Not a man was despatched to ascertain the exact truth. Nor a party sent out to reconnoitre; no sortie made, nor even a gun fired, though bodies of the enemy's horse and foot were seen hurrying from the place of conference . . . and several officers declared they could see distinctly through their field-glasses two bodies lying on the ground." Another officer, Lieutenant Warren, even claimed to have seen Macnaghten fall to the ground and Afghans "hacking at his body." However, the usually pessimistic, fatalistic Elphinstone preferred to believe the account of Macnaghten's fleeing escort, who, doubtless wishing to escape censure for deserting him, insisted that he and his companions had been seized, bound and carried off into the city. Elphinstone dispatched his adjutant general, Captain Grant, to assure the commanding officer of each regiment that though *ghazis* had disrupted the conference, the envoy and his colleagues were safe in the city and would soon return.

But, as the hours passed and there was no firm news of Macnaghten, few in the cantonments doubted that something terrible had occurred. Despite the pleas of many junior officers for an immediate attack on the city, all Elphinstone did was to ensure that "the garrison was got ready and remained under arms all day," as he himself wrote. He also ordered the arrest of any high-ranking Afghans who had come into the cantonments to trade. The order caused chaos with Afghans scrambling over the icy ground to get away. By evening a great noise rose from the city, which sepoy Sita Ram likened to "the noise of the wind before a storm." It was the *ghazis* readying themselves to resist the attack they thought the British would surely mount to avenge Macnaghten's murder. Elphinstone, however, interpreted the yelling as a warning that the Afghans themselves were about to attack and ordered his troops to man the defenses. No assault came, and the night passed uneasily as rumor and counter-rumor flew around the cantonments.

Meanwhile Lawrence and the badly bruised Mackenzie had been subjected to a terrifying ordeal since their capture and incarceration in a dungeon in the Mahmud Khan Fort. As Lawrence later recalled, "[We] sat down together in a corner of the room, but the mob on the outside soon discovered us, and coming up to the small grated window, commenced cursing us and spitting at us through the bars, calling on the soldiers who were guarding us to deliver us up to them as a sacrifice. A severed human hand, clearly that of a European, was then held up for us to look at, while they shrieked out, 'Your own will soon be in a similar plight.' A blunderbuss was then passed through the bars, and was just about being fired, when one of our guard struck it up. Towards nightfall the crowd of bloodthirsty wretches gradually melted away."

Not long after, the captives were visited by several chiefs, "who spoke kindly to us, assuring us no harm would befall us" and who asserted that Macnaghten and Trevor were safe in the city. The mood changed with the arrival of Amenoolah Khan, who threatened the two officers "with instant death, saying: 'We'll blow you from guns; any death will be too good for you.'" However, he eventually departed, and toward nightfall Lawrence and Mackenzie's jailors, having "in a gentlemanly manner" relieved them of their watches and rings, gave them sheepskin cloaks to keep out the cold and shared their food with them, after which they lay down. Mentally and physically exhausted, they soon fell sound asleep, but just after midnight they were roused and taken into the city to Akbar Khan's house through streets "as silent and deserted as a city of the dead."

Akbar Khan himself was in bed. He received them courteously, assuring them that Macnaghten and Trevor were both well, though Mackenzie noticed "a constraint in his manner." They were then shown into another room, where Captain Skinner was being held, and at last received confirmation of Macnaghten's fate. Lawrence rushed forward to seize Skinner's hands. "But being startled by the gravity of his looks," Lawrence recounted, "I asked him 'what was the matter?' 'Matter!', he replied, 'Don't you know?' 'No!' said I: 'nothing more than that we have been lucky enough to escape with our lives, and are prisoners.' 'The Envoy is dead,' said Skinner, slowly and solemnly. 'I saw his head brought into this very courtyard.'" He also told Lawrence and Mackenzie that the envoy's mutilated body had been "dragged through the city, and his head stuck up for all to gaze upon in the Char Chowk [Grand Bazaar], the most frequented and open part of Kabul."

Skinner was convinced that Akbar Khan himself had killed Macnaghten using one of the pistols the envoy had given him and that had previously been Lawrence's. Though Akbar Khan never formally admitted his guilt and even Lawrence later had doubts, he likely was the instigator of Macnaghten's death. Mohan Lal reported that he later heard Akbar Khan privately boasting "that he was the assassin of the Envoy" and also claimed that Akbar Khan had confessed his guilt in a letter. However, whether it had always been his intention to kill rather than capture the envoy, and whether he killed him by accident or perhaps in the grip of what Lieutenant Eyre called his "tiger passions," is less certain. An account by Akbar Khan's cousin in a letter that later fell into British hands rings true: "The Sirdar [Akbar Khan] at last said to the Envoy; 'Come, I must take you to the Nawab's.' The Envoy was alarmed and rose up. Mohammed Akbar seized him by the hands saying: 'I cannot allow you to return to cantonments.' The Sirdar wished to carry him off alive, but was unable; then he drew a double-barrelled pistol from his belt, and discharged both barrels at the Envoy, after which he struck him two or three blows with his sword, and the Envoy was thus killed on the spot."

The day after Macnaghten's death, the Afghan chiefs sought to revive negotiations with the British. Akbar Khan, Amenoolah Khan and other leaders dispatched a letter to the cantonments together with a draft treaty stating the terms on which they would allow the British army safe conduct to Peshawar. The British were immediately to quit Kabul, Kandahar, Ghazni and Jalalabad, while Dost Mohammed and his family were to be allowed to return to Afghanistan. Shah Shuja could stay or go as he chose. There was also to be a further exchange of hostages, and the British were to pay the chiefs large sums as the price for being allowed to travel unmolested through the passes.

Before dispatching the draft treaty, the chiefs had shown it to some of the British officers they were holding. Disguised in Afghan robes for their safety—a device that fooled no one so that their escort had to beat off a "savage mob who yelled and screamed on all sides" demanding their blood—Mackenzie and Lawrence had been smuggled from Akbar Khan's house to that of Nawab Zaman Khan, where they had found not only a gathering of the chiefs but also Captains Conolly and Airey, given up as hostages a few days earlier. Conolly confirmed Skinner's report that Macnaghten's body was dangling for all to see in the Grand Bazaar, adding that Trevor's corpse was also on display.

Led by Akbar Khan, the chiefs vehemently accused the captives "of treachery and everything that was bad," insisting that the overtures they had made to Macnaghten had only been a test of his good faith—a test he had failed. Discussion then moved to the treaty. The chiefs told their captives they "would now grant us no terms save on the surrender of the whole of the married families as hostages, all the guns, ammunition and treasure." The officers attempted to persuade the chiefs to modify their demands and in particular to convince them that to surrender their women would be "utterly abhorrent to our feelings and at variance with our customs." They succeeded in the latter, and, for the moment at least, that demand was removed. Lawrence was also allowed to write a short letter to Lady Sale informing her of the deaths of Macnaghten and Trevor and enclosing another from Conolly to Lady Macnaghten. Lawrence and Mackenzie were then taken back to Akbar Khan's house.

THE ARRIVAL OF these letters on Christmas Eve—the day that the chiefs sent in the new draft treaty—finally convinced Elphinstone that the envoy was dead. He turned to Eldred Pottinger, still suffering from the wounds he had received during his flight from Charikar. In Pottinger's own words, "[I was] hauled out of my sick room and obliged to negotiate for the safety of a parcel of fools who were doing all they could to ensure their destruction" and "would not hear my advice." As he soon discovered, there was little to negotiate. Though Pottinger and others urged an immediate assault on Kabul, Elphinstone and his senior officers, including Brigadiers Shelton and Antequil, were convinced there was no alternative but to accept the humiliating terms set out in the treaty.

Emboldened by this supine acquiescence, the chiefs at once increased their demands, this time going well beyond the terms agreed previously with Macnaghten. All the money in the British treasury was to be turned over to them. The British were to surrender most of their artillery and all their spare muskets. In addition, the chiefs returned to their demand that all the senior married men with their women and children should remain as hostages until Dost Mohammed and the other Afghan prisoners held by the British arrived safely in Kabul. Once again, Elphinstone's inclination was to agree to everything that was asked. He even contemplated handing over female hostages, offering two thousand rupees a month to any man who would surrender his wife. According to Lady Sale, Captain Anderson's response was that "he would rather put a pistol to his wife's head and shoot her," while her own son-in-law, Lieutenant Sturt, declared that she and his wife would "only be taken at the point of the bayonet." Only Lieutenant Eyre offered himself, his wife and child as hostages "if it was to be productive of great good." Faced by such resistance, Elphinstone told the chiefs he could never consent to such a measure.

On 26 December messengers working for the British brought letters into the cantonments addressed to Macnaghten from political officers at Jalalabad and Peshawar. They reported that reinforcements were on their way from India. Pottinger seized on this news to try once more to convince Elphinstone to resist the Afghan demands. He also argued that the Afghan chiefs were disunited and that Shah Shuja's position was strengthening. Elphinstone was sufficiently swayed to summon a council of war, at which Pottinger pleaded with the military command not to negotiate with the enemy. They had no right, he said, to bind the hands of the British government by committing it to withdrawing from Afghanistan or to order Sale in Jalalabad and Nott in Kandahar to abandon their posts. He pointed out that Nott had been designated commander in chief—a fact that his inability to get to Kabul did not alter—so that Elphinstone had no authority over him anyway. Neither, Pottinger insisted, did they have any right to expend huge sums of public money to buy their own safety. Furthermore, the enemy was clearly not to be trusted and would probably betray them. The only sensible—and honorable—courses were either to occupy the Balla Hissar and attempt to hold out there or to abandon their baggage, fight their way over ninety miles to Jalalabad and there await the promised reinforcements from India.

Elphinstone was almost convinced by Pottinger's arguments, but Shelton was not. He insisted that neither of Pottinger's plans was practical and that the safety of the British force was worth paying any sum of money for. The other senior officers agreed, and Elphinstone ordered Pottinger to resume negotiations with the chiefs to conclude the treaty, despite his view that they would thereby "be dishonoured and disgraced and the stigma of cowardice fixed on us ever." Lady Sale was similarly depressed that the only options the military leaders would contemplate were "a disgraceful treaty or a disastrous retreat."

On 29 December a haggard Captain Lawrence arrived in the cantonments, disguised as an Afghan with a floppy turban "leaving only an eye exposed" and in Lady Sale's view looking "ten years older from anxiety." Pottinger had secured his release by insisting that the bills to be drawn on the government of India to enable the payment of the huge sums demanded by the chiefs must be signed by Lawrence as Macnaghten's secretary. Lawrence got down to work but took care to stipulate that the bills could be cashed "only on the presentation of certificates from our political agent at Peshawar *of the safe arrival there of our troops.*"

The Afghans continued to pressure the British, demanding the immediate surrender of their artillery with the exception of the few pieces they were to be allowed to keep. Pottinger, still hoping something might occur to avoid capitulation, procrastinated, handing over the guns two by two on successive days. However, there was little he could do. He and other officers and men could only watch as muskets, ammunition and wagons were also surrendered to the Afghans, together with fresh hostages. Captains Walsh, Drummond, Warburton and Webb joined the other British officers in captivity, though on their arrival in Kabul Captains Skinner and Mackenzie were allowed to return to the cantonments. Warburton must have been worrying about his pregnant Afghan wife, a cousin of Akbar Khan, whom he had not seen since Burnes's murder on 2 November. That day he had been in the cantonments when the mob besieged his house, where his wife was, and set it alight, and he had little way of knowing where she was or even whether she was still alive.

The wounded and the sick—many of the latter had frostbitten toes, fingers, noses and cheeks, for which, according to Colin Mackenzie, the harassed army doctors found the traditional Afghan remedy of a cold poultice of cow dung "most efficacious"—and two doctors to care for them were sent into captivity in the city on 29 and 30 December because there was insufficient transport to take them on the retreat. On New Year's Day 1842, after Elphinstone had insisted Pottinger write to Sale ordering him to withdraw from Jalalabad, the ratified treaty bearing the seals of eighteen chiefs finally arrived in the cantonments. The text contained everything the Afghans had demanded except the surrender of British families. In return they guaranteed the British forces safe passage out of their country. Mackenzie described how a miserable Pottinger "signed the treaty in soldierly obedience, knowing full well that he would be held responsible for that which was the work of others."

The first article of the treaty demanded "that the British troops shall speedily quit the territories of Afghanistan and march to India, and shall not return; and twenty-four hours after receiving the carriage-cattle [camels and ponies] the army shall start." In fact the British had been making efforts to prepare for what would be a ninety-mile trek in subzero temperatures through snow that already lay at least a foot deep around Kabul and would be far deeper in the passes. *Ghazis* milled about outside, harassing merchants and sometimes attempting to rush the cantonment gates. Captain Johnson captured the daily indignities and obstacles in his diary: "Very busy, buying camels and yaboos [ponies] . . . The Ghazis still infest our gates and insult us in every possible way—stop our supplies coming in from the town and abuse and ill-treat those who bring them. No notice taken by our military leader." He complained that "the chiefs say they cannot control their men, and that if their people misbehave themselves at our gates, or around our walls, we must fire upon them. No orders, however, given by General Elphinstone to punish our insulting foe, who naturally attribute our forbearance to dastardly cowardice."

As the British forces struggled to make their preparations while await-ing the provisions promised by the chiefs, warnings flooded in just as they had before the murders of Burnes and Macnaghten. Johnson wrote: "Sev-eral of my native friends from the city come daily to see me. And all agree, without one dissenting voice, that we have brought the whole of our misfor-tunes upon ourselves, through the apathy and imbecility displayed at the commencement of the outbreak. They also tell me that our safety on the retreat depends solely on ourselves—that no dependence is to be placed on the promises of any of the chiefs, and more especially Mohammed Akbar Khan. Every one of them will now . . . do his utmost to destroy us." Mohan Lal, from his hiding place in the city, was also warning that the chiefs were not to be trusted and that the British would be attacked as soon as they left the cantonments. Lady Sale noted a report "that the chiefs do not mean to keep faith: and that it is their intention to get all our women into their pos-session; and to kill every man except one, who is to have his hands and legs cut off, and is to be placed with a letter *in terrorem* at the entrance of the Khyber passes, to deter all Feringhees from entering the country again." A further warning stated that Akbar Khan "would annihilate the whole army, except one man, who should reach Jalalabad to tell the tale."

As the first days of January passed in a mood of bleak foreboding, conditions in the bitterly cold cantonments were miserable. Every night the soldiers and civilians expected orders to march the next day, but they did not come. Whether for genuine practical reasons or because they saw advantages in further weakening the British by delaying their retreat, the chiefs kept asserting that they had neither completed the arrangements necessary to ensure the safety of the retreating British force nor gathered sufficient provisions. Shah Shuja, who had already warned Lawrence that the chiefs were not to be trusted, sent a messenger to the cantonments, to try to persuade Lady Macnaghten on no account to ride on the retreat but to seek sanctuary "with as many ladies as would accompany her" in the Balla Hissar. When Pottinger learned of this, he persuaded Lawrence to join him in making one final attempt to convince Elphinstone that, on moving out of the cantonments, the entire force should march at once for the protection of the Balla Hissar, where the king would be bound to ad-mit them. Elphinstone's response was "Can you guarantee us supplies?" When the officers said they could not although they were "pretty sure of sufficient supplies," Elphinstone replied, "No, we retreat!"

On the evening of 5 January, although the chiefs had still not sent either the promised supplies or strong escort to protect the retreating column from the *ghazis*, Elphinstone decided, against the advice of Pottinger and others, to wait no longer. He ordered every fighting man to carry three days' provisions in his rucksack and for the entire force to be ready to march at daybreak. He also ordered Sturt to cut an opening through the eastern ramparts of the cantonments to provide an additional exit point for the troops and camp followers. That night, Sturt wrote a letter to his father-in-law, Brigadier Sale, in which he revealed his apprehension about the coming retreat: "We shall have a fight—but courage! Man will not help us—God only can."

With his mind set firmly on departure, Elphinstone seems to have had little regard for the fate of Shah Shuja, who, realizing that the British were about to abandon him, wrote plaintively to Brigadier Antequil, the commander of his forces, asking "if it were well to forsake him in the hour of need." The British could salve their consciences by arguing that the treaty provided for Shah Shuja to depart with them if he wished, but sensibly enough the king had no intention of leaving the relative safety of the Balla Hissar to risk himself in the passes. With his protectors deaf to his appeals and on the point of marching, his best, indeed only, hope for the moment was to seek an accommodation with the chiefs and hope they would observe it. Lady Sale had no sympathy for him, writing coldly of what she suspected would be his fate if he stayed: "The Afghans do not wish to put him to death, but only to deprive him of sight."

On that final night in Kabul, Lady Sale, whose last few meals had been cooked "with the wood of a mahogany dining-table" as furniture was broken up for firewood, was inspecting a selection of books her son-in-law hoped to save by sending them to a friend in the city. She picked up a volume by the Scottish poet Thomas Campbell, by chance opening it at a poem whose words were to haunt her "day and night." It was Campbell's "Hohenlinden," of which the final verse read:

> *Few, few shall part where many meet.*
> *The snow shall be their winding sheet;*
> *And every turf beneath their feet*
> *Shall be a soldier's sepulchre.*

CHAPTER FIFTEEN

The spectacle then presented by that waving sea of animated beings, the majority of whom a few fleeting hours would transform
into a line of lifeless carcasses to guide the future traveller on his
way, can never be forgotten.

—LIEUTENANT VINCENT EYRE, 8 JANUARY 1842

THOUGH THE FIRST bugle sounded at five A.M., not until around
nine A.M. on the bright, frosty morning of Thursday, 6 January did the
first British troops leave the cantonments to begin their long-anticipated
retreat. Though Shelton had wanted all the baggage loaded and prepared
by moonrise, it was not ready until eight A.M., while Elphinstone—still
vainly hoping for the promised Afghan escort—declined to order the retreat to begin until pressed by Captain Mackenzie.

Brigadier Antequil commanded the vanguard, which was followed
by the main column including the baggage train under Brigadier Shelton,
and then the rear guard. The only artillery the Afghans had agreed to allow the British to take—six horse artillery guns and three mule-borne
mountain guns—were divided between the three groups. The retreating
force comprised 4,500 fighting men, of whom 690 were European, 2,840
sepoy infantry and 970 sepoy cavalry. They were accompanied by 12,000
camp followers, who, Lieutenant Eyre wrote, "proved from the very first
mile a serious clog upon our movements, and . . . the main cause of our
subsequent misfortunes."

Compared to the jaunty optimism with which the Army of the Indus had arrived in Kabul nearly two and a half years earlier, Captain Lawrence saw around him "a crouching, drooping, dispirited army." Ahead lay a ninety-mile journey through a frozen landscape. Their route—difficult to negotiate even in summer—lay eastward through Begramee to Boothak, then southward through the high Khoord Kabul Pass, then eastward again to Tezeen and through the Jugdulluk Pass to Gandamack and eventually Jalalabad and safety.

Captain Lawrence had asked for and been given the responsibility of protecting the British women and children who were traveling toward the front of the main column, regarded as the safest place. Most of these women—some pregnant, some ill, some even traveling in their nightgowns—were to be carried in palanquins. However, Lady Sale and her daughter Alexandrina Sturt were riding on horseback. An Afghan well-wisher had advised them to wear turbans and common sheepskin coats (*poshteens*) over their clothes and to keep away from the main group of ladies, who, he warned, were likely to be attacked. Therefore that morning they were riding with some cavalrymen. Leaving the cantonments, Lady Sale was relieved that few Afghans had gathered to witness their departure and that those who had made no move to molest the column as it began picking its way over snowy ground so dazzling white it hurt the eyes. The cold was bitter and the landscape, in Lady Sale's words, "a swamp encrusted with ice." Lawrence pitied "the poor native soldiers and camp followers, walking up to their knees in snow and slush."

The eyewitness accounts of those who survived often conflict in the details. Survivors were in different places at different times. None could see the length of the straggling column. However, all the accounts convey the confusion and uncertainty at the start of the retreat and the terror and despair at its end. They also reveal their authors' frustrations at foolish decisions which contributed to the disaster, several made in the very first hours.

Elphinstone had planned that his retreating force should clear the wild Khoord Kabul Pass on the first day—a journey of fifteen miles. Speed was therefore imperative. However, when the retreat was just under way, Nawab Zaman Khan—the figurehead king appointed by the insurgents until Dost Mohammed's return—sent a message warning the British to defer their departure until there was an escort to protect them. Elphinstone, still racked by indecision, ordered Shelton to halt. This was too much for Captain Mackenzie, who decided that, with half the troops already out of the cantonments, it would be disastrous to stop the retreat. Therefore he countermanded the order. With the general's despairing cry of "Mackenzie, don't!—don't do it!" as the only response to his insubordination fading behind him, he galloped off to tell Shelton to resume the march.

In addition to Elphinstone's vacillation, there were practical obstacles to a swift and orderly departure. Barely half a mile from the cantonments the great, heaving mass of retreating people and animals—the baggage train included two thousand camels—came to a standstill because the bridge that Elphinstone had ordered to be built across the Kabul River was not ready. Sturt had repeatedly argued that the river—although deep in some places but just eight feet wide—was easily fordable, but his superiors had decided a bridge was needed. Sturt and his sappers had begun work in the early hours, laboring up to their hips in freezing water to clear boulders from the riverbed so they could construct a bridge out of gun carriages with doors and planks laid over them. However, Elphinstone, busy with his breakfast, had failed to authorize the sending of the gun carriages until after nine A.M., so that Sturt and his engineers could not complete the bridge until midday.

When the bridge was eventually ready, it simply proved a bottleneck with the thousands of camp followers jostling among the baggage wagons and gun carriages for their turn to cross amid "the oaths of the camel-drivers, the bewailings of the Hindustani servants, and the roar of camels," as an eyewitness wrote. The advance guard took until early afternoon to cross and leave the bridge free for the main column to follow. Lady Sale and her daughter wisely preferred to ride their horses through the water rather than joining those attempting to cross what she called the "rattling bridge." Captain Lawrence, meanwhile, was already finding it hard to keep his contingent of women and children together, with "some of the bearers hurrying on, others lagging behind with the palanquins and doolies containing the women and children." He saw the irony that to reach the road for Jalalabad, the column had to pass close to the citadel from which Shah Shuja was doubtless watching his allies' ignominious departure. He could not help casting "a long, lingering look at the Balla Hissar feeling assured that *even now* all might be retrieved if only the order was passed to march upon and occupy that fortress, instead of plunging into the dreadful defiles before us, to our certain destruction."

The order of march quickly dissolved into confusion with camp followers and baggage inextricably mixed up with the troops. Such was the chaos that the main column, with its long line of laden camels, was still leaving the cantonments by late afternoon. When winter darkness fell around four o'clock, the vanguard had only reached Begramee, some five miles away, where Elphinstone called a halt for the night. In the panic and disorder and under attack by Afghans bent on loot, servants had flung down their loads or abandoned baggage animals so that, as Lady Sale wrote, "private baggage, commissariat and ammunition were nearly annihilated at one fell swoop." With no equipment to pitch a proper camp, the women and children—most of them still in their litters for warmth—found places inside small tents. Lady Sale shared one with her daughter, son-in-law Sturt and two others, but the tent did not keep out the bitter wind. Doubling up her long legs beneath her in a straw chair provided by Captain Johnson, Lady Sale covered herself with her sheepskin coat and tried to sleep. Lawrence shared another tent with two other officers, all "thankful for the shelter and some cold meat and sherry which Lady Macnaghten was able to spare us, and without which we must have starved."

The unfortunate rear guard, whose task had been to man the cantonment walls until the rest of the column had left, were unable to depart until six o'clock in the evening, having first destroyed almost everything they could not carry except for the guns, which the ever honorable Elphinstone considered it would be a violation of the treaty to spike. As soon as they abandoned the walls, Afghans surged in, firing at the retreating troops, killing some fifty soldiers as they tried to protect a pile of baggage waiting to be carried over Sturt's bridge. Before long, the night sky was lit by "columns of lurid smoke and flame" as the Afghans set fire to the buildings in the cantonments. The rear guard remained under attack all the way to Begramee. As they fought their way forward in the darkness, they witnessed the fate of stragglers from the main column, encountering "literally a continuous lane of poor wretches, men, women, and children dead or dying from the cold and wounds, who, unable to move, entreated their comrades to kill them and put an end to their misery."

The rear guard finally struggled into the encampment on the bank of the Kabul River at about two A.M., "worn out by hunger and fatigue, and benumbed by cold," having abandoned much of their baggage and spiked two of their guns. They found no comfort in the camp, which was "one mass of confusion; no places marked out for the different regiments or baggage; the snow very deep on the ground; all order gone." With no shelter, food or fuel, the men could only huddle together in the snow, "too weary even to cry out in their suffering," as Lawrence reported. The night was pitch-black, but when dawn rose he was shocked to discover how many had died: "I found lying close to my tent, stiff, cold, and quite dead, in full regimentals, with his sword drawn in his hand, an old grey-haired conductor [noncommissioned officer] named Macgregor, who, utterly exhausted, had lain down there silently to die."

The cold was as great an enemy to the British force as were the Afghans, and they had no response to it. Before setting out, Pottinger had urged his fellow officers to have old horse blankets and other materials torn into strips that could be wound around the soldiers' feet and ankles in the Afghan fashion to protect them from the cold. However, like most of Pottinger's advice, the suggestion had been ignored. During the early stages of the retreat, Lieutenant Eyre observed how Mackenzie's loyal Afghan *jezailchis* cleared a small area of ground of snow, then "laid themselves down in a circle, closely packed together, with their feet meeting in the centre; all the warm clothing they could muster among them being spread equally over the whole. By these simple means sufficient animal warmth was generated to preserve them from being frostbitten; and Captain Mackenzie, who himself shared their homely bed, declared that he had felt scarcely any inconvenience from the cold." However, no one seems to have encouraged the European and Indian troops to sleep in this way.

At seven A.M. on 7 January, the force moved out once more in temperatures so low that, as Mackenzie described, "the very air we breathed froze in its passage out of the mouth and nostrils, forming a coating of small icicles on our moustaches and beards." Lawrence observed, "All discipline and order had ceased, and soldiers, camp followers, and baggage were all mingled together. More than half of the sepoys were, from cold and hunger, unable to handle their muskets, and throwing them away, mixed themselves up with the mass of non-combatants." Others had deserted during the night, and some of Shah Shuja's sappers and infantry abandoned their colors and slipped back to Kabul, "preferring becoming prisoners there to the certain death which they saw clearly must result from continuing any longer with the main body."

As the force slowly advanced toward the Khoord Kabul Pass, still five miles away, several hundred Afghans could be seen on either side of the column, moving parallel with it. Word went around that these were the escort promised by the chiefs to protect the retreating British. By now the bearers of the ladies' palanquins were becoming exhausted. The men carrying Lady Macnaghten declared they could go no farther, and Lawrence took her up on his own horse—a strong animal that had belonged to her husband. Overtaking a camel with empty straw panniers hanging down on either side of its ribs, Lawrence transferred the envoy's widow into one of these, balancing her weight by placing a bundle of clothes in the other pannier. Returning to the rest of the women and children, he discovered that one—Mrs. Boyd—was nowhere to be seen. He at once rode back to look for her and, encountering Brigadier Antequil, learned that Afghans had attacked the rear of the column, carrying off two cannon due to the cowardice of the Forty-fourth regiment, all Europeans, who had not fired one shot to defend them. Though an artillery officer and some of his men had later charged the enemy and succeeded in spiking the guns, a gloomy Antequil told Lawrence the incident "was too bad to speak about."

Meanwhile, the Afghans shadowing the retreating army had shown themselves not friends but foes, suddenly falling on the main column, killing stragglers and carrying off captives and baggage. A sergeant likened them to "hungry wolves." Worried the Afghans would cut off part of his force, Elphinstone sent back troops and cannon under Shelton to try to drive them off. At this time, Nawab Zaman Khan sent a further message to Pottinger, warning that the Khoord Kabul Pass was strongly occupied by Ghilzai tribesmen and promising to disperse the attackers and to supply food and fuel if Elphinstone stopped his march. Around this time too, the British observed a chief accompanied by several hundred horsemen watching the column. Pottinger sent Captain Skinner under a flag of truce to talk to him. As Pottinger must have suspected, it was Akbar Khan himself. He reproached Skinner over the precipitate departure of the British, telling him they were to blame for their predicament and claiming that he had come to defend them against their attackers. He also told Skinner that he wanted further hostages as surety that Sale would evacuate Jalalabad.

Learning of Akbar Khan's fresh demands, and in the light of Nawab Zaman Shah's warning, Pottinger persuaded Elphinstone to halt although it was only midday. He agreed to stop until nightfall, when he intended to march on again. However, later that afternoon another of his officers convinced him that the troops were too exhausted for a night march, and Elphinstone ordered his column to make camp where they were, at Boothak. "Here was another day entirely lost," Shelton complained. The retreating force was a mere ten miles from Kabul, having again covered only five miles that day. Furthermore, in addition to the two lost cannon, two more had had to be spiked and abandoned because the starving artillery horses were too weak to drag them any farther.

Lawrence eventually located the missing Mrs. Boyd but saw little other cause for cheerfulness. The conditions in the camp were terrible, he reported, with "thousands of human beings and animals all promiscuously huddled together in such a dense mass that it was hardly possible to move through them." That night the temperature dropped, according to an officer's thermometer, to minus ten degrees Fahrenheit. "Who can adequately describe the horror and sufferings of such a situation?" Lawrence asked. Lieutenant Eyre also wrote of the "monstrous, unmanageable, jumbling mass" and how night closed over the frozen, huddled people "with its attendant trains of horrors—starvation, cold, exhaustion, death." A sergeant major told how some sepoys "burnt the cane foundations of their caps and the butts of their muskets to get a little warmth, some of them suffering so much from the cold that he saw them thrust their poor frost-bitten hands into the fire until they were charred." A group of officers crouched over the ashes of a pistol case they had burned and drank wine to drive out the cold. At dawn the next morning, 8 January, further frozen corpses were found lying on the ground.

Shortly after sunrise Elphinstone dispatched Skinner to negotiate further with Akbar Khan, who now demanded that the British remain where they were or advance only as far as Tezeen until confirmation came that Sale had left Jalalabad. He also asked for four hostages, specifically naming Shelton and Lawrence. Meanwhile, several hundred Ghilzai tribesmen had been observed massing around the entrance to the Khoord Kabul Pass, but Major William Thain had led the Forty-fourth in a vigorous bayonet charge and succeeded in driving them off. Several officers thought the action proof that even at this eleventh hour the British could "if properly led have driven the enemy like sheep into Kabul, and [them-] selves have occupied the Balla Hissar," as Lawrence wrote. Elated by Thain's success, some artillerymen who had discovered an abandoned cask of brandy and, in Lady Sale's words, become "much too excited," wanted to pursue the fleeing enemy. Their commanding officer abused them as "drunkards," but the more tactful Sturt assured them that they were "fine fellows" and their bravery much appreciated but that their lives were too valuable to be risked. Lady Sale herself was grateful to be given a tumbler of sherry "which at any other time would have made me very unlady-like, but now merely warmed me" while "cups full of sherry were given to young children three and four years old without in the least affecting their heads."

Pottinger himself had ridden off to tell Akbar Khan that the British would agree to halt at Tezeen and there await news of Sale's evacuation of Jalalabad. He also offered himself as hostage in the place of Shelton, who was refusing to be handed over to the enemy. Akbar Khan agreed to modify his hostage demands. He would, he said, be satisfied with three: Pottinger, Lawrence and any other Pottinger cared to nominate. Pottinger chose Mackenzie. By midmorning, in what must have seemed a bizarre change in their circumstances, the three officers found themselves breakfasting on a hillside with Akbar Khan, who had courteously invited them to join him after requesting his men to relieve them of their pistols and rifles.

At about midday the retreating British army, in Eyre's words, "a living mass of men and animals," was again in motion toward the forbidding five-mile-long Khoord Kabul Pass, "shut in on either hand by a line of lofty hills, between whose precipitous sides the sun at this season could dart but a momentary ray. Down the centre dashed a mountain torrent, whose impetuous course the frost in vain attempted to arrest, though it succeeded in lining the edges with thick layers of ice, over which the snow lay consolidated in slippery masses." Eyre added, "The idea of threading the stupendous pass before us, in the face of an armed tribe of bloodthirsty barbarians, with such a dense, irregular multitude was frightful and the spectacle then presented by that waving sea of animated beings, the majority of whom a few fleeting hours would transform into a line of lifeless carcasses to guide the future traveller on his way, can never be forgotten by those who witnessed it."

Elphinstone believed that he had secured a cease-fire from Akbar Khan, who had promised to clear the pass of Ghilzais. However, either Akbar Khan's authority over the Ghilzais was not what he claimed, or he had lied.° Lady Sale described how the force—"the baggage mixed up with the advance guard and the camp followers surging ahead in terror"—had barely advanced half a mile into the pass before Ghilzais concealed behind small stone breastworks (*sangars*) began firing on them while others closed in, cutting and slashing with their long knives. Terrified men, women and children splashed through the icy stream, slithering and sliding over the snowy ground in a desperate attempt to get away. A survivor described how "dreadful indeed was the slaughter; wounded men covered with blood, vainly endeavoured to obtain a safer place in the advance, and only rendered the confusion greater. Baggage, ammunition, and even children were deserted, and to get out of the pass seemed the object of all."

At one point the pass became "completely choked." Soldiers were trapped beneath heavy fire from Afghans on the heights above. Even when able to advance, some were too numb with cold to be able to discharge their muskets to dislodge the attackers. The fleeing mass had to cross the Kabul River no fewer than twenty-eight times in their bid to reach the end of the pass. Lieutenant Sturt rode back to help another officer whose horse had been shot from under him, only to be shot himself in the groin and unhorsed. Ghilzais would have hacked him to pieces but for Lieutenant Mein, who, though wounded himself, stayed by his side until a sergeant came to help him. Together they dragged Sturt on a quilt through the remainder of the pass and then on ponyback into the camp. Here doctors admitted they could do nothing for him.

°Pottinger told Mackenzie that he had earlier heard Akbar Khan—unaware that Pottinger understood both languages—shout, "'Slay them' in Pashtu, though he called to them to stop firing in Persian."

Of the British women, Mrs. Eyre cleared the pass quickly because her horse took fright and bolted. Lady Sale and her daughter also got through speedily by urging their mounts on "as fast as they could go over a road where, at any other time, we should have walked our horses very carefully." "Fortunately," she wrote, "[I have] only one [musket] ball in my arm; three others passed though my poshteen near the shoulder without doing me any injury. The party that fired . . . was not above fifty yards from us." Most of the rest of the British women had by now exchanged their palanquins for panniers on camels led by sepoys. Their speed was at best two miles an hour. During the harrowing journey through the pass, several lost their children, temporarily or permanently. Afghans seized Captain Boyd's youngest son after the camel on which he was traveling was shot. However one young woman, Mrs. Mainwaring, clung doggedly to her child after the camel carrying them was hit. Lady Sale, who did not give praise lightly, described how she "not only had to walk a considerable distance with her child in her arms through the deep snow, but had also to pick her way over the bodies of the dead, dying and wounded . . . and constantly to cross the streams of water, wet up to the knees, pushed and shoved about by men and animals, the enemy keeping up a sharp fire and several persons being killed close to her."

Lieutenant Eyre estimated that three thousand soldiers and camp followers died in the pass that day. The victory went down in Afghan folklore. According to some villagers more than a century later: "When the battle entered the Khoord Kabul valley the British troops lost many of their people. Some were killed by the water, some by swords, some by guns but all by the hand of Allah." The three officer hostages, Lawrence, Pottinger and Mackenzie, saw for themselves the full horror of what was happening when some hours later their captors—a group of thirty horsemen in whose charge Akbar Khan had left them while he himself rode ahead, professedly to stop the Ghilzais' attack—led them into the pass. A massacre was under way. Lawrence described the scene: "Sepoys and camp followers were being stripped and plundered on all sides, and such as refused to give up their money and valuables were instantly stabbed or cut down by the ruthless enemy with their long knives. On seeing us the poor creatures cried out for help, many of them recognising me and calling out to me by name. But what could we do? We ourselves were quite helpless."

They passed the bodies of children hacked in two and other corpses stripped naked with their throats cut ear to ear. Nearing the middle of the Khoord Kabul Pass, they found an abandoned gun and around it many more bodies.

Despite their escorts, the hostages soon found themselves in danger as Ghilzai tribesmen clustered around. The tribesmen, according to Lawrence, "demanded that we should be given up to them for a sacrifice, brandishing their long blood-stained knives in our faces and telling us 'to look on the heaps of carcasses around us, as we should soon be ourselves among them.' 'You came to Kabul for fruit, did you? How do you like it now?' they cried." So worried were their escorts that they concealed the officers beneath the shadows of some overhanging rocks until, with darkness falling, the tribesmen began turning for home with their spoils. When they rode on again, a wounded English sergeant cried out to them for help. At first Lawrence thought he had only lost his left hand, but, raising him up, he found that "from the nape of his neck to his backbone, he had been cut in pieces." When Lawrence said there was nothing he could do for him, the man begged him to shoot him, but even this, Lawrence had to tell him, he could not do, to which the man gasped out, "Then leave me to die."

The captives were, however, able to help Captain Boyd's little son, brought to them on Akbar Khan's orders, and the two-year-old son of a private, taken from the arms of his dead mother lying blood-spattered on the ground. They also took charge of Mrs. Bourne, the pregnant wife of another private, whom one of Akbar Khan's men had saved from a Ghilzai as he was about to cut off her fingers for her rings. Mackenzie could scarcely persuade her to mount behind him on his horse she was "so stupefied from fear and cold." The officers wrapped her in a sheepskin coat, tying the sleeves of it together in front, but Mackenzie wrote of the difficulty of preventing her petticoats from riding up as they continued on their journey. She was so thirsty that he felt her licking the snowflakes falling on his shoulders. Finally, long after darkness had fallen, the captives and their escorts reached a small fort, where, after a scarcely digestible meal of a sheep's tail boiled in water and some half-baked bread, they covered themselves in sheepskins and tried to sleep.

Just beyond the far end of the Khoord Kabul Pass, those who had made it through were bivouacking in the thickly falling snow without food or fuel at an altitude of 7,200 feet. Only four tents remained to them. Elphinstone had one, and the others were supposedly meant for the women and wounded. The dying Sturt, calling desperately for water, was sharing one of them with thirty others, including his wife and mother-in-law, who were trying to ease his sufferings. Throughout the night the wounded Lieutenant Mein went to and fro to fetch water for him from a nearby stream, which Mackenzie was later told was running red with blood. He described how even the most fastidious of the women eagerly drank the blood-stained water as "all they could get." Many more perished that night from the bitter cold. Another officer wrote of his shock on waking to discover that two sepoys had frozen to death at his feet, having crept close trying to gain a little warmth from the edges of the *poshteen* that was covering him.

At first light the next morning, 9 January, many of the troops and camp followers moved off without waiting for orders, convinced their only chance of survival lay in pushing on quickly, though some were so frostbitten they could scarcely put a foot to the ground. Lady Sale described "the only order appearing to be, 'Come along; we are all going, and half the men are off, with the camp followers in advance!'" The rest of the force followed at eight A.M. Sturt died soon after, his end hastened by being jolted about in a pannier on a camel. Lady Sale and her daughter "had the sorrowful satisfaction of giving him Christian burial" in the snowy ground. He would be the only member of the entire force to receive such rites during the retreat. In the midst of this pitiful confusion, Akbar Khan sent a message to Elphinstone again promising provisions and protection if the force would halt. Ignoring Shelton's oft-made objections that delay would cause the total destruction of the column, Elphinstone sent orders that it was to halt. Remarkably enough, people obeyed, though "the general feeling was that there was no hope left."

That morning Lawrence and the hostages were taken to the nearby Khoord Kabul Fort, where Akbar Khan, clearly choosing his words with care, told them that he had a suggestion to make that, though motivated purely by feelings of humanity, he feared might be misconstrued. Clearly, he said, given the events of the previous day, the British could no longer protect the helpless women and children. Therefore he proposed that "the ladies and their husbands, the children, and the wounded officers should be made over to him," promising to keep them safe and later to send them under escort to Jalalabad. By *ladies*, Akbar of course meant the European women. He had no interest in female camp followers or the sepoys' families. Neither did the officers, men of their time, suppose he meant anything else. Though they may have been moved by the plight of the camp followers and sepoys' wives and children, whose suffering was even greater and whose numbers were far larger, it seems never to have occurred to any of them to intercede on their behalf.

Having seen such terrible sights along the way, the officers unhesitatingly approved the scheme, and Captain Skinner, arriving soon after from the British camp, also eagerly endorsed it. The officer hostages begged him to lose no time in returning to speak to Elphinstone. Though handing over women and children to an enemy who had so far failed to keep faith caused him some soul-searching, the chance of sparing them further suffering prompted Elphinstone to agree to the scheme. That same evening Skinner returned, bringing with him a party including Lady Macnaghten, Lady Sale, Mrs. Sturt, Mrs. Boyd, Mrs. Anderson, Mrs. Eyre, Mrs. Waller, Mrs. Trevor, Mrs. Mainwaring and Mrs. Ryley, some with their husbands and children, and several others: Sergeant Wade and his family, Captain Troup and Lieutenant Mein, who were both wounded, two unnamed wives of private soldiers, as well as Mackenzie's faithful Indian Christian servant, Jacob.

Though he had vigorously supported the scheme, now that it had come to pass, Lawrence found it "distressing beyond expression to see our countrywomen and their helpless children thus placed in the power of these ruffians. The extreme suffering of mind and body they had endured . . . was apparent in their worn and grief-stricken faces, many of them during these wretched days had tasted nothing but some dry biscuits and some sherry or brandy." With the exception of the formidable Lady Macnaghten, who had saved all her property, "they had lost everything except the clothes they were wearing." Lady Sale and her daughter, overwhelmed with grief at Sturt's death and scarcely in a fit state to decide whether to accept Akbar Khan's protection, had recognized there was "but faint hope of our ever getting safe to Jalalabad" and "followed the stream."

CHAPTER SIXTEEN

When Burnes came into this country, was not *your* father entreated by us to kill him; or he would go back to Hindustan, and on
some future day return with an army and take our country from
us? He would not listen to our advice, and what is the consequence? Let us, now that we have the opportunity, take advantage
of it, and kill those infidel dogs.

—AFGHAN CHIEFS TO AKBAR KHAN, 11 JANUARY 1842

ON THE MORNING of 10 January 1842, after a fourth night in subzero temperatures following their all-day halt near Khoord Kabul, the
remnants of Elphinstone's force set out once more for Jalalabad. Sergeant
Major Lissant described men whose frostbitten feet had "become like
large burnt pieces of wood" and whose hands were "so dreadfully swollen
and cracked they could not hold, much less use a musket." With many also
suffering the agonies of snowblindness—like having grains of hot sand
trapped beneath the eyelids—for which they tried rubbing their inflamed
eyes with snow, they were easy prey. As they entered the narrow Tunghee
Tareekee Gorge, a fifty-yard-long pinch-point, Ghilzais lying in wait on
the hills above fired volley after volley at them. Survivors later told Eyre:
"Fresh numbers fell at every volley, and the gorge was soon choked with
the dead and dying: the unfortunate sepoys, seeing no means of escape,
and driven to utter desperation, cast away their arms and accoutrements,
which only clogged their movements without contributing to their defence, and along with the camp followers fled for their lives. The Afghans

now rushed down upon their helpless and unresisting victims sword in hand and a general massacre took place. The last small remnant of the Native Infantry regiments were here scattered and destroyed; and the public treasure with all the remaining baggage fell into the hands of the enemy."

The leading troops managed to push on through the gorge and after five miles halted to allow the rest to catch up. Few appeared. Nearly the entire main and rear columns had been destroyed. Fifteen officers and 300 men had died in the defile, reducing the fighting force to fifty horse-artillerymen with one howitzer, 250 men of the Forty-fourth infantry regiment and 150 cavalrymen both British and Indian and a few other sepoys. Perhaps between 3,000 and 4,000 camp followers remained, their disorder and panic continuing to hamper the soldiers' movements.

Akbar Khan was still shadowing the retreat. A desperate Elphinstone dispatched Captain Skinner to demand why he was not protecting them as he had promised. Akbar Khan's response, which probably had some truth in it, was that neither he nor their own chiefs could restrain the Ghilzais. Yet again he had a proposal for the British—this time that the surviving troops should surrender their arms and place themselves under his protection, though he said he could do nothing for the camp followers. Elphinstone refused, and the column descended into another defile, the three-mile-long Huft-Kotul Gorge, in whose shadowy depths they found the butchered remains of camp followers who had rushed ahead. Before long, Ghilzais attacked the rear of the column led by Shelton, but he rallied his men to return their fire and succeeded in driving them off.

At around four P.M. the retreat reached the Tezeen Valley, where Akbar Khan again tried to persuade Elphinstone to order his men to lay down their arms. Again the general refused. Instead, at Shelton's suggestion, he decided on a forced march through the night in the hope of getting through the Jugdulluk Pass, some twenty-two miles away, before the Afghans had time to block or occupy it. After spiking the last remaining gun, to which they tied a wounded doctor too weak to go on whom they hoped the Afghans might take pity on, but who would freeze to death in the coming hours, the force moved off at seven P.M. The night was clear and bright and the snow not as deep on the ground as before. They covered the first seven miles without a shot being fired and began to hope that they might indeed slip away from their enemy. However, at Seh-Baba the Ghilzais attacked the rear, triggering panic among the camp followers, who surged forward in a great wave until the sound of further firing, this time from the front, caused them to stampede back again. In the confusion it was impossible for the soldiers to form up to defend themselves, and many fell dead or wounded.

Dawn was breaking on 11 January when the survivors reached Kutter-Sung—still ten miles from their goal of Jugdulluk. After a brief halt to allow the rearmost to catch up, Elphinstone ordered his men onward again after they had bade farewell to those too weak to continue. These included Surgeon General Dr. Duff, who, after being badly wounded in the left hand, had directed its amputation by another doctor wielding a penknife. Elphinstone again hoped the Afghans might spare the lives of those left behind, but all were to be murdered. As the depleted column marched on, it was yet again attacked from the rear. Shelton and his men once more held off the attackers while the rest of the column struggled to the village of Jugdulluk at the entrance to the pass. As heavy, one-and-a-half-ounce, jezail balls fired by Afghan sharpshooters hissed around them, Elphinstone—perhaps hoping to cause a distraction that would help Shelton and his men—ordered twenty of his mounted officers "to form line and show a front." While they did so a bullet smashed the jaw of the adjutant general, Captain Grant. As Grant slumped forward in his saddle, Captain Johnson caught him and lowered him to the ground. However, the line held until Shelton and his rear guard—fighting all the way—at last reached them, and they all took cover behind the walls of a ruined fort.

More and more Ghilzais had been occupying the surrounding heights, and their fire kept the troops pinned down behind the walls. As the hours passed, hunger and thirst tormented them. Although a stream was only 150 yards away, any attempt to reach it to drink meant death. Instead, as Johnson described, "Some snow was on the ground, which was greedily devoured; but instead of quenching, it increased our thirst." During a lull in the firing, Elphinstone sent Johnson to see whether the camp followers had any beasts left. Discovering three bullocks, he had them butchered and distributed among the starving European soldiers, who devoured the flesh "raw, and still reeking with blood."

A party of Afghan horsemen had meanwhile been observing events from a distance, and one of them now approached to say that they were Akbar Khan's men. Elphinstone sent Skinner to demand of Akbar Khan yet again why he was not restraining the Ghilzais. While Skinner was away, the Ghilzai attack intensified. The storm of bullets so terrified some camp followers that they ran out into the open, to be struck down immediately. Army paymaster Captain Bygrave, at the head of fifteen men of the Forty-fourth, their bayonets fixed, succeeded in chasing some Afghans from the nearby hills, and several times cavalrymen charged out to dislodge the enemy. The latter sorties also provided the chance of some food. Sergeant Major Lissant described how "as the horses fell both officers and men stripped their flesh off."

Toward late afternoon, Skinner returned with an invitation from Akbar Khan to Elphinstone and Shelton to join him at a conference with the chiefs at his camp two miles away. With the force now reduced to some 150 men of the Forty-fourth, 16 dismounted members of the Horse Artillery, 25 cavalry troopers and a few sepoys, and with little ammunition left, Elphinstone and Shelton agreed to go, taking the Persian-speaking Johnson as their interpreter. Sepoy Sita Ram wrote of the men's amazement that Elphinstone should put himself in Afghan hands after what had happened to Burnes and Macnaghten, and wrote that "when the General *sahib* left all discipline fell away."

Elphinstone and Shelton found their host in an apparently hospitable mood. He ordered a cloth to be spread on the frozen ground and offered his famished visitors mutton, rice and tea. When they had finished, he invited them to join the chiefs around a crackling fire, and discussions began. Elphinstone asked for food and water to be sent to his men. Akbar Khan agreed, though it was a promise he failed to keep. Perhaps knowing that Sale had not yet moved from Jalalabad, he then announced that the three officers must remain as further hostages to ensure Sale complied with the order to depart. Elphinstone argued that he must return to his men since it would otherwise appear as if he had deserted them. He offered to send Brigadier Antequil in his place, but Akbar Khan would not be swayed. That night he ordered a tent to be pitched for the three officers in which, wrapping themselves in their cloaks, they lay down and tried to sleep.

The next morning, 12 January, the conference resumed, with the frail Elphinstone reduced to pleading with Akbar Khan for the lives of his remaining troops. Akbar Khan promised to do what he could, but Johnson was shaken by the violent language of Ghilzai chiefs whom he overheard arguing with Akbar Khan. The chiefs seemed bent on exterminating the British, saying to Akbar Khan: "When Burnes came into this country, was not *your* father [Dost Mohammed] entreated by us to kill him; or he would go back to Hindustan, and on some future day return with an army and take our country from us? He would not listen to our advice, and what is the consequence? Let us, now that we have the opportunity, take advantage of it; and kill those infidel dogs."

Akbar Khan's father-in-law, the Ghilzai chief Mohammed Shah Khan, who seems to have been trying to assist him in reaching an accommodation with his fellow chiefs, suggested the British should pay them two hundred thousand rupees to guarantee their safe passage through the remaining passes to Jalalabad. Elphinstone readily agreed, but the chiefs were harder to convince. Meanwhile, Akbar Khan, who was denouncing the chiefs privately to the Britons as "dogs" who could not be trusted, proposed to Elphinstone and Shelton that toward dusk he and his own men should ride to the rescue of the surviving British troops and mounting them a man apiece behind them, bring them to safety. He claimed the Ghilzais would not dare attack for fear of hitting him or his men. Elphinstone and Shelton rejected the offer as dishonorable and— knowing how hard it would be to extract the soldiers from among the camp followers—impracticable.

Dusk was falling before Mohammed Shah Khan returned to tell Elphinstone that the chiefs had finally agreed, in return for payment, to allow his force to continue to Jalalabad unmolested. Akbar Khan said that he himself would ride with them, though somewhat ominously he advised Captain Johnson to summon any friends of his to join him in captivity rather than allow them to march on and face death—an offer Johnson refused. Elphinstone meanwhile wrote a letter to Brigadier Antequil ordering him to have the troops ready to march on at eight A.M. the next morning. At around seven P.M. that evening, before the letter had been sent, the sound of firing was plainly heard from the direction of the pass. In fact, Brigadier Antequil had already ordered the men to move out toward the Jugdulluk Pass. A dismayed Akbar Khan suggested "that he and the officers should follow them," to which Elphinstone agreed. However, almost at once Akbar Khan changed his mind, saying that "he feared their doing so would injure the troops by bringing after them the whole horde of Ghilzais then assembled in the valley."

Elphinstone and Shelton could not know what had been happening during their absence of more than twenty-four hours. Earlier that day, Captain Skinner, on his way to Akbar Khan's camp, had been shot in the face by a Ghilzai and subsequently died in agony. Meanwhile, Ghilzai marksmen had been firing almost constantly on the British troops, picking off man after man. Antequil had decided he could wait no longer for news of Elphinstone and had given the order to advance under cover of darkness. Again the sick and wounded were abandoned. Sergeant Major Lissant found it "heartrending to hear the poor fellows calling on their comrades to bring them on and not leave them to be cut to pieces by the enemy."

As Antequil and the depleted column of only some 145 men—about 120 men of the Forty-fourth and 25 cavalrymen—entered the two-mile-long Jugdulluk Pass, they suffered only the occasional volley of jezail fire. However, climbing in the darkness toward the head of the pass, they found two six-foot-high barricades of holly-oak blocking their way. According to Sergeant Major Lissant, all was immediately confusion, "horse and foot and camp followers all got into a heap, no one could move for some time . . . Numbers were trod to death, and the enemy getting among the rear slaughtering away at pleasure, the cries and screeches of the poor fellows were terrible." Desperate men tore at the prickly branches with bare, cold and bloodied hands as the fighting toward the rear intensified. Though the men "fought like gods, not men," in Sita Ram's words, twelve officers, including Brigadier Antequil, were killed as they struggled to hold the Afghans off. Among them was the one-legged Captain Dodgin, who killed five Afghans before succumbing. Sita Ram himself was knocked unconscious by a jezail ball that grazed his head. He later came round to find himself slung across a horse and on the way to Kabul to be sold as a slave. "What dreadful carnage I saw along the road—legs and arms protruding from the snow, Europeans and Hindustanis half-buried, horse and camels all dead!" he later wrote.

Only a few—a party of fifteen mounted officers who, as soon as there was a gap wide enough, abandoned their fellows, riding over them in their haste to get away, and subsequently a larger group of fifty to sixty officers and European soldiers—got through the barrier. Captain Lawrence was later told that some men, angered by the selfishness and cowardice of the fleeing officers, had fired at them. Sergeant Major Lissant described how, with all discipline lost, "every man was acting for himself." He and four others took refuge in a cave rather than march on.

The main body of fifty or sixty survivors hurried out of the pass toward Gandamack, several miles away, which they reached as dawn was rising. Among them was Captain Souter of the Forty-fourth, who had wrapped the regimental colors—thirty-six square feet of embroidered yellow silk—around his waist in a bid to preserve them. Ten years earlier, Burnes had admired the daisy-filled meadows of the Gandamack Valley and the surrounding pine-clad mountains, and only two years before, Captain Havelock had been captivated by its setting "in a delightful and well-watered valley, fertile, and planted with spreading mulberry trees." However, to desperate starving men on the run in deepest winter, it was no haven. Afghans poured from their dwellings to surround the soldiers, who had barely two rounds of ammunition apiece and only twenty muskets between them.

Forced from the road, the troops climbed a nearby hill. A local chief offered to negotiate, and Major Griffiths, the senior surviving officer, rode off to see him. Meanwhile, tribesmen pressed yet closer around the troops, jostling them. Captain Souter described how, ostensibly friendly at first, the Afghans then "commenced snatching swords and pistols from the officers; this we could not stand but drove them from the hill, and the fight commenced again. After two hours, during which we drove the Afghans several times down the hill, our little band (with the exception of about twenty men and a few officers of different regiments) being either killed or wounded, the enemy suddenly rushed upon us with their knives and an awful scene took place and ended in the massacre of all except myself, Sergeant Fair, (our mess sergeant) and seven men, that the more than usual humanity displayed by Afghans were induced to spare.

"In the conflict my poshteen flew upon and exposed the Colour; Thinking I was some great man from looking so flash, I was seized by two fellows (after my sword dropped from my hand by a severe cut on the shoulder and my pistol missing fire) who hurried me from this spot to a distance, took my clothes from off me except my trousers and cap, led me away to a village, by command of some horsemen that were on the road, and I was made over to the head man of the village who treated me well, and had my wound attended to." Major Griffiths and the civilian clerk he had taken with him as his interpreter were also saved.

The mounted group that had ridden ahead, abandoning their comrades, had been faring badly. Nine had been killed along the way, leaving six officers including two army doctors who managed to reach Futtehabad, only sixteen miles from Jalalabad. However, here the exhausted men made the mistake of pausing to eat bread offered them by the villagers. This allowed time for a party of Afghans to fetch their weapons and attack them. They cut two of the officers down at once. The remaining men fled, but, only four miles from Jalalabad, pursuing horsemen caught and killed three of them. The fourth man, the thirty-year-old Dr. William Brydon, had hidden behind some rocks during the pursuit and rode on alone. An assistant surgeon who had been seconded to Shah Shuja's army, he was a resourceful man. On leaving Kabul, he had "followed the Afghan custom of carrying a bag of parched grain mixed with raisins at their saddlebow" to provide nourishment as he rode. Along the way, he had searched for wild liquorice roots to chew to lessen his thirst.

Suddenly, as Brydon described in a letter to his brother, "I saw a great many people running towards me in all directions. I waited until they got pretty close and then pushed my horse into a gallop and ran the gauntlet for about two miles under a shower of large stones, sticks, and a few shots, in which I had my sword broken by a stone, my horse shot in the spine close to the tail and my body bruised all over by the stones." He was next attacked by an Afghan horseman, who, as Brydon flung his sword hilt at him, slashed at him with his *tulwar*, wounding him in the left hand and knee. "[I] stretched down the right [hand] to pick up the bridle. I suppose my foe thought it was for a pistol for he turned at once and made off as quick as he could." The bleeding Brydon continued on his way. But "suddenly all my energy seemed to forsake me, I became nervous and frightened at shadows, and I really think I would have fallen from my saddle but for the peak of it." Jalalabad at last came in sight, but, fearing that Sale and his force might have departed and it was in Afghan hands, Brydon dismounted and, crouching behind some fallen masonry, watched anxiously for a sign.

Sale and his garrison were indeed still there, though the past weeks had been testing ones. Since occupying Jalalabad in mid-November, they had been living in a state of constant watchfulness, sallying out to drive off groups of mounted Afghans when they pressed too close, strengthening their defenses and receiving a stream of disquieting information—some in letters, some merely rumors—about what was happening in Kabul. On 2 January a letter from Pottinger, dated a week earlier, had told them of Macnaghten's murder and also that negotiations with the chiefs were continuing and that the Kabul force intended to fall back on Jalalabad shortly. A few days later a further letter from Pottinger, written in French for greater security, had warned that the chiefs were proving faithless and that Sale should stand firm until he received further instructions. Also at this time Sale and his men had learned from an intercepted message from Akbar Khan to a local chief that "a holy war was proclaimed; and that all believers were adjured, in the name of the Prophet, to rise against the infidels" and inciting him to "slay the chief of the Feringhees in Jalalabad."

On 9 January a small band of Afghans had ridden up to the fort under a flag of truce and handed over a letter written in English, dated eleven days earlier and signed by both Elphinstone and Pottinger. It told Sale that it had been agreed with Akbar Khan that the British would depart from Afghanistan. Sale and his men were to march immediately for Peshawar since Elphinstone had undertaken that the Kabul force would not begin its own retreat until assured by Sale that his troops were beyond Afghanistan's borders. "Everything has been done in good faith. You will not be molested on your way; and to the safe-conduct which Akbar Khan has given, I trust for the passage of the troops under my immediate orders through the passes," Elphinstone had added.

Sale had called a council of war to help him decide how to respond to orders that Reverend Gleig called "as peremptory as ever came from the head-quarters of an army." Though the letter was obviously genuine, Sale and his officers decided that it must have been written under duress. In view of this and the clear evidence that Akbar Khan was inciting the tribes to attack Jalalabad, it would, they decided, be highly imprudent to act upon it. George Broadfoot wholeheartedly supported the decision, writing in his diary, "Our duty in every case is clear—to stand fast to the last." A few days earlier he had predicted the fate that would overtake the Kabul force if they were unwise enough to trust the Afghans, who would "probably inveigle them into the passes and attack them, and heavy indeed would be their loss without cattle, fuel or food, assailed night and day amidst the snow."

Therefore, instead of preparing to withdraw, Sale wrote to the commander in chief in India, Sir Jasper Nicolls, that in the absence of orders from India he saw no reason to obey the instruction from Kabul, which had been forced upon the British "with the knives at their throat." He asked for reinforcements from Peshawar before his ammunition and provisions ran out, and sensibly put his men to strengthening Jalalabad's defenses further. On 12 January a message arrived reporting that the Kabul force had left the cantonments but been delayed at Boothak and that, though Akbar Khan was escorting the column, they feared he was trying to rouse the tribes against them. It was the last letter Sale would receive from an army that by then had ceased to exist.

The following day, 13 January, as Brydon was cautiously approaching, some of Sale's men were digging a ditch around the northwestern bastion. Private Edward Teer, posted on sentry duty above the Kabul Gate on the west wall facing toward Gandamack, "suddenly descried a dark speck" and gave the alarm. Men grabbed their field glasses. According to the Reverend Gleig, they saw "leaning rather than sitting upon a miserable pony, a European, faint, as it seemed, from travel, if not sick, or perhaps wounded. It is impossible to describe the sort of thrill which ran through men's veins as they watched the movements of the stranger." The chaplain heard Colonel Dennie, who had been warning that "not a soul will escape from Kabul except one man; and he will come to tell us that the rest are destroyed," exclaim, "Did I not say so? here comes the messenger."

Cavalrymen galloped out to the slumped, swaying figure and, supporting him in the saddle, brought him in. Those gathering eagerly around learned that he was Dr. Brydon, "who at the moment believed himself to be," wrote Gleig, "the sole survivor of General Elphinstone's once magnificent little army." Havelock described how "his first few hasty sentences extinguished all hope in the hearts of the listeners regarding the fortune of the Kabul force. It was evident that it was annihilated." Brydon's physical state shocked them. His body was a mass of cuts and abrasions, and his feet were so swollen with frostbite he could scarcely stand. Two days earlier he had lost a boot, and the freezing metal of the stirrup had burned his foot despite the twine he had wound around the stirrup. As for his pony, its legs were collapsing beneath it, and it died soon after.

Sale, whose thoughts must have flown instantly to his wife and daughter, at once dispatched cavalry to look for any other survivors, but "not a straggler, however—not a living soul, man, woman or child—appeared," Reverend Gleig reported. They found only the mutilated corpses of Dr. Harpur and two of the officers who had been Brydon's companions. That night and for several thereafter, Sale ordered night lanterns to be hung from poles around the ramparts, while "from time to time," according to Gleig, "the bugles sounded the advance, in the hope that one or other of these beacons might guide some wanderer" through the darkness. No other Europeans came, but eventually about twenty sepoys reached Jalalabad. The bugle call, in the words of one of Sale's captains, was only "a dirge for our slaughtered soldiers."

CHAPTER SEVENTEEN

This is the work of God that has come to pass . . . so that the whole of Islam united with one heart have engaged in a war against the infidels.

—AKBAR KHAN TO THE CHIEFS, FEBRUARY 1842

THE MAIN GROUP of captives spent the nights of 9 and 10 January crammed into five dark rooms in the Khoord Kabul Fort, but compared to "the cold and misery [they] had been suffering in camp on the bare snow," it was, Eyre thought, "heaven." On 11 January their captors brought them toward Tezeen in the wake of the retreating British force. Though they could not know the full extent of the disaster overtaking the remnants of the Kabul force, they must have suspected the worst. "The snow was absolutely dyed with streaks and patches of blood for whole miles, and at every step we encountered the mangled bodies of British and Hindustani soldiers and helpless camp-followers, lying side by side . . . the red stream of life still trickling from many a gaping wound inflicted by the merciless Afghan knife," wrote Eyre. Lady Sale described the "sickening" smell of blood and guiding her horse "so as not to tread on the bodies."

Reaching the fort at Tezeen, the captives found Lieutenant Melville, who had surrendered to the Afghans the previous day having, Eyre noted unsympathetically, "received some slight sword cuts," as well as some four hundred sepoy cavalry who had deserted to the enemy and were camped outside the fort. The next day at Seh-Baba—where the Kabul force had been attacked during its night-time flight toward the Jugdulluk Pass—

gun carriages were still smoldering amid piles of bodies, including that of Dr. Duff, the surgeon whose hand had been amputated with a penknife. Camp followers sheltering among the rocks begged for food and clothing the captives could not provide. However, recognizing a wounded private, Mackenzie took him up behind him on his horse and when the horse tired, himself dismounted to walk through the snow even though one of his feet was badly frostbitten. They passed the night sixteen miles beyond Tezeen, crammed into one room and supplied with *chapattis* by an old woman who trebled her price when she saw how hungry the travelers were.

On 13 January—the day Dr. Brydon reached Jalalabad—they reached the village of Jugdulluk. Among the stone ruins where the British troops had crouched for shelter while Elphinstone and Shelton sought to negotiate with Akbar Khan, they discovered "a spectacle more terrible than any we had previously witnessed, the whole interior space being one crowded mass of bloody corpses," as Eyre wrote. In some ragged tents the prisoners found Elphinstone, Shelton and Johnson, whom Akbar Khan had left there under guard after seizing them, and learned for the first time that they were also captives. The next morning, joined by Akbar Khan himself, the entire party was taken northward into hills, where "long glittering icicles" hung from the rocks.

IN JALALABAD, DEEPLY shocked by Dr. Brydon's story, Sale feared that the triumphant Akbar Khan would soon attack the city. Indeed, he was so worried that he decided the best course was to attempt to negotiate the safe withdrawal of his garrison to India. Shah Shuja, in a bid to strengthen his position with the chiefs, had sent messengers with demands that Sale abide by the treaty between the British and the Afghans and depart. At a stormy council of war conducted over several days, Sale presented these as the justification for retreating. The majority of his officers initially supported him, but during the debate, in which "strong language" and "high words" flew, George Broadfoot argued passionately that retreat meant dishonor and managed to sway his fellow officers. Sale still disagreed but, finding himself outnumbered, gave in.

Fighting Bob's hopes now focused on the arrival of reinforcements from India. Ever since reaching Jalalabad, he had been dispatching *cossids* with messages asking for reinforcements, written on tiny slips of paper which could be sewn into saddles or "sometimes baked in a cake, sometimes inserted into a quill, which is concealed either in the beard or in an unusual receptacle behind," as a young lieutenant euphemistically described. However, his requests met with a mixed reception. At Government House in Calcutta, Lord Auckland was still unaware of the Kabul disaster, although warnings that all was not well had been reaching him for weeks. In late November George Clerk, a political officer posted at Ambala on India's northern frontier, had reported unrest in Kabul and the murder of Burnes. On his own initiative, Clerk had already dispatched two regiments—the Sixtieth and the Sixty-fourth Bengal Native Infantry—across the Sutlej River to Peshawar, close to the border with Afghanistan. Worried that these might not be sufficient, he subsequently ordered two further regiments—the Fifty-third and Thirtieth Bengal Native Infantry—north as well.

Auckland had initially been annoyed when he heard of Clerk's action. He doubted how a concentration of troops on the border could influence events in Kabul given that they could not reach the city until the snows had cleared the following spring. He was, anyway, opposed to rushing to commit further troops to Afghanistan. Lulled by Macnaghten's optimistic reports, he believed that any disturbances in Kabul were minor and would soon be quelled. Furthermore, he was awaiting the arrival of Lord Ellenborough, his successor as governor-general, following the change of government in Britain from the Whigs to the Tories. He was well aware that the new administration—Prime Minister Peel and the Duke of Wellington especially—had always opposed the British invasion of Afghanistan. He was reluctant to commit them to further interventions of which they would be bound to disapprove.

At the end of November, about a week after he had received Clerk's letter, further reports of unrest in Afghanistan reached Auckland. He wrote to Sir Jasper Nicolls, "It seems to me that we are not to think of marching fresh armies for the re-conquest of that which we are likely to lose." He still considered the number of troops in Afghanistan was sufficient to cope with the crisis and that reinforcements could not arrive in time to help. Therefore "safety to the force at Kabul can only come from itself." However he conceded that he was glad the additional regiments had been sent to Peshawar as "they may afford a strong point of support either for retreat or for advance—and whether Brigadier Sale's two regiments fall back upon them, or they advance to Jalalabad, there will be a respectable force for any object." Nicolls, long opposed to the Afghan invasion, agreed, writing: "I really would not advise our forcing either Shuja or ourselves upon a nation so distant and in all respects so dissimilar both to our Sepoys and ourselves . . . that we have no base of operations has always been clear; but now, were we to march a reinforcement on the best horses, we could not be sure of carrying the Khyber Pass, and if snow has fallen, the road to Kabul would still be closed."

On 4 December an account from Lady Sale detailing the deteriorating situation in Kabul up to 9 November shook Auckland. Perhaps for the first time he understood the peril. He immediately wrote to Macnaghten—a letter the envoy probably never received—that it seemed to him "far too hazardous and too costly in money and in life" for the British to remain in Afghanistan in the face of "the universal opinion, national and religious," that they should leave, and that it was time to consider "in what manner all that belongs to India may be most immediately and most honourably withdrawn from the country." Worry was by now taking its toll on the governor-general, who had hoped to sail home to England leaving a quiescent Afghanistan behind him. He was said to pace the veranda of Government House for hours in the daytime, and at night to lie on the lawn and press his face into the grass for comfort. His sister Emily thought that he looked ten years older.

Lack of reliable news sharpened Auckland's anxiety. No official reports from Kabul reached him in December—only private letters from Jalalabad and Peshawar, often confusing and contradictory. In January he appointed General George Pollock, commander of the Agra garrison, to command the troops assembling on the border. The son of King George III's saddler, Pollock was a capable veteran company soldier who had served in India since 1803. He had not been Auckland's first choice. Despite Nicolls's attempts to dissuade him, Auckland's eye had fallen on a man in the Elphinstone mold: the elderly Major General James Lumley, then recovering from serious illness. Believing himself unfit for such a strenuous post, Lumley had sensibly asked to be examined by army doctors, who had agreed with him.

On 20 January Auckland finally learned of Macnaghten's murder and of the British agreement to evacuate Kabul. His sister wrote, "Poor Macnaghten's death has been a great shock; we knew him so well, and it has been such an atrocious act of treachery." Auckland himself wrote that "this calamity" was "as inexplicable as it [was] painful" and immediately asked Nicolls to send another brigade to the border "to be prepared to march onwards if necessary." However, he was contemplating only rescue—not retribution. Writing to the president of the Board of Control in London, he assured him, "My present purpose is that only of gathering strength, and I will rather attempt to stem than immediately to turn the course of events."

However, Auckland shortly learned that it was too late to stem the tide. On 30 January a dispatch from Jalalabad announced the annihilation of the Kabul force. Auckland could scarcely believe it, expressing his amazement that an army of well-trained, well-armed British troops could be wiped out by tribesmen with only muskets and spears. The news of the disaster unleashed a torrent of criticism in the press in India. William Peel, a naval officer and the son of the British prime minister, who was passing through India as part of Britain's forces for the Opium War in China, complained in a letter home that he found the India press "vile" and that it was "astonishing that [in India] where we are but a handful and have scarcely any strength of our own, persons should be allowed to publish what they please and which must necessarily, as slander will always find more readers, and they are only intent on making money, turn with abuse and the most vulgar remarks upon the principal officers of the government."

Auckland issued a proclamation denouncing "a faithless enemy, stained by the foul crime of assassination," and setting out the measures he was taking. These included raising eight thousand new recruits and an additional regiment of irregular cavalry. However, as his private secretary John Colvin wrote to George Clerk that day, he did not intend "to re-enter Afghanistan with a view to re-conquest, retaliation, punishment, or any other name by which a second invasion might be described," at least for the present.

A fresh reason for Auckland's caution, in addition to his reluctance to commit Lord Ellenborough, was the news he had just received of a reckless and abortive attempt to force the Khyber Pass by British troops.

Brigadier Charles Wild had reached Peshawar in late December with the four Bengal Native Infantry regiments sent by Clerk. Responding to Sale's urgent entreaties and without waiting for further forces to join him, on 18 January he had advanced into the Khyber. Lacking artillery, he had taken with him a few ramshackle cannon lent him by General Avitabile, governor of Peshawar, who had also supplied him with some auxiliary Sikh troops. The Sikh guns had failed to work properly, the Sikh troops, who had a deep-seated fear of the pass, had mutinied and his own men had panicked under Afghan fire. Wild had been wounded, and the entire force had fallen back, confirming all Auckland's fears about the dangers of acting in haste.

Fortunately, General Pollock was neither rash nor impulsive. On 5 February he reached Peshawar to find morale low and eighteen hundred of his troops in the hospital, many with malaria. His orders from Auckland were to do no more than secure the safe withdrawal of Sale's garrison from Jalalabad and protect the frontier. These were, in fact, Auckland's last orders as governor-general. On 28 February Lord Ellenborough's ship anchored off Calcutta, and Auckland prepared to depart. In a letter to his old colleague Hobhouse he wrote of the unparalleled "horror and disaster of what had happened." The situation in Afghanistan was "irretrievable," but the governor-general did not blame himself since "the tone of all those whose observation should have been best, of Macnaghten, Burnes, General Elphinstone, Pottinger, was that of unlimited confidence in the growing improvement of our position at Kabul."

Ellenborough, who had first learned "the disastrous intelligence from Kabul of the murder of Sir W. Macnaghten and the destruction of the British and Native troops" when his ship moored off Madras, discussed the issues with a "greatly depressed" Auckland during the two weeks before the latter embarked for home. Three days after his predecessor's departure, Ellenborough wrote to Nicolls that future strategy "rested solely on military considerations . . . In the first instance regard to the safety of [the various garrisons] . . . and finally, to the re-establishment of our military reputation by the infliction of some signal and decisive blow upon the Afghans, which may make it appear to them, and to our own subjects and to our allies, that we have the power of inflicting punishment upon those who commit atrocities . . . and that we withdraw ultimately from Afghanistan, not from any deficiency of means to maintain our position but because we are satisfied that the King we have set up has not, as we were erroneously led to imagine, the support of the nation over which he has been placed."

IN BRITAIN IN late 1841, Peel's new government was deep in discussion about how to deal with the ongoing economic crisis that was being exacerbated by another harsh winter. Among the measures under consideration was the reintroduction of an income tax, first imposed as a temporary measure to fund the war against Napoleon and abandoned after his defeat. (The tax was reimposed in the summer of 1842.) As yet the government was still unaware of the Afghan disaster—the first reports of unrest in Kabul did not reach London until early January 1842. By late February the government knew of the danger to the Kabul force but not until 10 March did it learn that Macnaghten was dead and that some catastrophe had overtaken the garrison. The Duke of Wellington complained that "there must have been either the grossest treachery, or the most inconceivable imbecility, and very likely a mixture of both." Yet even then, the full extent of the catastrophe was not understood. Reports in the *Times* suggesting disaster in Afghanistan met with public incredulity, even hostility. An officer wrote to the newspaper abusing it for publishing "a tissue of bazaar reports injudiciously forwarded to Britain." However, on 5 April the paper published a private letter from Dr. Brydon to his brother Tom, written soon after reaching Jalalabad, that provided incontestable evidence of the army's destruction.

By then the government knew the worst. On 31 March Wellington wrote to Ellenborough urging him to restore Britain's fallen reputation and lamenting, "Our enemies in France, the United States, and wherever found are now rejoicing in triumph upon our disasters and degradation." A week later, Prime Minister Sir Robert Peel, while approving such sentiments, wrote more coolly to Ellenborough, "We shall lose nothing . . . by acting cautiously and deliberately—by securing ourselves against the risk of even greater disasters in Hindustan, or of reiterated failure in our attempt to inflict just retribution."

Ellenborough would not receive this advice for some time and meanwhile had to navigate his own course through the immediate and complex problems confronting him: how best to relieve Sale and extricate the other garrisons still in Afghanistan, how to rescue the hostages, what to do about the erstwhile British protégé Shah Shuja, still in the Balla Hissar, and how to demonstrate to the watching world that the British would not tolerate the massacre of their troops.

For the four hundred-strong British garrison in the citadel at Ghazni, it was already too late. On 6 March, after besieging Ghilzais had cut off the water supply, the commanding officer, Lieutenant Colonel Thomas Palmer, agreed to depart on the promise of safe passage to Peshawar sworn on the Koran. However, as soon as the garrison left the fortress it was attacked and, after suffering many casualties, surrendered. Ten officers were taken hostage, and many of their men massacred or sold into slavery. News of Ghazni's fall reached Ellenborough in early April, and so seriously did he take it that almost immediately he left Calcutta to be closer to the northwest frontier and thus shorten the lines of communication.

At Jalalabad, as Sale had anticipated, Akbar Khan had indeed turned his attention to ejecting the British. Though he had needed time to raise sufficient troops, he had succeeded by reminding his fellow chiefs that this was jihad, writing, "This is the work of God that has come to pass . . . so that the whole of Islam united with one heart have engaged in a war against the infidels." By early March he was blockading Jalalabad, though lack of siege cannon prevented him from launching a frontal assault.

At Kandahar the taciturn and determined Nott was also holding out. He had forcibly evicted some six thousand citizens from the city to make his position more secure. Nevertheless, he was besieged, and a relief force on its way to Kandahar via the Bolan Pass and Quetta was initially repulsed with heavy losses, only finally forcing its way to Kandahar in May.

At Peshawar Pollock was preparing his forces. Though he refused to be pressured by Sale's appeals for help into advancing before his preparations were complete—a decision for which many would criticize him—he could at least reassure Sale that help was coming. On 31 March, after waiting for the arrival of cavalry, horse-artillery and sufficient ammunition—he was insistent that every man had two hundred rounds—Pollock set out. At three thirty on the morning of 5 April, as quietly as possible without bugle blast or drum-beat, the three columns of Pollock's force approached the Khyber Pass.

As Pollock was well aware, the Khyberees, had constructed a giant *sangar*, a barrier of stones reinforced with branches and mud to block the mouth of the pass, where their white flag symbolizing "Victory or Death" was flying. He had decided the best tactic was one favored by the Afghans themselves: to occupy the high ground. "Fancy English troops crowning heights . . . yet they can and will do it," an excited young officer who would lose his life in the action wrote the night before. Pollock's plan was a success. While the Khyberees guarding the *sangar* still slept, British troops were already halfway up the cliffs overlooking the entrance. Outmaneuvered, the Khyberees fled, and the main force pushed through the pass scarcely having to fight, becoming the first troops in modern times to force the Khyber—others had bribed or negotiated their passage.

However, at Jalalabad, spies reported that Pollock had been repulsed. When, on 6 April, the garrison heard Akbar Khan's guns firing a salute, they assumed these reports must be correct. In fact, the cannonade was celebrating the death of Shah Shuja. Under increasing pressure from chiefs on all sides—Barakzai and Sadozai—to prove he had truly broken with the British and was not "sinking Islam," the king had unwisely agreed to quit the safety of the Balla Hissar to lead fresh troops against the unbelievers at Jalalabad. Early on the morning of 5 April, a son of Nawab Zaman Khan—seemingly without the knowledge or consent of the nawab, appointed king by the conspirators early in the rising and who had even sent his wife to Shah Shuja to promise on the Koran that he would be safe—had shot the king down as he was being carried in his royal litter to join the Afghan troops encamped in the hills outside Kabul.

Believing that the relief of Jalalabad was not, after all, imminent, some of Sale's officers argued that same day that their best chance of survival was to attack Akbar Khan. Though initially reluctant, Sale finally agreed. Just then news arrived that Pollock had indeed forced the Khyber Pass, and Fighting Bob urged on preparations for the assault on Akbar Khan with renewed energy. On the night of 6 April soldiers were told to draw up wills, if they wished, "to be attested by officers by midnight," and rubbish was strewn over the ground to deaden the sound of gun carriages being moved. Shortly before dawn the next day, three infantry columns supported by two hundred cavalry and artillery, marched through Jalalabad's Kabul Gate. Akbar Khan's camp lay two and a half miles away, but his men had occupied some forts between Jalalabad and his camp. Sale, astride a white charger, ordered Dennie and his regiment, the Thirteenth Light Infantry, supported by artillery, to attack the nearest of the forts while the rest pressed on. The prescient Dennie, who had foreseen the fate of his comrades at Kabul, met his own end during the assault. However, Sale's attack on Akbar Khan's camp succeeded. Though his cavalry resisted for a while, artillery fire finally drove them off, and Sale seized and burned the camp, where his men found four guns taken from the massacred Kabul garrison. The action would cause Ellenborough to glorify the men of Jalalabad as the "Illustrious Garrison" and to dash off a letter to Sir Robert Peel rejoicing that "at last we have got a victory and our military character is re-established."

On 16 April Pollock and his men entered Jalalabad. Their arrival was regarded with mixed feelings. Thomas Seaton, an officer of the garrison, wrote, "They had not arrived in time to help us in our imminent peril, and they had lost the grand opportunity of joining with us to crush the man whose treachery had destroyed our brethren in arms, and so many thousands of unarmed camp-followers, whose bones were scattered in the Kabul passes . . . So when . . . Pollock's force arrived, there was a hearty welcome, but a sly bit of sarcasm in the tune—an old Jacobite air—to which the band of the 13th played them in, 'Ye're o'er lang o' comin.'"

Brydon was also not altogether delighted that Pollock had reached Jalalabad. Political officers had already been quizzing him about his account of the retreat, and he suspected Pollock would wish to hold a formal inquiry into what had happened. These suspicions seemed to be confirmed when Pollock sent his aide-de-camp to ask Brydon to call on him. Uncertain what to reveal about the behavior of some individuals during the retreat and especially about the decisions made by the commanding officers, the doctor turned for advice to a friend, Lieutenant Francis Cunningham. Together they decided what it would be judicious for Brydon to say to avoid, as Cunningham wrote, "useless and unpleasant controversy." However, they had no need to be anxious. Brydon returned far sooner than Cunningham had expected with an amused expression.

"He had not been asked a single question about the retreat, but had been closely pressed to testify to the actual death of a Dr. Harcourt of the HM 44th who had married Pollock's daughter who would be unable to draw the interest on certain bonds without such a certificate."

A WEEK EARLIER, the defeated Akbar Khan had set out north, taking the most important of his hostages with him. He might have been surprised to learn of a rumor circulating around the Jalalabad garrison that he "intended to bring Lady Sale . . . before the walls, and put her to torture within sight, and so compel Sale to surrender." On hearing of it himself, Sale told an officer with deep emotion, "I—I will have every gun turned on her; my old bones shall be buried beneath the ruins of the fort here; but I will never surrender."

By then the hostages had been in captivity for three months, during which Lady Sale had continued to keep her sharply observed, unhysterical journal. In the first days, shunted from mud fort to mud fort, they had seen huddles of starving, naked people who, they were told, "had sustained life by feeding on their dead comrades." However, on 17 January they had reached the stronghold of Budeeabad—belonging to Akbar Khan's father-in-law, the Ghilzai chief, Mohammed Shah Khan—at the head of the Lughman Valley, some forty miles from Jalalabad. Here they had remained for eleven weeks, the officers and ladies sharing five rooms, while others found what shelter they could in stables and sheds. Some, including a sergeant major who had only joined the army "in consequence of having committed a murder," according to Mackenzie, were so badly wounded that they died within a few days.

Lady Sale was glad that at last she could at least wash her face; "it was rather a painful process," though, "as the cold and glare of the sun on the snow had three times peeled my face, from which the skin came off in strips." She also described how the captives made coffee substitute from rice and barley. Their food consisted of rice, flour and the flesh of the two lambs killed daily that Lawrence rationed out between them. Despite the privations, the officers and ladies were attended by Hindu servants who had chosen to accompany them into captivity. However, a few weeks later, the Afghans insisted on turning out of the fort any servant too ill and frostbitten to work—and there were many. Eyre described how "the limbs of many of these poor wretches had completely withered . . . the feet of others had dropped off from the ankle." He thought their expulsion "a cruel scene."

As time passed, the captives grew desperate for news, trying to piece together what was happening from rumors and scraps of information. Akbar Khan himself told them that the only European to reach Jalalabad was Dr. Brydon.* From the thin and ill-looking Major Griffiths and Captain Souter, brought to Budeeabad in mid-February, they learned of the final massacre at Gandamack, while Sergeant Major Lissant, also brought to join them, had his own stories of the retreat to tell. However, Akbar Khan did permit Lady Sale to correspond with her husband. Sale's letters—though he must have written with care, knowing the Afghans would read them—reported that Jalalabad was holding out and that General Pollock was marching to relieve the garrison. Sale also sent his wife boxes of clothes as well as books to ease the boredom of captivity.

Clean clothes were especially welcome since, as Lady Sale noted, "very few of us . . . are not covered with crawlers." They soon became adept at distinguishing different types of vermin—calling lice "infantry" and fleas "light cavalry." Despite their common plight, some of the women showed little generosity. Mrs. Eyre, who only had one gown, asked another with several trunks full to lend her one but was refused. The owner of the trunks was probably Lady Macnaghten, who had somehow preserved most of her baggage, including valuable shawls and her jewels. Lady Sale also seems to have been selfish. Captain Mackenzie asked her to lend Mrs. Eyre a needle so that she could sew clothes from material sent by Akbar, but his diplomacy failed.

On 19 February a powerful earthquake struck. The bedridden Elphinstone was carried to safety in the arms of his servant, a private of the Forty-fourth. The ceiling of a room that Lady Sale had luckily just vacated fell in. Rushing outside to look for her daughter, she found everyone safe. She reported that even one of Lady Macnaghten's cats was dug out

---

*According to Lady Sale, among others, Akbar Khan had predicted that only one survivor would reach Jalalabad. It is possible that he engineered this outcome. He was certainly intelligent enough to appreciate its potential effect on British morale.

alive from the ruins. Shelton admonished Mackenzie for a breach of military protocol "in a solemn tone to make him feel the enormity of his offence." "Mackenzie, you went downstairs *first* today." To which Mackenzie replied, "I'm sorry; it's the fashion in earthquakes, Brigadier." That night the captives slept in the open.

The same earthquake did much to nullify the work that Broadfoot had been doing to strengthen Jalalabad's defenses. Luckily, Akbar Khan did not take advantage of the destruction to attack, and Broadfoot and his sappers were able to rectify the damage. Though Akbar's camp out on the plains was largely untouched, many of his men had hurried home to their villages to check on their families. The quake was also felt as far away as Peshawar, disturbing some of Pollock's young officers as they played quoits and obliging others "to hold on to the ropes of our tents to prevent falling." It also raised a great dust cloud over the city, where houses and towers collapsed. Pollock himself had a narrow escape when a beam crashed down on a desk at which he had been working a few moments earlier.

In succeeding weeks aftershocks shook the earth, so that sometimes Lady Sale felt "a tremulous motion as of a ship that has been heavily struck by a sea" or the sensation "of a heavy ball rolling over our heads, as if on the roof of our individual room, accompanied by the sound of distant thunder." Sometimes there were other alarms for the captives—rumors that Jalalabad had fallen, which made Lady Sale extremely anxious, and lurid tales of the cruelty of Akbar Khan, who, she wrote, "is known to have had a man flayed alive in his presence, commencing at the feet."

The prisoners tried to judge their own situation from the attitude of their jailors, who were sometimes kind, sometimes talked of ransom but at other times robbed them and threatened them with being sold as slaves. On 6 April they learned of Shah Shuja's murder, and three days later, the owner of their fortress prison, Mohammed Shah Khan, arrived to confirm stories they had already heard that Sale's men had destroyed Akbar Khan's camp. Mohammed Shah Khan told them that many of the chiefs wanted to kill them but that Akbar Khan was resisting. Instead, he intended moving them somewhere more remote from where the British could never rescue them. As the captives soon learned, Akbar Khan's plans extended only to the most valuable of his prisoners: the officers and "ladies." The soldiers, their wives and children were to remain behind.

On 10 April these choice hostages, relieved of their remaining valuables, left Budeeabad. Barely four miles into their journey, according to Lawrence, "a horseman was seen advancing from the south-east at full gallop, waving his turban and shouting out some phrases in Persian which threw our escort into the most intense excitement. They wheeled round flourishing their arms, and I really thought for a few minutes that it was a preconcerted signal for commencing our indiscriminate slaughter."

In fact, the messenger was bringing orders from Akbar Khan to return the prisoners to Budeeabad because he feared the other chiefs might attempt to seize them. However, on returning to the fort they were ordered not to unpack and the next morning rode out once more to their uncertain future.

CHAPTER EIGHTEEN

The object of the combined march of your army and Major General Nott's upon Kabul will be to exhibit our strength where we suffered defeat, to inflict just, but not vindictive retribution upon the Afghans.
> —LORD ELLENBOROUGH TO GENERAL POLLOCK,
> 23 JULY 1842.

ELLENBOROUGH'S SATISFACTION THAT Pollock had forced the Khyber Pass did not encourage him to be rash. On 19 April he instructed Nott to evacuate Kandahar and retreat via Quetta as soon as he was able—a "peremptory order" that came "like a thunderclap," as Nott's political officer Rawlinson wrote. Nott informed Ellenborough that as he was short of everything, especially transport—which he had repeatedly requested—the earliest he could march his troops back through Quetta was October.

The governor-general also instructed Pollock and Sale to move their troops from Jalalabad closer to the Indian border unless negotiations over the hostages or military considerations made such a step unwise. Pollock was horrified and wrote to Nott urging him to remain in Kandahar. The letter no longer exists, but Pollock many years later explained his reasons: "I felt at the time that to retire would be our ruin—the whole country would have risen to endeavour to destroy us. I therefore determined on remaining at Jalalabad until an opportunity offered for our advance, if practicable . . . Stopping Nott for a few days, after his receipt of orders to

retire, was perhaps a very bold step . . . but I felt it pretty certain that if we worked together in earnest, the game would be ours."

Even after learning that Sale had routed Akbar Khan, Ellenborough still did not alter his opinion that the British forces should fall back toward India. Instead, he hoped Sale's victory could be regarded as the "signal and decisive blow upon the Afghans" he had promised on his arrival in Calcutta. However, Ellenborough knew that he risked public and political odium if he appeared to be abandoning the hostages, and in a further letter to Pollock of 28 April, he implied that the general might, under certain circumstances, advance on Kabul. The many crossings-out and marginal notes on drafts of that letter show his nervousness about taking such a step. Pollock grasped at the prospect, replying, "I trust that I am not wrong in considering this letter as leaving to me discretionary powers" and insisting that immediate withdrawal "would be construed into a defeat, and our character as a powerful nation would be entirely lost in this part of the world."

POLLOCK MEANWHILE HAD opened negotiations with Akbar Khan for the release of his hostages, who had been taken through drenching rain to the fort at Tezeen. Here on 20 April, as the fort's walls rattled and shook during yet another earthquake, Mrs. Waller, the wife of an artillery officer, gave birth to a girl—the fourth British child born in captivity. She had little time to recuperate before Akbar Khan decided to move his prisoners south into the Zandeh Valley. When the officers complained that dragging ill and exhausted women and children about was inhuman, Akbar Khan's father-in-law, Mohammed Shah Khan, retorted, according to Eyre, that "wherever he went we must all follow; and if our horses failed, we must trudge on foot; and if we lagged behind, he would drag us along by force." Akbar Khan seemingly rebuked Mohammed Shah for his rudeness to the hostages but certainly did not alter his plans.

The journey into the Zandeh Valley was General Elphinstone's last. On the evening of 23 April, suffering from violent dysentery for which opium and the bitter liquid of a boiled pomegranate provided only temporary relief, he died. Throughout his captivity he had repeatedly spoken of his wish to have perished with his men on the retreat. Akbar Khan ordered the body to be wrapped in felt blankets, packed around with highly scented wormwood leaves inside a rough wooden casket and sent to Jalalabad with a small escort. Private Miller, one of Elphinstone's batmen (soldier-servants), disguised himself as an Afghan to accompany the body. Near Jugdulluk, Ghilzais attacked, broke open the coffin and stripped and stoned the corpse. Only the warnings of Akbar Khan's men of the punishment he would inflict deterred them from burning it. Hearing what had happened, Akbar Khan dispatched a much larger escort to repack the body. The cortege, accompanied still by Miller despite his having been wounded, finally reached Jalalabad, where Elphinstone was buried with full military honors.

Akbar Khan's gesture in returning the body for burial was an indication of his desire to bring negotiations with Pollock to a satisfactory conclusion. He talked at length and in private to Lawrence about his anxiety to make terms. Captain Lawrence responded that as a gesture of goodwill Akbar Khan should send the women and children to Jalalabad while retaining the men. However, Akbar Khan replied that the other chiefs would never permit it and were in fact demanding the prisoners be assembled in one place so that each "could kill a captive with his own hands."

Akbar Khan's own position among the chiefs was growing precarious. Following Shah Shuja's murder, Prince Futteh Jung—Shah Shuja's second son—had declared himself his father's successor. From the Balla Hissar he was demanding that all the European hostages be handed over to him. The powerful Amenoolah Khan—one of the original instigators of the uprising—had suddenly switched his allegiance from Akbar Khan to Futteh Jung, whom he joined in the Balla Hissar. Akbar Khan's response was to besiege them in the citadel until an intervention from Nawab Zaman Khan made him desist.

Neither were Akbar Khan's negotiations with the British prospering. Just after Elphinstone's death, he had dispatched Colin Mackenzie on parole to Jalalabad carrying a letter setting out his terms for freeing the hostages. Mackenzie was a deeply religious man who regularly conducted services for the captives. He had been selected as emissary because the chiefs "had got it into their heads that I was a Mullah and they thought I would come back." Mackenzie was warmly greeted on his arrival at Jalalabad, though his louse-ridden clothes were immediately taken away and burned. The proposals he brought from Akbar Khan—to release the prisoners either if the British withdrew from Afghanistan or when his father, Dost Mohammed, returned from exile—were less well received. Pollock had no authority from Ellenborough to agree to either suggestion and sent Mackenzie back with a counterproposal: a payment of two hundred thousand rupees for the prisoners' release.

On his return Mackenzie learned that during his absence Captain and Mrs. Anderson had been reunited with their young daughter, whom they had lost during the frantic fighting in the Khoord Kabul Pass four months earlier. The child had been taken to the Kabul slave market for sale. Alerted by British prisoners in Kabul, Nawab Zaman Khan had purchased her for four hundred rupees and taken her into his household. Akbar Khan had recently taken Troup and Pottinger with him to Kabul, where they had seen the girl and persuaded Nawab Zaman Khan to return her to her parents. She was healthy but spoke only Persian and had been taught to say, "My father and mother are infidels, but I am a Mussalman."

Disappointed that Pollock was only offering money, Akbar Khan sent Mackenzie back to Jalalabad with further and more complex proposals, including an amnesty for himself and his close associates and—on the basis that the British intended withdrawing from Afghanistan—their recognition of him as the country's interim ruler. He also asked for a handsome annual payment and a large lump sum. Pollock's reply to Akbar Khan was noncommittal, offering little more than the two hundred thousand rupees already proposed. Unknown to Pollock, even this was more than Ellenborough was prepared to countenance. Ellenborough's attitude toward negotiating with the enemy had been hardening. In mid-May he wrote to Pollock warning him not even to consider making terms with a man who not only was Macnaghten's "acknowledged murderer" but had "deceived and betrayed a British army into a position in which it was destroyed." The most for which "so great a criminal" could hope was that the British would spare his life.

By this time Akbar Khan, still fearing the other chiefs would seize his valuable hostages, had moved them to a fort only three miles from Kabul. The obvious route was through the Khoord Kabul Pass, but finding it "absolutely impassable from the stench of dead bodies," as Eyre wrote, the escort brought the hostages another way. On their arrival the hostages were shown some cattle sheds and told these were the only accommodation available. A "greatly incensed" Lady Sale objected, and Akbar Khan ordered the fort's owner to house the captives in his own family's quarters and took some of the officers to his own house in Kabul. The prisoners were allowed to walk in the fort's gardens, and the men bathed in a stream running through it. Soon new arrivals swelled their numbers, including the British soldiers, women and children left behind at Budeeabad, who all looked "miserably thin and weak."

Now encamped close to Kabul, Akbar Khan resumed his attacks on Futteh Jung, bombarding the Balla Hissar and detonating a mine beneath one of its great towers. During the truce that followed, in an increasingly farcical situation, the leaders of the various factions occupied different towers within the citadel: Futteh Jung and Amenoolah Khan for the Sadozais, Akbar Khan and Nawab Zaman Khan representing the rival Barakzai factions, Mohammed Shah Khan, Akbar Khan's father-in-law, for the Ghilzais and Shirin Khan for the Kizzilbashis. By late June, having coaxed the volatile Amenoolah Khan to support him once more and through judicious bribery, Akbar Khan had strengthened his position. He used the opportunity to gain control of as many of the British prisoners in Kabul as he could. They included Captain John Conolly and five other British hostages, whom, realizing their value as bargaining chips, he purchased from Kabul's chief mullah, as well as the sick and wounded left behind when Elphinstone's column had begun its retreat in January.

By then Ellenborough was well aware that Nott and Pollock were finding excuses not to withdraw from Afghanistan. In June he wrote to Prime Minister Peel complaining, "We shall be unable now to bring back the two armies until the cool season" and railing about the malign influence of political officers who, "poisoned by vain ambition," needed to learn that they were not free agents and that "there is a government." He also alleged that Nott and Pollock had "not a grain of military talent" and that had the latter not fallen into the hands of the politicals, "he would otherwise have been before now on the left bank of the Indus, and safe."

Yet Ellenborough should not have been surprised. Nott's stubbornness was legendary, while Sir Jasper Nicolls, Ellenborough's commander in chief, had warned him weeks before that Pollock was his own man and would "stand alone."

However, as the weeks passed, Ellenborough began to change his mind. If his generals had withdrawn their troops immediately after Sale's defeat of Akbar Khan as he had wanted, he could successfully have claimed that the Afghans had been punished. However, to pull out of Afghanistan now, after months of doing nothing, would smack of failure, especially when political and public opinion in India and at home was clamoring for action to rescue the hostages and inflict revenge. On 4 July Ellenborough sent Nott and Pollock revised orders. Though his instructions to withdraw to India still stood, Nott could retreat via Kabul if he wished and—if he did—Pollock could advance to the capital in a joint operation with him. He had not consulted his commander in chief, Sir Jasper Nicolls, who complained in his diary, "[Ellenborough's] want of decent attention to my position is inexcusable."

Ellenborough explained his equivocatory reasoning in a letter to the Duke of Wellington, who had been foremost among those urging him to restore Britain's reputation in the East: "The case is one in which, at this distance, I could not direct an advance, but, at the same time, I should hardly be justified in continuing to prohibit it." To Sir Robert Peel he wrote an unusually long seven-page letter justifying his action and arguing that if Nott and Pollock succeeded they could reclaim the honor of the British army "in triumph upon the scene of its late disaster."

Nott, as Ellenborough knew he would, chose to advance on Kabul. Fearing that Nott might already have departed for India instead, Pollock sent letter after letter to Kandahar, sometimes using rice water as "invisible ink." Then in mid-August he received Nott's confirmation that he was indeed going to Kabul.

The governor-general still continued to limit his generals' objectives, instructing Pollock, "The object of the combined march of your army and Major General Nott's upon Kabul will be to exhibit our strength where we suffered defeat, to inflict just, but not vindictive retribution upon the Afghans, and to recover the guns and colours as well as the prisoners lost by our army." That done, come what may, Nott and Pollock were "to obey the positive orders of your government to withdraw your army from Afghanistan." Also they were not to involve themselves in internal politics. Any British commitments or obligations had died with Shah Shuja, and they had to concur with "whatever government or person the Afghans may prefer."

When Akbar Khan discovered that the British intended to advance, not withdraw, he flew into a rage, threatening to sell all the captives to the slave markets in Turkestan. However, on calmer reflection he realized his best course was to maintain a dialogue with Pollock. Mackenzie was very ill with typhus, so Akbar Khan sent Lawrence and Troup as his new envoys to Jalalabad.

Preoccupied with planning for the advance, Pollock saw no point in further negotiations and gave Lawrence and Troup a noncommittal reply. He was well aware from messages sent by the British agent Mohan Lal of the chaotic political situation in Kabul. Lal had also been intriguing among the chiefs, trying to detach them from Akbar Khan and seeking promises that the hostages would be neither killed nor sold. Realizing Lal was a spy and that he had access to British funds, on 22 June Akbar Khan had seized him and had him tortured in the Balla Hissar. However, Lal was still managing to communicate with Pollock, describing merciless beatings and how Akbar Khan had extracted thousands of rupees from him and was threatening to blind him unless he provided more. Pollock warned Akbar Khan that the British would hold him accountable for Lal's well-being, and the torture ceased, though Lal remained a prisoner. During his incarceration Lal was comforted by John Conolly, shortly to die of a heart attack not long after hearing that his brother Arthur, still a captive of the psychotic emir of Bokhara, had been publicly beheaded, together with his fellow prisoner Colonel Charles Stoddart. The news that the Afghans had destroyed a British army had convinced the emir that the British were weak and hence keeping the two officers alive any longer was pointless.

On 7 August Nott finally left Kandahar for Kabul, leading what he proudly described as "a compact and well-tried force" of six thousand, having dispatched the remainder of his army to Quetta. Ahead of him lay a difficult three hundred miles. On 20 August Pollock and Sale marched out of Jalalabad with eight thousand men to begin their shorter journey of some ninety miles. Pollock had ordered baggage be kept to a minimum, eliminating the sideboards, dressing tables and trunks of dress uniforms that had so encumbered the Army of the Indus. The troops were, in Private Teer's words, "eager to march anywhere" to escape Jalalabad's heat and stench and its clouds of flies. According to the Reverend Gleig, they came "in myriads . . . The very air became black with them; and they entered into men's food, and crawled over their persons, polluting whatever they touched. It was a season of intense suffering . . . and the sufferers from a burning heat sought shelter against it by digging holes in the ground and sleeping in them at the hazard of being buried alive, as in one instance, at least, actually befell."

Akbar Khan's reaction to the British advance was to order all his hostages taken north toward Bamiyan with an escort commanded by a deserter from Shah Shuja's infantry, Saleh Mohammed. The group had recently been joined by five officers given as hostages before the retreat from Kabul and also the officers taken prisoner at Ghazni, whose commanding officer, Colonel Palmer, had been badly tortured because the Afghans had suspected him of having buried treasure in the citadel. The youngest hostage to set out into the mountainous northern wilds was Lady Sale's granddaughter, born to Alexandrina Sturt just a month earlier. On previous journeys the women had sometimes been insulted by Afghans affronted by their bare faces and heads. This time they wore Afghan dress, "the outer garment of which consists of a large and white sheet completely shrouding the body, to which is attached the *bourkha*, or veil, of white muslin, with only a small open space of network opposite the eyes to peep through," as Eyre described.

On 30 August Nott saw his first serious fighting when an army of twelve thousand men, led by the governor of Ghazni, advanced to confront him, but his men routed the Afghans. Ghazni itself fell six days later without a fight. Nott ordered his engineers to destroy the citadel. The flames were still rising as his army marched onward, carrying with them, as explicitly commanded by Ellenborough, the sandalwood gates of the ancient tomb of Sultan Mahmud of Ghazni, supposedly looted from the Indian temple at Somnath centuries earlier. He hoped to gain great kudos by returning them to India. An irritated officer complained that the gates were "an endless trouble to us, as they were very large and heavy, and all our bullocks weak, very sulky and would not work. Consequently the men had in many cases to pull them along."

By this time Pollock had reached Gandamack to find it "literally covered with skeletons, most of them bleached by exposure to the rain and sun, but many having hair of a colour which enabled us to recognise the remains of our own countrymen." On 1 September Futteh Jung rode into the British encampment to ask for sanctuary. Having been robbed of his gold, silver and jewels and virtually imprisoned in the Balla Hissar by Akbar Khan, he had managed to escape and gone in search of Pollock's advancing army. Though Ellenborough had warned Pollock not to take sides, he treated the new arrival with deference, even ordering a salute to be fired in his honor.

By 12 September Pollock was encamped near the entrance to the narrow Tezeen Pass. As an officer recalled, that night Afghan sharpshooters fired on the British from the heights above, "their bullets . . . flying like hail among our tents," while their war chant of *Huk! Huk! Huk!* resounded all night long. The next day the British had advanced barely two miles into the pass "when suddenly a long sheet of flame issued from the heights on each side, and a thousand balls came whizzing and whistling about our heads. The hills were lined with the enemy in great force."

This "great force" was perhaps the largest yet to confront the British in Afghanistan: sixteen thousand men, commanded by Akbar Khan himself, in a last desperate bid to hold back the avenging British. Once again, Pollock employed the tactic he had used in forcing the Khyber of denying his attackers the high ground by sending troops to storm the heights. "Up we went, helter, skelter . . . and in a short time we were up and at them," wrote an officer. The Afghans roared insults of "dogs, kafirs and the like" at the onrushing British, but at the sight of their bayonets they fled, scrambling yet higher to get away: "The Afghans would stand like statues against firing but the sight of the bristling line of cold steel they could not endure!" Then at a signal from the valley floor, the assault force flung themselves to the ground as Pollock's howitzers hurled shrapnel shells onto the ridges above them. Looking to the crest, an officer saw an Afghan carrying "a large blood-red standard in a very exposed position . . . brandishing his tulwar in his right hand and daring the soldiers to come on." The British rushed forward again, driving the enemy from ridge to ridge. Broadfoot and his Gurkhas were among the pursuers, so that, according to an officer, "far in the distance were to be seen small parties of these diminutive warriors, driving strong bodies of Afghans before them."

The troops seized Akbar Khan's camp and burned his tent, where, as so often related in military tales, a feast had apparently already been laid out for him to celebrate his anticipated victory. Akbar Khan himself fled northward, leaving Pollock to pass unopposed through the Khoord Kabul defile, where an officer described an "awful scene of slaughter . . . the remains of the poor victims of Elphinstone's imbecility and of Afghan treachery lay in frightful numbers, some on their backs at full length, having evidently met the happiest fate, instantaneous death; others with their limbs contracted . . . as if they had died in agony . . . groups of skeletons and bodies were huddled together, near what had evidently been a fire, by which they had endeavoured to postpone the awful fate which overtook them, and hundreds of others lying around—freezing to death! The greatest portion . . . were mere skeletons, but there were many to which the flesh still clung and whose features were recognisable."

On 15 September Pollock's army camped on the Kabul racecourse laid out by the British when they had happily anticipated time for leisure pursuits. Mohan Lal, who had escaped from his prison a week earlier, arrived to tell Pollock what he knew of the hostages' whereabouts. Pollock dispatched six hundred Kizzilbashi soldiers provided by Lal's friend and protector Shirin Khan, under his military secretary Richmond Shakespear, to locate them. Unknown to Pollock or Lal, the prisoners, who had reached Bamiyan, in the territory of the Hazaras, on 2 September, were already free, though still in considerable danger.*

Their liberty was the result of their jailer's greed. Captain Johnson had been trying to convince Saleh Mohammed that the British would reward him well if he released the prisoners. Guessing it would probably be expedient to side with the British once more, Saleh Mohammed had recently taken to dressing in a European officer's blue frock coat and was showing himself receptive. However, he was also still receiving orders from Akbar Khan. On 11 September he confided in Pottinger he had received two letters. The first, from Akbar Khan, ordered him to take the hostages north into the Hindu Kush and sell them to the Uzbeks. The second, from Mohan Lal, offered him a pension for life if he released his

---

*Mohan Lal later became a vocal critic of the errors made by the British administration in India during the Afghan campaign. His frankness won him few favors in India, but the home government in Britain rewarded his services with a handsome pension of one thousand pounds a year. He died in Delhi in 1877 at the age of sixty-five.

prisoners. Realizing that this was their chance for freedom, Pottinger summoned the other officers, and the men borrowed Lady Sale's room for a private conference during which they succeeded in convincing Saleh Mohammed that Lal's letter was genuine. Five officers signed a bond guaranteeing him one thousand rupees a month and twenty thousand rupees subject to the hostages' safe arrival at Kabul—money that he would never receive—and he gave them back their freedom for the first time in more than eight months.

As yet the former prisoners had no way of knowing what had been happening in the wider world, and their first fear was that they might be attacked, recaptured and even sold into slavery. Johnson wrote they "were determined rather to die at Bamiyan than to perish in a dungeon in Turkestan" and immediately "laid in provisions, dug wells, filled the ditches round the fort with water, and were all prepared for a siege." Pottinger, meanwhile, with remarkable confidence summoned local Hazara leaders to demand their allegiance. When the governor of the province refused, Johnson described how the former hostages "deposed him and set up another!"

On 15 September they learned that Akbar Khan was in flight from the British and decided to try to reach Kabul. Saleh Mohammed obtained some muskets so they could defend themselves if attacked, but when Lawrence asked for volunteers from the released private soldiers to form a guard, the men were silent, causing Lady Sale to exclaim, "You had better give *me* [a musket] and I will lead the party." The next day the group of twenty officers, half of whom were wounded, fifty-one other ranks, twelve women and twenty-two children set out for Kabul, fearful that at any moment they might encounter Akbar Khan's retreating forces. However, that night a messenger brought word that Shakespear was on his way to find them, and their spirits rose.

The following day, while they were resting, they saw a cloud of dust on the skyline. They hoped it was Shakespear but took up defensive positions until, as Lawrence wrote, the dust indeed "announced the advance of our friends." An emotional Shakespear, dressed in Afghan clothing, rushed to embrace Lady Sale, only to be rebuked by Shelton, curmudgeonly to the last, for not first paying his respects to him as the senior commanding officer. Knowing that strong bands of Afghans were not far away, Shakespear urged the group to keep going as fast as they could. Three days later, they met Sale at the head of a party of dragoons. Lady Sale wrote with rare emotion of her reunion with her husband: "happiness so long delayed, as to be almost unexpected, was actually painful, and accompanied by a choking sensation which could not obtain the relief of tears." Pollock had originally intended to dispatch Nott, not Sale, in Shakespear's wake. However, Nott had reached Kabul on 17 September to find, to his disappointment, that Pollock had beaten him, and objected that his men were tired, adding, in a clear reference to Ellenborough's previous lack of concern for the hostages, that since the government "had thrown the prisoners overboard, why then should he rescue them?"

On their way to Pollock's camp, the former captives passed through Kabul, where, as Eyre noted, "the streets were almost empty, and an unnatural silence prevailed . . . We passed the spot where Sir Alexander Burnes's house had stood.—It was now a heap of rubbish.—The garden in which he took so much interest and pride, was a desolate waste." Reaching the camp, they were greeted by a twenty-one-gun salute, and soldiers crowded around congratulating them on their rescue. Captain Warburton was soon united with his Afghan wife and baby son, born in a Ghilzai fort between Jugdulluk and Gandamack eight weeks earlier. His wife had fled their burning house in the city after insurgents had set it alight on the day of Burnes's murder. Since then well-wishers had concealed her, even though her cousin Akbar Khan had sworn to punish her for marrying an infidel; he had sent his soldiers to raid houses where she was believed to be hiding, "thrusting in all directions with their lances and swords, trying to find out her hiding-place" so that "she had often to run away from one house thus treated to take shelter in another," as her son later wrote in his memoirs. The other British hostages in and around Kabul had also been rescued, including some two thousand sepoys and camp followers, many crippled through frostbite, found begging in the streets of Kabul.

All that remained was to deliver retribution. Pollock sent troops to seize and sack the fortified town of Istalif, where Amenoolah Khan was believed to have fled. There the soldiers released a further five hundred sepoys being kept captive in terrible conditions and exacted such revenge that a young lieutenant described how the brutality made him feel like a licensed assassin. On 9 October Pollock ordered his engineers to destroy

Kabul's seventeenth-century Grand Bazaar, where Macnaghten's mutilated remains had been displayed, though he told them to position the charges in such a way that the surrounding portions of the city would be unharmed. According to one of Pollock's men, the bazaar was still "a splendid arcade, six hundred feet long, with two thousand shops, all roofed over from end to end with glass," where mouth-watering fruit and other delicacies were piled. Pollock's decision to flatten it annoyed Nott, who thought it would have made more military sense to blow up the Balla Hissar. Nevertheless, the bazaar went up in smoke and flames. Despite Pollock's orders that there was to be no looting, an officer described how when people heard the explosions "the cry went forth that Kabul was given up to plunder. Both camps rushed into the city, and the consequence has been the almost total destruction of all parts of the town." Lal was deeply upset that the houses and shops of many who had befriended him were destroyed.

On 12 October Pollock and Nott led their forces from Kabul back toward India. Futteh Jung had wisely decided to go with them, leaving young Prince Shapur, another of Shah Shuja's sons, on the throne. Though the British had nominally recognized Shapur, they left him neither military nor financial support. Akbar Khan soon arrived in Kabul to chase him from the throne, and in early 1843 Dost Mohammed returned from exile to resume his place as emir. About to leave India behind him, Dost Mohammed would tell his British "hosts": "I have been struck with the magnitude of your resources, your ships, your arsenals; but what I cannot understand is why the rulers of an empire so vast and flourishing should have gone across the Indus to deprive me of my poor and barren country."

The retreating British force reached Jalalabad safely, transiting passes that were, according to an officer, "strewn with skeletons of men and animals . . . Our gun-wheels ground to dust the bones of the dead . . . In some places the Affghans . . . had placed the skeletons in the arms one of the other, or sometimes sitting or standing against the rocks as if they were holding a conversation!" In Jalalabad they delayed several days to pull down the fortifications Broadfoot and his sappers had so carefully constructed before entering the Khyber Pass. Though the vanguard got through the pass without difficulty, Khyberees fell on the rear, picking off stragglers and carrying off baggage. A young lieutenant and an ensign became the last men to die in action during a conflict that had claimed so many thousands of lives.

In India Lord Ellenborough planned great celebrations. He issued a proclamation effectively damning Auckland's policies and praising his own and—to emphasize further the contrasting success of himself and his predecessor—dated it 1 October, the day of Auckland's Simla Manifesto announcing the British invasion of Afghanistan four years earlier. Ellenborough also issued a note to the princes of India glorifying the return to India of the gates of Somnath, "so long the memorial of your humiliation." The gates were eventually discovered to be not the originals but later replicas of those plundered from India, and they were ignominiously dumped in a warehouse in Agra.

The governor-general traveled from Simla to greet the returning British troops in December 1842 as they crossed the Sutlej River over a bridge of boats. At Ferozepore—where in 1838 the Army of the Indus had paraded before Lord Auckland and Ranjit Singh—Ellenborough had ordered the erection of a ceremonial bamboo arch flanked by an honor guard of gorgeously caparisoned elephants, through which the troops—many openly amused at the extravagance of it all—marched. Spectators might have been forgiven for believing they were witnessing the celebration of a great victory rather than an epilogue to failure, as the Reverend Gleig observed: "the end of a war begun for no wise purpose, carried on with a strange mixture of rashness and timidity, and brought to a close, after suffering and disaster, without much of glory attaching either to the government which directed, or the great body of the troops which waged it."

EPILOGUE

Remember the rights of the savage as we call him . . . remember the happiness of his humble home . . . the sanctity of life in the hill villages of Afghanistan among the winter snows is as inviolable in the eyes of Almighty God as can be your own.
—WILLIAM GLADSTONE, PRIME MINISTER OF BRITAIN, 1879

NOW WAS THE time for analysis and blame-sharing. Sir Jasper Nicolls, commander in chief in India, wrote to Ellenborough, succinctly listing eight reasons for the campaign's failure.

1st: Making war with a peace establishment.
2nd: Making war without a safe base of operations.
3rd: Carrying our native army . . . into a strange and cold climate, where they and we were foreigners, and both considered as infidels.
4th: Invading a poor country, and one unequal to supply our wants, especially our large establishment of cattle.
5th: Giving undue power to political agents.
6th: Want of forethought and undue confidence in the Afghans on the part of Sir William Macnaghten.
7th: Placing our magazines, even our treasure, in indefensible places.
8th: Great military neglect and mismanagement after the outbreak.

His reasons, all valid, contain a mix of the political and the military, the strategic and the tactical. There is no doubt that the military disaster on the scale that occurred on the retreat from Kabul could have been avoided by better leadership of the army in Kabul.

Back in Britain, politicians and others concentrated on the political and moral aspects, both more subjective and more difficult to analyze. Sir John Kaye, the historian who collected many of the primary documents and indeed published in full those that had been expurgated or omitted from the government's publication justifying the war in 1839, saw the hand of God in the outcome: "The calamity of 1842 was retribution sufficient . . . to stamp in indelible characters upon the page of history, the great truth that the policy which was pursued in Afghanistan was unjust, and that, therefore, it was signally disastrous. It was . . . an unrighteous usurpation, and the curse of God was on it from the first. Our successes at the outset were a part of the curse. They lapped us in false security, and deluded us to our overthrow. This is the great lesson . . . 'The Lord God of recompenses shall surely requite.'"

Henry Lushington, another commentator, wrote in a book-long analysis of the conflict in 1844: "We entered Afghanistan to effect a change of dynasty—we withdrew from it professing our readiness to acknowledge any government which the Afghans may themselves think fit to establish. We entered it above all to establish a government friendly to ourselves. Are the Afghans our friends now? . . . Except for the anarchy we have left in the place of order, the hatred in the place of kindness, all is as it was before . . . The received code of international morality is not even in the nineteenth century very strict. One principle however seems to be admitted in the theory, if not the practice of civilised men, that an aggressive war—a war undertaken against unoffending parties with a view to our own benefit only—is unjust, and conversely that a war to be just must partake the character of a defensive war. It may be defensive in various ways . . . either preventing an injury which it is attempted to inflict, or of exacting reparation for one inflicted, and taking the necessary security against its future infliction but in one way or other defensive it must be." He could find no justification for the campaign being a defensive war since "the Afghans had not injured us either nationally or individually." He believed that individuals could not place the blame for the war solely on the government: "The crime . . . is one of which the responsibility is shared by every Englishman. It is no new thing to say that a nation and especially a free nation is generally accountable for the conduct of its government."

Lushington placed particular emphasis on the impact of misjudgment. "The great error of Sir William Macnaghten," he wrote, "appears to us to have been the attempt to bestow too soon and without sufficient means of coercing those who had hitherto lived at the expense of their weaker neighbours, the unappreciated blessings of an organised and powerful government upon the people of Afghanistan . . . We have received a severe lesson which we may make a useful one if we choose to learn from it well, if not we shall perpetrate injustices again and again."

A report produced while the war was still in progress by one of the committees of the East India Company, which, as Hobhouse had confessed, had been largely ignored in the conduct of the war, stated, "This war of robbery is waged by the English government through the intervention of the government of India without the knowledge of England or of Parliament . . . and therefore evading the check placed by the constitution on the exercise of the prerogative of the crown in declaring war. It presents, therefore, a new crime in the annals of nations—a secret war. It had been made by a people without their knowledge, against another people who had committed no offence. Effects . . . : loss of England's character for fair dealing; loss of her character of success; the Mussulman population is rendered hostile." The *Times* in May 1842 commented, "This nation spent £15 million on a less than profitable effort after self-aggrandisement in Afghanistan, and spends £30,000 a year on a system of education satisfactory to nobody." However, calls for a full parliamentary inquiry into the background to the war and into the doctoring of the government papers, led by, among others, a newly elected Tory member of Parliament named Benjamin Disraeli, came to nothing.

Outside Britain there was general satisfaction at Britain's unexpected reverses in Afghanistan. In the United States the Afghan War took up numerous column inches in the nation's newspapers, large and small. Outrage at the "odium" and "wickedness" of the British intervention and admiration for the "indomitable love of independence" of the Afghans were almost universal. Atrocities committed by the British as they sought retribution were equally condemned. Afghanistan became somewhat of an issue in the 1842 congressional elections with British attitudes and actions being seen as emblematic of behavior America should avoid. The U.S. administration, however, made no protest to Britain. It was more concerned with negotiating a major treaty with Britain—the Webster-Ashburton Treaty—regulating outstanding issues between the two countries, including the definition of parts of the border between the United States and Canada, and securing favorable trading rights under British aegis in Asia, and in particular China, following Britain's victory in the Opium Wars and the secession to them of Hong Kong.

WITH THE BENEFIT of hindsight, among the more important lessons the British should have learned from the First Afghan War were many that resonate today. Their leaders were not honest with themselves or their public about their motivation, providing partial and misleading information to both Parliament and public. In their own minds they exaggerated the threats to their position in India and exaggerated the power of their available troops to cope with the demands an Afghan campaign would make on them.

The British entered Afghanistan without clear objectives or a defined exit strategy or timetable. In what could be termed *regime change*, they endeavored to impose on the country a ruler unpopular with his people. The Duke of Wellington correctly prophesied that Britain's difficulties would begin when its military success ended. These successes led them into an open-ended commitment to a ruler whom they had not chosen well and, when they realized this, hesitated to replace or "guide" sufficiently. They alienated an increasingly hostile population excited into jihad against the infidel British by Islamic clerics and their followers, the *ghazis*, ready to martyr themselves.

British intelligence was poor. Although they saw Russia as their main rival in Central Asia, there was no Russian speaker anywhere in their administration in India. Their knowledge of the terrain was sketchy, and they were ignorant until too late of the tribal nature of the politics of the country which barely merited that name, being split up between semiautonomous tribes, people looking very different from each other and speaking mutually incomprehensible languages. They did not understand that these tribes united only rarely and that when they did so it was against a foreign invader such as themselves.

Many senior British officers' only experience of action had been in the defeat of Napoleon's vast armies on the plains of Europe a quarter of a century before. When, beaten in conventional warfare, the Afghans changed their tactics into those of the guerrilla fighter, these same British officers found it difficult to react to an enemy who picked off their soldiers, highly visible in their red coats, from vantage points high above the passes, their long-barreled jezails accurate at far greater range than the British Brown Besses. The British learned that it was both difficult to recruit and train Afghan troops to support Shah Shuja and when they did so found their loyalty and performance in battle was unreliable, one officer complaining, "They would never be fit for anything."

In general, British troops struggled to distinguish between hostile and peaceful Afghans, both in Kabul and in the countryside, even when, as was not always the case, they tried hard to make such distinctions. As a consequence innocent civilians were punished and killed, and even more of the population were turned into ready recruits for the enemy. The British and the Afghans alike had problems in understanding each other's cultures and characters. The British stereotyped the Afghans as cunning, corrupt and deceitful and thus found it difficult to believe in the motives of those who were in fact well disposed toward them. The Afghans accepted British protestations of their reputation for straight dealing at face value and were thus the more let down when the British proved duplicitous and Machiavellian.* The Afghan propensity for assassination as well as the taking and subsequent trading between themselves of hostages initially appalled the British, but later they at times found themselves complicit in plans for targeted assassination as the easiest way to rid themselves of troublesome opponents. The attitudes and ambitions of Persia and the passage of forces and weapons across the Helmand River as well as the porous, imprecise border complicated British policies.

---

*So convinced had the Afghans become of English duplicity and cunning that Taliban troops in 2005 nicknamed one of their leaders "Mullah Dadullah"—"The Lame Englishman"—on account of his war wound and particular deviousness.

Changes of government in Britain changed policy in Afghanistan. Politicians—even those who favored the intervention—were concerned about cost as timescales extended, preferring to take the short rather than the long-term view. In Kabul, too, British civilian officials and military commanders bickered about the division of responsibilities between them. Civilian officials such as Macnaghten, whose careers depended on the success of the mission, created a *conspiracy of optimism*.* Generals protested in vain against withdrawal of forces to a level that led to an overstretching of resources and a consequent inability to control more than a few strategic outposts outside Kabul, rather than the whole countryside. Sometimes even these outposts were overrun.

The British found it easier to purchase acquiescence to their own and Shah Shuja's activities than to win over Afghan hearts and minds. Therefore, perhaps the biggest British miscalculation was—in response to cost-cutting pressures from home—unilaterally to reduce some of the subsidies paid to Afghan tribal chiefs. Their economy measure was immediately followed by an Afghan rising.

The long time taken for communications between London and the governor-general's administration in Calcutta and then from Calcutta to those in command in the field in Afghanistan inevitably hampered effective decision making—a problem exacerbated by the fact that the British did not choose their senior officials and generals well. On the military side the deficiencies of Elphinstone and Shelton are so obvious as to require no recapitulation. Among the civilians, the supreme command lay with Lord Auckland, as governor-general. Two phrases used by the Roman historian Tacitus in his assessment of Galba—one of the unsuccessful Roman emperors in the year of the four emperors, A.D. 69—could have been used of Auckland: *magis extra vitia quam cum virtutibus* (a man rather without vices than possessing virtues) and *capax imperii nisi imperasset* (considered capable of exercising power if he had not been called upon to do so).

Auckland, a pleasant character, had proved a good administrator in less demanding posts in the government in London. However, even if the post of governor-general was slightly less powerful than that of Roman

*The term *conspiracy of optimism* was used by a recent former British ambassador in Kabul to describe current official perceptions of the present coalition intervention.

emperor, he was insufficiently strong a character or leader when placed in supreme command of policy in India, thousands of miles and many weeks in terms of communication away from London, to withstand either the conspiracy of optimism generated by Macnaghten from Kabul or pressures from home both to economize and to expedite success and withdrawal. It was not that he was a complete failure—he did restrain some of Macnaghten's plans for operations beyond Afghan borders—but that he was not equipped temperamentally or intellectually to dominate the situation. He preferred to acquiesce in his subordinates' plans to continue existing policies when they began to go awry, rather than ordering either a halt or a thorough review.*

Chief among Auckland's subordinates was Macnaghten. Though an undoubtedly clever man, he was out of both his milieu and his depth in Afghanistan. Nearly all his career had been spent in the secretariat in Calcutta, and he had little experience of independent command. His ingrained optimism led him throughout to minimize or ignore difficulties. He underestimated the military capabilities of the Afghans and overestimated those of the British and Indian troops, leaving him both to accept troop reductions and deployments when he should not have and to propose grandiose operations beyond Shah Shuja's borders—for example, against Herat—which were entirely unfeasible. Though he understood the importance of making it appear to the Afghan population that Shah Shuja was a true king and thus ensured that his troops led the army on its marches and made the first ceremonial entries into cities, in promoting the invasion and Shah Shuja himself, he was far too optimistic in his assessment of Shah Shuja's abilities and of the ease with which the diverse and stubborn Afghans could be induced to accept as a ruler a man they considered to have an aura of ill fortune.

As for Alexander Burnes, as well as courage, he had needed great self-confidence, resourcefulness and strength of judgment to succeed in his youthful journeys in Central Asia. Such qualities rarely go hand in hand with humility. What is more, Burnes seems to have allowed all the praise and attention he had received in London to turn his head to the

---

*Auckland was strongly criticized on his return to Britain. However, after a further change of government he again became First Lord of the Admiralty. He died unexpectedly on New Year's Day, 1849.

extent that in his subsequent career he found it easier to antagonize less celebrated but more senior colleagues than to devote enough of his time and charm to convince them of the undoubted soundness of many of his views, particularly those in regard to Dost Mohammed. Thwarted, and urged on by his unrequited ambition, he preferred, to the detriment of his historical reputation, to acquiesce, albeit sulkily, in policies that he believed wrong. He did so in the hope of obtaining, by his temporary passivity, high office in which he would remedy others' deficient policies, thus fulfilling his youthful promise—something fate never allowed him the opportunity to do.

DESPITE ALL THE soul-searching about British actions at home and abroad, not long after the last British regiments had returned to India down through the Khyber Pass, the British in India returned to their expansionist policies. Their confidence restored by the success of the army of retribution and at the urging of Governor-General Lord Ellenborough, they moved west into Sind, where the emirs, emboldened by British defeats in Afghanistan, had increased tolls on the Indus and then indulged in what the British saw as a variety of provocations. The last straw had been an assault in February 1843 on a British mission led by Colonel James Outram. This in the government's view justified them in "introducing to a brigand infested land, the firm but just administration of the East India Company."

Lord Ellenborough dispatched an expeditionary force of 2,500 men led by General Sir Charles Napier, who pronounced before departing, "We have no right to seize Sind yet we shall do so, and a very advantageous, humane and useful piece of rascality it will be." Known to his troops variously as "Old Fagin" or "the Devil's Brother" because of his wild unkempt appearance and large hooked nose, Napier was as good as his word, swiftly defeating the emirs, after which the British soon annexed Sind.* The Indus was now open to British navigation and commerce.

---

*Napier never sent the punning telegram consisting of the single word PECCAVI, which was an invention of the humorous magazine *Punch*. Recipients would at once have recognized the word as Latin for "I have sinned" and realized Napier was actually saying, "I have Sind."

Karachi, never relinquished by the British, began its rise from a fishing port with three thousand inhabitants to Pakistan's leading commercial center and port with a population of around 15 million today.

The next people to suffer the advance of the British were their old allies the Sikhs. Their lands had fallen into near anarchy as contenders strove to replace Ranjit Singh, one of whom unwisely led a plundering raid into British territory. The British invaded in November 1845 and defeated the Sikhs in bloody battles in which General "Fighting Bob" Sale and Major Broadfoot were both killed.[*] The British withdrew, although imposing restrictions on Sikh power and stationing garrisons at strategic points in their territories. They also took control of Kashmir, seized earlier by Ranjit Singh from the Afghans, and shortly afterward ceded the territory, whose inhabitants were mostly Muslims, to one of their vassal rulers, the Hindu maharaja of Jammu, in return for a substantial payment. This action would have unforeseen consequences at the partition of India at its independence in 1947. The rulers of the princely states were allowed to opt to join either India or Pakistan. The maharaja of Jammu, as a Hindu, opted for India for not only Jammu but also Kashmir, whose Muslim majority would have preferred to join Pakistan. This led to a Pakistani invasion of part of Kashmir and to an unresolved border dispute bedevilling the relationship between India and Pakistan that continues to the present.

In 1848 the Sikhs rebelled against the British restrictions. The British defeated them once more in a series of hard-fought battles and in March 1849 annexed the Sikh territories. During the Sikh wars Dost Mohammed had occupied Peshawar, abandoned by the Sikhs as they focused all their efforts on confronting the British. However, after the Sikh defeat he relinquished the city to the British, effectively giving up his claim to the area.

In 1856 the Persians again occupied Herat. In a three-month war, a British maritime expeditionary force operating in the Persian Gulf and led by Colonel James Outram coerced the Persians into relinquishing Herat once more and promising to abandon any interference in Afghanistan.

A year later part of the East India Company's Bengal army mutinied,

---

[*]Lady Sale died in 1853 in Cape Town.

precipitating what has come to be seen as the first major Indian struggle for independence from the British. Some historians see Britain's retreat from Kabul as a factor in the rebellion, showing as it did that the East India Company's forces could be defeated. The conflict was bloody, and atrocities were committed on both sides, in one of which Lady Sale's daughter Alexandrina and her new husband were ambushed and decapitated. Eventually the British, with the assistance of a considerable body of Indian troops—in particular newly recruited Sikhs—as well as Gurkhas, put the rising down. Among the veterans of the Afghan War who played leading roles in the suppression were Henry Havelock, James Outram and Vincent Eyre. Dr. Brydon survived another siege—that of the British residency in Lucknow—although badly wounded. In the reorganization that followed the end of the fighting, the East India Company's authority and army were transferred to the British Crown.

During the rising Dost Mohammed had again wisely resisted calls from the more hotheaded of his advisers to retake Peshawar. Perhaps as a consequence of his forbearance, the British did not intervene when, in 1863, he finally conquered Herat. He did not live long to enjoy his success, however, dying only a few weeks later. Throughout his reign Dost Mohammed had proved a pragmatic, capable ruler. Astute in his assessment of both the powers on his borders and of his Afghan subjects and their intricate tribal politics, he knew how far he could go in imposing his rule on the latter and in unifying his country. He also knew the importance of religion and used its power to good effect against his infidel opponents. Dost Mohammed had been eager to court the British as his allies and turned to others only when rejected by them. After the war he sensibly held back from attempting to profit from British preoccupation with either the Sikh wars or rebellion in India.

After a familiar fratricidal succession struggle, one of Dost Mohammed's younger sons, Sher Ali, emerged as the new emir. (Akbar Khan, Dost Mohammed's favorite son, had died in 1845 at the age of twenty-nine.)

THE IMPROVED RELATIONS between Britain and Russia continued during the 1840s, but by 1854 differences between the two over the "Eastern question"—the potential breakup of the Ottoman Turkish

Empire—led to the Crimean War, in which Britain, allied with the Ottoman Turks and the French, fought Russia. The 1856 Treaty of Paris concluding the conflict ended for the present Russian ambitions to extend
southwest. In the east, under Nicholas I, who died in March 1855, and his
son and successor, Alexander II, Russia had continued after the end of the
First Afghan War to expand into Central Asia, pushing a line of fortresses
through the Kazakh steppes and establishing a presence on the Aral Sea.
In 1869 Bokhara was compelled to accept czarist suzerainty, and Russian
power reached the banks of the Amu Darya, or Oxus, River. Although the
British had refused to commit themselves to aid Afghanistan in fighting
the Russians if they crossed the Amu Darya, in 1874 British policy changed
with the election of a Tory prime minister, Benjamin Disraeli, who advocated a forward, interventionist policy in Afghanistan and elsewhere.

In 1875, in a remarkable coup, Disraeli succeeded in buying the
virtually bankrupt Khedive of Egypt's 40-percent stake in the company
owning the Suez Canal, opened in 1869. In doing so, he did much to safe-
guard a new and quicker route from Britain to India, increasing the importance as a coaling station of the port of Aden (Yemen) seized by Lord
Auckland during the period of the Afghan War. In 1876 Disraeli's government sanctioned the British occupation, annexation and fortification of
Quetta and the surrounding area.

When Sher Ali acquiesced in 1878 in the arrival of an uninvited Russian diplomatic mission in Kabul, the British demanded that he should
receive one from them as well. Sher Ali asked them to delay because he
was in mourning for his eldest son, but the British claimed that this and
what they considered subsequent unsatisfactory responses to their diplomatic initiatives were provocatory, and in that year dispatched three
invading columns numbering some forty-five thousand men into Afghanistan, opening the Second Anglo-Afghan War forty years after the first
began. In London George Lawrence, the veteran of the first war, in-
veighed against this second intervention: "I regret to think that the lapse
of years has apparently had the effect . . . that a reaction has set in, and
that a new generation has arisen which, instead of profiting by the solemn
lessons of the past, is willing and eager to embroil us . . . in the affairs of
that turbulent and unhappy country."

Kandahar soon fell to the southernmost of the invasion columns.

Other British forces had advanced through the Khyber Pass when Sher Ali died as he was trying to cross the border into Russian territory to secure a meeting with the czar himself. The emir was succeeded by his son Yakub Khan. He agreed to meet the British at Gandamack, where in 1842 the Forty-fourth Foot had stood and died. Eventually he agreed to allow Britain to direct Afghan foreign policy and to control the main passes into Afghanistan from British India, as well as to accept a British mission in Kabul. In return, he was to receive a subsidy and the usual vague promises of British support against (other) foreign intervention.

In the summer of 1879 the British mission led by Sir Pierre Louis Napoleon Cavagnari, the thirty-nine-year-old son of an Italian father and Irish mother, headed into Kabul with a military escort of seventy-five men. At the same time, the nearest major British force was pulling back from the Khyber Pass in an attempt to escape an outbreak of cholera. Transmitting his message for part of its journey by a newly established telegraph line, Cavagnari reported his entrance to the city on 24 July: WE RECEIVED THE MOST BRILLIANT RECEPTION. WE PROCEEDED ON ELEPHANTS WITH A LARGE ESCORT OF CAVALRY. OUTSIDE THE CITY TWO BATTERIES OF ARTILLERY, NINE REGIMENTS OF INFANTRY WERE DRAWN UP . . . THEIR BANDS PLAYING THE BRITISH NATIONAL ANTHEM. LARGE CROWD ASSEMBLED AND WAS ORDERLY AND RESPECTFUL. EMIR ENQUIRED AFTER VICEROY'S HEALTH AND QUEEN AND ROYAL FAMILY. EMIR'S DEMEANOUR WAS MOST FRIENDLY. Later Cavagnari telegraphed, NOTWITHSTANDING ALL PEOPLE SAY AGAINST HIM, I PERSONALLY BELIEVE YAKUB KHAN WILL TURN OUT TO BE A VERY GOOD ALLY AND THAT WE SHALL BE ABLE TO KEEP HIM TO HIS ENGAGEMENTS. On 2 September his dispatch, tinted *couleur de rose* in a way reminiscent of Macnaghten, was ALL WELL IN THE KABUL EMBASSY.

Early the next day Afghan soldiers, incensed at being paid neither by the emir nor by the British, and at rumors circulated by the Kabul mullahs that the British were intent on religious conversion, attacked Cavagnari's residence. Before midafternoon, despite desperate sorties, the residency was ablaze and all the Europeans were dead. The Afghans gave the surviving Indian troops a chance to surrender, which they refused. Instead, they made one last sally, and within five minutes they too were all killed. The only survivor was an Indian subofficer who had been away from the mission on detached duty and escaped to bring news of the massacre to the British forces.

Immediately British troops under General Frederick Roberts—the son of Abraham Roberts who had resigned as commander of Shah Shuja's contingent after quarreling with Macnaghten—marched on Kabul. Although outnumbered five to one, his force led by Highlanders and Gurkhas defeated an Afghan army and occupied the city on 12 October 1879. Yakub Khan abdicated at once and, like previous unsuccessful Afghan rulers, was sent into exile in India. Several of those who had paraded Cavagnari's head through the streets were publicly executed in the burned rubble of Cavagnari's residency. Buildings within the Balla Hissar were demolished, and probably accidentally—rumors said the cause was an artillery officer's pipe—a main ammunition dump within the Balla Hissar exploded, causing many casualties.

All the while, mullahs were preaching jihad against the British. Posters appeared overnight on city walls signed by "the Leader of the Mujhaddin." In December sentries posted on top of the partially destroyed Balla Hissar saw three Afghan tribal armies approaching the city. Roberts forced them into retreat, showing a decisiveness that had been sorely lacking in Kabul four decades earlier.*

The next spring in Kabul, British officers debated whom to install as emir. Their choice eventually fell on Abdur-ur-Rahman, a grandson of Dost Mohammed. In London the opposition leader, William Gladstone, became prime minister in April 1880 after defeating Disraeli. His response to a report by a British journalist of atrocities committed by the country's troops in Kohst, near the site of the future Tora Bora cave complex, was to inveigh against the results of Disraeli's policies: "Remember the rights of the savage as we call him . . . remember the happiness of his humble home . . . the sanctity of life in the hill villages of Afghanistan among the winter snows is as inviolable in the eyes of Almighty God as can be your own."

General Roberts wrote, "[I] dreaded that a change of government might mean a reversal of the policy which I believed to be the best for the

---

*During one of the running engagements, a British officer, General Hugh Gough, was saved from a bullet by a suit of chain mail, probably but not certainly the last British soldier to be saved by personal armor until the advent of Kevlar and similar modern body armor.

security of our position in India." Not long thereafter, the British indeed suffered a major setback, but not as a result of government policy. Nor was it at Kabul, but in the south on the Helmand River not far from Kandahar, on high ground near a village near Maiwand. A British force of some 2,500 men was defeated on 27 July 1880 in open battle by a much larger Afghan army, including many white-clothed *ghazis*. The Afghans broke the much-vaunted red British squares—just as they had done at Bemaru in late 1841—and drove their soldiers back to Kandahar with nearly one thousand killed.* According to Afghan folklore, at the height of the battle a young Pushtun woman urged on the troops, waving her veil as a standard. "Young love, if you are martyred in the battle of Maiwand, I will make a coffin for you from the tresses of my hair. [If you do not fall] by God someone is saving you as a token of shame." The Pushtun woman's story and slogan are reportedly still being used by the Taliban to encourage their fighters.

Kandahar prepared for a siege. As soon as Roberts in Kabul heard the news from Maiwand, he hastily put together a force of ten thousand men. Leaving behind all wheeled artillery and heavy baggage for the sake of speed, he marched the troops over three hundred miles to Kandahar in just under three weeks in the blistering summer heat. The day after he arrived, he attacked the Afghan forces. With Gurkhas and Highlanders again to the fore, Roberts and his men routed their enemy, who fled, abandoning their camp.

In response to Prime Minister Gladstone's command, before 1880 had ended the British army was withdrawing from Afghanistan. The only tangible benefits of their expenditure of many lives and much treasure were the installation of an emir more friendly on the surface to the British and the securing of the control of the key passes into Afghanistan from the south and east.

BRITAIN CONTINUED TO see Russia as a threat to its Indian empire. In 1885, the year Gladstone lost office, a crisis over the Panjdeh oases on the far northwestern border of Afghanistan almost led to war—so

---

*Sir Arthur Conan Doyle has Sherlock Holmes identify Dr. Watson on their first meeting as a veteran of the Second Afghan War, and in the 1960s, much to Afghan surprise, the "Baker Street Irregulars" asked the bemused Afghans to place a monument to the fictional Dr. Watson on the Maiwand battlefield.

much so that the British stationery office, planning ahead, had already printed documents declaring war before both sides pulled back from the brink. In the aftermath, the British and Russians recognized the need to delineate the boundary between Afghanistan and the Russian-held or influenced territories. After some haggling a border was agreed. In the far northeast where the Russians had been pressing forward in the Wakhan, a thin sliver of land was handed to Afghanistan to prevent the Russian border anywhere abutting that of British India.

The British also persuaded the emir to agree to a boundary commission to fix the frontier between British India and Afghanistan. The task was given to Sir Mortimer Durand, the son of Henry Durand, the hero of Ghazni. The line he drew split in two many of the tribal areas such as Waziristan. Though the principles were agreed between the two sides centrally, the surveyors who went into the border areas to fix the boundaries on the ground met a great deal of hostility and often came under attack. This unrest built up over the next few years into a series of major conflicts with the frontier tribes, who besieged outlying British forts and attacked supply columns in Chitral, Tirah, Waziristan and the Swat Valley.

Winston Churchill, on leave from his regiment to act as a war correspondent, observed through a German-manufactured telescope one initially unsuccessful British attack on a hilltop position in the Mamund Valley. As the soldiers rose from the shelter of the rocks behind which they had been firing, an officer spun around and fell, his face covered with blood. Two of the men ran to help him. "A soldier who had continued firing sprang into the air and falling began to bleed with strange and terrible rapidity from his mouth and chest. Another turned on his back, kicking and twisting." Others began to pull the injured away, "dragging them roughly over the sharp rocks in spite of their screams and groans." Another officer was immediately shot. Several Sikhs ran forward to help him. Suddenly, a mob of "howling" Afghans emerged over the crest of the hill thirty yards away and "charged sword in hand, hurling great stones." Those carrying them dropped one officer and two wounded sepoys. "The officer's body sprawled upon the ground. A tall man in dirty white linen pounced on him with a sword. It was a horrible sight."

Churchill also described the problems of campaigning in the heat: "September in these valleys is as hot as it is easy to imagine . . . Slowly the hours pass away. The heat is intense. The air glitters over the scorched plain, as over the funnel of an engine the wind blows with a fierce warmth, and instead of bringing relief raises only whirling dust devils, which scatter the shelters and half-choke their occupants. The water is tepid and fails to quench the thirst. At last the shadows begin to lengthen as the sun sinks towards the western mountains. Everyone revives."

The campaigns were conducted with no quarter given on either side to prisoners. Rudyard Kipling described the leveling effect of guerrilla warfare such as this.

ARITHMETIC ON THE FRONTIER

> *A great and glorious thing it is*
>   *To learn, for seven years or so,*
> *The Lord knows what of that and this,*
>   *Ere reckoned fit to face the foe—*
> *The flying bullet down the Pass,*
> *That whistles clear: "All flesh is grass."*
>
>   *Three hundred pounds per annum spent*
>   *On making brain and body meeter*
> *For all the murderous intent*
>   *Comprised in "villanous saltpetre!"*
> *And after—ask the Yusufzaies*
> *What comes of all our 'ologies.*
>
>   *A scrimmage in a Border Station—*
>   *A canter down some dark defile—*
> *Two thousand pounds of education*
>   *Drops to a ten-rupee jezail—*
> *The Crammer's boast, the Squadron's pride,*
> *Shot like a rabbit in a ride!*
>
>   *No proposition Euclid wrote,*
>   *No formulae the text-books know,*
> *Will turn the bullet from your coat,*
>   *Or ward the tulwar's downward blow*
> *Strike hard who cares—shoot straight who can—*
> *The odds are on the cheaper man.*

Kipling also gave chilling advice to British soldiers in another poem:

When you're wounded on Afghanistan's plains
*   And the women come out to cut up what remains*
Just roll to your rifle and blow out your brains
*   An' go to your Gawd like a soldier.*

Part of the British policy was, in Churchill's words, to make the tribesmen's villages "hostages for their good behaviour." When they rebelled the British punished them by destroying their crops, wells and fortifications. Churchill told how, as his column left the area, "not a tower, not a fort was to be seen, the villages were destroyed. The crops had been trampled down. They had lost heavily in killed and wounded and the winter was at hand."

Even though Churchill approved of the campaign, he wrote home to his family, "There is no doubt we are a very cruel people." Lord Roberts, the successful general of the Second Afghan War, wrote, "Burning houses and destroying crops unless followed up by some sort of authority and jurisdiction, mean . . . for us a rich harvest of hatred and revenge."*

These risings had begun to take on a more overtly religious dimension. Not least responsible was Abdur-ur-Rahman, the emir in Kabul, who covertly encouraged the frontier tribes. He ensured the wide circulation of a book he had written, which emphasized that jihad was the highest duty of all Muslims and which extolled those dying in the fight who would be "placed in the throat of green-winged birds who circle in the air and make their nests in the branches of the most blessed tree in Paradise."†

At the end of the campaign Churchill, who was nearly killed when a bullet went through his hat, praised the benefits the new roads driven into the mountains would bring in terms of trade: "As the sun of civilisation rose above the hills, the fair flowers of commerce unfolded and the

---

*According to current on-the-spot reporters, some of the frontier villages that suffered most in the fighting with the British at that time are among those that have given the greatest support to Taliban and Al-Qaeda fighters.
†Many of the insurrection's leaders were mullahs. Some, such as Mullah Sadullah in Swat—nicknamed by the British "the Mad Fakir"—were Muslims of the Wahhabi sect.

streams of supply and demand, hitherto congealed by the frost of barbarism, were thawed." But when the main British force left the frontier mountains behind them, together with their roads, their garrisons and a trail of destruction, they were also leaving a legacy of hatred and resentment among subdued but still defiant tribespeople.

ABDUR-UR-RAHMAN DIED IN 1901 and was succeeded by his short, obese, eldest son Habibullah. On his only visit to India in 1907 the nightlife enchanted him, and he was accompanied at parties by an attendant with a bag of jewels that he distributed to any woman who caught his eye. Despite such attractions, he remained levelheaded enough during the visit to refuse to endorse an Anglo-Russian convention, reached without Afghan involvement, which put an effective end to the Russo-British "Great Game."

Among the key points of the convention, reached in the face of German and Turkish threats to the wider interests of the signatories, were that Russia agreed Afghanistan was outside its sphere of influence and agreed to confer with Britain about any matters concerning Russo-Afghan relations. In turn, the British agreed not to annex Afghanistan and not to interfere in its internal affairs. Also the British and Russians agreed, without consulting Persia, to divide that country into two spheres of influence, with the British zone including those parts touching the western border with Afghanistan. They also agreed that if a third party threatened Persia, they would each occupy their spheres of influence. Both Britain and the Soviet Union used this convention as the justification for jointly occupying Persia—by then known as Iran—and deposing its shah in the Second World War, citing German threats and the need to protect their oil supplies.*

Under Habibullah some progress was made toward development in Afghanistan. During the First World War Habibullah wisely resisted the

---

*The long history of British meddling in Persia goes some way toward explaining why, instead of, as many others have done, seeing Britain as a kind of secondary force in the Middle East and Afghanistan, Iran's propaganda quite often portrays Britain as a cunning and malevolent old lion manipulating a stronger but less sophisticated United States.

Germans' pressure to join the war on their side, although he did allow a German mission into the country for a brief time in 1915–16. It was said that German spies tried to raise jihad among Afghan tribesmen by claiming that the kaiser had become a Muslim and it was thus their duty to support him against the British.

Soon after the end of the First World War, Habibullah was assassinated near Jalalabad on a hunting trip. The killer is still unknown. Some said it was his brother Nasrullah's doing, and he was imprisoned; others that it was a pro-Turkish, anti-British clique; yet others blamed the British. The upshot was that the emir's third son, twenty-seven-year-old Amanullah, succeeded. Partly to divert the tribes' attention from the internal factionalism, Amanullah proclaimed jihad against the British in the mosque in Kabul to enthusiastic cries of "death or freedom!" from onlookers. He called on the frontier tribes to rise up on his behalf, and his chief general, Nadir Shah, sent soldiers across the frontier on 4 May 1919, initiating the Third Anglo-Afghan War.

It was a short-lived affair. The British used old First World War fighter aircraft to attack the Afghans, aircraft so underpowered they could not get high enough to fly over the mountains; they flew instead along the valleys, where they were fired on from above by Afghan marksmen on the ridges. On 24 May an old Handley-Page bomber attacked Kabul. Amanullah protested to the British, pointing out how recently they had considered the bombing of civilians a crime: "One of your aeroplanes bombarded our royal palace . . . causing great excitement and panic among our loyal people. Many other favourite buildings in our . . . unprotected town were bombed. It is a matter for great regret that the throwing of bombs by Zeppelins on London was denounced as a most savage act and the bombardment of places of worship and sacred spots was considered a most abominable operation while now we see with our own eyes that such operations were a habit which is prevalent among a civilised people of the west."

On the ground, the British forces soon repulsed the Afghans, who in early July sued for a truce. At the ensuing conference the British, exhausted by the First World War and fearing Communist influence in Afghanistan following the 1917 Russian Revolution, allowed Amanullah to remain on his throne and conceded that he would now control Afghanistan's foreign policy.

Amanullah set out on a campaign to reform his country, basing his measures on those of Atatürk in Turkey. He insisted on men wearing Western dress and sometimes carried shears to cut off nonregulation items of clothing. He opened education to women and allowed them to choose whom to marry. Factories were established and foreign commercial advisers encouraged. On a visit to Europe in 1928 his queen, Soraya, appeared unveiled with bare arms and wearing a V-necked dress as her husband sought further development projects. Conservative mullahs used pictures of the queen to show how decadent the emir was becoming.

On his return Amanullah called for monogamy, the full emancipation of women and for all women to go bareheaded. Following his execution of five conservative mullahs who had protested, a rebellion broke out against him. Amanullah pulled back on some of his emancipatory reforms, but to no avail. He was soon in exile in Italy with his queen. Civil war followed. General Nadir Shah eventually established himself as king but was in turn assassinated in 1933. He was succeeded by his nineteen-year-old French-educated son, Mohammed Zahir Shah, who ruled at first under the guidance of his paternal uncles. Advised by other members of his family, in particular his cousin Daoud, he reigned for the next forty years until, in 1973 Daoud, who was eager to speed the pace of commercial and constitutional change, ousted him in a coup.

The forty years of Mohammed Zahir's reign saw, in addition to a gradually increasing internal prosperity, major changes on both Afghanistan's northern and southern borders. In 1947 the British departed, and modern India and Pakistan came into being. The Durand line remained as the border with Afghanistan, giving the Pakistanis the dominating heights the British had appropriated for themselves and continuing the partition of the lands of the local tribes, which explains the near inevitability of the fighting in Afghanistan spilling over the artificial frontier with Pakistan. The Pakistanis also continued with what had evolved into an arm's-length British approach to the control of the frontier tribes. Nevertheless, tensions between Pakistan and Afghanistan grew over the years in regard to transport and other costs for the transit through Pakistan of Afghan imports and exports, and more particularly about claims for Pushtun autonomy.

Afghans increasingly turned to Russia as a trading partner, and, as the Cold War intensified and Pakistan drew closer to the United States, the Russians were eager once more to expand their influence in Afghanistan, which again became a buffer state, this time between communism and capitalism, with both Russia and the United States competing for influence. The Afghan armed forces used Russian weapons, most of their officers were Russian-trained and the army's technical language was Russian. The United States became directly involved in many aid projects in Afghanistan, such as that for the irrigation of the Helmand Valley.

After he came to power, Daoud, who had had Soviet support in his coup against his cousin, tried to resist Russian pressure for increased influence in Afghanistan's internal as well as external affairs. His reward was to be deposed and murdered in April 1978 in a military-backed Russian-inspired coup, which led to the establishment of a Communist regime. Traditional tribal and Islamic factions rose in sporadic rebellion against the new government's policies, such as land reform and female emancipation, until in December 1979 the Russians—claiming to be answering appeals from the people and government of Afghanistan and to be concerned about instability spilling over their own borders—invaded. Like the British in 1839, the Russian high command expected to be out of Afghanistan within a year, in the interim having pacified the country and helped the Communist government establish itself.

Instead, the Russians stayed for eight years, fighting an insurgency backed by the United States and Islamic countries that took advantage of the safe havens provided by the tribal territories on the opposite side of the Durand line in Pakistan. When the Russians finally departed on the eve of the breakup of the Soviet Union, more than 1.5 million people had died. Many more were refugees in Pakistan, and Afghanistan's infrastructure had been destroyed, relegating the country to an almost medieval condition.

After the Russian departure, the previously Russian-backed president, Najibullah, clung to power. His forces successfully repulsed mujahideen attacks, in particular a four-month-long assault on Jalalabad—the only major battle into which Osama bin Laden is known to have led his Arab forces into action himself. However, Najibullah's regime was overthrown, and he was murdered in spring 1992. A standoff between guerrilla leaders followed, foremost among them Rashid Dostum, Ahmad Shah

Massud and the more fundamentalist Gulbaddin Hekmatyar. During this period fighting with heavy weapons took place in civilian areas without regard to who was caught in the crossfire, and atrocities were common. One of the most notorious was the attack by Massud's men on the Hazara suburb of Kabul. Amid the rubble of the Kabul zoo, Hekmatyar kept one of the lions alive by sometimes throwing it a prisoner in the way of the Roman emperors.

Against this background the power of the Taliban began to grow as they were perceived as a relatively corruption-free movement with more regard for civilian welfare than any other group and with leaders whose lives were simple and followed religious principles, albeit fundamentalist ones. Many Afghans were prepared to accept the restrictions these principles placed on their freedoms as a price worth paying for the stability the Taliban brought to their ravaged country. The Taliban's primary leader, Mullah Mohammed Omar, had been brought up near the site of the Battle of Maiwand, in which the Afghans had defeated the British, in a village whose inhabitants relished telling stories of the defeat of the infidel.

The Taliban took Kabul in the summer of 1996 and gradually increased their hold on the country. A few months earlier, Osama bin Laden, who had been out of Afghanistan for six years, returned. He had played no part in the founding of the Taliban and initially returned to an area near Tora Bora outside their control. His focus was on international jihad against the United States, that of the Taliban an internal one on Afghanistan. However the Taliban, perhaps influenced by the Pushtun code of hospitality and mindful of his role in the fight against the Russians, refused to surrender bin Laden to the United States following the first of his international attacks. Thereafter his name and that of the Taliban became synonymous to the wider public.

The coalition invasion of Afghanistan in 2001 was thus an inevitable consequence of 9/11. British forces, still numbering among them a Gurkha regiment from Nepal as well as of course many Highlanders, followed the United States into Afghanistan, where they have lived and died for the past decade, over 160 years after British forces first entered the country.

The Afghans see the last two centuries of interaction with the European powers and the United States as one continuum. A British officer reported recently how an Afghan government minister had reproached him that the British had burned down the covered market in Kabul. Fearing some hasty action by his nation's troops, he eventually discovered that the remark had referred to the burning of the bazaar by the British at the end of the First Afghan War. Along the route of the catastrophic retreat Afghans today show coins seized from the British baggage train, which have passed down their families, and recount the deeds of their ancestors in slaying the infidel British, while pointing to the sites of the battles. Invoking events long past, a recent Taliban recruiting slogan asked Afghans, "Do you want to be remembered as a son of Dost Moham-med or a son of Shah Shuja?"

ACKNOWLEDGMENTS

I WROTE THIS book with my husband Michael, my partner in writing and in life, whose recollections of traveling through the barren passes from Kabul to Peshawar first made me want to tell this story. I also want to acknowledge the voices of the past. I could not have written this without the letters, diaries and papers of those who experienced the traumatic events of Britain's first military intervention in Afghanistan. I am indebted to the staff of the British National Archives, the British Library, the Bodleian Library, the London Library and the National Army Museum for their help, patience and professionalism in helping me track such sources down—whether an army chaplain's memoirs or a message scribbled in Latin by a beleaguered British officer on a strip of paper to be smuggled out of Afghanistan to India.

For helping me understand the reality of fighting in Afghanistan in the twenty-first century, I am very grateful to several young Britons currently serving there for sharing their experiences and perceptions.

I must also thank friends for commenting on the text, especially Kim Lewison, Neil Munro and Clinton Leeks.

Lastly, my warm thanks to George Gibson, Mike O'Connor and their colleagues at Walker & Company and Bloomsbury USA, and to my agents Michael Carlisle of Inkwell Management, New York, and Bill Hamilton of A. M. Heath and Co. in London.

NOTES AND SOURCES

As this book is intended primarily for the general reader I reference quotes from the following primary sources only where their origin might otherwise be unclear in the context. (Full details of the editions used are in the bibliography.)

Atkinson, J. *The Expedition into Afghanistan*
Broadfoot, W. *The Career of Major George Broadfoot* (compiled from Broadfoot's own papers by Major W. Broadfoot)
Dennie, Colonel W., *Personal Narrative of the Campaigns in Afghanistan, Sinde, Beloochistan etc.*
Durand, Sir H. M. *The First Afghan War and Its Causes*
Eyre, V. *The Military Operations at Kabul*
Gleig, Reverend G. R. *Sale's Brigade in Afghanistan*
Harlan, J. *Central Asia—Personal Narrative of General Josiah Harlan, 1823–1841*
———. *A Memoir of India and Afghanistan*
Havelock, H. *Narrative of the War in Afghanistan in 1838–39*
Johnson, Captain. Diary in *Blackwoods Magazine*, March 1906
Kennedy, Dr. R. H. *Narrative of the Campaign of the Army of the Indus in Sind and Kabul in 1838–9*
Lal, M. *Journal of a Tour Through the Punjab, Afghanistan and Parts of Persia*
———. *Life of the Amir Dost Mohammed Khan of Kabul*
Lawrence, Sir G. *Reminiscences of Forty-Three Years in India*
Mackenzie, H. *Storms and Sunshine of a Soldier's Life*, which includes long extracts from Colin Mackenzie's journals. (A detailed letter from Mackenzie to Eyre describing Macnaghten's assassination is included at Appendix 15 in Stocqueler's compendium of official papers and personal narratives, *Memorials of Affghanistan* [sic].)
Masson, C. *Narrative of Various Journeys in Balochistan, Afghanistan and the Punjab and Kalat*
Ram, Subedar Sita. *From Sepoy to Subedar*. (The authenticity of this account had been queried because of some inconsistencies and inaccuracies. However, like most historians, I have accepted its veracity. Any errors seem to me to be attributable to the distance in time between the events described and when they were set down.)
Sale, Lady. *A Journal of the Disasters in Afghanistan, 1841–2*
Stocqueler, J. H. *Life of Sir William Nott*, which includes much of Nott's *Memoirs and Correspondence*. (All quotes from Nott come from this book unless otherwise stated.)

Sir John Kaye's detailed *History of the War in Afghanistan* was published shortly after the war (in 1851, revised in 1857) and used and attributed many contemporary primary sources. Despite the heated debates about the war that were still continuing at the time Kaye's history was published, the authenticity of the documents he quotes was never queried. This is important since some, for example Eldred Pottinger's journal of Herat, were subsequently destroyed in a fire in his study.

ABBREVIATIONS

AUCK   Auckland Papers, British Library
BROU   Broughton Papers, British Library
ELLEN   Ellenborough Papers, British National Archives (formerly Public Record Office [PRO])
P. P.   Parliamentary Papers for 1839, 1843 and 1859 about the Afghan War and its background. (The 1859 papers are a full edition—produced at Parliament's request by Sir John Kaye—of those published in 1839, from which some documents were completely missing and some had been edited, leading to them being called "garbled.")
WELLES   Wellesley Papers, British Library

PRELUDE

1   "The consequence . . . that country": Quoted in Sir J. W. Kaye, *History of the War in Afghanistan*, vol. 1, p. 378.

1   "The colours . . . subjects": Major Hamlet Wade, quoted in H. Mackenzie, *Storms and Sunshine of a Soldier's Life*, vol. 1, p. 272.

2   Learning . . . Mecca: Hawkins's account of his journey to and life at the Mogul court is from *Early Travels in India*, edited by W. Foster, pp. 81 and 83.

3   "the abandoned . . . wealth . . . every spark . . . extinguished": T. Wilkinson, *Two Monsoons*, p. 4.

5   "a delegation . . . the East": Quoted in J. H. Waller, *Beyond the Khyber Pass*, p. xxv.

6   "He is . . . govern": Queen Victoria's letter to her uncle the Belgian king of 11 June 1844, Benson and Asher, *The Letters of Queen Victoria—1837–1861*, vol. 2, p. 14.

7   "Poor . . . she . . . shrink": Quoted in J. Morris, *Heaven's Command*, p. 26.

7   Although the United States, of which Michigan became the twenty-sixth state in 1837, and its 17 million population might seem at this stage of history to have been remote from jockeyings for power in Central Asia, this is not entirely the case. British cotton manufacturers preferred the less brittle, longer-staple, American cotton to that produced in India. Slaves in the southern cotton fields were laboring to produce the raw material for Britain's cotton mills which fueled its commercial aspirations. Also, many academic historians have seen parallels between America's push westward and Russian expansion south and east into Central Asia. In the case of Georgia, where gold had been discovered in the western hills, American expansion was by a treaty at least as "unequal" as that by which the British compelled the Chinese to cede Hong Kong. It forced the Cherokee from their homes in Georgia onto the so-called Trail of Tears in late spring 1838 on which a quarter of the thirteen thousand who set out died.

CHAPTER ONE

Unless otherwise indicated, all quotes describing Mountstuart Elphinstone's journey are from his *Account of the Kingdom of Caubul*.

10   "[I] pushed him . . . passage": Quoted in Sir J. W. Kaye, *History of the War in Afghanistan*, vol 1, p. 69.

10   "imperious superiority": M. Lal, *Life of the Amir Dost Mohammed*, p. 8.

10   "to allow . . . French": 22 August 1809, Treaty No. 6, P. P. Indian Papers No. 2, 1839.

11   "it was better . . . guilt and shame": Quoted in J. H. Waller, *Beyond the Khyber Pass*, p. 17.

13 "nothing . . . a bird": B. Gascoigne, *The Great Moghuls*, p. 13.

15 "They know . . . each other!": Colonel W. H. Dennie, *Personal Narrative of the Campaigns in Afghanistan*, p. 62.

16 "the dire . . . polygamy": Sir P. Sykes, *A History of Afghanistan*, vol. 1, p. 392.

19 "the beard . . . of tears": Captain James Abbott, quoted in G. Bruce, *Retreat from Kabul*, p.16.

20 "Peradventure . . . wordly affairs": J. H. Stocqueler, *Life of Sir William Nott*, p. 104.

20 "Russia . . . the keys": Quoted in J. A. Norris, *The First Afghan War*, p. 28.

CHAPTER TWO

Where not otherwise indicated, all quotes describing Burnes's journey are from his own account, *Travels into Bokhara*.

21 "Commerce . . . enlightened community": Quoted in N. Fergusson, *Empire*, p. xviii.

21 "No British . . . in triumph": 9 December 1829, Edward Law (Lord Ellenborough), *Political Diary*, vol. 2., p. 144.

21 "Mind . . . languages, sir!": Sir G. Lawrence, *Forty-Three Years in India*, p. 2.

22 "on the . . . honour": Sir J. W. Kaye, *Lives of Indian Officers*, vol. 2, p. 17.

22 "The navigation . . . view": A. Burnes, *Travels into Bokhara*, vol. 3, p. 2.

22 "might . . . Central Asia": 12 January 1830, quoted in J. A. Norris, *The First Afghan War*, p. 40.

23 "since . . . by water": A. Burnes, *Travels into Bokhara*, vol. 3, p. 3.

23 "the scheme . . . war": Quoted in Sir J. W. Kaye, *History of the War in Afghanistan*, vol. 1, p. 176.

23 "its facilities . . . your researches": J. Lunt, *Bokhara Burnes*, p. 38.

23 "Alas! . . . its conquest": Ibid.

25 "horses . . . to England . . . excited . . . elephants": Burnes, *Travels into Bokhara*, vol. 3, pp. 152–53.

28 "The Home . . . they want": Burnes's letter to his sister of September 1831, Kaye, *Lives of Indian Officers*, vol. 2, p. 20.

CHAPTER THREE

Where not otherwise indicated, all quotes describing Burnes's journey are from his *Cabool Being a Personal Narrative of a Journey to and Residence in That City in the Years 1836–38.*

37 Everything . . . saddled": Quoted in J. A. Norris, *The First Afghan War*, p. 68.

37 "religiously . . . neighbours": 20 October 1832, P. P. 1839 Indian Papers No. 3.

41 "fly . . . elephant": J. H. Waller, *Beyond the Khyber Pass*, p. 79.

43 "the law . . . of nations": L. Mitchell, *Literary Review*, October 2010, p. 6.

43 "doing . . . in India": Quoted in Sir J. W. Kaye, *History of the War in Afghanistan*, vol. 1, p. 167.

43 "the right . . . obligations . . . it is . . . extensive": Quoted in Anon., *Progress and Present Position of Russia in the East*, pp. 150–51.

44 "to interfere . . . Afghanistan": Quoted in Norris, *The First Afghan War*, p. 90.

44 "would not . . . possessions": Quoted in ibid., p. 85.

44 "a dry . . . Sanskrit": Quoted in *Dictionary of National Biography* entry for Macnaghten and J. Lunt, *Scarlet Lancer*, p. 171.

44 "dry . . . rude": Quoted in Lunt, *Scarlet Lancer*, p. 171.

45 "The field . . . Paradise . . . reckless . . . Sikhs . . . [I hope] . . . own": 31 May 1836, P. P. 1839, Indian Papers No. 5.

45 "depute some gentleman . . . My friend . . . benefit": 22 August 1836, P. P. 1839, Indian Papers No. 5.

45 "the best . . . Afghanistan": Lord Auckland to Dost Mohammed, 15 May 1837, P. P. 1839, Indian Papers No. 5.

46 "All . . . applied": H. Mackenzie, *Storms and Sunshine of a Soldier's Life*, p. 145.

47 "a narrow . . . of the pass": G. Lawrence, *Reminiscences of Forty-Three Years in India*, p. 33–34.

48 "either . . . men:": G. Whitteridge, *Charles Masson of Afghanistan*, p. 123.

48 "My house . . . each other": Undated letter dispatched April 1837, P. P. 1859.

49 "In any case . . . sovereign": 15 May 1837, ibid.

50 "under any . . . Ranjit Singh": 11 September 1837, ibid.

50 "placing . . . bosom": Quoted in P. Macrory, *Kabul Catastrophe*, p. 57.

50 "In a settlement . . . ends": 23 December 1837, P. P. 1859.

51 "The chiefs . . . Kandahar?": Quoted in Kaye, *History*, vol. 1, p. 190.

51 "In the critical . . . Indus": 23 December 1837, P. P. 1859.

51 "We are . . . here . . . Herat . . . dinner": Quoted in Kaye, *History*, vol. 1, p. 196.

51 "knew . . . and us": Ibid.

52 "the one strong man . . . now . . . side": Quoted in J. Lunt, *Bokhara Burnes*, p. 182.

52 "conform . . . guidance": 20 January 1838, P. P. 1859.

52 "asked . . . return": Quoted in Lunt, *Bokhara Burnes*, p. 183.

52 "had often . . . own": Quoted in Kaye, *History*, vol. 1, p. 206.

53 "at a . . . Turkestan . . . Were the Afghans . . . British?": Quoted in ibid., p. 205.

54 "I expected . . . disappointed": 23 April 1838, P. P. 1859.

54 "I came . . . arrived": Quoted in Kaye, *History*, vol. 1, p. 183.

CHAPTER FOUR

55 "It is . . . Russia's": Quoted in J. A. Norris, *The First Afghan War*, p. 176.

55 "If dirt . . . filth": Lieutenant A. Conolly, *Journey to the North of India*, vol. 2, pp. 3–4.

56 "We gave . . . come": Sir J. W. Kaye, *History of the War in Afghanistan*, vol. 1, p. 162.

56 By late November . . . a course: All quotes in these paragraphs are from Pottinger's journal, quoted in Kaye, *History*, vol. 1, pp. 229, 231 and 245.

58 "leave . . . fate . . . intrigue . . . frontiers . . . attempt . . . Afghanistan . . . most expedient": Lord Auckland's partly unpublished memo of 12 May 1838, quoted in Kaye, *History*, vol. 1, p. 319 and partly given in P. P. 1839, Indian Papers No. 4.

59 "where . . . Hindustan": Kaye, *History*, vol. 1, p. 312.

59 "this would . . . milk": Quoted in ibid., p. 326.

59 Negotiations . . . great deal": All quotes in these two paragraphs are from a letter of 2 June 1838, P. P. 1859 except for "not as . . . produced," which is from a letter in Sir J. W. Kaye, *Lives of Indian Officers*, vol. 2, p. 65.

61 "55 high-bred horses . . . paces . . . musk . . . quinces": Tripartite Treaty, P. P. 1839, Indian Papers No. 1.

61 "oppose . . . ability": Ibid.

62 "the fact . . . consequence": Macnaghten's letter of 17 July 1838, quoted in Kaye, *History*, vol. 2, p. 347.

62 "could be induced . . . countrymen": Kaye, *History*, vol. 1, p. 328.

62 "Every . . . weakness": Letter to Sir Charles Metcalfe, in ibid., p. 359.

62 "Make . . . *west*": Quoted in A. Bilgrami, *Afghanistan and British India*, p. 15.

63 "We are . . . England": 22 July 1838, Quoted in Kaye, *History*, vol. 1, pp 366–67.

64 "no result . . . support": Colvin to Pottinger, 15 August 1838, AUCK 37694, folio 15.

64 "I shall . . . wisely": Auckland to Skinner, 21 August 1838, ibid., folio 10.

64 "an adventurer . . . Kandahar": Kaye, History, vol. 1, 209.

64 Following . . . is gone": All quotes in this paragraph are from ibid, pp. 284–45 and 382.

65 The Simla Manifesto of 1 October 1838 was widely reproduced, e.g., as an annex to H. Havelock's book.

65 *justice . . . necessity* . . . "in a manner . . . language": P. Macrory, *Kabul Catastrophe*, p. 81.

66 "Auckland has . . . British": Quoted in P. Hopkirk, *The Great Game*, p. 190.

67 "to prosecute . . . frontier": 8 November 1838, the full text is quoted in Kaye, *History*, vol. 1, pp. 383–84.

67 Lord Auckland wrote to the Secret Committee on 13 August 1838 warning of unrest in neighboring states, P. P. 1839, No. 4.

67 "I could . . . Russia": Auckland to Hobhouse, 13 October 1838, BROU 36473, folios 331–38.

67 "The Afghan . . . with it": Evidence before the Official Salaries Committee of the House of Commons, 1850, quoted in H. Mackenzie, *Storms and Sunshine of a Soldier's Life*, p. 302.

67 "the Russian fiend . . . empire": Quoted in Hopkirk, *The Great Game*, p. 192.

67 "You must . . . ground": Quoted in J. Stewart, *Crimson Snow*, p. 39.

68 "You will . . . hopeless . . . If you succeed . . . out": Quoted in Kaye, *History*, vol. 1, p. 379.

68 "an act . . . folly": G. Bruce, *Retreat from Kabul*, p. 25.

68 "We have . . . establish it": Quoted in Norris, *The First Afghan War*, p. 228.

68 "rocks . . . snow": Quoted in Kaye, *History*, vol. 1, p. 378.

68 "act of infatuation": Quoted in J. H. Waller, *Beyond the Khyber Pass,* p. 128.

68 "The consequences . . . country": Duke of Wellington to Mr. Tucker, in ibid.

CHAPTER FIVE

69 "all dressed . . . jewels": E. Eden, *Up the Country*, p. 205.

69 "dreadfully . . . drum": Ibid., pp. 204–5.

70 "I . . . needed . . . I think . . . under": Quoted in P. Macrory, *Kabul Catastrophe*, p. 84.

71 "From beneath . . . elephants . . . gorgeously . . . cloth": D. H. Mackinnon, *Military Service and Adventures in the Far East by a Cavalry Officer*, pp. 62 and 65.

72 "exactly . . . eye": Eden, *Up the Country*, p. 198.

72 "slight . . . debauchery": Mackinnon, *Military Service and Adventures*, p. 62.

72 "of frosted . . . gold": Ibid., p. 66.

72 "I could . . . Lady J's": Eden, *Up the Country*, p. 208.

72 "unbridled . . . spirits": Mackinnon, *Military Service and Adventures*, p. 62.

72 "horrible . . . swallow it:" Eden, *Up the Country*, p. 207.

72 "Nobody . . . vanities": Ibid., p. 209.

72 "I don't . . . instructions": Macrory, *Kabul Catastrophe*, p. 84.

72 "What . . . bags! . . . What resounding . . . them": G. Bruce, *Retreat from Kabul*, p. 29.

73 "regarded . . . cologne": Macrory, *Kabul Catastrophe*, p. 86.

73 "always . . . in India": Letter of General Nott quoted in Stocqueler, *Life of Sir William Nott*, p. 106.

75 "the ramrod . . . cartridges": F. G. Greenwood, *Narrative of the Late Victorious Campaigns*, p. 216.

75 [To cross . . . deserted . . . were . . . unclean": Quoted in Subedar Sita Ram, *From Sepoy to Subedar*, pp. 85 and 88.

75 "I should . . . visited . . . What . . . moon": T. W. E. Holdsworth, *The Campaign of the Indus*, p. 3.

76 "neither . . . frontier" Sir: J. W. Kaye, *History of the War in Afghanistan*, vol. 1, p. 401.

76 The task . . . Indus: All quotes in this paragraph are from W. Broadfoot, *The Career of Major George Broadfoot*, p. 7.

77 "Not content . . . this": Quoted in Kaye, *History*, vol. 1, p. 419.

77 "the cool . . . sand": J. Atkinson, *The Expedition into Afghanistan*, p. 105.

78 "marched . . . abstinence": Sir H. Durand, *The First Afghan War and Its Causes*, p. 92.

78 "Our . . . water": S. Ram, *From Sepoy to Subedar*, p. 88.

78 "could never . . . nation": Quoted in Kaye, *History*, vol. 1, p. 425.

79 "not . . . seen," Letter of General Nott, quoted in Stocqueler, *Life of Sir William Nott*, p. 111.

80 "in . . . putrefaction": Holdsworth, *The Campaign of the Indus*, p. 68.

80 "to wrap . . . kebabs in": Ibid., p. 52.

80 "if . . . Ocean": Bengal Hurkaru and Chronicle, January 1834, quoted in P. Macrory and G. Pottinger, *The Ten-Rupee Jezail*, p. 192.

80 "as long as I live": Nott's letter of 9 April 1839, quoted in Stocqueler, *Life of Sir William Nott*, p. 121.

82 "commenced . . . do so": Major J. Outram, *Rough Notes of the Campaign in Sind and Affghanistan*, p. 122.

82 "no . . . cattle": W. Hough, *March and Operations of the Army of the Indus*, p. 90.

83 "without . . . expect": Sir G. Lawrence, *Forty-Three Years in India*, p. 11.

83 "The truth . . . ruler . . . he . . . laws": Quoted in Ram, *From Sepoy to Subedar*, p. 90.

83 "horrible": Letter of 8 June 1839, quoted in Holdsworth, *The Campaign of the Indus*, pp. 74–76.

83 "First . . . Mind": Undated memo, BROU 36470, folios 19–21.

84 "dug . . . latter . . . the sheet-anchors . . . historians": Kaye, *History*, vol. 1., pp. 203–4.

84 "All my . . . set up!": Quoted in Sir John Kaye, *Lives of Indian Officers*, vol. 2, p. 65.

84 "the garbled": Kaye, *History*, vol. 1, pp. 202–4 for his views on the "garbled" official correspondence relating to the reasons for going to war.

84 "mutilated" and "eviscerated": H. Lushington, *A Great Country's Little Wars in Afghanistan and Scinde*, p. 62.

CHAPTER SIX

86 "You . . . king?": Quoted in Sir G. Lawrence, *Forty-Three Years in India*, pp. 12–13.

88 "Were huddled . . . beheaded": M. Lal, *Life of the Amir Dost Mohammed*, p. 104.

89 "There . . . over": T. W. E. Holdsworth, *The Campaign of the Indus*, p. 22.

89 "when the morning . . . horizon": Sir H. M. Durand, *The First Afghan War and Its Causes*, pp. 177–78.

90 "The fire . . . bullets": Holdsworth, *The Campaign of the Indus*, p. 92.

90 "stunned . . . concussion . . . Don't . . . failure!": Quoted in Colonel W. Dennie, *Personal Narrative of the Campaigns in Afghanistan*, p. 77.

90 "*literally* . . . pieces": Lieutenant Stock, quoted in G. Bruce, *Retreat from Kabul*, p. 66.

91 "pretty . . . interesting . . . inexpressibles": Quoted in H. E. Fane, *Five Years in India*, p. 172.

91 "one . . . globe": Quoted in W. Hough, *March and Operations of the Army of the Indus*, p. 203.

91 "the smell . . . gone": Quoted in J. Atkinson, *The Expedition into Afghanistan*, p. 220.

92 "If you . . . here": Quoted in ibid., p. 232.

93 "peaches . . . England": Fane, *Five Years in India*, p. 183.

93 "We may . . . over": 19 September 1839, quoted in G. Pottinger, *The Afghan Connection*, p. 95.

CHAPTER SEVEN

94 On the . . . dimensions": All quotes in this paragraph are from H. Havelock, *Narrative of the War in Afghanistan*, pp. 114–15.

96 "hemmed . . . River . . . men . . . buy": J. Atkinson, *The Expedition into Afghanistan*, p. 270.

96 "owing . . . Kabul . . . on . . . placed": W. Hough, *March and Operations of the Army of the Indus*, p. 252.

98 "either the grossest": Major J. Outram, *Rough Notes of the Campaign in Sind and Afghanistan*, p. 120.

98 "he had . . . force!": Quoted in Sir G. Lawrence, *Forty-Three Years in India*, p. 24.

99 "the plans . . . monarch:" General Orders, 18 November 1839, given in full in Havelock, *Narrative of the War in Afghanistan*, pp. 317–23.

100 "days . . . Delhi": Quoted in Sir J. W. Kaye, *History of the War in Afghanistan*, vol. 2, p. 28.

100 "I wished . . . catastrophe!": Quoted in ibid., p. 23.

100 "Shah . . . subjects": Letter of 14 October 1839, quoted in *Journal of Indian History*, vol. 12, no. 2, 1933, pp. 263–68.

103 "In Persia . . . is!": Quoted in M. Lal, *Life of the Amir Dost Mohammed*, p. 140.

104 "with . . . cat": Brigadier Shelton, quoted in Kaye, *History*, vol. 2, p. 208.

106 "rending . . . honour": C. Noelle, *State and Tribe in Nineteenth-Century Afghanistan*, p. 48.

106 "A beautiful . . . swim . . . A woman . . . love": L. Dupree, *Afghanistan*, p. 3.

107 "I have . . . spoken to . . . Be silent . . .
ourselves": Quoted in Sir J. W. Kaye,
Lives of Indian Officers, vol. 2. pp. 47–49.

CHAPTER EIGHT

109 "Much good . . . everywhere": C. de
Grunwald, *Tsar Nicholas I*, p. 194.

110 "it would . . . sea [the British]": J. A.
Norris, *The First Afghan War*, p. 19.

110 "Why is . . . lost": Colvin to Burnes,
17 January 1839, AUCK 37695, folio
34.

111 "There is . . . force": Wade to Auckland,
31 January 1839, BROU 36473, folios
431–33.

111 "extremely . . . footing": Auckland to
Hobhouse, 25 May 1839, BROU 36474,
folios 7–12.

111 "I only . . . support": Auckland to
Macnaghten, 7 December 1839, AUCK
37697, folio 12.

111 "should you . . . proceedings": 29
February 1840, quoted in Norris, *The
First Afghan War*, p. 310.

112 "we must . . . aggression": 15 April 1840,
quoted in ibid., p. 313.

112 "If . . . us": Hobhouse to Auckland, 4
May 1840, AUCK 37700, folios 74–75.

112 The truth . . . plentiful)": All unattributed
quotes in this paragraph are from C.
Noelle, *State and Tribe in Nineteenth-
Century Afghanistan*, pp. 19–21.

113 "Our . . . perch": Letter of 27 November
1839, quoted in *Journal of Indian
History*, Vol. 13, no. 3, 1933, pp. 405–22.

113 B. Woodward, in *Obama's Wars*,
discusses government corruption today
in Afghanistan, pp. 65–67 and 208.

114 "bad . . . Shuja": Sir J. W. Kaye, *History
of the War in Afghanistan*, vol. 2, p. 18.

114 "the apple . . . British": C. Noelle, *State
and Tribe in Nineteenth-Century
Afghanistan*, p. 47.

115 "the Afghans . . . match": Quoted in
Kaye, *History*, vol. 2, p. 83.

CHAPTER NINE

117 "his head . . . feet": H. Mackenzie,
Storms and Sunshine of a Soldier's Life,
p. 116.

117 "Herat . . . behaviour": Letter of 20
August 1840, quoted in *Journal of
Indian History*, vol. 13, no. 3, 1933,
pp. 417–18.

117 At this . . . income": All quotes in these
two paragraphs are from G. Buist, *Outline
of the Operations of the British Troops in
Scinde and Affghanistan*, pp. 288–91.

119 "so much . . . mind": Sir J. W. Kaye,
History of the War in Afghanistan, vol.
2, p. 83.

119 "For God's . . . fight?": Quoted in ibid.,
p. 84.

119 "this brilliant . . . effect": Quoted in
J. A. Norris, *The First Afghan War*,
p. 334.

119 "You may . . . hurt": Quoted in Kaye,
History, vol. 2, p. 86.

120 "Sheets of . . . anything": Quoted in Sir
J. W. Kaye, *Lives of Indian Officers*, vol.
2, p. 47.

121 "Front! Draw swords": Quoted in Sir
G. Lawrence, *Forty-Three Years in
India*, p. 45.

123 "no mercy . . . country": Quoted in H. R.
Gupta, *Punjab, Central Asia and the
First Afghan War*, p. 142,

123 "a wonderful fellow": Quoted in P.
Macrory, *Kabul Catastrophe*, p. 116.

123 "with liberality . . . had . . . victim":
Quoted in Kaye, *History*, vol. 2, p. 98.

CHAPTER TEN

125 "For God's . . . away": Quoted in
W. Broadfoot, *The Career of Major
George Broadfoot*, p. 28.

125 "We have . . . administration": Quoted in
Sir J. W. Kaye, *History of the War in
Afghanistan*, vol. 2, p. 100.

126 "hardly . . . state . . . perpetually . . .
resources": Quoted in ibid., p. 130.

126 "perfect children . . . should . . .
consequence": Quoted in ibid.,
p. 127.

127 "must . . . Afghanistan": Quoted in ibid.,
p. 116.

127 The terms . . . expressions: All quotes in
this paragraph are from ibid., pp. 118,
123 and 125.

128 "The country . . . Beersheba": Quoted in
ibid., p. 130.

128 "All . . . basis": Quoted in P. Macrory, *Kabul Catastrophe*, p. 132.

128 "most . . . situations": Quoted in Kaye, *History*, vol. 2, p. 137.

128 "a highly paid . . . them out": Quoted in Sir J. W. Kaye, *Lives of Indian Officers*, vol. 2, p. 57.

128 "smoked . . . jellies . . . if rotundity . . . them": Quoted in ibid., p. 58.

128 "I am . . . bayonet": Quoted in Kaye, *History*, vol. 2. p. 119.

128 "when he . . . credit": Quoted in ibid., p. 68.

129 "pure trickery": Letter to Burnes's brother-in-law, quoted in G. J. Alder, *Historical Journal*, vol. 15, no. 2, June 1972, p. 237.

129 "and thus furnish . . . worms": Burnes's preface to his posthumously published account of his Kabul mission, ibid., p. 238.

129 "the best . . . send you": Colvin to Macnaghten, 13 December 1840, AUCK 37703, folio 23.

129 "a very . . . regiment . . . feeble . . . Kabul": Quoted in J. Lunt, *Scarlet Lancer*, pp. 197–98.

130 "remarkably . . . manners": Auckland to Macnaghten, 28 November 1840, AUCK 37702, folios 128–30.

130 "The part . . . war . . . the duty . . . operations . . . as its . . . dependence": Auckland to Elphinstone, 18 December 1840, AUCK 37703, folio 33.

130 "You will . . . peace": Quoted in Sir G. Lawrence, *Forty-Three Years in India*, p. 53.

130 "more . . . murdered": H. Palmer, *Indian Life and Sketches*, p. 23.

131 "The colours . . . impression": Quoted in H. Mackenzie, *Storms and Sunshine of a Soldier's Life*, p. 272.

132 "to maintain . . . without . . . to attempt . . . policy": Quoted in Kaye, *History*, vol. 2, p. 146.

133 "We cannot . . . alarming": Quoted in ibid., p. 149.

133 "a distinguished . . . officer . . . accompanied. . . . O'Groats": Quoted in G. Buist, *Outline of the Operations in Sinde and Afghanistan*, p. 293.

133 "an awful outlay": Quoted in Kaye, *History*, vol. 2, p. 151.

133 "part of . . . withdrawn": Quoted in Lady Sale, *A Journal of the Disasters in Afghanistan, 1841–2*, p. 23.

134 "Can there . . . Budget?": Quoted in N. McCord, *British History, 1815–1906*, p. 154.

134 However . . . Poles": All quotes in this paragraph are from C. de Grunwald, *Tsar Nicholas I*, p. 196.

135 "from financial . . . difficulties": 21 August 1841, AUCK 37706, folios 55–56.

135 "the necessities . . . alternative": Quoted in V. Eyre, *The Military Operations at Kabul*, p. xiv.

136 "useless . . . distressing": Letter of 26 July 1841, quoted in Mackenzie, *Storms and Sunshine*, p. 216.

136 "coming tempest": Quoted in C. Noelle, *State and Tribe in Nineteenth-Century Afghanistan*, p. 50.

138 "Wade . . . it": Quoted in Mackenzie, *Storms and Sunshine*, p. 189.

139 "a number . . . purposes": Quoted in Lady Sale, *A Journal of the Disaster in Afghanistan*, p. 439.

139 "so early . . . wont": Ibid., p. 20.

139 "The storm . . . subside . . . there . . . helm": Quoted in Sir H. M. Durand, *The First Afghan War and Its Causes*, p. 338.

140 "Ay! . . . Macnaghten": Quoted in P. Macrory and G. Pottinger, *The Ten-Rupee Jezail*, pp. 57–58.

140 "there was . . . injure him": Quoted in J. H. Stocqueler, *Memorials of Affghanistan [sic]*, appendix 12, "Narrative of the Murder of Sir Alexander Burnes by His Servant Bowh Sing," p. cxl.

CHAPTER ELEVEN

143 "that there . . . regiment . . . This is . . . Burnes": Quoted in J. H. Stocqueler, *Memorials of Affghanistan [sic]*, Appendix 12, "Narrative of the Murder of Sir Alexander Burnes by his servant Bowh Sing," p. cxli.

146 "crying . . . murdered": Sir G. Lawrence, *Forty-Three Years in India*, p. 64.

148 "stirring . . . perdition": James Burnes to James Carnac, 1 February 1842, WELLES 37313, folio 135.

148 "Since . . . tomorrow . . . Our . . . done":
Quoted in Sir J. W. Kaye, *History of the War in Afghanistan*, vol. 2, p. 187.

150 "be impolitic": Quoted in Stocqueler, *Memorials of Affghanistan*, Appendix 7, "Narrative of the Events in Kabul by a Quondam Captive," p. lxxi.

150 "From the . . . troops": P. Macrory, *Kabul Catastrophe*, p. 162.

151 "from where. . . . mad . . . had forgot . . . king": Quoted in Stocqueler, *Memorials of Affghanistan*, Appendix 7, p. lxvi.

152 "suddenly . . . body": Mackenzie's letter to Eyre of 19 November 1842, V. Eyre, *The Military Operations at Kabul*, p. 377.

152 "rather . . . going": Ibid.

153 "*Feringhee* . . . European): Ibid.

153 "and then . . . him": Quoted in H. Mackenzie, *Storms and Sunshine of a Soldier's Life*, p, 208.

154 "It behoves . . . terms": Quoted in Kaye, *History*, vol. 2, p. 197.

154 "there was . . . hourly": Quoted in Stocqueler, *Memorials of Affghanistan*, appendix 7, p. lxxii.

155 "very . . . awful . . . Do not . . . fast": Quoted in Kaye, *History*, 2, pp. 199–200.

156 "*beegahs* . . . swords": Quoted in ibid., p. 230.

156 "We came . . . religion": Quoted in ibid., p. 231

157 "Most . . . day . . . the enemy . . . dawn": J. Haughton's account of his survival, *Char-ee-kar and Service There with the Fourth Goorkha Regiment.*

CHAPTER TWELVE

158 "It is . . . country": Quoted in Sir J. W. Kaye, *History of the War in Afghanistan*, vol. 2, p. 254.

158 "contumacious . . . actuated . . . feelings": Quoted in ibid., p. 209.

162 "I have . . . chance!": Letter of 17 November 1841, J. H. Stocqueler, *Life of Sir William Nott*, pp. 361–62.

162 "The despatch . . . destruction": Quoted in P. Macrory and G. Pottinger, *The Ten-Rupee Jezail*, p. 201.

163 "If . . . befall us": Quoted in Sir G. Lawrence, *Forty-Three Years in India*, p. 84.

165 "Dust to dust": Quoted in H. Mackenzie, *Storms and Sunshine of a Soldier's Life*, p. 221.

165 "swarms . . . cavalry": V. Eyre, *The Military Operations at Kabul*, p. 104.

167 "none . . . stiff": Quoted in J. Bruce, *Retreat from Kabul*, p. 150.

169 "something . . . favour": Quoted in Kaye, *History*, vol. 2, p. 237.

169 "We learn . . . delay": Quoted in ibid., p. 235.

170 "I beg . . . to you": Quoted in ibid., p. 254.

CHAPTER THIRTEEN

172 "We shall . . . with us": Quoted in Sir J. W. Kaye, *History of the War in Afghanistan*, vol. 2, p. 281.

172 "At . . . judgement": Quoted in Ibid., p. 255.

175 Macnaghten . . . the cavalry: All quotes in these two paragraphs are from ibid., pp. 272–74.

175 "The military . . . *moment*": Quoted in H. Mackenzie, *Storms and Sunshine of a Soldier's Life*, p. 236.

175 The following . . . with us": All quotes in these four paragraphs are from Kaye, *History*, vol. 2, pp. 278–81.

177 "exceedingly . . . cold": J. H. Stocqueler, *Memorials of Affghanistan*, [*sic*], appendix 7, "Narrative of the Events in Kabul by a Quondam Captive," p. xciv.

179 "You can . . . rupees . . . If . . . tomorrow": Quoted in Kaye, *History*, vol. 2, pp. 295–96.

180 "The sending . . . agreement": Quoted in Ibid., p. 297–98.

181 "the gilded bait": Stocqueler, *Memorials of Affghanistan*, appendix 7, p. cii.

181 "A plot! . . . that!": Quoted in Mackenzie, *Storms and Sunshine*, p. 241.

181 "not . . . plot . . . Leave . . . you": Quoted in Kaye, *History*, vol. 2, pp. 301–2.

183 "Why not! . . . betrayed . . . person": Mackenzie's letter to Eyre, in Stocqueler, *Memorials of Affghanistan*, appendix 15, p. cliii.

183 "Oh . . . alarmed": Quoted in Sir G. Lawrence, *Forty-Three Years in India*, p. 118.

184 "armed . . . teeth . . . slippery . . . glass": Ibid., p. 119.

CHAPTER FOURTEEN

185 "hacking . . . body": Quoted in V. Eyre, *The Military Operations at Kabul*, p. 183.

186 "with instant . . . for you": H. Mackenzie, *Storms and Sunshine of a Soldier's Life*, p. 246.

186 "in a . . . manner": J. H. Stocqueler, *Memorials of Affghanistan* [sic], appendix 7, "Narrative of the Events in Kabul by a Quondam Captive," p. civ.

186 "as silent . . . dead": Mackenzie, *Storms and Sunshine*, p. 247.

187 "The Sirdar . . . spot": Quoted in ibid., p. 247.

188 "savage . . . sides": Sir G. Lawrence, *Forty-Three Years in India*, p. 127.

188 "of treachery . . . bad . . . would . . . treasure": Mackenzie, *Storms and Sunshine*, pp. 248–49.

188 "utterly . . . customs": Lawrence, *Forty-Three Years in India*, p. 128.

189 "[I was] hauled . . . advice": Quoted in G. Pottinger, *The Afghan Connection*, p. 154.

189 "if . . . good": Lady Sale, *A Journal of the Disasters in Afghanistan, 1841–2*, p. 201.

190 "be dishonoured . . . ever": J. Cunningham, *The Last Man*, p. 75.

192 "with . . . her . . . Can . . . supplies? . . . pretty . . . retreat!": Lawrence, *Forty-Three Years in India*, pp. 142–43.

193 "We shall . . . can": Quoted in Cunningham, *The Last Man*, p. 83.

193 "if it were . . . need": Eyre, *The Military Operations at Kabul*, p. 189.

CHAPTER FIFTEEN

196 "the oaths . . . camels": J. H. Stocqueler, *Memorials of Affghanistan* [sic], appendix 7, "Narrative of the Events in Kabul by a Quondam Captive," p. cix.

197 "columns . . . flame": Ibid.

197 "literally . . . misery": Sir G. Lawrence, *Forty-Three Years in India*, p. 145.

198 "worn out . . . cold": Ibid.

198 "one mass . . . order gone": Stocqueler, *Memorials of Affghanistan*, appendix 7, p. cx.

199 "hungry wolves": Sergeant Major Lissant's account, *Army Quarterly*, October 1928, p. 145.

200 "Here . . . lost": Quoted in Sir J. W. Kaye, *History of the War in Afghanistan*, vol. 2, p. 369.

200 "burnt . . . charred": Major General Sir T. Seaton, *From Cadet to Colonel*, quoting a sergeant-major, p. 223.

202 "dreadful . . . of all": Stocqueler, *Memorials of Affghanistan*, appendix 7, p. cxii.

202 "completely choked": Lady Sale, *A Journal of the Disasters in Afghanistan, 1841–2*, p. 240.

203 "When . . . Allah": *Journal of the Foklore Institute*, June 1967.

204 "Despite . . . to die": All quotes in this paragraph are from Lawrence, *Forty-Three Years in India*, p. 146.

205 "the general . . . left": H. Mackenzie, *Storms and Sunshine of a Soldier's Life*, p. 267.

206 "the ladies . . . to him": Lawrence, *Forty-Three Years in India*, p. 157.

CHAPTER SIXTEEN

207 "When . . . dogs": Quoted in Lady Sale, *A Journal of the Disasters in Afghanistan, 1841–2*, p. 269.

207 "become . . . wood . . . so . . . musket": This quote, as well as all others in this chapter attributed to Sergeant Major Lissant, comes from his account in the *Army Quarterly*, October 1928.

209 "to form . . . front": H. Mackenzie, *Storms and Sunshine of a Soldier's Life*, p. 269.

209 "raw . . . blood": J. H. Stocqueler, *Memorials of Affghanistan* [sic], appendix 7, "Narrative of the Events in Kabul by a Quondam Captive," p. xcvi.

211 "dogs": Sale, *A Journal of the Disasters in Afghanistan*, p. 271.

212 "that he . . . them . . . he . . . valley": Ibid., p. 270.

213 "commenced . . . attended to": Manuscript letter from Captain J. A. Souter to his wife.

214 "followed . . . saddlebow": Dr. Brydon's account printed for private circulation.

214 "I saw . . . stones": Brydon's letter to his brother, 20 January 1842, *Journal of the*

Society for Army Historical Research,
vol. 51, 1973.

214 "[I] stretched . . . could . . . suddenly . . .
of it": Dr. Brydon's account printed for
private circulation.

215 "a holy . . . infidels . . . slay . . . Jalalabad":
Reverend G. R. Gleig, *Sales's Brigade in
Afghanistan,* p. 133.

215 "Everything . . . passes": Quoted in ibid.,
p. 134.

215 "as peremptory . . . army": Ibid., p. 135.

216 "with . . . throat": P. Macrory, *Kabul
Catastrophe,* p. 236.

216 "suddenly . . . speck": E. Teer, *The Siege
of Jellalabad,* p. 17.

216 "leaning . . . stranger . . . not a soul . . .
messenger . . . who . . . army": Reverend
Gleig, *Sales's Brigade in Afghanistan,*
pp. 137–38.

216 "his first . . . annihilated": Quoted in D.
S. Richards, *The Savage Frontier,* p. 145.

217 "not a. . . . appeared . . . from time . . .
wanderer": Reverend Gleig, *Sales's
Brigade in Afghanistan,* p. 140.

217 "a dirge . . . soldiers": Major General
Sir T. Seaton, *From Cadet to Colonel,*
p. 214.

CHAPTER SEVENTEEN

220 "sometimes . . . behind": J. S. Cumming,
A Six Years' Diary, p. 170.

220 At the end . . . closed": All quotes in this
paragraph are from J. A. Norris, *The
First Afghan War,* pp. 382–83 or Sir
J. W. Kaye, *History of the War in
Afghanistan,* vol. 3, p. 14.

221 "far . . . life . . . the universal . . .
religious . . . in what . . . country":
Auckland to Macnaghten, 4 December
1841, AUCK 37706, folios 202–3.

222 "Poor Macnaghten . . . treachery":
Quoted in M. Fowler, *Below the Peacock
Fan,* p. 83.

222 "this calamity . . . as . . . painful":
Auckland to Lyall, 23 January 1842,
AUCK 37707, folio 118.

222 "My present . . . events": Auckland to
Fitzgerald, 23 January 1842, AUCK
37707, folio 123.

222 "vile . . . astonishing . . . government":
Quoted in D. Crane, *Men of War,* p. 179.

222 "a faithless . . . assassination":
Proclamation of 31 January 1842, Norris,
The First Afghan War, pp. 387–88.

222 "to re-enter . . . described": Colvin to
Clerk, 31 January 1842, AUCK 37707,
folio 134.

223 "horror . . . happened . . . irretrievable . . .
the tone . . . Kabul": 18 February 1842,
AUCK 37707, folios 187–88.

223 "the disastrous . . . troops": Ellenborough
to Peel, 21 February 1842, ELLEN PRO
30.12.89.

223 "greatly depressed": Auckland to
Hobhouse, 1 February 1842, AUCK
37707, folio 188.

223 "rested . . . placed": Quoted in Kaye,
History, vol. 3, p. 192.

224 "there must . . . both": Quoted in Norris,
The First Afghan War, p. 395.

224 "a tissue . . . Britain": Captain H.
Tuckett, quoted in J. Cunningham, *The
Last Man,* p. 125.

224 "Our enemies . . . degradation":
Wellington to Ellenborough, 31 March
1842, Norris, *The First Afghan War,*
pp. 397–98.

224 "We shall . . . retribution": Peel to
Ellenborough, 6 April 1842, ELLEN
PRO 30.12.37.

225 "this is . . . infidels": Quoted in M. E.
Yapp, "Revolutions of 1841–2 in Afghanistan," *Bulletin of the London School of
Oriental Studies,* vol. 27, no. 2, 1964,
p. 356.

226 "Fancy . . . do it": Quoted in Cumming,
A Six Years' Diary, p. 185.

226 "sinking Islam": Quoted in Yapp,
"Revolutions of 1841–2 in Afghanistan,"
p. 353.

226 "to be . . . midnight": E. Teer, *The Siege
of Jellalabad,* p. 30.

227 "at last . . . re-established": 21 April
1842, ELLEN PRO 30.12.89.

227 "They had not . . . o'comin' ": Major
General Sir T. Seaton, *From Cadet to
Colonel,* pp. 213–14.

227 "useless . . . controversy . . . He had . . .
certificate": Cunningham, *The Last Man,*
p. 127.

228 "intended . . . surrender . . . I . . .
surrender": Quoted in Seaton, *From
Cadet to Colonel,* pp. 214–15.

230 "in a solemn . . . earthquakes, Brigadier":
     P. Macrory, *Kabul Catastrophe*, p. 248.

230 "to hold . . . falling": J. Brasyer, *Memoirs*,
     p. 11.

CHAPTER EIGHTEEN

232 "The object . . . Afghans": ELLEN PRO
     30.12.98.

232 "peremptory order . . . like . . .
     thunderclap": Quoted in Sir J. W. Kaye,
     History of the War in Afghanistan, vol.
     3, p. 203.

232 "I felt . . . ours": Quoted in P. Macrory
     and G. Pottinger, *The Ten-Rupee Jezail*,
     p. 174.

233 "signal . . . Afghans": Quoted in ibid.,
     p. 192.

233 The much amended drafts of
     Ellenborough's letter to Pollock are in
     ELLEN PRO 30.12.89.

233 "I trust . . . powers . . . would be . . .
     world": 13 May 1842, quoted in Kaye,
     History, vol. 3, p. 199.

235 "My father . . . Mussalman": Quoted in
     H. Mackenzie, *Storms and Sunshine of a
     Soldier's Life*, p. 347.

235 "acknowledged murderer . . .
     deceived . . . destroyed . . . so great a
     criminal": 15 May 1842, ELLEN PRO
     30.12.98.

236 "miserably . . . weak": V. Eyre, *The
     Military Operations of Kabul*, p. 318.

236 "we shall . . . safe": All quotations in this
     paragraphs are from Ellenborough's
     letter of 7 June 1842, ELLEN PRO
     30.12.89.

236 "stand alone": Quoted in Macrory
     and Pottinger, *The Ten Rupee Jezail*,
     p. 173.

237 "[Ellenborough's] want . . . inexcusable":
     Quoted in P. Macrory, *Kabul
     Catastrophe*, p. 254.

237 "the case . . . prohibit it": 6 July 1842,
     ELLEN PRO 30.12.89.

237 "in triumph . . . disaster": Ibid.

237 "The governor-general . . . prefer":
     All quotes in this paragraph are
     from Ellenborough's letters of 23
     and 29 July 1842, ELLEN PRO
     30.12.98.

238 "eager . . . anywhere": E. Teer, *The Siege
     of Jellalabad*, p. 36.

239 "an endless . . . along": Quoted in
     *Journal of the Society for Historical
     Research*, vol. 55, 1977, p. 83.

239 "literally . . . countrymen": Augustus
     Abbott, quoted in Macrory and
     Pottinger, *The Ten-Rupee Jezail*, p. 179.

240 By 12 September . . . before them": All
     quotes in these two paragraphs are from
     F. G. Greenwood, *Narrative of the Late
     Victorious Campaigns in Afghanistan*,
     pp. 212–13, 217–19.

241 "awful . . . recognisable": Major General
     Sir T. Seaton, *From Cadet to Colonel*,
     pp. 222–23.

243 "had thrown . . . rescue them?": Quoted
     in Kaye, *History*, vol. 3, p. 349.

243 "thrusting . . . place . . . she . . . another":
     Colonel Sir R. Warburton [Mrs.
     Warburton's son] *Eighteen Years in the
     Khyber, 1879–1898*, p. 5.

244 "a splendid . . . glass": J. Brasyer,
     Memoirs, p. 12.

244 "the cry . . . town": Major Rawlinson,
     quoted in Kaye, *History*, vol. 3, p. 369.

244 "I have . . . country": Quoted in P. G.
     Fredericks, *The Sepoy and the Cossack*,
     p. 118.

244 "strewn . . . conversation!": Diary of N.
     Chamberlain, 15 October 1842, quoted
     in G. W. Forrest, *Life of Field-Marshal
     Sir Neville Chamberlain*, p. 153.

245 "so . . . humiliation": Kaye, *History*, vol.
     3, p. 350.

EPILOGUE

246 "1st . . . outbreak": P. Macrory, *Kabul
     Catastrophe*, p. 267.

247 "The calamity . . . requite'": Sir J. W.
     Kaye, *History of the War in Afghanistan*,
     vol. 3, p. 402.

247 Henry Lushington . . . again and again":
     Quotes in these two paragraphs are
     from H. Lushington, *A Great Country's
     Little Wars in England, Afghanistan
     and Scinde*, pp. 24, 27, 75, 124 and
     168.

248 "This . . . hostile": H. B. Hanna, *The
     Second Afghan War*, vol. 1, p. 1.

248 Outside Britain . . . Hong Kong: Further
     details of the United States' reaction are
     contained in Dr. L. Marshall's article
     "American Public Opinion and the First

Afghan War," *Pakistan Journal of American Studies*, vol. 2, no. 1, March 1984, pp. 1–11.

250 "They would . . . anything": Burnes, quoted in Sir J. W. Kaye, *Lives of Indian Officers*, vol. 2, p. 65.

253 "introducing . . . Company . . . We . . . be": Quoted in D. S. Richards, *The Savage Frontier*, pp. 58–59.

256 "I . . . country": Quoted in J. Stewart, *Crimson Snow*, p. 216.

257 In the summer . . . EMBASSY: All quotes in this paragraph are from Richards, *The Savage Frontier*, p. 84.

258 "Remember . . . own": Quoted in F. Morley, *Life of Gladstone*, vol. 3, p. 595.

258 "[I] . . . India": Quoted in Richards, *The Savage Frontier*, p. 101.

259 "Young . . . shame": There are several different versions of these verses. See L. Dupree, *Afghanistan*, p. 411 and D. Loyn, *Butcher and Bolt*, p. 120.

260 Winston Churchill . . . sight": All quotes in this paragraph are from W. S. Churchill, *The Story of the Malakand Field Force*, pp. 126–27.

260 "September . . . revives": Ibid., pp. 114–15.

262 Part . . . hand": All quotes in this paragraph are from ibid., pp. 165 and 188.

262 "There is . . . people": Quoted in J. Morris, *Pax Britannica*, p. 418.

262 "Burning . . . revenge": Quoted in D. Loyn, *Butcher and Bolt*, p. 160.

262 "placed . . . Paradise": Quoted in ibid., p. 147.

262 "As . . . thawed": Churchill, *The Story of the Malakand Field Force*, p. 192.

264 "One . . . west": Quoted in Richards, *The Savage Frontier*, p. 163.

268 "Do you . . . Shah Shuja?": Quoted in Loyn, *Butcher and Bolt*, p. 272.

BIBLIOGRAPHY

BOOKS

Allen, C. *Soldier Sahibs*. London: John Murray, 2000.

Allen, Reverend I. N. *Diary of a March Through Scinde and Afghanistan*. London, 1843.

Anon. (author J. McNeill). *Progress and Present Position of Russia in the East*. London, 1836.

Atkinson, J. *The Expedition into Afghanistan*. London: W. H. Allen, 1841.

Barr, Lieutenant W. *Journal of a March from Delhi to Peshawar and from Thence to Kabul*. London: J. Madden, 1844.

Barthorp, M. *The Northwest Frontier, British India and Afghanistan, 1839–1947*. Poole: New Orchards Editions, 1982.

Benson, A. C., and Asher, Viscount. *The Letters of Queen Victoria—1837–1861*. Vols. 1 and 2. London: John Murray, 1908.

Bilgrami, A. *Afghanistan and British India, 1793–1907*. New Delhi: Sterling Publishing, 1972.

Blanch, L. *The Sabres of Paradise*. New York: Viking Press, 1960.

Brasyer, J. *The Memoirs of J. Brasyer*. London: Gowars, 1892.

Broadfoot, W. *The Career of Major George Broadfoot*. London: John Murray, 1888.

Bruce, G. *Retreat from Kabul*. London: Mayflower, 1967.

Buist, G. *Outline of the Operations of the British Troops in Scinde and Affghanistan*. Bombay, 1843.

Burnes, Sir A. *Cabool Being a Personal Narrative of a Journey to and Residence in That City in the Years 1836–38*. London: John Murray, 1842.

———. *Travels into Bokhara*. Vols. 1, 2 and 3. London: John Murray, 1834.

Chakravarty, S. *Afghanistan and the Great Game*. Delhi: New Century, 2002.

Churchill, W. S. *The Story of the Malakand Field Force*. 1890; reprint, London: Leo Cooper, 1989.

Conolly, Lieutenant A. *Journey to the North of India*. Vols. 1 and 2. London: Richard Bentley, 1834.

Crane, D. *Men of War*. London: HarperCollins, 2009.

Crankshaw, E. *The Shadow of the Winter Palace*. London: Penguin, 1976.

Cumming, J. S. *A Six Years' Diary*. London: Martin and Hood, 1847.

Cunningham, J. *The Last Man. The Life and Times of Surgeon William Brydon*. Oxford: New Cherwell Press, 2003.

Dennie, Colonel W. *Personal Narrative of the Campaigns in Afghanistan, Sinde, Beloochistan etc.* Dublin: William Curry Jun., 1843.

Docherty, P. *The Khyber Pass*. London: Faber, 2007.

Dupree, L. *Afghanistan*. Princeton, NJ: Princeton University Press, 1973.

Durand, Sir H. M. *The First Afghan War and Its Causes*. London: Longman Green, 1879.

Eden, E. *Up the Country*. London: Curzon, 1978

Edwards-Stuart, I. *A John Company General—Life of Lieutenant-General Sir Abraham Roberts.* Bognor Regis, UK: New Horizon, 1983.

Elphinstone, M. *Account of the Kingdom of Caubul.* Vols. 1 and 2. London: Richard Bentley, 1842.

Eyre, V. *The Military Operations at Kabul.* London: John Murray, 1843.

Fane, Colonel H. E. *Five Years in India.* London: Henry Colbourn, 1842.

Fergusson, N. *Empire.* London: Allen Lane, 2003.

Fieldhouse, D. K. *The Colonial Empires.* London: Weidenfeld and Nicolson, 1966.

Forrest, G. W. *Life of Field-Marshal Sir Neville Chamberlain.* Edinburgh and London: William Blackwood and Sons, 1909.

Foster, W., ed. *Early Travels in India.* New Delhi: Munshiram Manoharlal Publishers, 1985. (This book reproduces the diaries of several early British travelers to India.)

Fowler, M. *Below the Peacock Fan.* London: Penguin, 1988.

Frazer, J. B. *Military Memoirs of Lieutenant-Colonel James Skinner.* Vols. 1 and 2. London, 1851.

Fredericks, P. G. *The Sepoy and the Cossack.* London: W. H. Allen, 1971.

Gascoigne, B. *The Great Moghuls.* London: Jonathan Cape, 1991.

Gleig, Reverend G. R. *Sales's Brigade in Afghanistan.* London: John Murray, 1846.

Greenwood, F. G. *Narrative of the Late Victorious Campaigns in Afghanistan.* London: Henry Colburn, 1844.

Grunwald, C. de. *Tsar Nicholas I.* London: MacGibbon and Kee, 1954.

Gupta, H. R. *Panjab, Central Asia and the First Afghan War.* 1943; reprint, Chandigarh, India: Panjab University Press, 1987. (The 1943 edition included a preface by J. K. Nehru.)

Hanna, H. B. *The Second Afghan War.* Vol. 1. London: Constable, 1899.

Harlan, J. *Central Asia—Personal Narrative of General Josiah Harlan, 1823–1841.* Ed. F. Ross. London: Luzac, 1939.

———. *A Memoir of India and Afghanistan.* London: R. Baldwin, 1842.

Haughton, J. *Char-ee-kar and Service There with the Fourth Goorkha Regiment in 1841.* London: Provost, 1879.

Havelock, H. *Narrative of the War in Afghanistan in 1838–39.* Vols. 1 and 2. London: Henry Colburn, 1840.

Holdsworth, T. W. E. *The Campaign of the Indus.* Published privately, 1840.

Honigberger, J. M. *Thirty-Five Years in the East.* Vols. 1 and 2. London: H. Bailliere, 1852.

Hopkirk, P. *The Great Game.* London: John Murray, 1990.

Hough, W. *March and Operations of the Army of the Indus, 1838–1839.* London: W. H. Allen, 1841.

Iqbal, A. *Circumstances Leading to the First Afghan War.* Lahore: Research Society of Pakistan, 1975.

Kaye, Sir J. W. *History of the War in Afghanistan.* Vols. 1, 2 and 3. London: W. H. Allen, 1857.

———. *Lives of Indian Officers.* Vols. 1 and 2. London: Strahan, 1867.

Kekewich, M. *Retreat and Retribution in Afghanistan, 1842.* Barnsley, UK: Pen and Sword Books, 2011.

Kennedy, P. M. *The Rise and Fall of the Great Powers.* London: Unwin Hyman, 1988.

Kennedy, Dr. R. H. *Narrative of the Campaign of the Army of the Indus in Sind and Kabul in 1838–9.* Vols. I and II. Bombay: T. B. Jervis, 1841.

Lal, M. *Journal of a Tour Through the Punjab, Afghanistan and Parts of Persia.* Calcutta, 1844.

———. *Life of the Amir Dost Mohammed Khan of Kabul.* London: Longman, 1846.

Law, E. (Lord Ellenborough). *Political Diary.* Vols. 1 and 2. London: Richard Bentley and Sons, 1881.

Lawrence, Sir G. *Reminiscences of Forty-Three Years in India.* London: John Murray, 1874.

Low, C. R. *The Afghan War, 1838–42, from the Journal and Correspondence of Major-General A. Abbott.* London: Richard Bentley and Son, 1879.

———. *Life and Correspondence of Field Marshal Sir George Pollock.* London: W. H. Allen, 1873.

Loyn, D. *Butcher and Bolt.* London: Windmill Books, 2009.

Lunt, J. *Bokhara Burnes*. London: Faber and Faber, 1969.
———. *Scarlet Lancer*. London: Rupert Hart Davies, 1964.
Lushington, H. *A Great Country's Little Wars in England, Afghanistan and Scinde*. London: J. W. Parker, 1844.
Mackenzie, H. *Storms and Sunshine of a Soldier's Life*. Vol. I. Edinburgh: David Douglas, 1884.
Mackinnon, D. H. *Military Service and Adventures in the Far East by a Cavalry Officer*. Vols. 1 and 2. London: Charles Ollier, 1847.
Macrory, P. *Kabul Catastrophe*. Oxford: Oxford University Press, 1986.
Macrory, P., and Pottinger, G. *The Ten-Rupee Jezail*. Norwich: M. Russell, 1993.
Martin, D. R. *The Postal History of the First Afghan War, 1838–42*. Postal History Society, 1964.
Mason, P. *A Matter of Honour*. London: Peregrin, 1976.
Masson, C. *Narrative of Various Journeys in Balochistan, Afghanistan and the Punjab and Kalat*. Vols. 1–4. Oxford: Oxford University Press, 1977.
McCord, N. *British History, 1815–1906*. Oxford: Oxford University Press, 1991.
Moore, G. *Vincent of the 41st*. Bedford, UK: Jaycopy, 1979.
Morley, J. *Life of Gladstone*. Vols. 1–3. London, 1903.
Morris, J. *Heaven's Command*. London: Faber and Faber, 1973.
———. *Pax Britannica*. London: Faber and Faber, 1975.
Noelle, C. *State and Tribe in Nineteenth-Century Afghanistan*. Richmond, London: Curzon, 1997.
Norris, J. A. *The First Afghan War, 1838–1842*. Cambridge: Cambridge University Press, 1967.
Outram, Major J. *Rough Notes of the Campaign in Sind and Affghanistan in 1838–9*. Bombay: Amercan Mission Press, 1840.
Palmer, H. *Indian Life and Sketches, 1816–66*. Mussorie, India: Mafasilite Printing Works, 1888.
Pearse, Major H. W. *The First Forcing of the Khaibar Pass, 1838–1839*. London: J. J. Keliher, n.d.
Pipes, R. *Russia under the Old Regime*. London: Peregrin, 1977.
Pottinger, G. *The Afghan Connection*. Edinburgh: Edinburgh Scottish Academic Press, 1983.
Ram, Subedar Sita. *From Sepoy to Subedar*. Ed. J. Lunt. 1873; reprint, Delhi: Vikas, 1970.
Richards, D. S. *The Savage Frontier*. London: Macmillan, 1990.
Sale, Lady. *A Journal of the Disasters in Afghanistan, 1841–2*. London: John Murray, 1843.
Seaton, Major General Sir Tas. *From Cadet to Colonel*. London: George Routledge and Sons, ndp.
Seton-Watson, H. *The Russian Empire, 1801–1917*. Oxford: Oxford University Press, 1967.
Smith, Sir H. *The Autobiography of Lieutenant-General Sir H. Smith*. Vols. 1 and 2. London: John Murray, 1902.
Stacy, Colonel L. R. *Narrative of Services in Beloochistan and Affghanistan*. London: W. H. Allen, 1848.
Stewart, J. *Crimson Snow*. Stroud, UK: History Press, 2008.
Stocqueler, J. H. *Memorials of Affghanistan [sic], 1842*. Calcutta: Ostell and Lepage, 1843.
———, ed. *Life of Sir William Nott. (Memoirs and Correspondence.)* London: Hurst and Blackett, 1854.
Sykes, Sir P. *A History of Afghanistan*. Vols. I and 2. London: Macmillan, 1940.
Teer, E. *The Siege of Jellalabad, 1841–42*. London: Soldiers and Sailors Help Society, 1904.
Vigne, G. T. *A Personal Narrative of a Visit to Ghuzni, Kabul and Afghanistan and a Residence at the Court of Dost Mohammed*. London: Whittaker, 1840.
Waller, J. H. *Beyond the Khyber Pass*. New York: Random House, 1990.
Warburton, Colonel Sir R. *Eighteen Years in the Khyber, 1879–1898*. Lahore: Pakistan Branch of Oxford University Press, 1970.
Westwood, J. N. *Endurance and Endeavour—Russian History, 1812–1971*. Oxford: Oxford University Press, 1973.

Whitteridge, G. *Charles Masson of Afghanistan*. Warminster, UK: Aris and Philips, 1986.
Wilkinson, T. *Two Monsoons*. London: Duckworth, 1976.
Woodruff, P. *The Men Who Ruled India*. Vols. 1 and 2. London: Jonathan Cape, 1963.
Woodward, B. *Obama's Wars*. London: Simon and Schuster, 2010.
Yafa, S. *Big Cotton*. London: Penguin, 2005.

PUBLISHED PARLIAMENTARY PAPERS

1839
—Correspondence Relating to Persia and Afghanistan
—Indian Papers Nos. 1, 2 (Treaties), 3, 4, 5, 6, 7
1843
—Copy of Further Papers Relating to Military Operations in Afghanistan, 17 February 1843
1859
—East India (Cabaul and Afghanistan), 8 June 1859

JOURNAL ARTICLES

Alder, C. J. "The Garbled Blue Books of 1839—Myth or Reality?" *Historical Journal*, vol. 15, no. 2, June 1972, pp. 229–59.
Army Quarterly. "The Retreat from Kabul (A Survivor's Story)—Statement of Sergeant-Major Lissant, 4 April 1842," vol. 37, October 1928, pp. 143–50.
Bearden, Milton. "Afghanistan, Graveyard of Empires," *Foreign Affairs*, vol. 80, no. 6, November–December 2001, pp. 17–30.
Disalker, D. "Some Letters about the First Afghan War," *Journal of Indian History*, vol. 12, no. 2, 1933, pp. 251–86 and vol. 13, no. 3, 1933, pp. 405–22.
Dupree, Louis. "Afghan and British Military Tactics in the First Anglo-Afghan War," *Army Quarterly*, vol. 107, April 1977, pp. 214–21.
———. "The First Anglo-Afghan War and the British Retreat of 1842," *East and West*, new series, vol. 26, nos, 3–4, September–December 1976, pp. 55–65.
———. "The Retreat of the British Army to Jalalabad in 1842—History and Folklore," *Journal of the Folklore Institute*, vol. 4, no. 1, June 1967, pp. 50–74.
de L. Fforde, C. W. "Memoirs of Captain C. W. Ford," *Journal of the Society for Army Historical Research*, vol. 55, 1977, pp. 73–84.
Irvine, W., ed. "Captain Johnson's Diary." *Blackwoods Magazine*, March 1906, pp. 347–68.
Marshall, Dr. L. "American Public Opinion and the First Afghan War," *Pakistan Journal of American Studies* (Islamabad: Area Study Center for Africa, North and South America, Quaid-i-Azam University), vol. 2, no. 1, March 1984, pp. 1–11.
Regimental Magazine of the Lancashire Regiment. "Padre to the 40th Regiment—Rev. I. N. Allen," vol. 3, no. 3, Autumn 1966, pp. 119–23
RUSI Journal. "Letters Concerning the 44th Regiment During the Retreat from Cabul in the First Afghan War," 1915, pp. 404–41.
Yapp, M. E. "Disturbances in Eastern Afghanistan, 1839–1842," *Bulletin of London School of Oriental Studies*, vol. 25, no. 1/3, 1962, pp. 499–523.
———. "Disturbances in Western Afghanistan, 1839–1841," *Bulletin of London School of Oriental Studies*, vol. 26, no. 2, 1963, pp. 288–313.
———. "Revolutions of 1841–2 in Afghanistan," *Bulletin of London School of Oriental Studies*, vol. 27, no. 2, 1964, pp. 333–81.

MANUSCRIPTS, UNPUBLISHED AND PRIVATELY PRINTED MATERIAL, MICROFILMS, ETC.

National Army Museum

Anon. Typescript note on Afghan War (NAM 6112/317).

Carey, R. Letter to his father (NAM 1959-12-146).

Brydon, Dr. W. Account of the retreat from Kabul printed for private circulation (MFN 8301-60).

Dawes, M. "Manuscript Journal" (NAM 6508-50).

"The Gordon Creeds in Afghanistan, 1839 and 1878–79, ed. W. Troudale (92 CRE).

Haslock, Color-Sergeant D., 41st Foot. "Memoirs, 1825–1848" (MFN 8109-63).

Horwood, Lieutenant W. S. Letter to his father (NAM 75005-76).

Lawrence, Captain G. Letter of 3 March 1842 to Lieutenant Colonel Gardner enclosing two "strip letters" sewn into saddles for concealment (NAM 1960-OS-287).

McCabe, Bernard. "More than Twice a Hero" (J. W. Sewell) (92 McCabe).

Moore, G. "Vincent of the 41st Class" (92 VIN).

Translation of "Native Report" detailing events at Kabul from 15 to 25 December 1841 (NAM 1960-OS-287).

Neil, J. M. E. "Recollections of 40 Years Service in the East" (92 NEI).

Sale, Brigadier R. Letters of 22 January 1842 and 26 January 1842 to Sir Jasper Nicolls (NAM 1960-OS-287).

Souter, Lieutenant J. A. Manuscript letter to his wife. Among "Letters Concerning the 44th Regiment during the Retreat from Kabul in the First Afghan War."

Stacy, L. R. "Narrative of Services in Balochsitan and Afghanistan" (92 STA).

Warburton, Col. Sir R. "Eighteen Years in the Khyber, 1879–1898." Lahore: Pakistan Branch, Oxford University Press, 1970.

British Library

Auckland Papers

Broughton Papers

Eyre Papers

Nicolls Papers

Palmerston Papers

Wellesley Papers

British National Archives

Ellenborough Papers

Eyre's manuscript notes on the Kabul massacre

INDEX

British relationship with, 83, 84, 255,
    263
envoy in Kabul, 51–52
invasion of Afghanistan, 266
and Khiva, 109–10, 111–12
military adviser support of Persia, 56
and Ottoman Turkish Empire, 255–56
and Persia, 263
southern expansion, 6, 19–20, 256
treat with Ottoman Turkish Empire
    and Britain, 134

S

Sadozai family clan, 16, 18–19, 159
Sale, "Fighting Bob"
    and Akbar Khan's blockade of
        Jalalabad, 225, 226–27
    attack on Ghazni, 90
    biographical info, 88–89
    death of, 254
    Ellenborough's instructions to, 232, 233
    and Elphinstone, 159–60, 191, 210,
        215–16
    in Jalalabad, 161–62, 215–17, 219–20
    Kohistan defeat, 120–21
    orders to secure Khoord Kabul Pass,
        136, 137–39
    return to India from Kabul, 133–34,
        136
Sale, Lady Florentia
    on Afghan fighting skills, 163
    arrival in Kabul, 107–8
    Auckland's information from, 221
    on battle for Rikabashi Fort, 160–61
    on Bemaru Hills battles, 163, 166
    death of, 254
    on debate about abandoning canton-
        ments to winter in Balla Hissar, 168
    on horses as meat, 173
    as hostage of Akbar Khan, 206, 218,
        228–31, 236, 239
    on Kabul insurrection, 148, 150, 158
    as leader of released hostages, 242

losing hope of getting out of Kabul
    alive, 179
and Macnaghten, 139–40
on options for treaty or retreat, 190
on retreat, 195, 201, 203
reunion with her husband, 243
on Shah Shuja's fate when British
    retreated, 193
on Shelton, 159
on surrender talks and terms, 170,
    172–73, 178
Saleh Mohammed, 239, 241–42
Salisbury, Lord, 67–68
Second Anglo-Afghan War, 256–59,
    261–63
Secret Committee of the East India
    Company, 4, 44, 45, 111
Seh-Baba, Afghanistan, 209, 218–19
sepoys. *See* Indian soldiers
Seven Years' War, 3
Seyyid Keramat Ali, 40–41
Shah Shuja
    Afghan people's dislike of, 82–83,
        86–87, 95, 114
    agreements for reclaiming kingship,
        59–61, 62
    and Amenoolah, 142
    Auckland's recommendation for king
        of Afghanistan, 58
    beheading of Islamic warriors, 88
    biographical info, 16, 17–18
    Britain's support for, 1, 32, 37–38, 249
    British abandonment of, 193
    British lack of respect for, 102
    and British surrender, 175, 176, 177
    Burnes on, 32, 59–60, 63, 114, 120
    conspiring with Ranjit Singh, 37–38
    death of, 226
    defection of infantry, 119–20
    and Dost Mohammed, 37–38, 123
    Elphinstone's meetings with, 14–15, 17
    entrance into Kandahar, 82
    exile in Ludhiana, 27, 32

A NOTE ON THE AUTHOR

DIANA PRESTON is an Oxford University–educated historian and the author of *Before the Fallout: From Marie Curie to Hiroshima*, which won the 2006 Los Angeles Times Book Prize for Science and Technology; *Cleopatra and Antony*; *Lusitania: An Epic Tragedy*; *The Boxer Rebellion*; *A First Rate Tragedy*; and *The Road to Culloden Moor*. She is the coauthor, with her husband, Michael Preston, of *A Pirate of Exquisite Mind* and *Taj Mahal*.